HISTORY OF RELIGION

HISTORY OF RELIGION

A SKETCH OF PRIMITIVE RELIGIOUS BELIEFS AND PRACTICES, AND OF THE ORIGIN AND CHARACTER OF THE GREAT SYSTEMS

By

ALLAN MENZIES D.D.

GYAN

Published by

GYAN

Gyan Publishing House
5, Ansari Road
Daryaganj, New Delhi-110002
Phone: 011-47034999, 9811692060
E-mail: books@gyanbooks.com

Distribution Network
gyanbooks.com
India, USA, Canada, UK, Australia, France

ISBN : 978-81-212-6432-7 (PB)
First Published, 1909

2nd Impression 2022

Printed at: Gyan Press, Delhi.

HISTORY OF RELIGION
Author: ALLAN MENZIES D.D.

HISTORY OF RELIGION

A SKETCH OF PRIMITIVE RELIGIOUS BELIEFS AND PRACTICES, AND OF THE ORIGIN AND CHARACTER OF THE GREAT SYSTEMS

BY ALLAN MENZIES D.D.

'Known unto God are all his works from the beginning of the world.'
—ACTS xv. 18.

1909

PREFACE

This book makes no pretence to be a guide to all the mythologies, or to all the religious practices which have prevailed in the world. It is intended to aid the student who desires to obtain a general idea of comparative religion, by exhibiting the subject as a connected and organic whole, and by indicating the leading points of view from which each of the great systems may best be understood. A certain amount of discussion is employed in order to bring clearly before the reader the great motives and ideas by which the various religions are inspired, and the movements of thought which they present. And the attempt is made to exhibit the great manifestations of human piety in their genealogical connection. The writer has ventured to deal with the religions of the Bible, each in its proper historical place, and trusts that he has not by doing so rendered any disservice either to Christian faith or to the science of religion. It is obvious that in a work claiming to be scientific, and appealing to men of every faith, all religions must be treated impartially, and that the same method must be applied to each of them.

In a field of study, every part of which is being illuminated almost every year by fresh discoveries, such a sketch as the present can be merely tentative, and must soon, in many of its parts, grow antiquated and be superseded. And where so much depends on the selection of some facts out of many which might have been employed, it will no doubt appear to readers who have some acquaintance with the subject, that here and there a better choice might have been made. The writer hopes that the great difficulty will not be overlooked with which he has had to contend, of compressing a vast subject into a compendious statement without allowing its life and interest to evaporate in the process.

For a fuller bibliography than is given in this volume the reader may consult the works of Dr. C. P. Tiele, and of Dr. Chantepie de la Saussaye. It will readily be believed that the writer of this volume has been indebted to many an author whom he has not named.

ST. ANDREWS, 1895.

PREFACE TO THE REVISED EDITION

SINCE this book first appeared twelve years ago it has been several times reprinted without change. Advantage has now been taken, however, of a call for a fresh issue, to introduce into it some alterations and additions, such as its stereotyped form allows. Some mistakes have been corrected, the names of recent books have been added to the bibliographies, and in some chapters, especially those dealing with the Semitic religions, considerable changes have been made. In going over the book for this purpose, I have seen very clearly that if it had been called for and written at this time instead of twelve years ago, some things which are in it need not have appeared, and additions might have been made which are not now possible. The last twelve years have made a great change in the study of religions; the prejudices with which it was regarded have almost passed away, powerful forces have been enlisted in its service, and admirable works have appeared dealing with various parts of the vast field. Yet I am glad to think that the attempt made in this book to furnish a simple introduction to a deeply important study, and especially to promote the understanding of the religions of the Bible by placing them in their connection with the religion of mankind at large, may still prove useful.

ST. ANDREWS, *June* 1907.

CONTENTS

PART I

THE RELIGION OF THE EARLY WORLD

CHAPTER I

INTRODUCTION

CHAPTER II

THE BEGINNING OF RELIGION

CHAPTER III

THE EARLIEST OBJECTS OF WORSHIP

CHAPTER IV

EARLY DEVELOPMENTS—BELIEF

CHAPTER V

EARLY DEVELOPMENTS—PRACTICES

CHAPTER VI

NATIONAL RELIGION

PART II

ISOLATED NATIONAL RELIGIONS

CHAPTER VII

BABYLON AND ASSYRIA

CHAPTER VIII

CHINA

CHAPTER IX

THE RELIGION OF ANCIENT EGYPT

PART III

THE SEMITIC GROUP

CHAPTER X

THE SEMITIC RELIGION

CHAPTER XI

CANAANITES AND PHENICIANS

CHAPTER XII

ISRAEL

CHAPTER XIII

ISLAM

PART IV

THE ARYAN GROUP

CHAPTER XIV

THE ARYAN RELIGION

CHAPTER XV

THE TEUTONS

CHAPTER XVI

GREECE

CHAPTER XVII

THE RELIGION OF ROME

CHAPTER XVIII

THE RELIGIONS OF INDIA

I. *The Vedic Religion*

CHAPTER XIX

INDIA

II. *Brahmanism*

CHAPTER XX

INDIA

III. *Buddhism*

CHAPTER XXI

PERSIA

PART V

UNIVERSAL RELIGION

CHAPTER XXII

CHRISTIANITY

CHAPTER XXIII

CONCLUSION

PART I

THE RELIGION OF THE EARLY WORLD

CHAPTER I

INTRODUCTION

THE science to which this little volume is devoted is a comparatively new one. It is scarcely half a century since the attention of Western Europe began to fix itself seriously on the great religions of the East, and the study of these ancient systems aroused reflection on the great facts that the world possesses not one religion only, but several, nay, many religions, and that these exhibit both great differences and great resemblances. The agitation of mind then awakened by the thought that other faiths might be compared with Christianity, has to a large extent passed away; and on the other hand fresh fields of knowledge have been opened to the student of the worships of mankind. By new methods of research the religions of Greece and Rome have come to be known as they never were before; and all the other religions of which we formerly knew anything have been led to tell their stories in a new way. A new study—that of the earliest human life on the earth—has brought to light many primitive beliefs and practices, which seem to explain early religious ideas; and the accounts of missionaries and others about savage tribes now existing in different parts of the world, are seen to be full of a significance which was not noticed formerly. We are thus in a very different position from our fathers for studying the religion of the world as a whole. To them their own religion was the true one and all the others were false. Calvin speaks of the "immense welter of errors" in which the whole world outside of Christianity is immersed; it is unnecessary for him to deal with these errors, he can at once proceed to set forth the true doctrine. The belief of the early fathers of the Church, that all worships but those of Judaism and Christianity were directed to demons, and that the demons bore sway in them, practically prevailed till our own day; and it could not but do so, since no other religions than those were really known. That ignorance has ceased, and we are responsible for forming a view of the subject according to the light that has been given us.

The science of religion, though of such recent origin, has already passed beyond its earliest stage, as a reference even to its earlier and its later names will show. "Comparative Religion" was the title given at first to the combined study of various religions. What had to be done, it was thought, was to compare them. The facts about them had to be collected, the systems arranged according to the best information procurable, and then laid side by side, that it might be seen what features they had in common and what each had to distinguish it from the others. Work of this kind is still abundantly necessary. The collection of materials and the specifying of the similarities and dissimilarities of the various faiths will long occupy many workers.

Unity of all Religion. — But recent works on the religions of the world regarded as a whole have been called "histories." We have the well-known *History of Religion* of M. Chantepie de la Saussaye, now in its third edition, and the *Comparative History of the Religions of Antiquity* of M. Tiele. A history of religion may be either of two things. The word history may be used as in the term Natural History, to denote a reasoned account of this department of human life, without attempting any chronological sequence; or it may be used as when we speak of the History of the Romans, an attempt being made to tell the story of religion in the world in the order of time. In either case the use of the term "history" indicates that the study now aims at something more than the accumulation of materials and the pointing out of resemblances and analogies, namely, at arranging the materials at its command so as to show them in an organic connection. This, it cannot be doubted, is the task which the science of religion is now called to attempt. What every one with any interest in the subject is striving after, is a knowledge of the religions of the world not as isolated systems which, though having many points of resemblance, may yet, for all we know, be of separate and independent growth, but as connected with each other and as forming parts of one whole. Our science, in fact, is seeking to grasp the religions of the world as manifestations of the religion of the world.[1]

In rising to this conception of its task, the science of religion is only obeying the impulse which dominates every department of study in modern times. What every science is doing is to seek to show the unity of law amid the multiplicity of the phenomena with which it has to deal, to gather up the many into one, or rather to show how the one has given rise to the many. In the study of religion, if it be really a science, this impulse of all science must surely be felt. Here also we must cherish the conviction that an order does exist amid the apparent disorder, if we could but find it. We must believe that the religious beliefs and practices of mankind are not a mere chaos, not a mere incessant out-

[1] The above statement is criticised by Mr L. H. Jordan in his excellent new work, *Comparative Religion*, p. 485, but is in the main a true account of what has taken place.

burst of unreason, consistent only in that it has appeared in every age and every country of the world, but that they form a cosmos, and may be known, if we take the right way, as a part of human life from which reason has never been absent, and in which a growing purpose has fulfilled and still fulfils itself. Some theories, it is true, from which the world formerly hoped much, are not now relied on, and the present tendency is to abstain from any general doctrine of the subject, and to be content with careful collection and arrangement of the facts in special parts of the field. Caution is no doubt most needful in the attempt to form a view of this great study as a whole. Yet something of this kind is possible, and is beyond all doubt much called for. It is the aim of this little work not only to describe the leading features of the great religions, but also to set forth some of the results which appear to have been reached regarding the relation in which these systems stand to each other.

The Growth of Religion Continuous.—We shall not pretend to set out on this enterprise without any assumptions. The first and principal assumption we make is that in religion as in other departments of human life there has been a development from the beginning, even till now, and that the growth of religion has gone on according to the ordinary laws of human progress. This is a position which, begin the study at whatever point he may, the student of this subject will find himself compelled to take up, if he is not to renounce altogether the idea of understanding it as a whole. To understand anything, means to the thought of the present day, to know how it has come to be what it is ; of any historical phenomenon at least it is certain that it cannot be understood except by tracing its history up to the root. We assume, therefore, until it be disproved, that in this as in other departments of human activity, growth has been continuous from the first. In every other branch of historical study, this assumption is made. The history of institutions is traced back in a continuous line to an age before there was any family or any such thing as property. The methods by which men have earned their subsistence on the earth are known equally far back; and there is no break in the development from the hooked stick to the steam plough. And should it not be the same in religion? Here also shall we not assume until we find it proved to be incorrect, that there has been no break in the growth of ideas and practices from the earliest days till now, and that the highest religion of the present day is part of that religion which man had at first? It is a part, indeed, which is in many ways far removed from the earliest religion, but what was most essential in the earliest belief still lives in it, and what was fittest to survive of its earliest motives, still prompts its worship. Should we adopt this view, we shall find many of the difficulties disappear which have frequently stood in the way of this study. When, according to the new tendency that seems to govern all modern thought, institutions and beliefs are regarded not as fixed things, but as things growing from something that was there before, and tending towards something that is coming, they cease to arouse contempt, or jealousy, or hatred. If we can regard religions as stages in the evolution of religion, then we have no motive either to depreciate or unduly to extol any of them. The earlier stages of the development will have a peculiar interest for us, just as we look with affection on the home of our ancestors even though we should not choose to dwell there. We shall not divide religions into the true one, Christianity, and the false ones, all the rest; no religion will be to us a mere superstition, nor shall we regard any as unguided by God. Feeling that we cannot understand our own religion aright without understanding those out of which it has been built up, we shall value these others for the part they have played in the great movement, and our own most of all, without which they could not be made perfect. In the light of this principle of growth we shall find good in the lowest, and shall see that the good and true rather than the evil and false, furnish the ultimate meaning of even the poorest systems.

We start then with the assumption that religion is a thing which has developed from the first, as law has, or as art has ; and the best method we can follow, if it should prove practicable, will be to follow its movement from the beginning. Without presuming to hope that everything will be made clear, or that we shall meet with no religious phenomena to which we cannot assign their place in the development, without indeed being too sure that we shall be able to find any plain path leading through the immeasurable forests of man's religious sentiments and practices, we may at least expect to find evidence of the direction which on the whole the growth of religion has followed.

Preliminary Definition of Religion.—But, before we can set out on this inquiry, we are met by the question, What is it that we suppose to have been thus developed? In order to trace any process of evolution it is necessary to define that which is evolved ; for it belongs to the very idea of evolution that the identity of the subject of it is not changed on the way up, but that the germ and the finished product are the same entity, only differing from each other in that the one has still to grow while the other is grown. Futile were it indeed to sketch a history of religion with the savage at one end of it and the Christian thinker at the other, if it could be said that in no point did the religion of the savage and that of the Christian coincide, but that the product was a thing of entirely different nature from the germ. It seems necessary, therefore, in the first place, to say what that is, of which we are to attempt the history ; or in other words, to say what we mean by religion.

It must not be forgotten that an adequate definition of a thing which is growing can only be reached when the growth is complete. During its growth it is showing what it is, and its higher as well as its lower manifestations are part of its nature. The world has not yet found out completely, but is still in the course of finding out, what religion is. Any definition propounded at this stage must, therefore, be of an elementary and provisional character. I propose then as a working definition of religion in the meantime, that it is "**The worship of higher powers.**" This appears at first sight a very meagre account of the matter; but if we consider what it implies, we shall find it is not so meagre. In the first place it involves an element of belief. No one will worship higher powers unless he believes that such powers exist. This is the intellectual factor. Not that the intellectual is distinguished in early forms of religion from the other factors, any more than grammar is distinguished by early man as an element of language. But something intellectual, some creed, is present implicitly even in the earliest worships. Should there be no belief in higher powers, true worship cannot continue. If it be continued in outward act, it has lost reality to the mind of the worshipper, and the result is an apparent or a sham religion, a worship devoid of one of the essential conditions of religion. This is true at every stage. But in the second place, these powers which are worshipped are "higher." Religion has respect, not to beings men regard as on a level with themselves or even beneath themselves, but to beings in some way above and beyond themselves, and whom they are disposed to approach with reverence. When objects appear to be worshipped for which the worshipper feels contempt, and which a moment afterwards he will maltreat or throw away, there also one of the essential conditions is absent, and such worship must be judged to fall short of religion. There may no doubt be some religion in it; the object he worships may appear to the savage, in whose mind there is little continuity, at one moment to be higher than himself and the next moment to be lower; but the result of the whole is something less than religion. And in the third place these higher powers are worshipped. That is to say, religion is not only belief in the higher powers but it is a cultivating of relations with them, it is a practical activity continuously directed to these beings. It is not only a thinking but also a doing; this also is essential to it. When worship is discontinued, religion ceases; a principle indeed not to be applied too narrowly, since the apparent cessation of worship may be merely its transition to another, possibly a higher form; but religion is not present unless there be not only a belief in higher powers but an effort of one kind or another to keep on good terms with them.

Criticism of other Definitions.—What has now been said will enable us to judge of several of the definitions of religion which have been put before the world in recent years. Without going back to the definitions offered by philosophers who wrote before the scientific study of our subject had begun, and limiting ourselves to those which have been propounded in the interests of our science, we notice that several make religion consist in an intellectual activity.[1] Thus Mr. Max Müller[2] says that "Religion is a

[1] Though Mr. Tylor defines religion as the "belief in spiritual beings," he is not to be charged with making it too much a matter of the intellect. He uses the word belief in a wide sense as including the practices it involves. In the word "spiritual," however, Mr. Tylor brings into the definition his theory of Animism, and thus makes it unserviceable for those who do not adopt that theory.

[2] *Introduction to the Science of Religion*, 1882, p. 13. The definition was put forward in the year 1873, and in his lectures on the Origin of Religion, 1882, Mr. Müller adhered to it as being in the main sound (p. 23).

mental faculty or disposition which, independent of, nay, in spite of, sense and reason, enables man to apprehend the Infinite under different names, and under varying disguises. Without that faculty . . . no religion would be possible." To this definition there are various strong objections. It implies that there is only one way in which men come to believe in higher beings; they arrive at that belief by finding something which transcends them and which they cannot understand; *i.e.* by an intellectual process. It may be doubted whether the sense of disappointment with the finite is the only road or even a common road, to belief in gods. Mr. Müller's omission, moreover, from his definition, of the practical side of religion, of the element of worship, is a fatal objection to it. Belief and worship are inseparable sides of religion, which does not come fully into existence till both are present. In a later work[1] Mr. Müller admits the force of this objection, urged by several scholars, to his definition, and modifies it as follows: "Religion consists in the perception of the infinite under such manifestations as are able to influence the moral character of man." In this form the definition recognises that worship, the practical activity in which man's moral character shows itself in fear, gratitude, love, contrition, is an essential part of religion, and that perceptions of the infinite apart from this are only one side of it. His original definition, however, has played too large a part in the history of our subject to be left without careful notice. The same objection applies to Mr. Herbert Spencer's account of the matter. Mr. Spencer finds the basis of all religion in the inscrutableness of the Power which the universe manifests to us. The belief common to all religions, he holds, is the presence of something which passes comprehension. The idea of the absolute and unconditioned he regards as accompanying all our consciousness of things

[1] *Natural Religion*, 1888, pp. 188, 193.

conditioned and limited, and as being not a negative notion, not merely the denial of limits, but a positive one. The unconditioned is that of which all our thoughts and ideas are manifestations, but which we never can know, with regard to which we cannot affirm anything but that it exists. This definition like that last noticed traces religion to the defects in man's knowledge, and rather to a negative than a positive element in his experience. It also comes under the objection that it traces religion rather to an intellectual than a practical motive, and omits the element of worship.

Other scholars have explained religion as the action of the curiosity of the human mind, of that impulse which prompts man to investigate the causes of things, and specially to seek for the first cause of all things. Here we touch what is certainly to be recognised as an invariable feature of religion; it always professes to explain the world, and to bring unity to man's mind by clearing up the problems which perplex him, and affording him a commanding point of view, from which he may see all the parts of the world and of life fall into their places. This, however, does not tell us what religion itself is. This curiosity, this impulse to know, are not specifically religious; they belong rather to philosophy. Other motives than those connected with knowledge entered from the first into man's worship. Curiosity impelled him to seek the first cause of things; in religion he saw something that promised to explain the world to him, and to explain him to himself. But it was something more than curiosity that made him regard that cause when found, as a god, and pay it reverence and sacrifice. What is the motive of worship? Wonder, no doubt, is always present in it, but what is there in it beyond wonder? No definition of religion can be regarded as complete in which the motive of worship is left undetermined. That is of the essence of the matter. There must be a moral as well as an intellectual quality which is characteristic of religion. What is religion morally? Acts of worship may be specified in which every conceivable moral quality seeks to express itself. The most contradictory motives, pride and anger and revenge, as well as fear or hunger or contrition, enter into such acts. But if religion is a matter of sentiment as well as of outward posture, these acts of worship cannot all be equally entitled to the name, and something is wanted to complete our definition.

Fuller Definition.—Let us add what seems to be wanting; and say that religion is the "**worship of higher powers from a sense of need**"! This will remind the reader of Schleiermacher's definition—"a sense of infinite dependence." It was always objected to that definition, that it made religion no more than a sentiment, a mood, but that besides this, it is both belief and action. But the truth Schleiermacher urged was one of essential importance to the matter. Belief in gods and acts of worship paid to them do not constitute religion unless the sentiment, the sense of need, be also there. These three together constitute religion both in the lowest and in the highest levels of civilisation.

A belief must exist, to take a step farther, that the being worshipped is capable of supplying what the worshipper requires. Men do not pray nor bring offerings to beings they suppose to be incapable of attending to them, or powerless to do them any good or evil. It is implied in every act of worship that the being addressed is a power who is able to do for the worshipper what he cannot do for himself. It is his inability to help himself or to supply his own needs that sends the worshipper to his god, who has a power he himself has not. If he could help himself he would not need religion, if his life were either perfectly prosperous and even, so that there was nothing left to wish for, or perfectly miserable and unsuccessful, so that there was no room for hope, he would not resort to higher powers; but neither of these two being the case, his life on the contrary being a mixed lot of good and evil, in which there are blessings his own forces cannot secure, and dangers from which no efforts of his own can save him, and the belief having arisen within him, in what way we need not now inquire, that higher powers exist who can, if they will, defend and prosper him, in this way he has religion, he keeps up intercourse with higher powers. And thus religion is not necessarily even in its most primitive form, a manifestation of mere selfishness. Though gifts are offered which are expected to please the higher beings, and though benefits are asked of which the worshipper is urgently in need, such transactions are not necessarily sordid any more than similar applications between human beings, between two friends, or between a parent and a child. Even the savage living in entire isolation, at war with every one and conscious of no needs but those of food and shelter, will not seek benefits from his god without some feeling of attachment, nor without some sense of strengthened friendship should the benefit be granted him. When once this sense of friendship has arisen, religion is present, the man has come to be in living relation with a higher power, whom he conceives, no doubt, after his own likeness, but nevertheless as greater than he is.

This then is what we conceive to be the essence of religion—the worship of higher powers, from a sense of need; and it is of this that we are to trace the history though only in the barest outlines. The definition itself suggests in what way the development may be expected to work itself out. According as the needs change their character, of which men are conscious, so will their religion also change. The gradual elevation and refinement of human needs, in the growth of civilisation, is the motive force of the development of religion. The deities themselves, their past history and their present character, the sacrifices offered to them, and the benefits aimed at in intercourse with them, all must grow up as man himself grows, from rudeness to refinement and from caprice to order. At its lowest, religion is perhaps an individual affair between the savage and his god, and has to do with material individual needs. At a higher stage (not always nor even commonly later in time) it is the affair of a family, of a tribe, or of a combination of tribes, and with each of these extensions the requests grow broader and less personal which have to be presented to the deity; the religion becomes a common worship for public ends. The needs of the nomad are other than those of the settled agriculturist, and those of the countryman differ from those of the citizen, and those of the Laplander from those of the Negro, and these differences will be reflected in the aspect of the deities and in the observances celebrated in their honour. When art begins to stir within a nation, the gods have to adapt themselves to the new taste. As society grows more humane, cruel and sanguinary religious observances, though they may long keep a hold of the ignorant and excitable, lose their support in the public conscience and are sentenced to change or to extinction. And when a new consciousness of personal human dignity springs up, and men come to feel the infinite value and the infinite responsibility of personal life, the old public religion is felt to be cold and distant, and religious services of a more personal and more intimate kind are sought for.

Thus **religion and civilisation advance together**; according as the civilisation is in any people, so is its religion. It is vain, broadly speaking, to look for the combination of primitive manners and customs with a lofty spiritual faith. The converse it is true may often seem to take place.

Religion, or rather religious creeds and practices, often seem to lag behind civilisation and to maintain themselves long after the reason and the conscience of a people has condemned them. That is because religion is what man values most in his life, and he is loath to change observances in which his affections are powerfully engaged. But religion must reflect the ideals of the society in which it exists; the needs which the society feels at the time must be the burden of its prayers; its sacrifices must be such as the general sentiment allows; its gods, to retain the allegiance of the community, must alter with time and prove themselves alive and in touch with their people. And if it be the case that civilisation has on the whole advanced upwards from the first; if, as Mr. Tylor assures us,[1] man began with his lowest and has in spite of occasional declines, on the whole been improving ever since, then of religion also the same will be true. It also will be found to begin with its rudest forms and gradually to grow better. Religion in fact is the inner side of civilisation, and expresses the essential spirit of human life in various ages and nations. The religion of a race is the truest expression of its character, and reflects most faithfully its attitude and aims and policy. The religion of an age shows what at that time constituted the object of man's aspiration and endeavour, as older hopes grew pale and new hopes rose on his sight. Thus the study of the religions of the world is the study of the very soul of its history; it is the study of the desires and aspirations which throughout the course of history men have not been ashamed, nay, which they have been proud and determined to confess. No more fascinating study could possibly engage us. It is true that the requirements for the adequate treatment of the subject are such as few indeed can hope to possess. He who would treat the history of religion aright ought to know thoroughly the

[1] *Primitive Culture*, chap. ii.

whole of the history of civilisation ; he should have explored the vast domain of savage life and thought, that has recently been opened up to us, and he should be at home in every century of every nation from the beginning of history. At a time like this, when new light is being poured every year on every part of our subject, no statement of it can be more than tentative and partial. The student will be directed at each step to sources of fuller information.

BOOKS RECOMMENDED. (GENERAL)

Outlines of the History of Religion to the Spread of the Universal Religions. By Dr C. P. Tiele. Translation. In Trübner's Oriental Series. Very condensed and in somewhat technical language; but the work of one of the greatest masters of the subject. A full Bibliography is appended to the various chapters.

Lehrbuch der Religionsgeschichte, von P. D. Chantepie de la Saussaye. Freiburg, 1887. The English translation has an altered title, viz. *Manual of the Science of Religion*, Longmans, 1891. The Third Edition (1905) is practically a different book, and consists of studies, each by an expert, of the various religions.

Religious Systems of the World (Sonnenschein, 1892) is a full collection of descriptions of the various religions, by persons specially acquainted with them ; of very unequal merit.

Mr. Max Müller's works cited above, also his more recent volumes of Gifford Lectures, contain a number of general discussions.

See also the Gifford Lectures of Mr. Ed. Caird, and the late Prof. Tiele.

Pfleiderer's *Philosophy of Religion*, 4 vols.

Pünjer, *Geschichte der christl. Religionsphilosophie*, 2 vols. 1880-38.

Rauwenhoff, *Wijsbegeerde van den Godsdienst*, 2 vols. 1887 (also in German).

M. Jastrow, *The Study of Religion*, 1901.

L. H. Jordan, *Comparative Religion, its Origin and Growth*, 1905.

Revue de l'histoire des religions, edited by M. J. Réville.

Archiv für Religionswissenschaft, edited by Alb. Dieterich.

CHAPTER II

THE BEGINNING OF RELIGION

Origin of Civilisation.—Every inhabited country, we are assured by ethnologists, was once peopled by savages; the stone age everywhere came before the age of metals. Antecedent to every civilisation that has sprung up on the earth is this dim period, the period of the cave dwellers and afterwards of the lake dwellers. There can be no chronology nor any exact knowledge of these early men, who lived by hunting, with stone weapons, animals which are now extinct. How from his earliest and most helpless state man came in various ways to help himself; how he discovered fire, how he improved his weapons and invented tools, how he learned to tame certain of the animals on which he had formerly made war, and instead of wandering about the world came to settle in one place and till the soil, and how family life came to be instituted, and the father as well as the mother to act as guardian to the children; all that is a vast history, which must be read in its own place. Immense, indeed, were the labours early man had to undergo, in wrestling his way up from a life like that of the brutes to a life in which his own distinctive nature could begin to display itself.

It was from the savage state that civilisation was by degrees produced. The theory that man was originally civilised and humane, and that it was by a fall, by a degeneration from that earliest condition, that the state of savagery made its appearance, is now generally abandoned. There may be instances of such degeneration having taken place; but on the whole, the conviction now obtains that civilisation is the result of progressive development, and was the result man conquered for himself by his age-long struggles with his environment. That development did not take place in all lands alike. In some it proceeded faster than in others, and its advances were due oftener to propagation from without, than to unaided growth from within; as one race came in contact with another new ideas were aroused of the possibilities of life in various directions. In some lands the development has scarcely taken place at all. There remain to this day races who are judged to be still in the primitive condition. Not all savage tribes are thought to be in that condition. The bushmen of Australia, the Andaman Islanders, and others,[1] are found to be in such a state in point of habits and acquirements that they must be considered as races which have fallen from a higher position, and present instances of degeneration. But a multitude of savage tribes remain in all quarters of the globe who do not appear to have been thus enfeebled, and who are held to be still in that state in which the dwellers in all parts of the earth were before civilisation began. They are races among whom civilisation did not spring up, as it did in China or in Peru. From these races we may learn in a general way what the ancestors of all the civilised nations were. It confirms this conclusion that we find in every civilised nation a number of phenomena, practices, beliefs, stories, which the mental condition of the nation as we know it does not account for, which manifestly are not outgrowths of the civilisation, but relics of an older state of life, which civilisation has not entirely obliterated; and that

[1] Instances in Tylor, *Primitive Culture*, chap. ii., where the theory of degeneration is fully discussed.

these practices, beliefs, and stories can be exactly matched by those of the savage races. The inference is drawn that civilisation has sprung from savage life, that, as Mr. Tylor says, "the savage state represents the early condition of mankind, out of which the higher culture has gradually been developed by causes still in operation." To trace the history of civilisation, therefore, it is necessary to go back to the earliest knowledge we have of human life upon the earth, and to ask what germs and rudiments can be discovered among savages of law, of institutions, of arts and sciences. Such works as Maine's *Ancient Law*, Tylor's *Primitive Culture*, Lubbock's *Origin of Civilisation*, show how fruitful this method is, and what floods of light it pours on the history of society.

Now what is true of civilisation generally will be true also of religion, which is one of its principal elements. If every country was once inhabited by savages, then **the original religion of every country** must have been **a religion of savages**; and in the later religion there will be features which have been carried on from the earlier one. This, indeed, we must in any case expect to find. No new religion can enter on its career on a soil quite unprepared, on which no gods have been worshipped before. (That would imply that there had been races in the world without religion, on which we shall speak presently.) A new faith has always to begin by adjusting itself to that which it found in possession of the soil, and it always adopts what it can of the old system. We should expect then that the great religions of the world should exhibit features which do not belong to their own structure, but which they inherited, with or against their will, from their uncivilised predecessors. And that is the case, as we shall see afterwards, with all the great religions. They are all full of survivals of the savage state. The old religious associations cling to the face of a land and refuse to be uprooted, whatever changes take place among the gods above. Superstitious practices continue among a race long after a truth has been preached there with which they are entirely inconsistent. Stories are long told about the gods, quite out of keeping with their character in the theology of the new faith, pointing to a time when not so much was expected of a god. In Mr. Lang's *Myth, Ritual, and Religion*, the reader will find an admirable collection of material showing how the popular elements of an old religion survive in a new one in which they are quite out of place. There is none of the great religions to which this does not apply.

Now, if it be the case that each of the great religions has been built upon a primitive religion formerly occupying the same ground, it might appear that we must, in order to understand any of the great religions, study first, in each case, the savage system which it superseded. It would be a serious prospect for the student if he had to make a separate study of a set of savage beliefs as an approach to each of the ten or twelve great religions. But this, as we shall see afterwards, is not the case. There is a great family likeness in the religions of savages, and we may even allow ourselves to speak not of the religions but of the religion of early races. In the next chapter an attempt will be made to describe that religion; but we may say here that there are some features which are generally, though by no means always found in it, and that these features may be regarded for practical purposes as the religion of the primitive world, which everywhere was the forerunner of the great systems. This is the jungle, as it were, overspreading all the early world, out of which like giant trees the great religions arose, and from which they derived and still derive a nourishment they cannot disown. Indeed, we may go much farther. In some of their leading doctrines, the great religions show the most striking affinity with one another. China and Egypt have some doctrines in common which are also found in the religion of the Incas ; the Aryan and the Semitic religions know them too. Should these doctrnes be found in the religion of savages, it will at least be a question whether the great religions all alike borrowed and developed them from that source, or whether any other explanation of the case can be found. Evidently we cannot make any progress with our subject till we have taken a general view of this religion of savages and come to some conclusions regarding it.

A few words must be said, by way of preface to this subject, on the mental habits of early races. We cannot hope to understand the thoughts of those people without knowing how they came to have such thoughts, how they were accustomed to think. Now of the savage we may say that he is just like a child who has not yet learned to think correctly, or to know things truly. He is making all kinds of experiments in thought, and being led into all sorts of errors and confusion ; and if the child takes years, the savage may take millenniums, to get free from these. He does not know the difference between one thing and another, between him self and the lower animals, or between an animal and a water-spout. He does not know how far things are away from him, nor what makes them move and act as they do ; why, for example, the sun and moon go round the sky, or why the wind blows. He cannot tell why things have this or that peculiar appearance ; why, for example, the rabbit has no tail, why the sky is red in the morning, why some stones are like men. And he wants to know all these things, and is for ever asking questions. But almost any answer will do for him, the first explanation that turns up is accepted ; and while a child finds out pretty soon if he has been told wrong, the savage is so ignorant that he cannot see the absurdest explanation to be false, but sticks to it seriously and goes on using it. There is no consistency in the contents of his mind, and inconsistency does not distress him. He has no classes and orders of things, but considers each thing by itself as it occurs, without putting it in its place with reference to other things. He has no idea of what is possible and what is impossible; these words in fact would have no meaning for him, since he is not aware of any laws by which events are governed. His imagination, accordingly, is not under any restraint; he hits upon all kinds of grotesque theories, and, having no critical faculty to test them, he repeats them and seriously believes them. The stories of the nursery, in which there are no impossibilities, in which a man may visit the sun and the winds in their homes and find them at their broth, in which the beasts can speak, in which the witch or the fairy knows at any distance what is going on and can turn up just at the nick of time, in which ghosts walk, in which anything can be changed into anything, a hero going through half-a-dozen transformations to escape from so many dangers,—these are to the savage not incredible nor foolish tales, to him they are very real, and very serious matters. He lives, in fact, we are told by the authorities on the subject, in the myth-making period of the world; in the period when such incidents as occur in the tales of fairyland and in the stories of mythology are matter of common belief, and even, it is thought, of common experience, so that when the story is put in a good form, it lives and is believed as a true record of what has actually taken place.

On one feature of the savage imagination in particular we must fix our attention. The savage regards all things as animated,—as animated with a life like his own. Of his own life he has no very exalted idea; he has no notion how different he really is from anything around him; as he is himself so he supposes other beings to be also, not only the animals but the trees and all that moves and even what does not move, even rocks and stones. He is living himself; he regards all these as living too. He imagines them like himself, and supposes them to have feelings and passions like his own, to reason as he does, and even if he is told they speak as he does, that is not incredible to him. Thus he lives in a world of infinite confusion, in which there are no laws, no classes of beings, no means of knowing what may happen, or of verifying any statement, where every effort of fancy may be believed. The mental world of savages has been compared to the ravings of a whole world turned lunatic. We survey it, however, without horror, because we know that reason is not unseated there, but striving towards her kingdom. That is the experience that had to be gone through, these are part of the experiments such as every child has still to make, by which the knowledge of the world is gradually arrived at.

Amid this apparent universal confusion a certain consistency of view is to be observed. It might be expected that the savage habit of thought, acting independently in different parts of the world, would lead to an infinite number of divergent and inconsistent views of the nature of things and of man's place in the world. But this is not found to be the case. Mr. Lang accounts as follows for the diffusion of the same stories all over the world: "An ancient identity of mental status, and the working of similar mental forces at the attempt to explain the same phenomena, will account without any theory of borrowing, or of transmission of myth, or of original unity of race, for the world-wide diffusion of many mythical conceptions." Mr. Tylor says that the same imaginative processes regularly recur, that world-wide myths show the regularity and the consistency of the human imagination. M. Réville, in his *Religions des peuples non-civilisés*, remarks that the character of savage religions is everywhere the same; that only the forms vary.

Now of the things that **all savages possess**, certainly **religion** is one. It is practically agreed that religion, the belief in and worship of gods, is universal at the savage stage; and the accounts which some travellers have given of tribes without religion are either set down to misunderstanding, or are thought to be insufficient to invalidate the assertion that religion is a universal feature of savage life.

How did it get there? How comes it that men so near the lowest human state, so devoid of all that has been since acquired, should yet be found to have this mode of thought universally diffused among them?

It has been ascribed to a **primitive revelation**. At the beginning, it is said, God, with the other gifts He gave to man, gave him religion; that is to say, gave him not only a disposition for reverence and piety, but a certain amount of religious knowledge, so that he set out with a stock of religious ideas which were not elaborated by his own efforts, but bestowed on him ready made. It is impossible, however, to conceive how this could be done. If the religion given at first was a lofty and pure one,—and no other need be thought of in such a connection,—then it implies a condition of human life far above the struggles and uncertainties of savage existence; and both the civilisation and the religion must have been lost afterwards. But how could all mankind forget a pure religion? Mankind in that case cannot have been fit for the possession of it; it was given prematurely. No. The history of early civilisation is the history of a struggle in which man has everything to conquer, and in which he is not remembering something he had lost, but advancing by new routes to a land he never reached before. And if civilisation was won for the first time, so was religion.

We may also put aside the theory that man had religion from the first as **an innate idea**, that he found information all ready and prepared in his mind of what it was proper to do in this direction, and how it was to be done. There was indeed a suggestion from within; but it was due not to any special faculty lying outside the essential structure of human nature, but to the constitution of the human mind itself. We cannot go into the philosophical question of the basis of religion in the human mind.[1] It would seem to be a **psychological necessity.** At all stages of his existence the world of which man is aware outside him, and the world of feelings and desires within him are in conflict. But the conviction lives within him that in some way they can be brought into harmony, and that a power exists which rules in both of these discordant realms and in which, if he can identify himself with it, he also will escape from their discord. If this be so, then this necessity to seek after a higher power must have begun to operate as soon as human consciousness appeared. The savage certainly was never unacquainted with the discrepancy between what he wanted and what the world would give him, between the inner man so full of desires and plans, and that outward nature which denied him his desires and thwarted his plans, and before which he felt so feeble and insecure. He also could not but be driven, if his life was to go on at all on any tolerable basis, to believe in something that had to do both with the world outside him and with the world of his heart, in a being which both had sympathy with his desires and power to give effect to them outwardly.

The whole of the early world did entertain such a belief. This is the first and the most important instance of uniformity of thought at a stage through which every nation

[1] See on this subject Prof. Edward Caird's Gifford Lectures, *The Evolution of Religion*, 1893.

once passed; all men at that stage believe in gods. We will not refuse the name of religion to this side of savage life, even should the needs be low and material which send the savage to his god, though his god be a being who in us would excite the very opposite of reverence, and though his treatment of his god be far from what to us seems worthy, or even though he strove to appease a multitude of spirits which he conceived as flitting about him, before he came to form a settled relation of confidence with one being whom he took for his own god. Where the sense of need has sent a human being to hold intercourse with a higher power, there we hold religion is making its appearance. And if this is universally the case among men at the savage stage, then religion is universal among the ancestors of all nations; it did not need to be invented when kings and priests appeared and wanted it as an instrument for their own purposes; it was there before there were any kings or priests, and is an inheritance which has come down to all mankind from the time when human intelligence first turned to the effort to understand the world.

Books Recommended

For this and the three following chapters

J. B. Tylor, *Anthropology*, Third Edition, 1891.
Frazer, *The Golden Bough* (1900).
A. Lang, *Myth, Ritual, and Religion*, new edition, 1899.
Th. Achelis, in De la Saussaye.
Waitz und Gerland, *Anthropologie der Naturvölker*, 1859-72.
Brinton, *Religions of Primitive Peoples*, 1897.
Of the reports of travellers and missionaries it is impossible here to give any indications.

CHAPTER III

THE EARLIEST OBJECTS OF WORSHIP

WE must now make some attempt to set forth the principal features of the religion of savages. It is an attempt of some difficulty; for savage religion is an immense and bewildering jungle of all manner of extraordinary growths. It is described in detail in large books, but if we try to sum it up in a short statement, we may be told that essential features have been omitted. No one set of savages has anything that can be called a system, and different sets of savages are not alike. For the present purpose we are obliged to include under the name, tribes who occupy various positions in the scale of human advancement, and tribes in all sorts of geographical positions, in hot climates and in cold, both rude savages and those who are nobler; and these will, of course, have a variety of ideas and needs, and in so far, different religions. After reading such a book as Mr. Frazer's *Golden Bough*, or turning over the pages of Waitz and Gerland's *Anthropologie der Naturvölker*, one is inclined to regard it as a hopeless task to reduce savage religion to any compact statement.

Mr. Tylor's orderly collections of materials bearing on different features of early religion are a help for which the student cannot be sufficiently thankful. After all, it is not the whole of savage religion that we are responsible for here, but only those parts of it that grew and survived in higher faiths. Remembering what has been said as to the uniformity of savage thought amid its great variety of forms, and looking for those parts of it which have proved to have life in them, rather than for what is merely curious and grotesque, we may venture on our task not without hope. In the present chapter we shall inquire what beings savages worship as gods. Of these we shall find that there are several classes; and it will be necessary to notice the great discussions which have arisen on the question which of these classes of deities was first worshipped by man. The objects worshipped by men in low stages of civilisation may be arranged in four classes, viz.—

1. Parts of nature (*a*) great, (*b*) small.
2. Spirits of ancestors and other spirits.
3. Objects supposed to be haunted by spirits (fetish-worship).
4. A Supreme Being.

1. **Nature-worship.**—It is not difficult to realise why early man turned to the great elements of nature as beings who could help him, and whom he ought, therefore, to cultivate. The farther we go back in civilisation, the less protection has man against the weather, the more do his subsistence and his comfort depend on the action of the sun, the winds, the rain. If, according to the habits of early thought, he conceived these beings as living like himself and as guided by feelings and motives similar to his own, he could not fail to wish to open up communication with them. That simple view, that they were living beings with feelings like his own, was enough to go upon. In his anxieties for food or warmth he could not fail to think of the beings who, he had observed, had power to supply

him with these comforts, of the rain which he had noticed was able to make food grow, of the sun whose warmth he knew. The thunderstorm was a being who had power to put an end to a long drought; the winds could break the trees, could dry up the wet earth, or could bring rain. Heaven was over all, and the Earth was the supporter and fertile producer of all; from her all life came. The moon as well as the sun was a friendly power, nay, in some climates, more friendly. Fire was a living being certainly, on whom much depended; and so was the great lake or the ocean. This is what M. Réville calls the great Nature-worship, in comparison with the minor Nature-worship to be noticed presently.

We do not now enter on the subject of mythology; that is to say, of the names men very early began to give to the great natural objects of worship, the characters they ascribed to them, the stories they told about them. That process of myth-making began very early, and is to be found at work in every part of the world. But at first it was simply the natural being itself, conceived as living, that was worshipped, not a spirit or a person thought to dwell in it. Of this, abundant evidence has survived in the great religions. Jupiter is just the sky, the Greek god Helios is just the sun, and the goddess Selene the moon. In China heaven itself is worshipped to this day. The Babylonians worshipped the stars. The Vedic gods are primarily the elements. From savage life examples of this earliest state of matters can also be quoted, though mythology has nearly everywhere greatly confused it. The Mincopies adore the sun as a beneficent deity, the moon as an inferior god. To the Natchez the sun is the supreme god; with some tribes of North America the chief god is heaven blowing, the sky with a wind in it, what Longfellow calls the "Great Spirit" or blowing. The Incas invoked together the Creator and the Sun and Thunder. Thunder was one of the great gods of the Germans. The Samoyede bows to the Sun every morning and every evening and says, "When thou arisest I also arise; when thou settest I also betake myself to rest." To the Ojibways Fire is a divine being, to be well entertained, with whom no liberties must be taken. In every land men are to be found who worship the Earth as a great deity, calling her by her own name and serving her with suitable rites. In the *Prometheus* of Æschylus the hero addresses his appeal as follows to the beings he regards as gods of old race who will sympathise with him against the upstart Zeus :—

> Ether of Heaven and Winds untired of wing,
> Rivers whose fountains fail not, and thou Sea,
> Laughing in waves innumerable ! O Earth,
> All-mother !—Yea and on the Sun I call,
> Whose orb scans all things ; look on me and see
> How I, a god, am wronged by gods.
>
> *Lewis Campbell*, line 85 *sq.*

The **minor Nature-worship** has to do with rivers and springs, with trees and groves, with crops and fruits, with rocks and stones, and with the lower animals. Here also we must bear in mind the habit of mind of early man, who regarded all things as animated and as like himself. It was not necessary for one who thought in this way to suppose that the spring was haunted by a nymph or the oak inhabited by a dryad, before he felt that the spring or the oak had a claim on him, and brought offerings to secure their friendship. The Nile and the Ganges did not become sacred by having a mythical being added to them as their spirit; they were themselves sacred beings. Every country is studded with names which reveal to the scholar the primeval sanctity of the spots they belong to; the mountain, the grove, and the individual tree, the rocky gorge, the rock, the grassy knoll, each was once an object of reverence. Britain is full of sacred wells, which once received prayers and offerings. There is no animal that has not once been worshipped. A marked feature of primitive life also is the worship of nature not in its particular objects but in its living processes. In a multitude of curious rites, some of which still survive in local usages, and have only recently been explained, primitive man brought himself into relations with nature in its growth, decay, and resurrection. He sympathised with it and imitated it, and he thus sought to make himself sure of the benefits which he saw bestowed by some power which he apprehended in its processes and believed able to further him.

2. **Ancestor-worship.**—A set of beings of a very different kind comes next. If man found in the world which he beheld outside him a number of objects he could make gods, his domestic experience forced him to consider certain beings of a different kind, of whom the outward world could tell him nothing. The worship of the dead, of ancestors, is diffused throughout nearly the whole of antiquity, it is practised by most savages. Man at an early stage does not fully realise the meaning of death. He interprets death after the analogy of dreams, in which he judges that the spirit leaves the body and traverses distant regions, coming back to the body again when the journey is ended. A vision is to him an instance of the same thing. He sees a friend, who, he afterwards learns, was far from him at the time, and he judges that it was the spirit of his friend which visited him. Thus there arises in his mind the conception of a human spirit which is able to leave the body and dwell at a distance from it. It is called by various names,—the shade, the image, the heart, as perhaps when Elisha says his heart went with Gehazi when he went to meet

Naaman the Syrian (2 Kings v. 26), the breath, the soul. When the breath or spirit goes away and stays away (in spite of efforts made to bring it back) the man dies. But the spirit is not dead. It has gone away and is staying somewhere else. The spirit resembles the body in shape, but it is of a thin and light consistence, and is able to move about and to pass through the smallest openings, to make unpleasant noises, and to cause its presence to be felt in a variety of ways. In the very earliest times, the savage regards the spirit which has left the house as an enemy, and uses a variety of precautions to keep it from coming back to trouble him (vampires, ghosts, *lemures*). Whether from such fear or from more liberal motives, much is done to please the spirits of the departed and to increase their comfort in the abodes to which they have gone. At their burial or cremation all they may be supposed to want where they are going, *i.e.* the things they used on earth, are made to accompany them; food and weapons are placed beside them; servants are killed whose spirits are to wait on them, even a wife, voluntarily or without being asked, gives up her earthly life to accompany her husband. Offerings of food and drink are made to them afterwards, prayers are addressed to them, memorials of them, of various kinds, are preserved in the houses they occupied.

It was the universal belief of the early world that the person continued to exist after the death of the body; and this furnished the materials for a religion which was more widely prevalent in antiquity than the worship of any god. In some forms of it, indeed, the spirit appears to have been treated as an enemy, and this worship might be judged to fall short of religion, which is the cultivation not the avoidance of intercourse with higher powers. The savage has no hope from the spirit, and does not seek his intercourse.

But in most forms of the belief in the continued life of the departed, other sentiments than fear prevail; natural affection is felt for the lost relative; the ancestor represents the family, to which the individual is called to subordinate and to some extent even to sacrifice himself, the spirit of the dead is the upholder of a family tradition which the living must hold sacred. Even in those cases in which nothing but fear is apparent, these latter sentiments may also be to some extent operative.

3. **Fetish-worship.**—The early world has still another kind of deity. In the case of all those we have considered, the god stands in some respect above the worshipper; man reverences the sun, spirit, or animal, for some quality in them that is admirable or that gives them a hold over him; they are in some ways beyond him. Among certain sets of savages, however, notably in South Africa, this feature of religion partially disappears, and objects are reverenced not for any intrinsic quality in them that makes them worthy of regard, but because of a spirit which is supposed to be connected with them. Stones, trees, twigs, pieces of bark, roots, corn, claws of birds, teeth, skin, feathers, articles of human manufacture, any conceivable object, will be held in reverence by the savage and regarded as embodying a spirit. Anything that strikes his fancy as being out of the common he will take up and add to his museum of objects, each of which has in it a hidden power. That power, be it repeated, is not connected with the natural quality of the object, but is due to a spirit which has come to reside in it, and which may very possibly leave it again. Having chosen this deity and set it up for worship, the man can use it as he thinks fit. He addresses prayers to it and extols its virtues; but should his enterprise not prosper, he will cast his deity aside as useless, and cease to worship it; he will address

it with torrents of abuse, and will even beat it, to make it serve him better. It is a deity at his disposal, to serve in the accomplishment of his desires; the individual keeps gods of his own to help him in his undertakings.

The name "fetishism" by which this kind of worship is known, is of Portuguese origin; it is derived from *feitiço*, "made," "artificial" (compare the old English *fetys*, used by Chaucer); and this term, used of the charms and armlets worn in the Roman Catholic religion of the period, was applied by the Portuguese sailors of the eighteenth century to the deities they saw worshipped by the negroes of the West Coast of Africa. De Brosses, a French savant of last century, brought the word fetishism into use as a term for the type of religion of the lowest races. The word has given rise to some confusion, having been applied by Comte and other writers to the worship of the heavenly bodies and of the great features of nature. It is best to limit it, as has been done above, to the worship of such natural objects as are reverenced not for their own power or excellence but because they are supposed to be occupied each by a spirit.

Can this be called religion? In the full sense of the term it cannot. We should remember that it is not the casual object, but the spirit connected with it that the savage worships; but even then we shall be obliged to hold that the fetish worshipper is rather seeking after religion than actually in possession of it.

4. **A Supreme Being.**—Is it necessary to add another class of deity to these three, and to say that besides nature-gods and spirits early man also worshipped a Supreme Being above all these? In most savage religions there is a principal deity to whom the others are subordinate. But if we carefully examine one by one the supreme gods of these religions, we shall find reason

to doubt whether they really have a common character so as to form a class by themselves. Many of them are nature gods who have out-grown the other deities of that class and come to occupy an isolated position. The North American Indians, as we saw, worship the Great Spirit, the heaven with its breath, to whom sun and moon and other ordinances of nature act as ministers. In many cases heaven is the highest god. In others again the sun is supreme. Ukko the great god of the Finns is a heaven- and rain-god. Perkunas the god of the Lithuanians is connected with thunder. On the other hand there are instances in which the supreme god appears to be a different being from the nature-god. The Samoyedes worship the sun and moon and the spirits of other parts of nature ; but they also believe in a good spirit who is above all. The Supreme Being of the islands of the Pacific bears in New Zealand the name of Tangaroa, and is spoken of in quite metaphysical terms as the uncreated and eternal Creator. Here we may suspect Christian influence. With the Zulus Unkulunkulu the Old-old one might be supposed to be a kind of first cause. But on looking nearer we find he is distinctly a man, the first man, the common ancestor ; beyond which idea speculation does not seem to go. Among many North American tribes it is usual to find an animal the chief deity, the hare or the musk-rat or the coyote. It is very common to find in savage beliefs a vague far-off god who is at the back of all the others, takes little part in the management of things, and receives little worship. But it is impossible to judge what that being was at an earlier time ; he may have been a nature-god or a spirit who has by degrees grown faint and come to occupy this position. We cannot judge from the supreme beings of savages, such as they are, that the belief in a supreme being was generally diffused in the world[1] in the earliest

[1] *Cf.* A. Lang, *The Making of Religion* (1898) ; Galloway, *Studies in the Philosophy of Religion* (1904), p. 123, *sq.*

times, and is not to be derived from any of the processes from which the other gods arose. We shall see afterwards how natural the tendency is which, where there are several gods, brings one of them to the front while the others lose importance. For a theory of primitive monotheism the supreme gods of savages certainly do not furnish sufficient evidence; they do not appear to have sprung all from the same source, but to have advanced from very different quarters to the supreme position, in obedience to that native instinct of man's mind which causes him, even when he believes in many gods, to make one of them supreme.

Which Gods were First Worshipped?—If then early man formed his gods from parts of nature and from spirits of departed ancestors or heroes, and even, should the more backward races now existing represent a stage of human life belonging to the early world, from spirits residing in outward objects, which of these is the original root of all the religions of the world? The claim has been made for each of these kinds of religion, that it came first.

1. **Fetish-gods came First.**—Till recently the view prevailed that all the religion of the world has sprung out of fetishism. First the savage took for his god some casual object, as we have described, then he chose higher objects, trees and mountains, rivers and lakes, and even the sun and stars. The heavens at last became his supreme fetish, and at a higher level, when he had learned about spirits, he would make a spirit his fetish, and so at last come to Monotheism.

This view is attractive because it places the beginning of religion in the lowest known form of it and thus makes for the belief that the course of the world's faith has been upward from the first. But it presents the gravest difficulties; for why should the savage make a god of a stick or a stone, and attribute to it supernatural powers? Who told him about a god, that he should call a stick god, or about supernatural powers, that he should suppose a stick to work wonders? There is nothing in the stick to suggest such notions; that he should make gods in this way, that the belief in wonderful powers should originate in this way, is surely quite incredible. Much more likely is it, surely, that he got the notion of God from some other quarter and applied it in his own grotesque and degraded way; than that the notion of God was taken first from such poor forms and applied afterwards to objects better suited to it. Religion and civilisation go hand in hand, and if civilisation can decay (and leading anthropologists declare that the debased tribes of Australia and West Africa show signs of a higher civilisation they have lost) then religion also may decay. A lower race may borrow religious ideas from a higher and adapt them to their own position, *i.e.* degrade them. And the progress of religion may still have been upwards on the whole, although retrograde movements have taken place in certain races. On these and other grounds it is now held with growing certainty that fetishism cannot be the original form of religion, and that the higher stages of it are not to be derived from that one. The races among whom fetishism is found exhibit a well-known feature of the decadence of religion, namely that the great god or gods have grown weak and faint, and smaller gods and spirits have crowded in to fill up the blank thus caused. Worship is transferred from the great beings who are the original gods of the tribe and whom it still professes in a vague way to believe, to numerous smaller beings, and from the good gods to the bad.

2. **Spirits, Human or Quasi-human, came First.**—Is the worship of spirits then the original form of religion? This has been powerfully maintained in this country by Mr. Herbert Spencer and Mr. Tylor. According to

Mr. Spencer "the rudimentary form of all religion is the propitiation of dead ancestors." Men concluded, as soon as they were capable of such reasoning, that the life they witnessed in plants and animals, in sun and moon and other parts of nature, was due to their being inhabited by the spirits of departed men. With all respect for the splendid exposition given by Mr. Spencer[1] of the early beliefs of mankind regarding spirits, it is impossible to think that he has made out his case when he treats the gods of early India and of Greece as deified ancestors. If the natural incredulity we feel at being told that Jupiter, Indra, the sun, the sacred mountain, and the stars all alike came to be worshipped because each of them represented some departed human hero, is not at once decisive, we have only to wait a little to see whether some other theory cannot account for these gods in a simpler way.

Mr. Tylor also derives all religion from the worship of spirits, but in a different way. His is the most comprehensive system of Animism, using that term in the narrower sense of soul-worship. Starting from the doctrine of souls, reached by early man in the way described above (p. 30 *sq.*), he argues that when once this notion was reached it would be applied to other beings as well as man. Not having learned to distinguish himself clearly from other beings, man would judge that they had souls like his own; and so every part of nature came to have its soul, and everything that went on in the universe was to be explained as the activity of souls. It was in this way, according to Mr. Tylor, that the view of the universal animation of nature, characteristic of early thought, was reached. "As the human body was held to live and act by virtue of its own inhabiting spirit-soul, so the operations of the world seemed to be carried on

[1] *Sociology*, vol. i. Also *Ecclesiastical Institutions*, p. 675; "ghost-propitiation is the origin of all religions."

by other spirits." At this point the soul is an unsubstantial essence inhabiting a body, it has its life and activity only in connection with the body; but the step was easily taken to the further belief in spirits like the souls, but not attached to any body. The spirits moved about freely, like the genii, demons, fairies, and beings of all kinds, with whom to the mind of antiquity the world was so crowded.

Three classes of spirits we have up to this point: those of ancestors, those attached to the various parts of the life of nature, and those existing independently. Can the higher nature-deities be accounted for by this theory as well as the minor spirits of the parts of nature? Mr. Tylor considers that they can; he declares that the "higher deities of polytheism have their place in the general animistic system of mankind." He acknowledges that, with few exceptions, great gods have a place as well as smaller gods in every non-civilised system of religion. But in origin and essence he holds they are the same. "The difference is rather of rank than of nature." As chiefs and kings are among men so are the great gods among the lesser spirits. The sun, the heavens, the stars, are living beings, because they have spirits as man has a soul, or as a spring has a spirit that haunts it. Thus in the doctrine of souls is found the origin of the whole of early religion. Mr. Tylor confesses, however, that it is impossible to trace the process by which the doctrine of souls gave rise to the belief in the great gods.

The weakness of this view is that it involves a denial that the great powers of nature could be worshipped before the process of reasoning had been completed which led to the belief that they had souls or spirits. But how did early man regard these great powers before this? Did they not appear to him adorable by the very impressions they made upon his various senses? Did he really need to argue out the belief that they had souls, before he felt drawn to wonder at them, and to seek to enter into relations with them?

Animism.—The word Animism, it should here be noticed, is used in the study of religions in a wider sense than that of Mr. Tylor. Many of the great religions are known to have arisen out of a primitive worship of spirits and to have advanced from that stage to a worship of gods. The god differs from the spirit in having a marked personal character, while the spirits form a vague and somewhat undistinguishable crowd; in having a regular *clientèle* of worshippers, whereas the spirit is only served by those who need to communicate with him; in having therefore a regular worship, while the spirit is only worshipped when the occasion arises; and in being served from feelings of attachment and trust, and not like the spirits from fear. When gods appear, some writers hold, then and not till then does religion begin; before that point is reached magic and exorcism are the forms used for addressing the unseen beings, but when it is reached we have worship; intercourse is deliberately sought with beings who hold regular relations with man. The word Animism is best employed to denote the worship of spirits as distinguished from that of gods. Whether or not early man derived his belief in the multitude of spirits by which he believed himself to be surrounded, from his belief in the separable human soul, there is no doubt that he did consider himself to be so surrounded. Animism in this sense is undoubtedly the beginning of some at least of the great religions.

3. **The Minor Nature-worship came First.—M. Réville** holds[1] that the tree and the river and other such beings were the first gods, and that the deification of the

[1] Réville, *Histoire des religions des peuples non-civilisés*, ii. 225.

great powers of nature came afterwards as an extension of the same principle. Mr. Max Müller seems to share this view when he says that man was led from the worship of semi-tangible objects, which provided him with semi-deities, to that of intangible objects, which gave him deities proper. The Germans, as a rule, hold the view that the great nature-worship came first, and that the sanctity of the tree and the river came to them from above, these objects being regarded as lesser living beings deserving to be worshipped as well as the greater ones. The English school let the sanctity of these objects come to them as it were from below; when man has come to believe in spirits, he concludes that they have spirits too, and worships the spirits he supposes to dwell in them. It does not seem that these theories are entirely exclusive of each other. French writers suppose that the minor nature-worship first sprang up of itself, half-animal man respecting the animals as rivals, the trees as fruit-bearers for his hunger, and so on, and that spirits were added to these beings when the great animistic movement of thought in which these writers believe, took place, of course at a very early period.[1]

The Great Nature-powers came First.—We come in the last place to that class of deities which we spoke of first—the powers of nature. By several great writers it is held that the worship of these is the original form of all religion. We shall give two of the leading theories on the subject, that of Mr. Max Müller and that of Ed. von Hartmann.

Mr. Max Müller has written very strongly against the view that fetishism is a primary form of religion, and holds that the worship of casual objects is not a stage of religion once universally prevalent, but is, on the contrary, a para-

[1] This view is the basis of M. André Lefèvre's *La Religion*. Paris, 1892.

sitical development and of accidental origin. He does not tell us what the original religion of mankind was. The work in which he deals most directly with this question[1] is concerned chiefly with the Indian faith, the early stages of which he regards as the most typical instance of the growth of religion generally. He does not, however, tell us definitely out of what earlier kind of religion that of the Aryans grew, which India best teaches us to know, or what religion they had before they developed that of the Vedic hymns. We may infer, however, what his view on this point is from the very interesting sketch he draws of the psychological advance man could make, in selecting objects of reverence, from one class of things to another (p. 179 *sqq.*). First, there are tangible objects, which, however, Mr. Max Müller denies that mankind as a whole ever did worship; such things as stones, shells, and bones. Then second, semi-tangible objects; such as trees, mountains, rivers, the sea, the earth, which supply the material for what may be called *semi-deities*. And third, intangible objects, such as the sky, the stars, the sun, the dawn, the moon; in these are to be seen the germs of *deities*. At each of these stages man is seeking not for something finite but for the infinite; from the first he has a presentiment of something far beyond; he grasps successive objects of worship not for themselves but for what they seem to tell of, though it is not there, and this sense of the infinite, even in poor and inadequate beliefs, is the germ of religion in him. When he rises after his long journey to fix his regards on the great powers of nature, he apprehends in them something great and transcendent. He applies to them great titles; he calls them *devas*, shining ones; *asuras*, living ones; and, at length, *amartas*, immortal ones. At first these were no more than descriptive titles, applied to the great visible phenomena of nature

[1] *Lectures on the Origin of Religion*, 1882.

as a class. They expressed the admiration and wonder the young mind of man felt itself compelled to pay to these magnificent beings. But by giving them these names he was led instinctively to regard them as persons; he ascribed to them human attributes and dramatic actions, so that they became definite, transcendent, living personalities. In these, more than in any former objects of his adoration, his craving for the infinite was satisfied. Thus the ancient Aryan advanced, "from the visible to the invisible, from the bright beings that could be touched, like the river that could be seen, like the thunder that could be heard, like the sun, to the devas that could no longer be touched or heard or seen. . . . The way was traced out by nature herself."

This famous theory is, when we come to examine it, rather puzzling. It does not account for the first beginnings of religion except by inference, and it does so in two contradictory ways; for, on the one hand, Mr. Max Müller enumerates tangible objects first as those from which men rose to higher objects, and on the other he denies that fetishism is a primitive formation. He suggests that there were earlier gods than the devas, but he tells us nothing about them, except that they were not fully deities; they were only semi-deities, or not deities at all. The worship of spirits he leaves entirely out of consideration; religion did not, in his view, begin with Animism. When he does tell us of the beginnings of religion, what is his view? The religion of the Aryans began, and it is a type—the other religions presumably began in the same way, *e.g.* those of China and of Egypt—by the impression made on man from without by great natural objects co-operating with his inner presentiment of the infinite, which they met to a greater degree than any objects he had tried before. Religion was due accordingly to æsthetic impressions from without, answering an æsthetic and intellectual inner need. Those needs, then, which led men to make gods of the great powers of earth and heaven were not of an animal or material nature, but belonged to the intellectual part of his constitution. Those who framed such a religion for themselves must have been raised above the pressing necessities and cares of savage life; they were not absorbed in the task of making their living, but had leisure to stand and admire the heavenly bodies, and to analyse the impressions made on them by the waters and the thunder. Nay, they had sufficient power of abstraction to form a class of such great beings, to bestow on them a common title, not only one but several progressive common titles, each expressing a deeper reflection than the last. Thus did they reflect on the nature of the cosmic powers, taken as a class. This, evidently, is not the beginning of religion. It is the religion of a comparatively lofty civilisation; lower stages of civilisation, and of religion also, must have preceded this one. Even the heavenly bodies, it appears to many scholars, must have been worshipped by men who regarded them not with æsthetic admiration and intellectual satisfaction only, but in the light of more pressing and practical interests.

We take **Edward von Hartmann** as the representative of those who, like Mr. Max Müller, trace the origin of religion to the worship of the heavenly powers, but who carry back that worship to the earliest stage. Writers who disagree with his philosophy take grave exception to his treatment of religion, for he regards religion, as he considers consciousness itself, not as an original and inseparable element of human nature, but as a thing acquired by man on his way upwards; and he finds the original motive of religion to have lain in egoistic eudæmonism, in the selfish desire of happiness, which at that stage of man's life determined all his actions. The account, however, given by Von Hartmann of the beginning of religion in the adoration of the powers of nature is of singular freshness and power, and we can deduct from it, after stating it, the peculiarities arising out of his philosophical system.

The first religion that existed in the world had for its objects the heavenly powers. The objects worshipped are known, indeed, before religion begins; the illusions of early thought have settled on the heavenly powers before they are worshipped; on the outward object the mind has conferred the character of a living and acting being, which it is henceforth to wear. This transformation, poetic fancy, not mere logic and not merely utilitarian considerations, has brought about. But religion only begins when man sets himself to worship these beings, and to this he is driven by his material needs. Religion begins in a being as yet without religion and without morality. The need for food is the motive that brings about the change, for that pure egoist early man has seen that the powers of nature are able to help or hinder him in his search for a living; the sun can set his plants growing or can burn them up, and the thunderstorm can revive them. His happiness depends on these powers, and he seeks to set up relations with them. He seeks to gain as an ally the heavenly power who is so able to further or to thwart his aims; he makes known to it his wishes by calling upon it, and he offers presents to it. He worships the heavenly powers, and religion has begun. Worship lends to these powers, though they were known before, a fixity and reality they did not formerly possess. Von Hartmann is inclined to trace all the various worships of these powers, which have prevailed in the most different parts of the earth, to the same original centre, while at the same time he maintains that even if all the instances of this worship cannot be referred to any common origin, it must have arisen in this way, wherever men of the same nature dwelt; the psychological necessity of this development accounts for the appearance of this same religion in different lands and among dissimilar races.

The worship of the heavenly powers, accordingly, is with this writer the original religion. While admitting that the worship of domestic spirits grew up in the way described by the English anthropologists, he denies that Animism is ever a religion by itself without being combined with higher beliefs. He denies also that fetishism could ever be an original religious product, or that men could ever pass from having no religion to the religion of fetishism. Wherever it appears, it is a religion of decay. All the religion in the world has come from the worship of nature, which, whether arising at one centre or at several, spread over the world, and is to be recognised, clearly or dimly, in the religions of all lands.

This view of the origin of religion is shared in the main by Otto Pfleiderer,[1] and other German writers. It was from the impressions made on man by the powers of nature, these scholars hold, and not from his belief in spirits, that his religion came. But it was not necessarily due to pure egoism, as Von Hartmann represents; the earliest religions need not, they hold, have been a mere attempt at bribery. The motives which first caused man to worship the heavenly powers surely arose from other needs than that for food alone. The intellectual craving, the desire to know the nature of the world he lived in, and to refer himself to the highest principle of it, as far as that could be attained; the æsthetic need, the desire to have to do with objects which filled his imagination; the moral need, the desire not to occupy a purely isolated position, but to place himself under some authority, and to feel some obligation, these also, though in the dimmest way, as matters of presentiment rather than clear con-

[1] *Philosophy of Religion*, vol. iii. chap. i.

sciousness, entered into the earliest worship of the heavenly powers. This view has the great advantage over that of Von Hartmann, that it makes the development of religion continuous from the first, instead of representing it as being originally a purely selfish thing, into which the character of affection and devotion only entered at some subsequent stage. If man's nature is essentially religious, then all that constitutes religion must have been with him from the first, in however unconscious and undeveloped form.

Conclusion.—We have enumerated the different kinds of gods worshipped by early man—fetishes, spirits, the powers of nature. We have found a general agreement that fetishism is not an original form of religion, but a product of the decay of higher forms in unfavourable conditions. As to the other two kinds of deities, it is impossible to deny that gods have been formed from the very first in each of these two ways. The domestic worship of the early world cannot be derived from nature-worship, but grew out of the belief awakened in early man, by the familiar experiences mentioned above. That the greater nature-worship, on the other hand, can be derived from the belief in spirits is an assertion which can never be proved, or even made probable; that it arose from the impressions produced on early man by the great objects and forces of nature, is a thing we can understand and believe. The minor nature-worship is also a very intelligible thing, even without Mr. Tylor's theory of souls to explain it. What more natural than that the savage should worship the great oak or the waterfall, or should think himself surrounded by invisible beings, even if he did not frame the latter on the model or the human soul? We arrive therefore at the conclusion that with the exception of the doctrines about death and the abode of spirits, we must regard the worship of nature as the root of the world's religion.

We must beware, however, of imputing to the thoughts of early men about their gods, any such qualities as consistency or regularity. The power of holding at one and the same time religious beliefs which are inconsistent with each other, is one which even in the most developed religions is by no means wanting; and how much more was this the case among men who lived before there was any exact thought! The savage could have a variety of gods of very different natures, who formed in his mind quite a happy family. When he found a new god, that did not oblige him to part with any old one; it was one god he was seeking, but he could not settle on one god as yet, when there were so many beings with a good claim to the position. He made his gods not out of nothing, but out of a great variety of experiences and impressions, and they acted and reacted on each other in an endless variety of ways. One god came to the front here and another there; an object was deified here from one reason and there from another; new gods in time turned old and were less thought of, while forgotten gods of former days came back to memory and were worshipped once more. Endless change, endless recurrences of growth and of decay filled up those great spaces and periods, measureless and trackless almost as the expanses of the ocean, that were covered by the prehistoric life of mankind.

Books Recommended

Of the large class of books reporting the manners and beliefs of special savage races we may specify—

D. G. Brinton, *The Myths of the New World*, 1868.

W. W. Gill, *Myths and Songs from the South Pacific*, 1876.

Kingsley, Miss, *West African Studies*, 1899.

Callaway, *The Religious System of the Amazulu*, 1863-72.

Duff Macdonald, *Africana, the Heart of Heathen Africa*, 1882.

G. Grey, *Journals of Two Expeditions of Discovery in North-Western and Western Australia*, 1841.

CHAPTER IV

EARLY DEVELOPMENTS—BELIEF

WE have seen from what materials early man made his gods. As the gods differed in their origin, they differed also from the very first in the mode of their development. The great nature-gods gave rise to one kind of religion, and the minor nature-gods to another, the thought of the departed members of the household to a third. But these various religions could not develop side by side without influencing each other. These different worships began in the very earliest times to get mixed up together; there is none of the great religions which we do not find to be a combination of them. It will be well to consider them in the first place separately.

1. **Growth of the Great Gods.**—Taking them in the order we have already followed, we come first to the great nature-worship, of which heaven, the sun, the moon, the stars, dawn and sunset, and then the phenomena of the weather, rain, storm, and thunder and lightning, are the objects. It cannot be too clearly borne in mind that what was worshipped was originally the natural object itself, regarded, after the earliest habit of thought, as living. To heaven itself, to the sun as he rose or set, to the storm itself, men addressed prayers and made offerings; and in many quarters, both among savages and in the great religions, the same thing occurs to this day.

But it was impossible for man to stop here, his imagination would not allow him to do so. In some races, imagination was more active than in others, but nowhere was it quite inoperative; and so it happened that man was led, here to a greater there to a less extent, beyond the direct and simple adoration of the powers of nature. When he began to give them names, a first and a great step was taken in advance of the original simplicity. A name is a power; if it is anything more than a mere title or label, and all primitive names are more than this, it brings with it associations of its own, and thus men are led to ascribe to the object indicated by the name, a new character and new powers. They proceed to argue about the name and draw conclusions from it as to the nature of the being they worship, and so come to think of their deity in quite a different manner. Even to classify objects together and give them a common title, "the bright ones," or "the living ones," as the early Aryans did, gives them an independent position of their own, and tempts the imagination to go further in describing them. Striving to find names for those beings he worships and thinks about so much, early man gives them the names of living creatures with whom he is familiar, and in this way he brings them much nearer to himself, and at the same time appears to himself to know a great deal more about them. The moon, for example, has horns, the moon is a cow. Heaven is over all, heaven is a father. And as he knows all about a cow, and all about a father, he at once has these deities made much more real to him, they have an independent existence to him. But, on the other hand, he has got something more in his deity than there is in the natural object. It is no longer the mere naked heaven or the mere moon he worships; but these beings with additions made to them by his own imagination.

As time goes on the additions grow more and more. Having got living persons for his deities, early man readily goes on to weave their histories and their relations. If the moon is a cow, the sun is a bull chasing her round the sky. This is an instance of a principle which obtains in many at least of the early religions and which it is important to remember, viz. that the powers of nature were first identified with animals. The zoomorphic stage of the nature-gods comes before the anthropomorphic (*cf.* the signs of the zodiac), and in many savage tribes it still survives.

But it is when the gods begin to be thought of after the likeness of human beings that the decisive step is made in their development. If heaven is a father, it is easy to go on from that. Earth will be the corresponding mother (an idea found all over the world); and all men will be their children. If the sun is invested with a name of masculine gender (but the sun is frequently feminine), he must do feats becoming such a character. If the storm is a male god, he will be a warrior or a huntsman. Thus the god acquires a personal character and an independent movement; what is told about him has reference, of course, to the natural object he sprang from, or the season with which he is connected; but the deity is becoming more and more separate from the natural object, and acquiring a character and history of his own. The stories connected with the god vary according to the habits and the imaginations of different peoples; in some cases the gods remain pure and exalted beings, in others savage and indecent myths are accumulated around them, and these primitive myths adhere to their persons long after they themselves have felt an upward tendency and acquired a civilised character with the moral elevation of their peoples. We shall see in many instances how the nature-gods were personified, made into beasts, made into men, and surrounded with myths and legends. That is the natural history of the nature-gods; the process through which they must pass if they grow at all.

Polytheism.—Another general feature of the worship of the great natural objects has to be mentioned. Each god has a history of his own; he has grown up separately as men concentrated their attention upon him. But as one god grows up after another, or as the gods who grow up in two countries are afterwards brought together, it comes to pass that there are many of them, and none of them is necessarily supreme. What is the worshipper to do? The least reflection will convince us that in any act of worship man fixes his attention on one object only. That belongs to the very nature of religion; as a child could not treat several men at once as its father, nor a servant be equally faithful to several masters, so man naturally tends to have one god. He turns to the highest he knows, who is most likely to be able to help him, and there cannot be two highests, but only one. But man's position in the early world does not allow him to be true to this religious instinct. As he sees one aspect of the world to-day, and another to-morrow, he cannot, when his god is a power of nature, always see the same god before him. But can he not worship another god when the first one is out of sight and out of mind? Though he worshipped heaven yesterday, can he not worship the sun to-day, or the storm, or the great sea? And though the former generation worshipped one of these beings in the foremost place, may not the existing generation devote itself principally to another? That power does not cease to be a deity which is not immediately before his mind. It is still a deity, and in a while he will turn to it again, and make it first. Thus it comes about by inevitable logic that when man gets his gods from nature, he has a number of them. When he gets a new god he does not deny the god he had before; he is not yet in a position to conclude that there can only be one god. When he is worshipping he feels as if there were only one; but this feeling applies at different times to a number of different beings, and from such inconsistency he lacks the power to free himself. The other is a god too; all the gods he has ever worshipped he may on occasion worship again. Nor can he refuse to recognise the gods of others; to them no doubt they are gods, if not to him; they are beings of the same class with his god. And thus early man is a polytheist. Polytheism is a complex product; it is the addition to each other of a number of cults which have grown up separately.

In Polytheism, however, very different religious positions are possible. Men may feel that the whole set of the gods in whose existence they believe have claims on them, and may regard themselves as worshippers of them all, resorting, as feeling and old association moves them, now to one and now to another, or defining the places or occasions at which each of them is to be sought, or in some other way adjusting their various claims; or, on the other hand, while believing in the existence of many gods, they may confine their worship to one. A man knows that there are many gods, but says that he has only to do with one of them. This is a religious position very frequently met with in antiquity. A circle of gods is believed in, but one of them comes into prominence at a time and is worshipped as supreme. This is called Kathenotheism: the worship of one god at a time. The title was invented by Mr. Max Müller, who also gives the title of Henotheism to that position in which many gods are believed in as existing, but worship is given to only one. The following are examples of the various positions:—

The language of **Polytheism** is—"Father Zeus that rulest from Ida, most glorious, most great, and thou sun that seest all things, and ye rivers and thou earth, and ye that in the underworld punish whosoever sweareth falsely—be ye witnesses."—*Iliad*, iii. 280.

The Jews at the time of Josiah were accomplished polytheists, as we may see from the catalogue of the worships suppressed at Jerusalem by that monarch, 2 Kings xxiii. The gods of each of the surrounding tribes appear to have been worshipped there, and the old gods of the separate tribes and families of Israel appear to have been kept up.

Kathenotheism.—The Vedic poets, as we shall see, speak of the god they are immediately addressing as supreme, and heap upon him all the highest attributes, while not thinking of denying the divinity of other gods.

The language of **Henotheism** is—"Thou, O Jehovah, art far above all the earth; thou art exalted far above all gods" (Ps. xcvii. 9). "There is none like unto Thee among the gods, O Lord! . . . Thou art great, and doest wondrous things: Thou art God alone" (Ps. lxxxvi. 8, 10). Here the other gods are recognised as existing, but only one is worshipped. Compare also St. Paul: "There are gods many, and lords many, but to us there is one God" (1 Cor. viii. 5, 6).

The language of **Monotheism** is—"All the gods of the peoples are idols: but Jehovah made the heavens" (Ps. xcvi. 5), and "Thou shalt have no other god before Me."

A further religious position to be noticed here is that of Dualism. Not all dualism comes from nature-worship, but in a land where a beneficent and a harmful natural force are in striking antagonism to each other, this may take place. Man, when he interprets the kindly influences of nature as the blessings of the good god, naturally interprets the agencies which blight or ruin as being also the manifestation of a living power, but of an evil one. Thanks to the good god alternate, in this case, with efforts to counteract or to appease the bad one; if the two appear to be nearly balanced, then neither is supreme, and both overawe the mind and receive worship. But in general we may remark that the greater nature-worship is of an elevating tendency. It brings man into relations with powers which are truly great, and places him even physically in the position of looking up, not down. Where the nature-power is a harsh one, a scorching sun, a tempestuous sea, the self-command and self-sacrifice called out by the worship of them may be, if not carried to extremes, a bracing discipline; but with some exceptions the nature-gods are good, and have to do with light and with kindness.

2. **The Minor Nature-worship.**—The worship of the great powers of nature has a universal character; it can be carried on anywhere; wandering tribes carry it with them; heaven and the sun and the winds can be addressed in every land. The minor nature-worship differs from it in this respect: an animal is only worshipped in the country where it occurs, and the worship of the tree, the well, the stone, is altogether local. With this local nature-worship the world was, in early times, thickly overspread; and manifold survivals of it are still to be found even in lands where the primitive religion has been longest superseded. This is the religion of local observance and local legend, which clings to the face of a country in spite of public changes of creed, and, when the old religion has departed, is found to have secured a shelter for itself in the new one.

In this minor nature-worship which spreads its network over all the early world, the character of primitive society is clearly represented; the small communities have their small local worships—each clan, almost each kraal, has its shrine, its god, and limits itself to its own sacred things. Religion is a bond connecting together the members of small groups of men, but separating them from the members of other groups. The following are some of the more important developments of this.

(*a*) **The Worship of Animals.**—Primitive man had to hold his own against the animals by force of strength and cunning; and he was well acquainted with them. He respected them for the qualities in which they excelled him, the hare for his swiftness, the beaver for his skill, the fox for his craftiness. What he worshipped however, was not the individuals of a species, but the species as a whole, typified perhaps in a great hare or a great fox, the mythical first parent of the species, and possessing its qualities in a supreme degree. And it happened apparently all over the world, at a very early stage, that men regarded themselves as related by the tie of descent, some to one species of animals and some to another. From this belief tribes took their names, each member tattooing the figure of his animal ancestor on his person. The Bechuanas, for example, are divided into crocodile-men, fish-, ape-, buffalo-, elephant-, and lion-men, and so on. The hairy or scaly ancestor is the "totem" of the tribe, and they consider that animal sacred, and will not eat the flesh of it. All who bear the same totem regard each other as of kindred blood, as descended from the same ancestor. The totem may also be a vegetable, in which case no member of the stock will gather or eat it.

Totemism is to be seen in operation at the present day in various parts of the world. North America is, perhaps, its classic land in modern times. It is, however, a stage of society and of religion through which all races have at one time or another passed.[1] From this two important consequences follow which will meet us again and again in our study of the great religions. The first is animal-worship, a phenomenon of frequent occurrence and of perplexing import. Mr. M'Lennan has shown that much at least of the widespread worship of animals is to be traced to an early totem-stage of society,[2] when animals were held sacred as the ancestors of men. In the second place, totemism explains the view taken in the early world of the nature of religious fellowship. In modern times people regard each other as brothers in religion when they believe the same doctrines. It is belief, an intellectual or spiritual agreement, that binds them together. The ancient religious union was of a quite different nature. People then regarded each other as brothers because they were of the same blood, descended from the same ancestor. In the Bible the Hebrews are all descended from Abraham, the Edomites from Esau, etc. That is the necessary condition of brotherhood in early times; only those could join in a religious rite who were of the same blood. For men of another blood there was another worship, another god. It is an earlier stage of this view, when men are of the same worship because they are descended from the same animal, and when they worship that animal.

(*b*) **Trees, Wells, Stones.**—The worship of each of these three is in itself a great subject, and we can do no more

[1] J. G. Frazer, "Totemism," in the *Encyclopædia Britannica*, vol. xxiii. It was formerly held that the Semites were an exception, having never passed through the totemistic stage. Mr. Robertson Smith, in his *Religion of the Semites*, maintains that, though they are past that stage when we first know them, the traces of it are apparent in their institutions, and that their sacrifices especially are based on ideas belonging to it. Wellhausen does not agree with him in this.

[2] *Fortnightly Review*, 1869-70. See also Mr. Lang's *Myth, Ritual and Religion* in many passages.

than mention the leading views which appear to have entered into them. Mannhardt in his *Feld- und Waldkulte* and Frazer in *The Golden Bough* have studied the survivals of tree-worship in the local customs of the peasantry of Europe. Early man appears to have worshipped trees as wonderful living beings; but his thought soon advanced to the conception of a tree-spirit, of which the tree itself was either the body or the dwelling, and which possessed various powers, such as that of commanding rain, or that of causing fertility in plants or in animals. From the tree-spirit, again, the tree-god was further formed, a being who was able to quit the sacred tree or who presided over many trees. Of these beliefs the fast-decaying usages of the Maypole and the Harvest May still remind us.

The well, in a similar manner, may first have been worshipped in and for itself, and then a nymph may have been added to it. The worship of wells consisted in throwing precious articles into them, or hanging such offerings on the surrounding trees, and asking some boon from the deity.[1] Rivers and lakes were also held sacred. The worship of stones, that is of stones not treated by art, but regarded as sacred in the form in which they were found, was widely diffused among early races; but this is a subject on which light is still called for. The Caaba of Mecca and the stone of the temple of Diana at Ephesus are famous isolated instances of it; but it has been suggested that the standing stones or menhirs which are found in every part of Europe, and in the south and west of Asia, were objects of this worship. In Palestine these stones are not found, though they occur in the neighbouring lands; and this is attributed

[1] In Mr. G. A. Gomme's *Ethnology in Folklore* many sacred wells are mentioned which are still, or were lately, frequented in England. St. Wallach's well and bath, in the parish of Glass, Morayshire, was much resorted to within living memory.

by Major Conder[1] to the zeal of the orthodox kings, who, we know from the Bible, destroyed all the monuments of idolatry in their territory.

What is common to these cults, and cannot be disregarded, is their local nature. This gives its colour to all the religion of early man. The god of the sacred tree cannot be worshipped anywhere else than where the tree stands, and he who would have his wishes granted by the well must come to it. The deity of this kind of religion has his abode at a certain spot, and he is a fixed, not a movable deity. There is a story, or a set of stories, connected with his shrine, and there are observances of one kind or another to be done there; and this goes on from age to age. Now a deity who is fixed to one spot will be worshipped by the people who dwell around that spot. The god will have his own people and dwell among them, and they alone will be his worshippers. And thus the surface of the earth comes to be parcelled out among a number of deities, each seated, like a little prince, at his own court among his own people. In passing from his own home to a distant spot, a man will leave the territory of his own god and enter on that of another, and as the god can only be worshipped at his own shrine, the man will leave his religion when he leaves his home, and either be compelled to serve the gods of strangers, or to perform no religious duties at all.[2] Thus the ideas connected with totemism meet and harmonise in many old countries with those connected with local shrines.[3] Those dwelling around

[1] *Scottish Review*, 1894, vol. xvii. p. 33, "Rude Stone Monuments in Syria."

[2] As illustrating this circle of ideas, compare the following passages in the Bible: Genesis xxviii.; Ruth i. 16; 1 Sam. xxvi. 19; 2 Kings v. 17; and of a later period, Psalm xlii.

[3] See on this whole subject Mr. Robertson Smith's *Religion of the Semites*.

the shrine form a kindred of one blood, of which the local god is both the progenitor and the living head. Religion is thus both strictly tribal and strictly local. It is for his brethren of the tribe, for those in whose veins the blood of the same divine ancestor runs, that a man's enthusiasm is kindled in acts of worship; it is his duty to his clan that he then realises, the prosperity of his clan that he desires. To those of other stems no religious bond unites him, they are men of another blood, of another worship. His religious duty is to love his neighbour, or fellow-tribesman, to hate his enemy, the man of another tribe. And on the other hand, as religion consists in approaches to a particular spot and the performance of certain rites, it is left behind when these rites are accomplished, and the man is away from his god. The sanctuary is regarded with extreme veneration, often with shrinking and terror, but distance makes a change, the religion alters with travel, and is left behind. This religion was on the whole a more exciting and intense thing than that of the great nature powers; and was far more interwoven with social life; but it also presented the greatest obstacles to progress, limiting men's affections to their own kin and their own land, and confining them in an inveterate conservatism.

3. **The State after Death.**—The belief that the human spirit was not extinguished at the death of the body, but entered on an existence without the body somewhere else, opened the door to a wide range of speculation; and the ideas arrived at by early man as to the place of spirits and the life beyond, are a principal part of that antique religion of which the great systems are the heirs. The funeral practices of prehistoric times, when various articles were placed in the tomb along with the body of the departed hero or father, and various sacrifices made to him at his burial or cremation and at anniversary festivals afterwards,

show that the spirits of the dead were conceived as carrying on the same kind of existence as they had led here, though an existence unsubstantial and of little power; "strengthless heads" Homer calls them. Food and drink were of use to them; for the finer part of it was supposed to reach them. The taste of blood revived them; and various pleasures were possible to them.[1] This belief, it will be seen, differs from all the modern doctrines of a continued existence. It is not the resurrection of the body that the savage believes in. He knows well enough that the body does not rise; but he also knows that the spirit can exist and move and do a number of things that were done in life, without the body. Nor can he be said to believe in the immortality of the soul. That term describes a free and unfettered existence after death, but to the savage the spirit after death has but a troubled and frail existence; it is tethered to certain spots on the earth, known to it formerly; it cannot do much, it lives under many limitations and constraints. Nor, again, can it be said that retribution after death is a true designation of the early belief. That may be found here and there in early times, but generally the other life is less under a divine government than this one; death takes a man away from his god as well as from his family, and the dead are left to themselves.

While, however, this is the general background of primitive belief about the other life, imagination is at work on the subject very early, and various features of that life are touched with more vivid colours, here in one way and there in another. The place where the departed stay, their occupations, their delights, are variously described; the land where they dwell is modelled on a land that is known, with the addition of ideal features; they do very much what they

[1] On this subject compare Mr. Tylor's *Primitive Culture*, twelfth and thirteenth chapters.

did on earth, hunt or feast, make music or carry on discussions. In some cases there is a judgment-seat before which the soul appears for its trial, and here of course the spirit-world must be divided into two parts or more, for the reception of those who are approved and of those who are condemned. The detailed description of the abodes of the blest and of the damned, by no means peculiar to Christianity, are later developments in the early world. Hell, Mr. Tylor says, is unknown to savage thought. The doctrine of transmigration, however, whether into plants or into lower animals, is of early growth.

Growth of the Great Religions out of these Beliefs.—These various developments of thought about the gods did, as a matter of fact, take place in primitive times, and that is almost all that can be said. In the religion of savages the various elements we have so briefly indicated cross and recross each other, in endless combinations; none of them is to be found entirely by itself. There is no fetish worship which is not accompanied by traces of an early belief in great gods; there is no belief in great gods which is not accompanied by a belief in lower spirits. With regard to every savage religion the student has to ask what the constituent elements of it are, in what way the various beliefs of the early world, beliefs arising from such different sources, meet in it and combine with one another.

In each of the higher religions, too, the same questions have to be asked. The beliefs which we have sketched are the materials out of which they also arose. They did not *originate* the belief in high gods with power over nature, nor the belief in the lesser spirits which busy themselves with man's affairs. They did not originate the belief in a life after death, nor was it left to them to appoint sacred seasons in the year, or to consecrate the spots to which worship has always clung. All these beliefs are prehistoric, and what remained for the great religions was not to bring them forward for the first time, but to surround them with a new kind of authority, and to establish as a matter of positive ordinance or revelation what had formerly grown up without any ordinance by the unconscious work of custom. It was not left for any of the great founders to plant religion in the world as a new thing, but only to add to the old religion new forms and new sanctions.

It may be said that if these are the elements of which religion as a whole is made, then religion arose at first out of illusions. That is no doubt true, in a sense. It was an illusion on the part of early man to suppose that the powers of heaven were animated beings who could be his allies and answer his appeals; it was an illusion to think that the tree or the stone contained a spirit, and an illusion to think that men's spirits can go and wander about the earth by themselves, leaving their bodies untenanted. But these illusions were after all only the outward and inadequate expression in which the spirit of religion then clothed itself. Religion must always express itself in terms of the knowledge which exists in the world at a particular time; and if the knowledge is defective to which the world has attained, religious beliefs must share in its defects. But, on the other hand, religion is something more than knowledge; it is also faith and communion, and these can be deep and true, even when the knowledge which provides their forms of expression is greatly mistaken. And when the forms of knowledge in which religion has clothed itself are found to be mistaken, religion has power to leave them behind and to adopt other forms, as the tree is clothed with fresh leaves in place of those which are withered.

Yet it would be wrong to admit that even in its character

as knowledge early religion was illusion and no more. The poetic faculty, the faculty which prompts us to find outside us what we feel to be within us and to assert its reality, led man right and not wrong. What he worshipped was not the bare object which met the eye and ear, but the thing as he conceived it. He conceived that there was without him that of which his inner consciousness bore witness, an ideal, a being not grasped by the senses, which could help him, with which he could hold intercourse, which had the power he himself had not. This, not the faulty outward expressions in which the sentiment clothed itself, was the living and growing element of his religion.

In addition to the books cited in this chapter, we may mention—

C. Bötticher, *Der Baumkultus der Hellenen*, 1856.

J. Ferguson, *Tree and Serpent Worship*, 1868.

" *Rude Stone Monuments in all Countries*, 1872.

CHAPTER V

EARLY DEVELOPMENTS—PRACTICES

In early religion it is important to remember that belief counted for much less than it now does; a man's religion consisted in the religious acts he did, and not in the beliefs or thoughts he cherished about his god. Worship, moreover, is that element of religion which in all ages and lands is apt to advance most slowly. Even in times of ferment of ideas and change of belief, we often see that the worship of a former time, be it simple or stately, goes on in its old forms, as if it were a thing that could not change. Men alter their beliefs more readily than their habits, especially the habits connected with their faith. If this is the case generally, it was much more the case in the early world than it is now. The religion of a shrine in old times consisted of a certain story about the god, and certain acts done before or near the object which represented him. There was no compulsion, however, to believe the story if a man did the acts or took part in them. As to his private beliefs no one inquired; if he took part in the proper acts of worship he counted as a religious man, unless he went so far as openly to flout the current opinions of his time.

Nor were the acts which went to make up religion of an elaborate or difficult nature. No minute ritual regulated in early times the approaches to the deity; they were a matter of common knowledge, and were fixed not by law, which did not yet exist in any form, but by public custom and public opinion. The manner in which a god is to be served is known of course to his own people who dwell around him; others do not know it. The immigrants from Assyria had to send for a Hebrew to teach them the ritual of the God of Palestine, as they were on his ground and did not know the right way to worship Him (2 Kings xvii. 24 *sqq.*). It is later that the rite becomes a mystery, known only to the professional guardian of the shrine or to the initiated few.

Sacrifice is an invariable feature of early religion. Wherever gods are worshipped, gifts and offerings are made to them of one kind or another. It is in this way that, in antiquity at least, the relation with the deity was renewed, if it had been slackened or broken, or strengthened and made sure. Sacrifice and worship are in the ancient world identical terms. The nature of the offering and the mode of presenting it are infinitely various, but there is always sacrifice in one form or another. Different deities of course receive different gifts; the tree has its roots watered, or trophies of battle or of the chase are hung upon its branches; horses are thrown into the sea. But of primitive sacrifice generally we may affirm that it consists of such food and drink as men themselves partake of. Whether it be the fruit of the field or the firstlings of the flock that is offered at the sacred stone, whether the offering is burnt before the god or set down and left near him, or whether he is summoned to come down from the sky or to travel from the far country to which he may have gone, it is of the materials of a meal that the sacrifice consists. In some cases it appears to be thought that the god consumes the offering, as when Fire is worshipped with offerings which he burns up, or when a fissure in the earth closes upon a victim; but in most cases it is only the spirit or finer essence of the sacrifice that the god enjoys; the rest he leaves to men. And thus sacrifice is generally accompanied by a meal. The offering is presented to the god whole, but the worshippers help to eat it. The god gets the savour of it which rises into the air towards him, while the more material part is devoured below. Every sacrifice is also a festival.[1] If this be the case it is unnecessary to spend much time in considering a number of theories formerly regarded with favour as to the original meaning and intention of sacrifice. The view that it is originally simply a bribe to the deity to induce him to afford some needed help, receives a good deal of countenance from primitive expressions. "*Do ut des*," "I give to thee that thou mayest give to me." "Here is butter, give us cows!" "By gifts are the gods persuaded, by gifts great kings." Was early sacrifice then simply a business transaction, in which man bringing a prayer to the deity brought a gift too, as he was accustomed to do to the great ones of the earth, in order that the deity might be well disposed towards him and grant his petition? Even if this was the case, if sacrifice were offered with the direct and almost the avowed intention of getting good value for it, yet if it takes the form of a meal, it is lifted above the most sordid form of bribery. There is a difference between slipping money into a man's hand and asking him to dinner, even if the object aimed at be in both cases the same; and when the invitations are numerous and formal, there must be a moral, not an immoral, relation between the two parties. Where the sacrifice is a meal, intercourse is sought for; a certain sympathy exists between worshipper and worshipped; they stand to each other not only in the relation of briber and bribed,

[1] Mr. Tylor (*Prim. Cult.* vol. ii. p. 397) states that "sacrifices to deities, from the lowest to the highest levels of culture, consist, to the extent of nine-tenths or more, of gifts of food and sacred banquets."

buyer and seller, but in that of patron and client, or of father and son.

But granting that early sacrifice was for the most part a meal, an observance, with a social element in it, between the god and the worshipper, what was the object of this meal, what was the motive for holding it? In some cases it looks as if the intention had been to strengthen the god, and to make him more vigorous, so that he might be able to do what was wanted of him. In the Vedic hymns this motive undeniably is to be met with. The notion is by no means unknown in early thought, that not only does man need God, but that God is also dependent on man, and capable of being aided and encouraged. In rites which are not strictly sacrifices, we notice men seeking to sympathise with their gods in what the gods are doing, and to take a share in it by doing similar things themselves. The Christmas and Easter fires in pagan times connected with the worship of the sun, are examples of this, and many other instances might be cited.

This, however, is not the principal motive of early sacrifice. All the incidents of it suggest that it is not merely a thing offered to the deity, but a thing in which man takes part; if it is a meal, it is one of which the god and the worshippers partake in common. In China the ancestors are invited to the family feast; their place is set for them; their share in the feast is placed before them. In the *Iliad*,[1] we have an account of a solemn religious act: after prayers the victims were slaughtered, choice slices were cut from them and cooked at the fire by the worshippers, who then ate and drank their fill; after this "all day long they worshipped the god with music, singing the beautiful pæan to Apollo, and his heart was glad to hear." In the Bible we know that the blood is poured out for the Deity

[1] I. 457 *sqq*.

and in various sacrifices the parts He is to have are specified, while the rest is to be eaten by the priests. In the earlier sacrifices of the Hebrews there are no priests; those who present the sacrifice consume it after the act of presentation, and the occasion is one of mirth and jollity, as at a banquet (1 Sam. ix. 12, 13, and the following description; see also Exod. xxxii. 5, 6). In fact it is a banquet. This is specially plain in the sacrifices of the Semites, as Mr. Robertson Smith has shown. Early Semitic usage exhibits clearly how sacrifice was an act of communion, in which the god and his human family proclaimed and renewed their unity with each other. The details may differ in other races, but in general it may be said that early sacrifice was an act done not by an individual, though plenty of individual sacrifices are also to be met with, but by a tribe, in which all the partakers of the blood of the tribe took part before the god who was their common ancestor, and who, as it were, presided over and shared in their feast. In some cases of totem-clans the totem animal is sacrificed, and all the members of the clan eat their animal ancestor (only on such a solemn occasion could the totem be eaten), and so renew their bond of membership and brotherhood. A covenant is made by sacrifice, to which the deity and all the members of his people are parties.

To these primitive conceptions others no doubt should be added. The mood was not always the same which prevailed when the tribe renewed its union with its god; that depended on circumstances. In general the sacrifice of early days is a joyous thing, but to a fierce god cruel rites belonged. When cannibalism was practised it also was such a primitive sacrifice, and the most powerful means, no doubt, of cementing the union of the god with the members of the tribe. When the god was noted for suffering, a tragic tone prevailed, and the sacrifice might have a dramatic character and represent the leading incident in the history of the god.

If we trace the history of sacrifice in any particular people we find two opposite tendencies at work in connection with it. On the one hand there is a disposition to smooth matters, to drop the harsher practices, to let an animal victim suffice where a man used to be sacrificed, to let the man off with some slight mutilation, such as circumcision; or to allow poor people to offer a less costly victim than the former custom claimed—the rite, in fact, becomes civilised, and adapts itself to the feelings of a humaner period. On the other hand there is a tendency to add to the value of the offerings, and to reckon the efficacy of sacrifice by its cost and painfulness. In periods of outward distress sacrifice attains a deeper earnestness, nothing is to be left undone, and no cost to be spared to bring the deity back to his people; darker customs which had become obsolete are revived again,[1] the ceremonial is made more elaborate, new kinds of sacrifice are introduced. The old social aspect of sacrifice grows faint; it becomes a propitiation or a trespass-offering; the notion is entertained that sacrifice is the more efficacious the more it has cost, or the more magnificent and awful its mode of presentation.

Prayer is the ordinary concomitant of sacrifice; the worshipper explains the reason of the gift, and urges the deity to accept it, and to grant the help that is needed. The prayers of the earliest stage are offered on emergencies, and often appear to be intended to attract the attention of the god who may be engaged in another direction. The requests they contain are of the most primary sort. Food is asked for, success in hunting or fishing, strength of arm, rain, a good harvest, children, etc. The prayers have a

[1] An instance of human sacrifice has just taken place in a remote part of Russia.

ring of urgency; they state the claims the worshipper has on the god, and mention his former offerings as well as the present one; they praise the power and the past acts of the deity, and adjure him by his whole relationship to his people (and also to their enemies) to grant their requests. As life grows more secure, the note of immediate urgency fades out of prayer; being a feature not of an occasional worship arising from some pressing need, but of a worship statedly offered at set times, it tends to run into forms, and to become fixed and to have the nature of a liturgy. Then it comes about that the words themselves are regarded as sacred, and that the efficacy of the sacrifice is supposed to be partly dependent on them. They are incantations which the deity cannot resist,—charms which in themselves have virtue to secure the desired result.

Sacred Places, Objects, Persons.—The early world had no temples, nor idols, nor priests. The worship of nature does not suggest the enclosing of a space for religious acts. The natural object itself being the sacred thing, worship is brought to it where it stands; the gift is carried to the tree or to the well, and if the deities are conceived as being above the earth, then the tops of hills are the spots where man can be nearest to them. High places are sacred in all lands. Groves and remote spots are also sacred. When man was carrying on his struggle with the wild beasts he would regard with terror the places where they had their lairs and strongholds; it was in this form that the feeling of mystery with which moderns regard places where they are cut off from all human intercourse, first appealed to man. After this earliest stage had passed, and the grove had come to be regarded as the dwelling of a deity, it became a place man did not dare to approach except with the necessary precautions. We may here explain a notion which plays a great part in early religion, but is not specially connected with any one institution of it, the notion, namely, of taboo. **Taboo** is a Polynesian term, and indicates that which man must not use or touch, because it belongs to a deity. The god's land must not be trodden, the animal dedicated to the god must not be eaten, the chief who represents the god must not be lightly treated or spoken of. These are examples of taboo where the inviolable object or person belongs to a good god, and where the taboo corresponds exactly with the rule of holiness.[1] But instances are still more numerous among savages of taboo attaching to an object because it is connected with a malignant power. The savage is surrounded on every side by such prohibitions; there is danger at every step that he may touch on what is forbidden to him, and draw down on himself unforeseen penalties. The nature of the early deities also excludes **idolatry** in connection with them; there is no need for a representation of a being who is visibly present, and can be extolled and worshipped in his own person. It was at a later stage, when the god came to be personified and separated in thought from his natural basis, that the need arose to make representations of him to aid the imagination. The stones of early religion are not idols. They are natural, not artificial stones; they are not images of the god, but the god himself, or at least that in which the divine spirit dwells,[2] or with which it associates itself for the purpose of worship. And, further, the earliest time knows no priests; there is no special class to whom alone the celebration of sacrifice is entrusted. It would be quite inconsistent with the whole view of sacrifice which then prevailed, to suppose that it could be done by proxy. It was a man's own act, by which he identified himself with his god and with his tribe, and that could only be done by a

[1] *Religion of the Semites*, by W. R. Smith, p. 142 *sqq.*

[2] *Ibid.* p. 192.

personal service. We often find kings and chiefs sacrificing. Agamemnon does so, Abraham and Saul do so, though the sacrifice of the latter is disapproved of by the priestly writer. David does so without being rebuked for it. The king or chief does this as the natural head of his clan; some one must take the leading part in the transaction. As religion is the principal part of politics, and the first business of the state is to keep itself right with the gods, the head of the state is its most natural representative on such an occasion. The head of a household also sacrifices for his house, not only to the spirits of the house, but in cases like that of Job, where there is no question of ancestor-worship. Early custom did not fix in any uniform manner by whose hands a sacrifice was to be made.

Magic.—In another direction, however, we see in the earliest times the growth of a class of persons with religious functions and attributes. While the ordinary worship of the gods does not require the services of any special class, there is everywhere found the man of special knowledge and gifts, to whom men resort for needs lying outside the scope of that worship. Every savage religion contains a certain amount of magic, of practices, that is to say, by which it is thought possible to influence or to foretell outward events. Early man is not limited in his views of what may happen by any accurate knowledge of natural laws, or of the sequence of cause and event, and he imagines it possible to influence nature in various ways. He imitates what he supposes to be the causes of things, judging that the event will also follow; or he uses such powers as he may have over spirits, to induce or compel them to accomplish his wishes; or he manipulates objects he believes to have a hidden virtue, in a way he believes calculated to bring about the desired result. Magic is thus related both to the cult of spirits and to that of casual objects, both to animism and to fetishism.

There is generally a special person in a tribe who knows these things, and is able to work them. It may be the chief or king,—there are many instances in which the chief is believed to have power to bring rain,—or it may be a separate functionary, medicine-man, sorcerer, diviner, seer, or whatever name be given him. He has more power over spirits than other men have, and is able to make them do what he likes. He can heal sickness, he can foretell the future, he can change a thing into something else, or a man into a lower animal or a tree, or anything; he can also assume such transformations himself at will. He uses means to bring about such results; he knows about herbs, he has stones or other objects endowed with special virtues, he also has recourse to rubbing, to making images of affected parts of the body, and to various other arts. Very frequently he is regarded as inspired. It is the spirit dwelling in him which brings about the wonderful results; without the spirit he could not do anything. While the details of course vary infinitely in different tribes, the figure of the worker of magic is an essential feature of any general sketch of early religion. He is often a person of great political importance; being supposed to be in closer alliance than any one else with spiritual beings, he has a power which is much dreaded, and which even the chief cannot disregard.

Of **Sacred Seasons** there can be but few in the earliest human life, when there is no fixed measure of time, nor any notion of regularity, but all depends on the occurrence of need and of danger. As soon as agriculture was engaged in, however, attention must have been fixed on the recurrence of the seasons, and the measures of time afforded by the moon must, at least, have been observed. The summer and the winter solstice, the equinoxes, the new moons, these were to the early cultivator epochs to be observed; and certain annual feasts are found to have come into use in very early times, epochs of man's simplest and earliest calendar, and occasions for tribal gatherings and for such fixed religious observances as we have described. A private religious emergency arising in the interval between two feasts is dealt with by means of a vow; the help of the deity, that is to say, is claimed at once, but the payment of the due consideration for it on man's part is deferred till the time of sacrifice comes round.[1]

Character of Early Religion.—We have now passed in review the principal observances and usages of primitive religion; but before concluding this chapter some remarks have to be made as to the position religion held in the life of ancient times, and as to the spirit and temper which it exhibited. In the first place, as we remarked above, religion was in these times the most important branch of the public service. Every uncommon occurrence had to be laid before the god, and no important step could be taken without consulting him; and it was a principal duty of the head of the state to keep the god on good terms with the tribe, and to apply to him for all the aid and protection the tribe required from him. In attending to this, however, the chief was acting for his tribesmen; where there was no chief these matters were not neglected, but were looked after by common spontaneous action by the members of the tribe. The god was their lord, their father, and they must always take him along with them. This identification of the god with the interests of his subjects is so close that the latter are troubled with no doubts as to whether or not their god is with them. If they observe the customary rules for cultivating his friendship, he must be with them; they never imagine that he can be estranged from them. It is the habitual attitude of early religion to take it for granted that the god goes with his people (he generally has no other

[1] Genesis xxviii. 20; Judges xi. 30; 2 Sam. xv. 8.

people to go with) and helps them against their adversaries. To doubt this and to resort to sacrifices of atonement to bring him back from his estrangement, is a later stage of religion. But if religion is in this way a public matter, a matter of the tribe and its concerns, what place is there in it for the individual? Individual cares and needs may form the subject of prayers and vows, but religion on the whole has to do with the tribe, not with the individual, or with the individual only as a member of the tribe. It is the duty of every one to take his part in the public approaches to the god; he must either do so or be cut off from his tribe. For his own griefs there is little comfort in the tribal worship; indeed, personal sorrows and perplexities meet with but little consideration in early religion. As the tribe is in no doubt of the goodwill of its god, and regards him as a firm ally not easily turned away, old religion has a confident and joyous air, strongly contrasting with the doubts and the contrition of modern faith. The acts of worship are feasts at which the members of the tribe rejoice and make merry before their god. To the delights of feasting those of dance and song are added ("The people sat down to eat and drink, and rose up to play"), and frequently the merrymaking goes to the pitch of frenzy; the worshippers dance themselves into an ecstasy; they feel the god taking possession of them, and are hurried along by the sacred inspiration to behaviour they would not dream of at any other time.

Early Religion and Morality.—How did this early religion bear upon morality? In how far was it a power for righteousness? There are two sides to this question. In the first place, the religion of the infant world was a strong influence for the restraint of individual excess. The god being the parent of the tribe, its customs had his sanction, he had no higher interest than its welfare, he was identified with all its enterprises, its battles were his battles also. The worship of the god therefore made strongly for loyalty to the tribe, and for the observance of its customs; it caused a man to forget his own interest where that of the tribe was concerned, and unhesitatingly to sacrifice himself for the public cause. But, on the other hand, primitive religion was an intensely conservative force; it subjected the whole life to the customs of the tribe, and discouraged spontaneity and independence in moral action. The duties it prescribed were of a conventional order; a man had no duties to those beyond his tribe, and to his fellow-tribesmen religion bade him rather walk by rule than consult his own feelings. Of the morality which consists in discipline and subordination to the community, early religion was an efficient school; to the higher morality, the law of which is found written in the heart, and which aims at rendering higher services than those of custom, it did not attain. The worship of the higher nature-powers, the heavenly powers of light and kindness, tending as it did to transcend the limits of place and of nationality, was destined powerfully to foster a more generous morality than that of the tribal worship, and this tendency was no doubt dimly felt by early man long before it was possible for him to follow it.

CHAPTER VI

NATIONAL RELIGION

WE now leave behind us the beliefs and practices of savage and barbarous tribes, and turn to those of mighty empires. The gulf which lies between these two parts of our subject is obviously a wide one; and in many instances there is no bridge by which the student can pass from one to the other. Often it is a matter of inference rather than of direct proof that the great systems are built out of the materials accumulated, as we have seen, in the prehistoric period. But the inference is sufficiently strong to rest upon; in some cases we are able to see quite clearly how the religion of the empire arose by an uninterrupted growth out of that of the tribe; and in the cases where this cannot be so fully made out, we yet judge that the result came about in a similar way. We pause therefore at this point to ask what is the nature of the transition at which we have arrived, or, in other words, what constitutes the difference between the primitive and the later religions? The difference is probably not one of magnitude only; it consists not merely in the fact that the religion of the empire is that of a much larger number of people than that of the tribe; there is a difference in character as well as in dimensions. With a view to the examination of this point it will be found convenient to consider some of the proposed classifications of religions, as most of these, though for different reasons, place the religions of the early world in a different category from those known to us historically.

The old-fashioned **Classification of Religions** was that of the true and the false. This our principle forbids us to accept, since we regard the various faiths of the world as stages in the development of religion, and therefore all relatively true.

Another division which has done good service is that into natural and revealed religion. By natural religion has generally been understood such religion as human reason could attain to without supernatural aid. But this description does not apply to any religious system that ever prevailed largely in any country; the actual religions have all been the work of custom and age-long tradition, not of the deliberate operation of reason. Natural religion therefore is a term which is of no use to us in classification; since none of the actual religions which we have to study answers to that title. Nor is revealed religion a term we can conveniently use in such a work as this. Many religions claim to be the result of revelation, but few make it at the outset of their career. The title tells us nothing about the original character of a religion, but only that at some period in its career the claim was made for it that its origin was supernatural. If we grouped the revealed religions together we might find that the members of the group had no similarity to each other beyond the accidental circumstance that the claim of revelation had been made for them. Besides, science cannot possibly take the revealed character of any religion for granted, but must examine each such faith to see if its growth cannot be accounted for without that assumption.

The term "natural" religion has, however, other meanings than that just mentioned, and some of these we may find to be of more service. It is proposed to divide religions into "natural" and "positive," or into those which have grown up and those which have been founded. The earlier religions were not due to the personal action of outstanding individuals (at least if they were, as surely they must have been in part, the individuals and their struggles are unrecorded), but were the work of unconscious growth, and were produced by forces, which, as they were at work in every part of the early world, may be called natural. These religions do not appeal to the authority of any founder, but are borne forward by custom and tradition. Some of the later systems, on the contrary, bear the names of their founders, and are said to have been introduced into the world at a certain time and place. Their beginning is fixed, and they have a body of beliefs and practices which belong to their original constitution, and possess authority for all subsequent generations of believers.

This classification promises well at first, but it is difficult to apply it; some religions pass imperceptibly from the stage of custom to that of statute, and in many religions both elements are so largely present that it is difficult to strike the balance between them. We are led to the conclusion that the real difference between the earlier and the later religions is a more vital one than any of these classifications would indicate. The authority and the positive character of the later systems is a symptom of the change which has produced them, but the change itself lies deeper. The higher form of religion is due to a great step which has been taken in civilisation; it is one of the features of the advance of society to a new stage.

Rise of National Religion.—It is an immense step in human progress when a set of barbarous tribes unite to form a nation. Under the strong hand of some chief or under the pressure of some great necessity, they give up the isolation which is both the weakness and the strength of the tribal state of society, they choose some strong place for their centre, they submit to a common government, and while still remembering their separate tribal traditions and usages, they learn to act as members of a greater community than the tribe. This is the beginning of civilisation proper. Law takes the place of custom; the state undertakes to punish crime, and private vengeance is discouraged; the state also undertakes the protection of the weak, so that humane sentiment appears, and a security is engendered in which the arts and sciences can spring up and flourish.

When this takes place a new type of religion also makes its appearance. While each of the tribes may long retain its own gods and its peculiar rites, some one god, perhaps the god of the strongest tribe, assumes a higher position than the rest; his worship becomes the central religion of the community, round which the other worships arrange themselves by degrees, until there comes to be a system embracing them all, but itself possessing a new character. In this way a national religion comes into existence. The details of this process are in every case beyond our observation. It is not perhaps for centuries after the national religion has come into operation, that reflection is turned towards it; not till the art of writing has come to some perfection is it described and formulated and made statutory; and by that time all accurate memory of its beginnings has faded away, and its origin is explained instead by a set of legends. But though its beginnings, like all beginnings, are obscure, the national religion is there. It has its history; the great man who brought the tribes together, or who first devised for them a higher form of worship, is remembered as its founder; the foundation is ascribed to the inspiration of the chief god himself; its sacred forms are written down and obtain the force of divine laws, the will of the deity is a thing clearly known and expressed in positive terms.

It is not asserted that this description will apply to the origin of all the national religions; the character and the circumstances of one nation differ from those of another, and it need not be supposed that they all reached their state worships in the same way. Some religions have become national by conquest rather than growth; while some which may truly be called national never attained to any national organisation. The process we have described, however, may be regarded as the typical one for the rise of a national out of tribal religions, and indicates to us what we may regard as the real and substantial difference between the stage with which we have been occupied and that to which we are now to turn. All other differences between the prehistoric and the historical religions may be traced to this one. Before the religion of a nation has systematised its doctrine and its ritual so as to merit the name of positive, before it has provided itself with a detailed ritual, or a fixed creed, or a regular priesthood, or a set of sacred books, the momentous step has already been taken, the new form of religious consciousness has appeared. Men have begun to believe not only in the tribal but in the national god or gods, and a national religion has come into existence.

The advance from tribal to national worship is one of the most momentous in the whole history of religion. The nature of the change involved in it may be summed up as follows.

1. Men obtain a **Greater God** than they had before. Formerly a man believed in the god of his tribe, one deity among many, as his tribe was one among many, each having its own god; but now he comes to know a god who is higher than the other tribal gods, as the king whom the tribes have united to obey is greater than the tribal chiefs.

The god stands at a greater distance than before from the worshipper; familiarity is lessened, and religion becomes capable of a deeper reverence and adoration. Although the worship of the tribal god is still kept up, yet if the new-born national consciousness is strong, the national form ot religion rather than the tribal will determine the religious sentiment of the individual.

2. **New Social Bond.**—The nature of the social force exerted by religion is altogether changed. In tribal religion the tie of the worshippers both to their god and to each other is that of blood; the god is their common lineal ancestor, whose blood is in the veins of all the tribesmen. The social bond supplied by such a religion is limited to the members of the tribe; a man's fellow-tribesmen are his brothers, but all other men are his enemies; with them he is at war as his god is. Social duty is a matter of blood relationship, and extends only to the kindred. When a national religion is arrived at, a social obligation of a new kind will evidently make its appearance. The national god is related by blood to only one of the tribes composing the nation; the bond between him and the other tribes must be of another nature. He has conquered their gods or they have voluntarily accepted him as their chief god; in any case it is not the tie of blood that binds them to him, but some more ideal tie, like that between a king and his subjects, or between a patron and his clients. And they now have a religious connection also with men who are not their kindred. The national worship is inconsistent with the gross materialism of the system of kinship, and places instead of it the belief in a god further above the world, and therefore more spiritual, and obligations to men which, as they are not derived from a common blood, are somewhat more purely moral.

3. **A Better God.**—The new god of the nation as

he is higher above the world is a being of higher and better character. He belongs to all the tribes, and is not the mere partisan of any; like the king, he is above tribal jealousies, and is interested in checking the violence of all, and securing justice to all. He may be appealed to by those who have suffered violence and who have no earthly helper; and thus he tends to become an ideal of justice and fatherly kindness, and to reflect in the world above the sentiments springing up in the world below, in favour of the repression of violence and the administration of even-handed justice.

In these directions the religion of the nation tends to rise above that of the tribe. The tribal worships may continue almost as they were, the tribal gods may still be worshipped, the tribal jealousies and conflicts still be carried on in spite of the new union, and all the superstitions of early religion may long survive; yet a new religious force has appeared which will in time produce a complete new system. The true principle of classification, therefore, must be drawn from the difference between tribal and national religion, as this is the most vital difference, and that from which all the others which we mentioned may be derived.

The transition thus sketched took place at widely different periods in different parts of the world; it began early and has taken place even in modern times, while very many tribes in various parts of the globe have not yet arrived at it. It is a transition of which it is manifestly impossible to exhibit the detail; in most cases the detail is not known, and it were a profitless task to trace how primitive religions met, united or remained apart, and how their crossings in one case led to a national religion, and in many others led to no such result. Much, no doubt, is to be found on such points in special works, and much still remains to be discovered. Various instances of the formation of national religions will meet us in our subsequent chapters.

The Inca Religion.—We give, however, at this point an example of the transition we have described, drawn from a quarter remote from the great movements of history, and in which the facts are plain and uncontested. Of the two great civilised communities of the New World, discovered by the Spaniards in the sixteenth century, Mexico presents a worship compounded of many elements, which, along with high and lofty morality and great magnificence of ritual, yet retains an extraordinary amount of cruelty and savage horror. In Peru, however, we find a state religion which superseded savage cults still remembered in the country, and from the *Royal Commentaries of the Incas*, written by the Inca Garcilaso de la Vega in the beginning of the seventeenth century,[1] we are able to describe the religion of Peru both before and after the Inca reformation.

"Before the Incas," this writer tells us, "each province, each nation, and each house had its own gods, different from one another, for they thought that a stranger's god could not attend to them but only their own." They worshipped all manner of deities; of these are mentioned herbs, plants, flowers, all kinds of trees, high hills, great rocks, and the chinks in them; caves, pebbles, emeralds. They also worshipped animals; the tiger, the lion, and the bear for their fierceness, and the monkey for his cunning; these they did not kill, but went down on the ground to worship them and would even suffer themselves to be devoured by them, since they regarded these animals as their own ancestors. All kinds of animals they treated in this way; there was not an animal, how filthy and vile soever,

[1] Printed by the Hakluyt Society.

so the quaint words tell us, they did not look on as a god. Other Indians, again, worshipped things from which they derived benefit, such as great fountains and rivers; some worshipped the earth, and called it mother, because it yielded their fruits; some the sea, calling it Mama-cocha; and a great number of other objects of adoration are mentioned. They sacrificed animals and maize, but also men and women, and these not only captives taken in war but also their own children, smearing the idol with the blood. (In other quarters of the globe this is a symbolic act showing that the idol and the worshippers all partake in the same life.) Some tribes were fiercer than others, and practised cannibalism more extensively. They were also well provided with sorcerers and witches.

All this the Incas altered. They were a princely family, regarding whose origin and accession to power various legends are told; the god they worshipped was the sun, and they considered and called themselves the children of the sun. Their father the sun, they said, had sent their forefathers to teach the tribes various things they very much needed to learn; to cultivate the fields, to breed flocks, to live in peace, to respect the wives and daughters of others, and to have no more than one wife. The Incas knew better, it was said, than the rest how to choose a god, and they declared that men should worship the sun, who gave light and heat and made things grow; they should be grateful for his benefits, and he would reward them if they were obedient. The Indians accordingly took the sun for their god "without father or brothers"; they considered the moon to be his sister and wife, but did not worship her. Besides this, we hear the Incas sought a supreme god, and called him "Pachacamac," that is "soul of the world." This being gave life to the world and supported it, but they did not build temples to him or offer him any sacrifice ; they worshipped him in their hearts as an unknown god.

The practice of the Inca religion as described to us by several Spanish writers falls a good deal short of this doctrine. Many beings were worshipped besides the sun ; a number of prayers were addressed to the Creator and the sun and thunder. Many sacred objects also were adored, such as embalmed bodies of ancestors and various idols. They practised all kinds of magic, and, worst of all, many boys and girls were offered in sacrifice, even before the Incas and on great public occasions. The reformation of the Incas is evidently not complete ; if it had not been arrested by the arrival of the Spaniards it may be that the purifying agency of the new religion would have found much still to do. Enough, however, is seen, to afford strong confirmation of the principle that religion gains infinitely in elevation when a national worship appears. The Incas were no doubt the heads of a tribe which had conquered others, and imposed its religion on them. The lesser conquered worships do not die out at once, but continue along with the central one. But the latter expresses the national spirit and aspirations ; and, as settled life fosters the growth of intelligence and of public spirit, the central worship must more and more supersede the others, while itself casting off its superstitious and backward elements and becoming reasonable and elevating.

It will be convenient to indicate at this stage the further line of study to be followed in this volume. As it is our aim to trace, however inadequately, the growth of the religion of the world as a whole, it is necessary that we should confine ourselves to those parts of religious history which lie in the line of that growth, or which serve in a conspicuous manner to illustrate the principles according to which it has taken place. It is by no means our purpose to give an account of all the religions of the world, nor do we seek to form a complete magazine of the curious phenomena with which this vast field of study is in every part so well supplied. If we have interposed the foregoing brief account of the religion of the Incas, it is not because of its own intrinsic importance, but because it supplies within so brief a compass such an apt example of that process which occurs so often in the growth of religion, by which the unorganised rites of a multitude of clans and families give way when the nation comes into being, to the higher and better religion of the state. In the same way the great religions of which we must next speak have, no doubt, only a loose connection with the central line of the world's religious progress. No work professing to deal ever so cursorily with our subject could omit to deal with the religion of China nor with that of Egypt; yet neither of these faiths perhaps has permanently enriched the religious consciousness of mankind. The religion of Babylonia, with which each of these is connected was also of isolated and independent growth, and is far away from us both in time and in historical connection. Like great and solitary mountains of ancient formation, each on a continent distant from ours, these faiths attract us not because we depend on them, but because they are interesting in themselves. It was out of the same jungle of primitive beliefs and rites, out of which our own religion has at length grown, that each of these lifted its head to such heights as it attained.

After disposing of these great systems we come to the developments, much later in point of time, which have led to the highest religion yet attained. And here two great races or groups of peoples have to be considered, each in its own way singularly gifted and each contributing in a distinctive manner to the growth of religion.

These are the Semitic and the Indo-European families. Under each of these heads we find several well-marked religions; and the nature of the case itself points out our further procedure. Taking up first the Semitic group,—including Islam,—since this part of the subject lies at a greater distance from ourselves, we shall inquire whether there is any common element in the various religions it comprises, or, in other words, if there is a Semitic religion which may be regarded as the origin from which the Semitic religions alike sprang, and which gave them a common character; and we shall then proceed to discuss the Semitic religions each by itself. We shall then discuss the common belief of the Aryans, and go on to the religions of the more important Aryan nations. Our last chapters will deal with Christianity and will point out the nature of the development which our study as a whole may have taught us to recognise in the religion of mankind.

Books Recommended

On the classification of Religions see Tiele's article on "Religion" in the *Encyclopædia Britannica*, Ninth Edition.

Alb. Reville Lectures on the Origin and Growth of Religion as illustrated by the Native Religions of Mexico and Peru. *Hibbert Lectures*, 1884.

De la Saussaye, Third edition, pp. 5-16, gives a good conspectus of the various classifications which have been proposed.

PART II

ISOLATED NATIONAL RELIGIONS

CHAPTER VII

BABYLON AND ASSYRIA

THE religion of Babylonia, of which that of Assyria is a late form, cannot be classed along with any other without some inconvenience. In point of remoteness in time it takes precedence even of the religions of China and of Egypt; like these great faiths it also is, in its earlier stage, a growth by itself in a land and people of its own, where apparently it grew up independently from rude beginnings. It is undoubtedly one of the Semitic religions; but it had a character of its own which other Semitic religions did not share, and of the simple and early Semitic religious attitude which will be set forth in another chapter it retained but little. It had an immense influence. Its ideas entered the religion of the Old Testament by several roads. Abram came to Canaan through Haran from Ur of the Chaldees; and in Canaan the religious ideas, myths, and legends of Babylon must have been well known. In a later period the tread of Babylonian soldiery was heard in Palestine many a time before the great captivity, in which Israel sat down and wept remembering Zion by the waters of Babylon. In Greece also we find that ideas which came from Babylon had become known, by way of Phenicia, at a very early period. Recent discoveries, however, seems to make it impossible to assign to the religion of Mesopotamia any other place than the first among the great faiths of the world. The ancient connection between Mesopotamia and Egypt, surmised till now rather than known, is coming to light, and it appears, at least, possible that the first of these countries may have to be regarded as the source of all the civilisations of antiquity. The pantheon of Egypt has striking similarities to that of Babylonia, and some of the Egyptian temples show traces of derivation from the lands of the Tigris and Euphrates. The similarities in the case of China are not so marked, but they are substantial. In Babylonia, therefore, we may be dealing not with one of three isolated religions, but with the mother of the other two. If, as Mr. Lockyer holds,[1] Egypt borrowed astronomy from Babylon in connection with temple-building, more than 5000 years B.C., the religion of Babylon must indeed be carried far into the past.

People and Literature.—Certain parts of Babylonian religion are much ruder and more superstitious than the exalted star-worship which is its central feature, and these have been ascribed to peoples who dwelt in Babylonia before the supposed Semitic conquest, viz. the Accadians in the north and the Sumerians to the south, peoples not related to the Semites in blood or in language, but generally called Turanian, and thought to be perhaps akin to the Chinese. The cuneiform writing which remained in use for millenniums after the Semitic immigration as the sacred literary form, was supposed to have been the invention of these peoples, who had also made some progress in plastic art.

[1] *Dawn of Astronomy*, 1894.

There is, however, no direct evidence of the alleged early Semitic invasion, and the Sumerian hypothesis of which it is a feature is now regarded by some with less confidence. Its feeble ray can be dispensed with in the light which is shining on ancient Babylonia from other quarters. For the information in question the world was formerly dependent on the scanty notices of Greek and Latin writers, but within the last half-century astonishing new sources of information have been opened up. Great libraries, made of brick tablets, have been discovered buried under the ruins of the cities of Babylonia and Assyria, and the gradual decipherment and arrangement of this old literature is proceeding as fast as able and devoted scholars can overtake it. Those who know the subject best declare that no complete history of Babylonian religion can yet be written. The texts now in our possession are not older than the eighth century B.C., and while they are known to embody many documents of much more remote age, yet the information is as yet too fragmentary and often of too doubtful interpretation, while the proportion it bears to the whole of Babylonian life is too little known to supply a solid foundation for history. With this caution we proceed to state the results which are considered likely to prove well founded. As we saw, several features remain in the religion in later times which appear to throw light back upon its early condition, and it may be best to begin with these before describing the noble structure presented on the whole by this religion.

1. **Worship of Spirits.**—The Babylonians, like the Chinese, believed the world to be thickly peopled with spirits of all kinds; and saw in each movement in nature the action of a "zi" or spirit. These spirits could be to some extent controlled; though their character was not known, yet certain charms and incantations were believed to have power over them, and communication with the unseen world took, there-

fore, the form of magic. The earliest portions of the sacred literature consist of spells or charms believed to possess this virtue, and these were never displaced from the collection; on the contrary, new spells were written even after higher spiritual beings were known and more ethical forms of addressing them had been devised. Especially were all pains and diseases ascribed to the agency of spirits, and the sick person naturally sent for an exorcist to expel the spirit which was tormenting him. Some spirits were more powerful than others, and the stronger spirit was invoked to rebuke and drive out the weaker. The spirit of heaven and the spirit of earth are adjured to conjure the plague-demon, the demon who was afflicting the eye, the heart, the head, or any other part of the body. Assertions are not wanting in the cuneiform literature that beliefs and practices of this kind formed no part of the true religion of Babylonia, and some scholars regard it as a late degeneration. The analogy of similar cases points, however, to the conclusion that magic is everywhere an early form of religion which is only overshadowed, not killed, when a great religion arises, and which tends to reappear.

2. **Animals.**—A step above this trafficking with spirits is the worship of animals, which Mr. Sayce considers to have been an early form of Babylonian religion, and to afford an explanation of various features in it. Like the gods of Egypt and those of Greece, many of the gods of Babylon have animal emblems; this appears both in the representations of them and in their legends. The winged bulls and eagle-headed men of Babylonian art represent the same rise of the gods which we know to have taken place in Egypt, from the animal to the semi-human, and then to the fully human form. An intermediate stage in Babylonia is that the god stands on the back of the animal with which presumably he was formerly identified. We have an

Assyrian Dagon whose head and shoulders are covered with a fish's skin; we have gods and goddesses who are human figures with the exception of their wings; we have winged dragons; we have the great bulls with human head and wings which stood as guardian deities to ward off evil spirits at the portal of a palace. The following animals were also connected with gods: the antelope, the serpent, which came to be the embodiment of cunning and wickedness, the goat, the pig, the vulture. We thus see that the rise from zoomorphism to anthropomorphism which the Greeks afterwards carried to the highest point attainable by the resources of art, began in Babylonia.

Like all early religions, that of Babylonia is broken up into a multiplicity of local worships. There is no common system, but each place has its own god or gods and its own sacred rites. In Egypt we shall find reason to believe that this state of matters had its origin in an early totemistic arrangement of society; whether the same was the case in Babylonia or not, it is vain to speculate. Babylonian religion as we see it has risen far above the direct worship of animals. Each god comes before us in a certain local connection and with a special character, but they tend to grow like each other, and their worship is organised on the same plan. The gods of Babylonia undoubtedly belonged to different towns, and though attempts were made in later times to bring them all together in an imperial Babylonian religion, and to settle their relations to each other, these attempts had little success. Here as everywhere it is the case that the individual gods are earlier than the system which seeks to connect them together.

The Great Gods.—The great gods of Babylonia belong to the elements and to the heavenly bodies. They are not, like the gods of the Semites, lords and masters, characters taken from human families; they are not husbands and fathers but creators and universal powers. Another mark about them is that they have originally no wives. When they come to have wives, these are simply doubles of themselves with no special character. A consort is given to the god by adding a feminine termination to his name, thus Bel receives Belit, Anu has Anat. Finally Babylonian religion is more and more directed to the heavenly bodies. It is Astral religion carried to its furthest point. This fixed the arrangement of its temples, the occupations of its priests.

We rapidly pass in review the **principal Gods**. One of the oldest is **Ea** of Eridu, a town which stood in old times at the head of the Persian Gulf. He is a god of the deep, whether it was that he was considered to have come over the water from another land, or whether he is connected with the belief which was held in Babylonia as elsewhere, that all things originally arose out of the abyss. In later forms of the legend his name appears as Oannes, and he is an amphibious being, half-fish, half-man, who rises from the deep and instructs men in arts and sciences. Works were preserved bearing his name, for he was an author. **Ana** the sky, is the god of Erech on the lower Euphrates. Like the Chinese, the men of Erech regarded the sky itself as the highest god, and the maker and ruler of all things. In Babylonia, however, the notion became spiritualised more than in China ; at first we hear that his dwelling became the refuge of the gods during the Deluge, but in later times he is regarded as a being quite above heaven and all created beings, and even all the gods. A third great god is **Bel** of Nippur, not the later Bel of Babylon, but an older one, identical with the Accadian Mul-lilla, the lord of the under-world. The earliest gods of this religion are those of the sea, the earth, and the sky. As they belong to different districts of the country, they can scarcely be called a trinity. A better approach to a trinity is formed by **Ea** of Eridu, **Davkina** his wife who is the earth, and the sun-god **Dumuzi**, their offspring. The son of Ea, also named Miri-Dugga or Merodach (Marduk), is identified with the Egyptian Osiris; they have the same symbol, each is a sun-god, and each has a sister who is also his wife, Merodach has Istar, and Osiris, Isis. In Sergul the principal deity was the fire-god, sometimes called **Savul**; in Cutha they worshipped **Nergal** the god of death, the "strong one" who had his throne beneath. Cutha was a favourite place of sepulture with the Babylonians. **Rimmon** was a god of wind, **Matu** of storms. There is a dragon **Tiamat**, with whom the great gods have to contend.

The **sun** and the **moon** were worshipped everywhere; each city had its own sun-god and its own moon-god. The preference generally shown by nomads for the moon is kept up in early Babylonia, where the moon-god is regarded as the father of the sun-god, and as the greater being. In Ur of the Chaldees the moon was the principal deity. There were also towns such as Larsa and Sippara, where the sun was the chief god; and many of the great gods of later times were originally sun-gods. The Chaldeans, moreover, were proverbially star-watchers, and a "zigurṛath" or observatory, a building of seven spheres corresponding to those of the planets as they pass through the signs of the zodiac and like them rising up to the seat of God at the North Star, was a regular part of the later Babylonian temple. To Babylonia is due the practice of the orientation of temples; that is to say, the arrangement of the building in such a way that its principal axis shall point exactly in a desired direction. Some of the Babylonian temples were oriented so that the sun should shine to the western end of them on the day of the spring equinox when the inundation of the rivers began on which the prosperity of the country so much depended. The temple was thus an astronomical instrument of a high degree of accuracy, and the priests who directed its building and served in it when built were men of science and learning. A religion which is connected with the heavenly bodies, though it does not fully supply the needs of the lower orders and has too little energy to cope with superstition, tends to produce a priesthood who form centres of enlightenment and civilisation throughout the country. This was in the highest degree the case in Babylonia. To these old astronomers the world owes the signs of the zodiac, which were fixed not later than in the fifth millennium B.C., and in which we see how early man beheld in the nightly heavens the creatures which on earth he regarded as divine, so that he worshipped them in both regions. The institution of the Sabbath is also Babylonian; whether it was connected with the changes of the moon, or with a week of days named after the seven planets, is not certain. Seven is a sacred number in Babylonia, as we find in many a connection.

Mythology.—We come lastly, in our attempt to enumerate those parts of Babylonian religion which have entered deeply into human thought, to the myths. The heroic legends and romances are the most interesting and the best-known portions of the newly-recovered literature. We have already noticed some fragments of mythology, such as the story of the fish-god who comes up daily from the sea the moon's being the father of the sun, and the family history of Ea and Davkina, with the sun their child. The two latter are evidently inconsistent with each other. But the story about the son of Ea and Davkina has an important further development. His name is Duzu or Dumuzu, and he is the **Tammuz** of whom we hear in the Bible (Ezekiel viii. 14), who is adored by women raising lamentations for him. He is said to be the sun-god of spring, to whom the heat of summer is fatal, and who dies in June. It is when moisture is failing from the ground that he is bemoaned. His home is in Eden, for Eden belongs to Babylonian legend, which places it near Eridu. There grows the great world-tree which the gods love; it rises from the centre of the world, and is nourished from springs which Ea himself replenishes. It is a cedar (Yggdrasil, the ash-tree, we shall find, occupies the same position with the Northern Teutons); it is sometimes found in a highly conventional form with the figure of a cherub at each side of it, each of whom holds in his hand a fruit. In this tree scholars recognise both the tree of life and the tree of knowledge with which we are familiar. The knowledge of the priests in Babylonia was not for every one, but was jealously guarded, and kept for the initiated alone.

From Tammuz we naturally pass to **Istar**, one of the few goddesses of old Babylonia, and by far the most famous of them. Istar was originally the goddess of the earth, and both mother and sister of the sun-god, for we are led to believe that she is at first the same as Davkina. The great myth of the **descent of Istar** describes how she goes down to the kingdom of the shades to seek the waters that shall give life again to her bridegroom Tammuz. The poem in which the narrative is preserved gives a description of the "house of darkness, where they behold no light," and then tells how, at the orders of Ninkigal or Allat, queen of Hades, Istar is deprived, successively, in spite of her remonstrances, of all her ornaments, and how the plague-demon Namtar is bidden to strike her with all manner of diseases. The result of Istar's disappearance under the earth is that all love and courtship cease both among men and the lower animals, and Ea himself is appealed to, to bring to an end so unnatural a state of affairs. A messenger is sent to the lower regions to cause the release of Istar and the re-ascent of Tammuz. This goddess, however, is known not only from this legend; she has many forms, and passed through various fortunes. The Istar of Erech herself lures Tammuz to his destruction. In early times Istar is also the evening star, the bright companion of the moon. Her leading character, however, seems to be that of a goddess of love. Fertility depends on her; she goes under the earth to find her lover. In this character she attracted in Babylonia a worship noted for impurity, which under the name of Ashtoreth is found also in Phenicia and in Syria. There is also, however, a warlike Istar, a strict goddess served by Amazons, and capable of identification with the Greek Artemis, as the Istar of love is identified with Aphrodite.

Much more primitive than the legend of Istar are some parts of the Babylonian accounts of the creation. There are several of these accounts, some newly discovered. In one the old god Ea peoples the original chaos with a variety of strange monsters. In another the birth of the gods is narrated as well as that of the world; we find also that chaos is itself conceived as a female monster, a dragon of evil, and the god has to do battle with this power of darkness and evil, and to bring light and the habitable world up from its realm. It is certainly true that the Babylonian legends of the creation are crude and inconsistent with each other, and that the account in Genesis belongs to a much higher order of thought. The Babylonian account of the deluge and the ark is more closely parallel to the Bible narrative; the two cannot possibly be independent of each other, and there may be no impropriety in holding that the Hebrew writers were acquainted with myths of general diffusion in the world they lived in.

The State Religion.—The Babylonian and Assyrian religion of which we hear in the Bible (*cf.* Isa. xl.-lxvi.) is the splendid worship of mighty empires; it has forgotten its humble beginnings, and under the guidance of large priestly and learned corporations has grown much in depth and purity. Of its outward magnificence the monuments furnish ample proof. The temple of Bel-Merodach at Babylon was a wonder of the world. Being the god of the prevailing city of the empire, Merodach was the greatest of all the gods, and was reverenced and extolled as befitted the friend and patron of the greatest of monarchs. His son Nebo was a prophet and a god of wisdom. What Merodach was to Babylon, Assur was to Assyria; in fact, he was the only god peculiar to Assyria. The rule that as religion grows in outward splendour it also gains in inward strength and spirituality is strikingly exemplified in the case before us. The gods have come to be moral powers, who really care for men, not only for the king, their earthly representative, but for their worshippers in general. Merodach is praised for his mercy; he not only accompanies the king in his wars, of which the inscriptions give us so many a wearisome catalogue, but he heals the sick, he brings relief to him who is mourning for his transgressions, and he brings life out of death and receives the soul committed to his mercy to a blessed dwelling above. Perhaps we pass here somewhat beyond the early period of the religion and touch on its ultimate phase. The penitential hymns of the later literature form a strong contrast to the magical incantations, which fill so much space in the Babylonian sacred literature. The confessions they contain are not very spiritual; the supplicant bewails his sufferings rather than his sins. Indeed, he rather infers from his sufferings that he has sinned, trodden, it may be, where he ought not to have trodden, or eaten what he should not have eaten, than confesses that he deserved to suffer for sins of which he is aware. What is implored is outward redress or ease, not inward peace. The removal of outward ills is taken as forgiveness. There can be no comparison between these hymns and those of the Bible. But what they do show is the rise in Babylonia of a religion for the individual. The gods are sought not only officially by the state or for state ends, but by the individual. They are believed to have regard to individual sufferings; and the friends of a dying person believe that the gods care for and will receive his soul.

Our knowledge of the religion of these lands is too imperfect to admit of wide conclusions being drawn from it. We know what the higher religion of Babylonia was; and we also see that the higher worship never entirely prevailed in this land; the god, like Bel or Assur, who bore the character of a human over-lord, never drove out the old set of spirits, nor brought the service of them to an end. As in the case of Egypt, so here the attempts made in the direction of a pure and spiritual worship met with no ultimate success. Babylon and Assyria never came so near to Monotheism as did Egypt three millenniums before Christ. Nabonidos, the last king of Babylon, collected all the gods together in his capital, and endeavoured to organise them in a system under Merodach as their head; but this led to religious discord rather than to peace, since the minor deities vehemently resented the removal of their images from their accustomed shrines, and were understood to refuse their aid to the state on the new conditions. The religion of Babylon was too much broken up into independent local cults to admit of such a unification. The highest that was reached was that one great god was adored in one city, another in another, with some depth and spirituality. To nations which had attained a higher faith, that of Babylon appeared to be an idolatrous worship of many gods. That is a harsh judgment. This religion also had life in it and advanced from a lower to a higher stage; from a timid trafficking with spirits to a service of gods who were ideal heads of human communities, and friends of individual men. It was not a mere system, as the world has been accustomed to think, of astrology and of divination of other kinds. But when Babylon and Assyria ceased to be independent powers, and became provinces of Persia, Bel bowed down and Nebo stooped, not to rise again. The world of that day had no need of them. It had already attained in more than one country to a higher religion than that of these deities.

Books Recommended

The Histories of Antiquity, viz.—

Maspéro, *Histoire ancienne des Peuples de l'Orient.*

Duncker, *The History of Antiquity*, from the German, by Evelyn Abbott.

Rawlinson, *The Five Great Monarchies of the Ancient Eastern World: Chdldea, Assyria, Babylonia, Media, and Persia.*

Ed. Meyer, *Geschichte des Alterthums*, 1884. The first volume embraces the History of the East to the foundation of the Persian Empire.

Schrader, *Die Keilinschriften und das alte Testament*, 1903.

Hilprecht, *Old Babylonian Inscriptions* chiefly from Nippur, 1893.

Records of the Past, 1, 3, 5, 7, 9, 11.

Sayce's *Hibbert Lectures*, 1887.

Tiele, *Egyptische en Mesopotamische Godsdiensten.*

Jastrow, *The Religion of Babylonia and Assyria*, 1898.

F. Jeremias in De la Saussaye, pp. 246-347.

Articles, "Semites" by M'Curdy, "Races of the Old Testament," and *Religion of Babylonia and Assyria*, by Jastrow, in Hastings' *Bible Dictionary*, vol. v.

CHAPTER VIII

CHINA

THE Chinese have always been a world in themselves, remote from other races of men; yet they developed a civilisation which is in many respects worthy to be compared with that of India or of the West. The people who made gunpowder and paper and who printed books, long before any of these things were done in Europe, might naturally think themselves the foremost nation of the earth. Their civilisation, however, has exercised no influence on the world outside of China, nor has it advanced to the higher achievements of the human mind. As their great wall secludes them from other nations, so do their mental habits prevent them from a free interchange of ideas with foreigners. The Mongolian race, indeed, from which, like the Hungarians and the Finns, they are descended, is so different from other races in many respects that some anthropologists suppose it to have a separate origin. Phlegmatic and matter-of-fact by nature, exact and careful in practical matters, and to a high degree imitative and industrious, the Chinese are singularly devoid of imagination and indisposed to philosophy. Their monosyllabic and uninflected language, belonging to one of the earliest strata of human speech, and ill fitted to express abstract or poetical ideas, is an index to their whole nature.

China has at present three religions, all recognised by

the State and represented in every part of the country—viz. Confucianism, Taoism, and Buddhism. For our purpose the first of these is very much the most important, as Taoism, originally a philosophy, quickly degenerated into a system of magic, and Buddhism is imported into China, and has to be spoken of elsewhere. Confucianism, being the direct descendant of the old state religion of China, is the native growth of the mind of the nation. Like the Chinese language, the state religion belongs to a very early formation, and presents the symptoms of a development which was rapid at first but was early arrested.

History of China.—Legend goes back to very remote antiquity and tells in a shadowy way of the arrival of the Chinese from the West (which scholars are agreed in regarding as a fact), and of early potentates, patterns to all their successors, who treated the people as their children, and invented for them the arts on which life in China most depends. History proper begins about 2000 B.C., though the Chinese had the art of writing a thousand years before that. Researches, however, which are now being made by several scholars, seem likely to lead to the conclusion that China received at least the seeds of civilisation and some religious ideas from Mesopotamia. Some of the resemblances of Chinese religion with that of Babylonia were pointed out in the last chapter. In a work like this and in the present state of knowledge it is necessary to deal with the religion of China as an isolated one. When the history of the country opens, the character, manners, and institutions of the people are already fixed. They are already civilised and have an organised religion, though how all this came about we cannot tell. The early kings are men of piety, inventors of arts, and authors of fundamental maxims of policy; but as time went on the kings grew worse and lost the affections of their people. In the twelfth century B.C.

the Chow dynasty came into power and gave China some of its best rulers, but it also soon fell off; the country broke up into a number of separate feudal principalities over which the central government lost all control, and in the sixth century Confucius is found wandering from one independent state to another. This confusion led in the third century B.C. to the displacement of the Chow by the Tsin dynasty. Shi-Hoang-Ti, fourth ruler of this line, one of the strongest rulers China ever had, assumed the title of Universal Emperor. He beat back the enemies of China beyond the frontier, began the building of the great wall, and broke down the power of the feudal rulers. It was found, however, that the feudal system still lived in the affections of the people, and as it was the religious books which mainly kept the past in veneration, the emperor ordered their destruction and enforced the edict with great rigour. The house of Han, however, which replaced that of Tsin in 206 B.C., recovered the ancient literature of the country from the hiding-places where copies of the books had been preserved, and established in accordance with them the very conservative constitution which has lasted to this day.

Sources.—The books thus condemned and thus recovered supply us with our knowledge of ancient China and of its religion. They are political rather than religious in their nature. China has no Bible, no book guarded by the ministers of religion as the basis of the system they conduct; the religious teachers of China, if there are any, are the literati, the books they preserve and study are the Classics. These are connected with the name of Confucius, who collected or edited them, and himself wrote one of them. They are not thought to be inspired, but are revered because of their immemorial antiquity. No people was ever more completely under the influence of a book, or set of books, than the Chinese. The learned class, who constitute the only nobility of China, receive their whole education from the books ascribed to Confucius; which, like other authoritative literatures, contains matter of various kinds.

The Chinese collection consists of the five Classics (King) and the four books (Shu). The former were edited by Confucius; the latter are by the disciples of that sage or by Mencius, a distinguished teacher in his school about a century after him. The five Classics are the most sacred of all. They are as follows:—

I.—1. The *Yih-king*, or Book of Changes. This is a divining book; it consists of a set of interpretations by princes of the twelfth century B.C., of a set of lineal figures. The system is in itself of childlike simplicity, but use and age have collected mysteries about it. It was exempted from the proscription of Shi-Hoang-Ti.

2. The *Shu-king*, or Book of History, contains speeches and documents of the early princes from the twenty-fourth to the eighth century B.C.

3. The *Shi-king*, or Book of Poetry, consists of a collection of 300 songs, selected by Confucius from a mass ten times as great. Some of these pieces are extremely old.

4. The *Le ke*, or Record of Rites. This book is said to have been composed by the duke of Chow in the twelfth century B.C., and is the principal source of information about the ancient state religion of China. It contains precepts not only for religious ceremonies, but also for social and domestic duties, and is the Chinaman's manual of conduct to the present day.

5. *Chun Tsew*, Spring and Autumn, contains the annals of the principality of Loo, of which Confucius was a native, from 721-480 B.C. They are extremely dry; and if we could understand the statement of Mencius that Confucius by writing them (for they are his own work) produced a great effect on the minds of his contemporaries, many things

about Chinese religion and manners would be clearer to us than they unfortunately are.

To these five Classics is sometimes added, as a sixth, the *Hsiao-king*, or Book of Filial Piety, a conversation on that subject between Confucius and a disciple.

It is impossible to tell how much Confucius did for these old books. Some hold that he did not change them much, nor put into them much of his own, and that, in fact, he was himself indebted to these books for all he is reported to have taught. On the other hand it is declared that he made the ancient books teach his own doctrine, and left out all that did not suit him; and, in confirmation of this view, the fact is pointed out that while these books as we have them teach pure Confucianism, another religion of a different spirit was growing up in China in Confucius's own day, which must have had some support in the old system. It may be that Confucius did not care to report to us all the features of the old religion, but only those of which he approved. But the information given us about that old religion is admittedly correct so far as it goes; and there is little doubt that what Confucius thought best in it, and what passed through him into the subsequent religion of China, was its most characteristic and most important part.

II.—The Classics of the second order comprise four books:—

1. The *Lun Yu*, or Digested Conversations of the Master; or, as Dr. Legge calls it, *The Confucian Analects.* It is from this book that we derive our information about the sage; it was compiled probably by the disciples of his disciples.

2. The *Ta-Heo*, or Great Learning, and

3. The *Chung Yung*, or Doctrine of the Mean, are smaller works, giving a more literary form to the doctrine of the sage.

4. The *Mang-tsze* contains the teachings of Mencius.

The State Religion of Ancient China.—Confucius never imagined himself to be a reformer of the religion of his country. The religion of China is in the main the same to this day[1] as it was before he appeared, and what is called Confucianism is simply that old system. That the worship of Confucius himself has been added to it does not involve any change of its structure. It is already well developed when we first see it, and what is very peculiar, it has already parted with all savage and irrational elements. There is no mythology; the universal legend of the marriage of heaven and earth is dimly recognisable, but there is no set of primitive stories about the gods. Of human sacrifice there is only one ancient instance; there are no rites with anything savage or cruel about them. Everything is proper, dignified, and well arranged. The deities are beings worthy to be worshipped, and they exact no meaningless services. There is nothing in any part of the religion to disturb the propriety of the worshipper or to suggest any doubts to his mind. In no other religion of the world do we find everything in such excellent order.

On the other hand, it is not a highly-developed religion. Its beliefs are those of extremely early times, and represent a stage of thought at which no other national religion stood still. The organisation common to developed systems is entirely wanting; there is no idol, no priestly class, no Bible, no theology; the most important doctrines are left so vague and undetermined that scholars interpret them in opposite ways. It is a religion in which, just as in the primitive stage, outward acts are everything, the doctrine nothing, and which is not regulated by an organised code but by custom and precedent. All these marks point to a formation in very early times, and to a very

[1] The working religion of the present day is fully described by Prof. de Groot in De la Saussaye, *Lehrbuch*, Third edition.

early arrest of growth, before the ordinary developments of mythology and doctrine, priesthood, ritual, and sacred literature had time to take place. They also point to the operation of some powerful cause, which, when the religion had developed its main features, was able to suppress older beliefs and practices, and lead the nation to devote itself altogether to the newer faith. How this took place we can only conjecture, but certainly it could never have been done unless the new faith and the national character had fitted each other perfectly. The classical religion may, as Prof. de Groot says, have come into existence along with the classical constitution set up by the Han dynasty 2000 years ago. But it must have been ready to enter into this position.

The objects of worship in the Chinese religion arrange themselves in three classes. The Chinaman of old worshipped and his descendant of to-day worships still—

1. Heaven.
2. Spirits of various kinds, other than human.
3. The spirits of dead ancestors.

1. **Heaven** (Thian) is the principal Chinese deity; in strictness we must say the sole deity, for there is no family of upper gods; heaven receives all the worship that is directed aloft. It is the clear vault, the friendly ever-present and all-seeing blue that is meant, not the windy nor the rainy sky, but that which is above all agitations, and which all beings of the air or of the earth look up to and serve. It is conceived as living. It is not a separable spirit, not a power behind, that is worshipped, but heaven itself,—the living heaven of that early thought, which has not yet come to distinguish between matter and spirit,—the living heaven which is over all, knows all, orders and governs all.

To this heaven other names are given, even in the oldest

writings—Ti, Ruler; or Shang-ti, Supreme Ruler. Did the Chinese conceive this ruler as identical with heaven, or as a personality dwelling in it or above it? It has been held that the two beliefs are not the same; that the Chinese of the earliest times worshipped the Supreme Ruler, *i.e.* the one God, Ti, and afterwards fell away from that position of pure monotheism and declined to the worship of the material object, heaven. The early Catholic missionaries argued that the Chinese Shang-ti was equivalent to the Christian "God," and signified a being other than the sky, the Supreme Power of the universe. The Chinese, however, generally denied that they made any such distinction,[1] and even declared that they could not understand it. The names Heaven and Supreme Ruler are used by them indiscriminately: one notices that Confucius does not use the personal form, but only speaks of heaven; "heaven," he says, when feeling distressed, "is destroying me." We have here, therefore, an early form of nature-worship.

The Supreme Power directs all things, and is an ever-present governor both in the natural and in the moral sphere. These two spheres indeed are not regarded as distinct. Nature reveals in all its changes the mind of its ruler, and human conduct is regarded as an outward thing, as a phenomenon on the same plane with the movements of nature; the two are supposed to be part of one system and to act directly on each other. As Heaven both governs the weather and looks after men's actions, for "every day

[1] Dr. Legge, while admitting that the Chinese originally worshipped the vault of heaven itself, maintains that they got past the early mode of thought which considers every natural object as animated, before the dawn of history, and became pure theists, believers in a supreme spiritual being. Confucius he considers to have held a lower religious position than his countrymen had already attained to. He also regards the worship of spirits and of ancestors as a later perversion and degradation of the original religion of one god.

heaven witnesses our actions and is present in the places where we are," these two aspects of providence are closely blended and are in fact the same. Heaven makes its will known in a natural way. It is one of the most peculiar features of Chinese religion that it knows no revelation, no miracles, no divine interferences. It has a belief in destiny, Ming; every one has his Ming, but it is only known when it is accomplished. "Does Heaven plainly declare its Ming?" Confucius is asked; and he replies, "No, heaven speaks not; by the order of events its will is known, not otherwise." Man learns by the external occurrences how Heaven is disposed towards him. When there is excessive rain or long drought, this shows that the harmony between Heaven and the earth is disturbed. It belongs to the emperor to put this right. He alone is entitled to offer sacrifice to Heaven; he stands in the closest relation to Heaven, who is the ancestor of his house; and when Heaven is seen to be displeased, the emperor must restore the harmony by governing his subjects better or by sacrifices. In an extreme case, when the emperor is seen to have fallen under the displeasure of Heaven, the conclusion is drawn that he must no longer be emperor. The people then are entitled to depose him and to set up a new ruler, through whom the necessary transactions with Heaven can be properly carried on. The belief has always been held in China, and is operative to this day, that it can be known when Heaven has rejected a ruler, and that it belongs to the people to carry that sentence into effect.

2. **The Spirits.**—The worship "of the spirits" is a primary religious duty for the Chinaman. The spirits, however, are an ill-defined set of beings; they are generally spoken of in the plural number, and sacrifice was offered to them as a body, no particular spirits being named. The spirits are connected with natural objects, every part of

nature has its spirit The sun, the moon, the five planets, clouds, rain, wind, the five great mountains, but also every smaller mountain, the rivers, each district, and a thousand other things, all have their spirits.[1] The spirits are not flitting about capriciously, but have been collected together and organised in a hierarchy, and this has loosened their connection with natural objects. They are spoken of as a set of beings who may be addressed as a body. A prince alone may sacrifice to the spirit of the earth, and to those of the mountains and rivers of his territory. But to the spirits in general all may and should pray; they assist those who pay them reverence and sacrifice to them. It will be seen that the worship of heaven and that of the spirits are kept separate. The former is the imperial worship; the emperor alone is competent to attend to it. The latter is the official worship of minor states. Nor are the two sets of deities wrought into a homogeneous system; we hear that the spirits, while subordinate to Shang-ti, are not his messengers. The surmise is not to be avoided that these two worships came originally from different circles of ideas, and have not been perfectly blended. The worship of heaven belongs to the higher nature-worship, that of the spirits to the lower; the latter is animistic, it is a worship of detached spirits, while the former is a worship of the natural object itself. The spirits are all good; there are scarcely any bad spirits in Chinese belief.

3. **Ancestors.**—The worship of ancestors is that which is assigned to the private individual. He does not approach Shang-ti any more than he would address the emperor on

[1] The Japanese official religion, 'Shin-to' (= way of the gods, as distinguished from Butsudo, way of Buddha *i.e.*, Japanese Buddhism), an easy worship of numberless spirits, without sacrifices and without any moral doctrine, is allied to this branch of the religion of China; as also is the religion of Corea.

earth; his working religion is directed to his ancestors. The Chinese believed in the continuance of the soul after death, and addressed solemn invitations to it to return to the body it had forsaken. Their belief can scarcely be described as that in personal immortality; it is the continuance of the family rather than of the person that is thought of. The individual does not look forward to his own future life or allow that to influence him; there is little trace of any belief in future rewards and punishments. China has no heaven and no hell. It is the past, not the future, that influences the present; the departed members of the family are believed to be still attached to it, and become its tutelary spirits. In every house there is a hall of ancestors, where worship and sacrifice is offered to them, and many even of the details of this worship remind us strongly of the way in which the Romans served their family heroes. Tablets belonging to the ancestors are placed in this hall; and to these they are supposed to come when properly invoked, so as to be present with the family. At every important family event they are summoned to attend. This worship has to be rendered by husband and wife jointly, so that marriage is necessary for its performance, and an early marriage is a religious duty.

The family sacrifice, like all sacrifices in China, is of the nature of a banquet, at which the living members of the family, and the spirits who have been summoned, eat and drink together. To heighten the illusion, the grandson was sometimes dressed in the clothes of the departed head of the house and made the principal figure of the celebration—

> The dead cannot in form be here,
> But there are those their part who bear;
> We lead them to the highest seat
> And beg that they will drink and eat;

So shall our sires our service own,
And deign our happiness to crown
With blessings still more bright.[1]

It is not only in the family that ancestors are adored. The emperor sacrifices in a public capacity to all the ancestors of his own line, and also to all his predecessors on the throne; a magistrate to all who have occupied his office before him. Ancient China possessed an elaborate ritual, and occasions of sacrifice were frequent. Every change of season, every portent of nature, every important step either in public or in private life, required its consecration. It is in accordance with the genius of the people that the sacrifices are not of the nature of propitiation, but expressions of gratitude and devotion merely. Asceticism has no place in this religion; everything in it is bright and sensible. He who is to offer a sacrifice prepares himself by prayer and retirement to do so worthily; but beyond this reasonable measure there is no afflicting of the soul, and in the prayers belonging to the occasion self-humiliation and confession have no place, but only thanksgivings and petitions. The petitions are for worldly benefits and furtherance; the sacrifices are means of procuring these from the heavenly powers. They consist chiefly of animal victims, but fruits are also used, and with the importance of the occasion the variety and costliness of the offerings increase. Elaborate music also accompanies great sacrifices, and is thought to be very acceptable to the heavenly powers. Religion is not separated from life in China. There is no special class to take care of it; every one has to attend himself to those sacrifices which are incumbent on him; this is a natural, matter-of-course part of a man's duty. As there is no Bible, there is no religious instruction, and the doctrine is quite vague and undefined. The ritual, however,

[1] *Shi-king*, II. vi. 5.

is fixed by tradition in every detail, and if a man attends to it he does his duty; religion is a set of acts properly and exactly done, the proper person sacrificing always to the proper object in the proper way.

Confucius was not a man who tried to change the religion of his country; indeed, he disliked to talk of religious subjects, and he practised reverently the religion which had long prevailed in China. His conversation was chiefly about what we should call worldly matters, and it is hard to see why the religion of China, the same after him as it had been before him, should be called by his name. What led to the connection was: (1) That he taught in a clear and simple way, as had never been done before, the theory of government and morals which lies at the root of Chinese religion, and thus did something, though unconsciously, to provide that religion with a doctrine. And (2) that he collected and edited the books which are the only literary documents the religion has, and which have formed ever since the study of the ruling classes in China. Receiving these books at his hands, they have naturally looked to him as the prophet of their faith.

His Life.—Kung-fu-tsze (*i.e.* Master Kong; the name was Latinised by the Jesuits) is better known to us than most other religious founders. He lived to the age of seventy-three, surrounded by admiring disciples, who remembered what they saw in him and heard from his lips; and this tradition is preserved in the *Lun Yu*, Digested Conversations,[1] a work compiled, as we observed, by disciples of the second generation. The supernatural element which in other cases gathered so quickly round a venerated figure, is here entirely absent; in China such growths do not take place. There may be some tendency to idealise the moral greatness of the sage, but there are also passages in which this tendency evidently has

[1] Dr. Legge, *Confucian Analects.*

not been at work; both in its candour and in the homeliness of much that is reported, the book invites confidence as a genuine record. We see the sage as the diligence of students in the present generation enables us to see Kant or Wordsworth; we hear his opinions on a great variety of subjects; we see how he behaved on occasions of state and at his meals in private, towards princes and towards common men; we laugh at his jokes and sigh with him at his privations.

He was born in 551 B.C. in a good rank of society, but was brought up in poverty, and owed all his success to his own merits. The bent of his mind showed itself early; as a child he amused himself with playing at ceremonies; at thirteen, he tells us, he bent his mind to learning, the subject of his studies being history and poetry, the ceremonies and the music of the empire. He early arrived at the views he always afterwards held as to the proper way to govern a people, and he believed with all the faith of an enthusiast that a vast improvement of society would follow the adoption of his method. It was to public employment that he aspired from an early period of life; but he did not readily find it in the unquiet times in which his lot was cast. He did enjoy office for certain brief periods, and marvellous things are told of the reformation of manners which at once attended his efforts as a governor. All got their due; there was no thieving, and there was no occasion to put the penal laws in execution, for no offenders showed themselves. What was the method which was held to have had such results? In the counsels which he gave to various rulers who applied to him this is set forth. He believed the power of example to be capable of effecting all that a ruler should desire. Punishments might be dispensed with, and excessive pains need not be bestowed on the machinery of government, but a prince who has "rectified" himself will soon have his people "rectified" too. The first task of a ruler is to "rectify names"; *i.e.* there is good government when the prince is really a prince and the minister a minister, when the father is a real father and the son a real son. The perfect order consists of the due observance by each rank of the duties belonging to it; there is to be a well-regulated hierarchy in which each understands his function and acts it out. The people are naturally good and docile, he held, and if they are well governed they will not do wrong even though rewards be offered for it. Thus by docile respect to tradition and authority, which all men are willing to pay if properly guided towards it, the pillars of the state are established.

His Doctrine.—This is the truth which Confucius preached most earnestly. He spoke of heaven but seldom, and of the spirits he professed no certain knowledge; he declared towards the end of his life that he had not prayed for many years. He was a diligent frequenter of all religious ceremonies and a strong upholder of the old order, but his interest in these things was not speculative or mystical, but entirely practical. He regarded himself as a teacher of virtue, not of religious doctrine; his watchword was "propriety," the dutiful observance of all right and customary rules of conduct. Yet there is not wanting an ideal element in his doctrine. He enounces the theory, of which the whole of Chinese religion is the outward expression, that the universe in all its parts, in nature and in man, is an order; that that order is declared to man alike in the ordinances of outward nature, in the constitution of society with its various ranks and classes, and in the ritual of religion; and that it is the whole duty of man to know that order and to conform himself to it. The theory is one in which the state is all, the individual nothing, and in which the present is entirely crushed under the dead hand of the past, and all originality and progress condemned even before they appear. If religion has been delivered from all that is unseemly and irrational, it has also, at least to Western eyes, lost much of its interest; the enthusiasms and excitements of early religion have departed, and no new enthusiasm has come in their place; no great god-wrought deliverance thrills the memory of posterity, no local cults excite exceptional devotion, no divine historical figure attracts to itself personal affection. Religion has cast off fear but has not yet risen to the inspiration of love. The domestic worship came nearest to this, for the other worships are cold and distant indeed; but that worship was a powerful influence for the prevention of progress. The Christian text which hallows individual daring and innovation, by bidding a man put his convictions above his father and mother, would be a shocking impiety to Chinese ears.

A temple was built to Confucius after his death and his worship was added to the state religion. The attempt made by the emperor Shi-Hoang-Ti in the third century after his death to suppress his memory and the books connected with his name, was, though conducted with great vigour, unsuccessful. The teaching of Mencius (371-288 B.C.), the most distinguished of his disciples, added no new element to that of Confucius. Two movements, however, have to be noticed, which in different ways aimed at giving something richer and deeper than Confucianism, and to which China owes the two additional religions of Taoism and Buddhism.

Taoism looks to Lao-tsze as its founder; but it has no personal founder and is composed of older elements. Lao was a philosopher who lived at the same time with Confucius, though half a century older; Confucius met him, as we hear in the *Analects*, and spoke of him with great respect. His work, the *Tao-te-king*, has been preserved, and though few profess to understand it, a general idea of his thought may be gathered from it. Lao, like Confucius, founds on the existing system; he quotes largely from older works, and there are sayings common to both the sages. Metaphysical thought, however, which with Confucius was implied rather than reasoned out, here stands in the forefront. Lao's system is a philosophy applied practically. Tao, the ruling idea of the system, from which both it and the religion which followed it are named, is variously rendered Reason, Nature, the way; the last is the nearest, though by no means a full rendering of it. By the manifold operations attributed to it, it reminds us of the Indian Brahma, and the riddle of Lao's obscurity has been proposed to be solved by the supposition that he was dealing with a doctrine imported from India which Chinese forms of speech could but imperfectly express.[1] Tao is not personal, but something that precedes all persons, all particular beings. It was there before heaven was; all things are from it and return to it at last. It is the principle at the root and the beginning of all things, by which they move, without haste or struggle, ambition or confusion. Existing first absolute and undeveloped, it has now been expressed; men can know it, and the secret of all goodness, all success both for the individual and for the state, is to know Tao and live in it. This makes a man superior to all rules and conventions; at home with himself he is superior to the world; he does not dissipate his energies in learning a great number of outward things, but acts spontaneously from an inner impulse. In this way the philosopher looked for a return of society to simpler manners; he even imagined that men might consent to put away the material arts of which they thought so much, and content themselves with living according to wisdom and being governed by the wisest.

[1] "Lao-Tzeu et le Brahmanism," by E. Quinet in the *Transactions of the Basel Conference*, 1904.

and show a much deeper insight than the cold teaching of Confucius. Lao taught the golden rule: "Recompense injury," he said, "with kindness." Confucius, on being asked about this, did not agree with Lao, but declared that kindness ought to be recompensed with kindness, but injury with justice, as if private morality ought not to rise higher than public policy. "Resent it not when you are reviled," Lao teaches; and "He who overcomes others is strong; he who overcomes himself is mighty." "He who knows when he has enough is rich." "The weakest things in the world subjugate the strongest." The *Book of Recompenses*, which is the practical manual of Taoists and is universally read in China, sets up a high ideal of goodness, and claims to be studied with devotion and earnestness. The task of self-discipline is represented as one requiring faith and courage, the continuous efforts of a lifetime, and unceasing watchfulness. If we judge Taoism either by its philosophy or by its morals, we must assign it a high rank among the efforts which have been made to guide men in the way of wisdom. As a religion, however, it is a dismal failure, and shows how little philosophy and morals can do without a historical religious framework to support them. Taoism was not at first a religion, and was not fitted to become one, as it neither offered any sacred objects of its own for pious sentiment to cling to, nor, like Confucianism, leant upon the state system. The religion which looks to Lao as its chief figure is not based on his teaching; at most it is connected with some of his less important doctrines. It did not take a place in the world till five centuries after the philosopher's death, and its rise was due partly to the emperor named above, who was opposed to Confucius, and partly to teachers who brought forward isolated doctrines of Lao's system which admitted of a popular application. When the religion appears it is a system not of philosophy but of magic. Lao had spoken of immortality as the portion of those who lived according to Tao; under the Chin dynasty (220 B.C.) Taoism is engaged in a search for the fairy islands, where the herb of immortality is to be found; in the first century of our era the head of Taoism is devising a pill which shall renew his youth. When Buddhism enters China, in the same century Taoism borrows from it the apparatus of religion, temples, monasteries, and liturgies, and sets out on its career as a church.

It was not without reason that **Buddhism** was sent for, if we are truly informed, by the rulers of China, or that it spread over the country, in the first century of our era. Neither Confucianism nor Taoism is a religion, in the full sense of the term, as supplying by intercourse with higher beings an inspiration for life. The former is regulative and no more; the latter is a mere set of devices for obtaining benefits from mysterious powers. Buddhism, on the contrary, appeals, as we shall see when we consider it in connection with India, to unselfish motives, and insists on the solemn responsibilities of individual life in such a way as to raise the value of the human person. As it appeared in China it is richer than we shall find it in India; it has a god, unknown to southern Buddhism, and it has a goddess Kouan Yin, "the being who hears the cries of men," sometimes represented with a child on her knee, just like a Western Madonna. While still essentially monastic, it offers salvation and a way of life to all. To faith in Buddha the merciful one is also added a belief in the paradise in which he receives believers. Thus a popular worship is provided, which neither of the older beliefs supplied.

It remains true that China has no religion worthy of the name. The phenomenon may there be witnessed, which is seen with certain differences also in Japan, that several religions exist side by side, all of which are supported by the state and live together without rivalry, and to all of which a man may belong at the same time. This could not be the case if any of the three appealed strongly to patriotic sentiment, or gave full expression to the ideals of the nation.

Books Recommended

In the Sacred Books of the East, vols. iii., xvi., xxvii., and xxviii. contain translations of Chinese Classics, by Dr Legge. The same writer has published three convenient volumes of his own, containing: 1. The Life and Teachings of Confucius. 2. The Life and Works of Mencius. 3. The Shi-King.

Dr. Legge has also written a popular work, *The Religions of China*, 1880. Also *The Notions of the Chinese concerning God and Spirits*, 1852.

The best account of the old State Religion is that of J. H. Plath, *Die Religion und der Cultus der alten Chinesen*, 1862.

Réville, *La Religion chinoise* (1889). The third volume of his History.

R. K. Douglas, *Confucianism and Taoism*, 1876. S.P.C.K.

De Groot, in De la Saussaye.

De Groot, *The Religious System of China*, vols. i.-iv., 1892-1901.

Beal, *Buddhism in China*, 1884.

Murray's *Guide to Japan*.

J. Edkins' *Religion in China*, 1878, the account of a modern missionary, may be consulted.

On Taoism, Pfizmaier, *Die Lösung der Leichname und Schwerter*, 1870; and *Die Tao-lehre von dem wahren Menschen und den Unsterblichen*, 1870.

Vols. xxxix.-xl. of the *S.B.E.* give Taoist Texts.

CHAPTER IX

THE RELIGION OF ANCIENT EGYPT

EGYPT is a land of still more ancient civilisation than China, and its civilisation is of more interest to us, since from it the nations of the West obtained in part the seeds of their arts and sciences. Even to antiquity everything Egyptian appeared venerable and mysterious, and the air of mystery is not yet removed from the country of the Nile. We have discovered the sources of the river and have learned to read the writing on Egyptian monuments; but the sphinx has other riddles than these—riddles not yet solved. Who are the Egyptians, and where did they come from? In ancient times they were thought to have descended from the interior of Africa; now the opinion gains ground that they were at a very early period connected with the ancestors of the Semitic races; their language is thought to show signs of this remote relationship. How, by whom, and when were they formed into a nation? No one can tell; they come before us four thousand years before Christ, a fully-formed nation, with an elaborately organised public service, and with a civilisation both broad and rich. And lastly, What is the religion of Egypt? What are the earliest gods of the land, and in what relation do the various gods which were worshipped in it stand to each other? That question cannot at the present time be fully answered. Even should it be proved, as it appears likely to be, that Egyptian civilisation was derived originally from Mesopotamia, much will still be dark and enigmatical. The foremost scholars in Egyptology confess that no history of Egyptian religion can as yet be written. Those who have tried to sketch it differ from each other as widely as possible, some alleging monotheism as its starting-point, and some the worship of animals. The religion also comes into view at the early period we have mentioned as a fully-formed and stately public system, whose youthful struggles, if it had any, are long past. What is most peculiar in that religion is, that it embraces elements which appear at first sight to have nothing whatever in common, nay, to be quite irreconcilable with each other. We shall do well not to attempt any construction of Egyptian religion as a whole, but to content ourselves with examining one after another the various elements, almost amounting to different religions, which are found in it side by side. We shall no doubt learn something of the relations in which they stood to each other, but it may prove that we shall find ourselves unable to adopt any of the theological theories by which Egyptian priests or Greek philosophers sought to combine them in one system.

History and Literature.—The principal thing to be remembered, in order to understand the history of ancient Egypt, is that the country was divided into a number of provinces or nomes, which, there is every reason to think, were originally independent of each other. Of these nomes there were about twenty in Upper Egypt—that is, in the long gorge of the Nile from Elephantine in the south to Memphis in the north; and about the same number in Lower Egypt—that is, in the flatter country from Memphis to the sea. King Mena or Menes, founder of the first dynasty, whose date, if he was a historical character at all, and not a mythic founder like Minos of Crete, Manu of India, or Mannus of Germany, cannot be later than 3200 B.C., is said to have united for the first time the two crowns of Upper and Lower Egypt. But though they became united under one ruler, the nomes never forgot their independence, nor did they cease to maintain their separate existence as states within the empire, each having its own army, its own ruler, its own system of taxation, its own worship. The supreme power resided now in one nome and now in another. The first two dynasties belonged to that of Abydos; the succeeding dynasties, to which the earliest monuments belong, so that Egypt here begins its real history, had their seat at Memphis. The twelfth dynasty, which is known to us, but is both preceded and followed by a gap of half a millennium in Egyptian history, made Thebes the capital. Thebes was also the seat of the eighteenth and nineteenth dynasties, which came after the foreign domination of the shepherd kings, and under which Egypt was at the summit of its power. Ramses II. and his successors, the Pharaohs of the book of Genesis, belong to the nineteenth dynasty.

How splendid the Imperial Court of Egypt was at various periods, the monuments tell us; these palaces, temples, and tombs are in proportion to a power which considered itself to have the world at its feet, and to be the manifestation of the greatest gods. Literature is at the same high level of development with the other arts, and writing is used for every branch of the public service. This, the most ancient of the literatures of the world, is spread over the immense surfaces of ancient temples and tombs, and stored up in masses of papyrus rolls, much of which is still to be explored. Our knowledge of ancient Egypt and its religion is still in its infancy. The story of the decipherment of the various characters and of the recovery of the early language of Egypt is one of the most wonderful triumphs of scholarship. Only one remark, however, do we now make in connection with

Egyptian writing, namely, that it illustrates in a singular manner the conservatism of the Egyptian people, a feature of their character which is strikingly manifested in their religion also. The ancient Egyptian did not cast away an old usage when a new one, even a very superior one, had been introduced. Long after metals had come into use, he still employed for various purposes, especially those connected with religion, implements of stone. The flint knives found in mummy-cases are connected with the work of embalming, and show the retention of an archaic usage. The same is true of the matter of writing. The earliest Egyptian writing was that which is called hieroglyphic, or picture-writing. In this system what is written down does not represent the sounds of words the writer uses, but the ideas in his mind; it is writing without words; a clumsy system we should say, and presenting the greatest possible difficulties to the reader. At a very early time, however, what is called hieratic writing was invented, in which the symbols used represent not things but sounds, though the symbols used are adapted from those of the earlier picture-writing. It is in this hieratic character that the great mass of Egyptian literature is preserved to us; but here again we find that the new system did not banish the old one from use. Especially in religious inscriptions and documents, the matter is given both in the newer writing and in the older; the piece is written twice, first in hieroglyphic, the old and sacred form, and then in hieratic, the new form, which could be easily read. In the matter of different objects of worship, too, it may perhaps be found that the same aversion to discard anything old and sacred manifests itself, the same disposition rather to carry on the old and the new together.

I. Animal Worship

We begin with that element in Egyptian religion which is to our eyes least rational. In the ages before and after the Christian era, when a number of Greek and Latin writers tell us about Egypt, we find that the religion of the country is described as consisting mainly in the worship of animals. This excited the wonder of these writers in no small degree. Herodotus asserts that the Egyptians counted all animals sacred, and gives a list of those which were specially worshipped. The hippopotamus, he says, is sacred at Papremis, the crocodile at Thebes; and some animals are sacred all over the country. He has much to tell of the manner in which the sacred animals are fed and tended, and of the honours paid to them at their death. Lucian says: "In Egypt the temple is a building of great size and splendour, adorned with precious stones and decorated with gold and with inscriptions; but if you go in and look for the god, you find an ape or an ibis or a goat or a cat." The same statement is made by Clement of Alexandria; and Celsus, the early Roman assailant of Christianity, speaks to the same effect. Thus the popular religion of Egypt, before and after the Christian era, had animals for its principal objects. A representative of the sacred species sat or crawled or hopped in the temple, and in that nome that animal was not eaten. In the nome in which the cat was sacred all cats were inviolable; any insult offered to a cat roused the whole population to frenzy, and one who killed a cat, even though he was a stranger in the place and un acquainted with its manners, forfeited his own life. In the next nome the cat was not sacred but some other animal; and these local differences of religion might occasion war between one nome and another. Juvenal gives in his fifteenth satire an account of a religious war of old standing between two neighbouring nomes, each of which hated and insulted the animal which was worshipped in the other. This may explain why it was impossible for the Israelites to offer sacrifice to Jehovah in Egypt. They had to go out into the wilderness, off Egyptian soil, before they could sacrifice animals Egypt held sacred.

The worship of a sacred animal in its own nome, a member of the species dwelling in the temple and the others enjoying respect and protection throughout that nome, this is the normal state of affairs. Sometimes an individual animal acquires sacredness for Egypt generally, as the bull Apis of Memphis, the bull Mnevis of Heliopolis, or the goat of Mendes. These, though originally local deities, might obtain a wider reverence if the nome they belonged to rose to greater power. Animals of every size and kind were worshipped in Egypt. Besides the large animals we have mentioned, the ape, the dog, the little shrew-mouse, each had its local sacredness; also snakes, frogs, and various kinds of fishes. The beetle (*scarab*) can by no means be left without mention; and a number of trees and shrubs were also sacred,[1] but, very curiously, not the palm.

It will be observed that our account of Egyptian animal worship is drawn from very late sources and applies to a late period of the religion. The religion of the earlier ages of Egypt is of quite a different kind; the kings and priests who wrote the inscriptions of the monuments tell us nothing about animal worship. Is that because such worship did not flourish in their day? Not necessarily. Perhaps they knew it well, but were not interested in it, or did not wish to encourage it. The Egyptians certainly did not believe the worship of animals

[1] A very complete list of the sacred animals and trees will be found in Wilkinson's *Ancient Egyptians*, vol. iii. p. 258 *sqq.*

to have been a late innovation. Manetho, an Egyptian priest who wrote in the third century B.C., says that the worship of animals was introduced under the second king of the second dynasty. That is as if we should say that an old custom of which we did not know the origin was introduced into Britain in the days of King Arthur. The priests of Manetho's day wished animal worship to be considered a corruption of the original religion of their country, but they could not specify the time at which it had come in, and placed its origin in the mythical period of history. The story of Manetho therefore goes to prove that the origin of animal worship is anterior to written records.

But we have other evidence to the same effect. The earliest representations of the deities of Egypt on the monuments testify in a way which can scarcely be mistaken that these great beings had originally some connection with members of the animal kingdom. The great gods of Egypt are designated on the monuments in three ways. Their ultimate form is human, the god is a man or woman, and as the human figures of all the deities are drawn after one conventional male and one conventional female pattern, a symbol is added to the head to show which god or goddess is meant. Hathor is a woman with a cow's horns on her head, Seb has a duck on his head, and so on. But an earlier form of the written symbols of the deities is that which represents them partly in human and partly in animal form. Horus appears as a man with the head of a hawk, Hathor as a woman with the head and horns of a cow, Bast is a woman with the head of a cat, Osiris has the head of a bull or of an ibis, Chnum of a ram, Amon has the head now of a ram now of a hawk. Deities so occur with human bodies and the heads of mythical animals such as the phœnix. But along with these semi-human, semi-animal figures there are found still simpler symbols for the deities; they are drawn as animals. It is only about the twelfth dynasty that the change to the higher form takes place, but even after the step was made of representing the gods as half-human, the older pictures of them were not discarded, but placed side by side with the new ones. Thus we find on the same stone two representations of Horus, one of which gives him as a man with a hawk's head, while the other makes him simply a hawk; and similar double representations of the other gods occur. If the gods of Egypt were thus conceived and represented, in the earliest times, then the animal worship described by the Greek and Roman writers was not the invention of a late age of decadence, but had its roots at least far back in the past. The early gods of Egypt were animals, whatever else, whatever more they were. It may be that the animal worship of the later and weaker Egyptian periods was a revival, such as takes place in weak periods, of a style of worship which in earlier centuries had to a large extent disappeared in favour of a more spiritual faith.[1] Of this only an Egyptologist can judge, but at any rate animal worship was not a new thing in Egypt, but a very old thing.

Theories Accounting for Animal Worship.—What did this worship mean? and how are we to account for it? The Egyptians themselves, and the ancient writers who turned their attention to Egypt, accounted for it by a variety of theories; and various theories are still held on the subject. We can only enumerate the principal ones. (1) The beasts were worshipped for their qualities, as is said to have been the case in Peru before the Incas (p. 84); each was reverenced for that divine excellence or virtue which appeared to be

[1] This is held by Le Page Renouf, in his Hibbert Lectures, *On the Origin and Growth of Religion, as Illustrated by the Religion of Ancient Egypt.*

manifestly resident in it. Thus the dog was worshipped for his watchfulness and faithfulness; the hawk for its darting flight through the upper air, like the flashing of the sun-light or of the sun-god himself; the cow as a great kind mother; the beetle for that wonderful procedure in the reproduction of his kind, in which he so strikingly brings life out of decay. (2) The beasts are not worshipped themselves; they are only the emblems of the deities with whom they are connected, and it is the deity who is worshipped, not the animal. This may be quite true of later practice, but is by no means a satisfactory explanation of its origin; for how was it arranged, and who was it that ordained at first, that the jackal should be the emblem of Anubis, the cat of Bast, the crocodile of Sebak, and so on? (3) Various mythological and quasi-historical accounts of the origin of the practice are given, such as that men long ago chose different animals for their standards in war, or that some early king, wishing to keep his subjects disunited, ordered that each nome should serve a different animal. It is also told as a story of early times that the gods when they walked on earth assumed the forms of various animals; thus the gods are still in the animals. The gods hid in the beasts in order to be near men and see how they did. But men found them out and worshipped them in the disguise they had assumed. (4) The gods cannot be present in the world and cannot be satisfactorily worshipped unless they have bodies to dwell in—that is involved in Egyptian psychology; and as the gods would be too much alike if they all occupied human bodies, they chose the bodies of different animals.

These theories of animal worship are evidently later inventions, to account for a state of matters the real origin of which was not known. Philosophical priests could not accommodate themselves to the animal worship of the temples without a doctrine to justify it to their minds. But those who resorted to such theories about animal worship could have nothing to do with calling the system into existence. We may be sure that a refined and cultivated people did not take up animal worship and cling to it, in spite of its repulsive features, with such tenacity as the Egyptians did, because of a speculative idea of the likeness of certain beasts to certain gods, or to express pantheistic views of the emanations of deity in animal forms. The system, in fact, cannot have sprung up after the Egyptians became civilised, and could not continue to exist among a civilised people, if it was not hallowed by an immemorial antiquity. Only as a mystery, a thing of which the origin was not known, could such a worship continue among such a people.

A new explanation of Egyptian animal worship has been put forward in recent times by the Anthropological school of students of religion,[1] and is rapidly gaining ground. The religious circumstances of Egypt as narrated by Juvenal and Diodorus have the strongest resemblance to the totemistic state of society described above (p. 55 *sq.*) Here, as in Peru before the Incas, or among the North American Indians of to-day, we have a number of communities each with its special sacred animal, which it does not eat, but reverences and defends. Other traces of totemistic arrangements may be suspected here and there in Egyptian observances, but even did the analogy extend no further than to the facts just mentioned, there would be a case for considering whether the nomes were not first peopled by a set of totemistic clans, who, even after they were united in one people, preserved their early separate

[2] See A. Lang, *Myth, Ritual, and Religion*, Second Edition. Frazer's *Totemism*. Most of the modern Egyptologists incline to the theory that animal worship, though not the only, was one of the chief sources of Egyptian religion. Pietschmann first took up this ground.

traditions. The sacred animals of the nomes would then be "the totems of the clans which first settled in these localities." Later developments of religion never displaced these venerable emblems, if this be so, of tribal life.[1]

II. The Great Gods

A very different set of gods are those made known to us by the monuments and books. It is the principal problem of this religion to explain how, along with the sacred animal, the cat or ibis or crocodile, there was worshipped in the Egyptian temple the celestial being, the god of heaven or of the sun, whose nature is light, who is righteous and good, and who more and more fills the mind of the worshipper with noble adoration, and leads him towards the high truths of theism. These high gods of Egypt were represented, as we have seen, from the earliest times of which we have any knowledge, under animal forms. As far back as we can see, Hathor is a cow, and Horus a hawk, and Anubis a jackal. Did beast worship spring by a process of degradation from the worship of the high gods? We have seen how difficult it is to maintain such a view. Did the higher worship then spring by a process of development out of the lower? That also would be hard to prove, for the high gods of Egypt are not beasts, however magnified and spiritualised, but beings of a different order; they are the sky, the sun, the moon, the dawn. And as in our opening chapters we saw reason to believe that the worship of the great powers of nature is an original thing with early man, and explains itself without being derived from lower forms of religion, so we must judge with regard to Egypt too. Even if some of the great Gods came from Mesopotamia, that helps us but little to understand their history after they arrived in Egypt. In

[1] Compare the worship of animals in Babylonia, pp. 92, 93.

this field also we are driven to recognise two religions, different in nature and of independent origin, existing side by side, and seeking to come to terms with each other; and the combination of the two is a process in Egyptian religion which took place before the period of which we have knowledge. It is prehistoric.

It was formerly considered that the nature-gods of Egypt had very little mythology connected with them; only one considerable story of their doings was known; most of them had no history beyond the few phrases applied by primitive thought to the great natural phenomena to qualify them to be regarded as living and active beings. But as more inscriptions are read, more divine myths are coming to light, and further discoveries of the same kind may be still in store for us. These different myths, however, are formed after the same pattern. The great gods of Egypt are simple beings and easy to understand, and they were never formed into an organised system like the gods of Greece, but remain in separate dynasties or families, and are very like each other. Many of them are sun-gods, or gods of the morning and evening, and their stories cannot differ very widely from each other, but they belong to different districts of the country; that is what constitutes their difference from each other, and keeps them separate.

The Great Gods also are Local.—The nature-god as well as the animal-god was worshipped in his own nome, where he dwelt in the midst of his own community of worshippers; he was not recognised in other nomes unless there were special reasons for it. But at the earliest period of our knowledge of Egypt this simple early arrangement has already undergone many modifications. Each nome has its own special deity. Set is the god of Oxyrhynchus, Neith of Sais, but more gods than one are worshipped in each nome. Generally there are three; in many places there is an ennead, a nine of gods, but the nine is a round number; there might be one or two less or more. The god of a nome which had risen to a commanding position extended his influence beyond his own nome, and came to share the temples of other gods, so that he was at home in a number of places. Ra is said to have fourteen persons—that is, fourteen views of his person have been developed in so many different districts. But if one god could thus be divided into several, the converse also took place; two or more gods were combined, by the simple addition of their names together, to form a new god. We have Ra-harmachis, Amon-ra, Ptah-Sokar-Osiris, and some even more elaborately compounded deities.

Thus there was a constant tendency to the production of new deities; even the attempts to combine existing deities only add to the number. No attempt in the direction of a system of gods had any success; local deities could not be suppressed; the nomes retained their separate deities and religious establishments to the end. There never was a religious organisation of Egypt generally; a priest could in some cases pass from the religion of one nome to that of another, but there was never a high priest of Egypt as a whole, however much a king might wish to organise all the worships of the country in one system. This local character of the Egyptian high gods was a source of weakness in these great beings, and never ceased to check their upward movement.

The temple of a nome had, as a rule, three gods, and these formed a family, the chief god having his consort and the third being their son. Of these triads we may mention some:—

Amen-Mut-Chonsu	are the triad of	Thebes.
Ptah-Sechet-Imhotep	,,	Memphis.

Osiris-Isis-Horus	are the triad of	Abydos (Philæ).
Sebak-Hathor-Chonsu	"	Ombos.
Har-hat-Hathor-Har-sem-ta	"	Edfu.

The son is the successor of his father, and it is his destiny in turn to marry his mother and so to reproduce himself, that is his own successor; and so though constantly dying he is ever renewed. The mother, not being a sun-god, does not die. If we remember that the gods have to do with the sun these things need not shock us, nor need we wonder at the statement which is very frequently met with, that a god is self-begotten, or that he produces his own members.

Mythology.—A few words may be said about Egyptian mythology in general before we speak of some of the principal gods. The usual stories of the beginning of things are not wanting, as when the principal god is said to have been born from a primeval egg, or a whole family of gods to be the children of Seb and Nut; Seb, the earth, being in Egypt the male, and Nut, heaven, the female, of these earliest parents of all things. More than one god, moreover, is held to have been an earthly king, and to be the founder of the royal house which now pays him homage. "The days of Ra," for example, are spoken of as a golden age in which perfect justice and happiness prevailed. Many stories too may be found which profess to furnish an explanation of some feature of nature or some institution of society, to account for the names of places or of animals, or for the presence of the five days which were added to the twelve lunar months in Egypt to produce a satisfactory solar year. Many old stories of the gods have magical efficacy when told in certain situations; one is good against poison, but must be told in a certain way, to produce the effect. After these stories of the gods' early reign of peace, come those relating to less happy periods, when the old god grew weak and began to have enemies, when gods and men became disobedient to him, when a war broke out among the gods, which is not yet brought to an end but breaks out ever afresh; or when the old god succumbed to his enemies, and his successor had to set out to avenge him. In some of these stories very primitive and savage traits appear, which show that they originated in a rude state of society. But they are about men, not about beasts, as we might have expected of Egyptian mythology, and the men are undoubtedly solar heroes; it is the fortunes of the daily (not the yearly) sun, his splendid and beneficent reign, his decline, his conflict with the powers of darkness, his decease and his resurrection, or the vengeance exacted on his behalf by his successor, that are spoken of, in connection now with one god and now with another.

Dynasties of Gods.—In the history of Egyptian religion one set of such gods succeeds another as the prevailing dynasty, according as the seat of empire in the country shifts to a new nome. These religious changes could take place without great convulsions. It was only the attempt to extinguish old established worships that was fiercely resisted, not the addition of a new god, even as superior to those already seated in the temple. In the earliest times known to us Ra of Heliopolis is the chief god of Egypt; Osiris of Thinis (Abydos) is also a great god, but the most characteristic development of Osiris-worship belongs to a later period. Ptah of Memphis comes to the front in the earliest dynasties. Much later is the rise of Amon to the first place, which he held when the Greeks and Romans had to do with Egypt. A very short account only, can be given of the sets of gods of which these are the heads.

Ra.—Ra means "sun"; his seat is Heliopolis or "On," where Joseph's master Potiphera, or "Priest of Ra," lived.

Heliopolis is the "house of the obelisk," the obelisk being a representation of the sun. First a kindly old king, he is later a warrior; he has to contend with the serpent Apep, the dragon of darkness who appears pierced by the shafts of Ra. But as Ra sinks in the conflict he is comforted by Hathor, the goddess of the western sky, and avenged by Horus, the ever young and ever victorious winged sun.[1] But Ra is a god of the under as well as the upper world. King Pi'anchi, of the twenty-second dynasty, entered into the great temple of Ra at Heliopolis and penetrated to the inmost chamber of it, afterwards sealing it up again. We are told what he saw there.[2] He looked upon "his father Ra," and saw the two boats intended for the daily journey of the god. Ra travels in his boat through the sky, but also at night through the under-world, of which also he is lord. The progress of the god of light through the world of darkness is a theme which was worked out later in much detail in connection with Osiris; but it forms part of the earliest known religious conceptions of the Egyptians, and Ra's voyage through the "Am Duat" or under-world, is described in considerable detail. Many figures accompany him in this voyage, and many are the obstacles to be overcome during the successive hours of night before he reaches again the gates of day. The souls of men who have died are also led by him through those nether spaces; by a hidden knowledge, if they have been at pains to possess themselves of it, they are able to keep close to Ra on the perilous journey. He gives them fields to cultivate in the plains beneath, and they are made glad

[1] There are in Egyptian religion several gods called Horus; this, the oldest one, is fused with Ra, the first sun-god, in the double name Ra-Harmachis, a being to whom the highest attributes are given. The symbol of this god is a recumbent lion with a man's head, the figure in which also the kings of Egypt are represented.

[2] See the inscription in *Records of the Past*, ii. 98.

by his appearance at the appointed hour in the nights that follow.

Osiris, the sun-god of Abydos, is also reported to have been a human being who was exalted to divine honours. (The god of the under-world and judge of the dead, who bears the same name, is a different figure; of him we shall speak afterwards.) He is the most interesting and the best known of the gods of Egypt; his myth is found at length in Plutarch, with the mystical interpretations proposed for it in ancient times; he is also the god in whom the affinity of Egyptian with Babylonian religion appears most clearly: cf. p. 95. Born, according to the myth we mentioned above, at one birth with four other gods, of the venerable parents Seb and Nut, he from the first has **Isis** for his wife and sister, and his brother **Set** is also born along with him, with whom he lives in perpetual hostility. Neither can quite overcome the other, and many are the incidents of their warfare. As a rule the gods of Egypt are serene and good beings; here only dualism shows itself. Osiris is the good power both morally and in the sphere of outward nature, while Set is the embodiment of all that the Egyptian regards as evil,—darkness, the desert, the hot south wind, sickness, and red hair. It is not the case that Set was an imported god and belonged to Semitic invaders, but these invaders found him more suited to their notions of deity than any other god of Egypt, and sought to make him supreme, in which, however, they could not succeed. The story of the dismemberment of Osiris and of the search of Isis for his loved remains, which she buried in fourteen different places where she found them, is one which is found connected with other names in other lands. **Horus** is the avenger of his father. Here we have this deity in three stages—Horus the child in his mother's arms,

Horus the avenger, and Horus the successor of his father, the complete sun-god.

This family of gods is more human and living to us than that of Ra or than any other set of Egyptian deities. We see with special clearness in this case the operation of the principle according to which the contrast of light and darkness when represented in the gods passes into that of moral good and evil, so that the god of light becomes the great upholder of righteousness and dispenser of beneficence. The good god of Egyptian religion, moreover, is accompanied by a goddess who is somewhat more than the pale reflection of the male god, as most Egyptian goddesses are. The incidents of the legend also lend to the divine characters a tragic depth in which the prosperous and happy gods of Egypt do not generally share.

Ptah is the god of Memphis, and adjoining his temple is the chapel of the bull Apis, who is called the "second life of Ptah." If these two resided side by side, some theory of their relationship was needed, and the bull became the earthly representative of the unseen deity. Each had a worship of prehistoric antiquity, and it is vain to theorise on their original relation to each other. As for Ptah, his name means "he who forms," and the Greeks called him by the name of their own Hephaistos, the artificer. In later times he came to be identified with the sun, and was called the "honourable," "golden," "beautiful," and "of comely face"; but earlier he seems rather to have to do with the hidden source of the world's heat, the elemental warmth which is at the beginning of all life. He also is, like Ra and Osiris, a god of the under-world to which men go after death. He is said to open the mouth of the dead—that is to say, that he hears them and judges them. But in the upper-world too he has to do with justice; he is called the "Lord of the Ell," a title connecting him with measurements and boundaries, matters of the greatest importance in Egypt. His son is **Imhotep**, he who comes in peace; the Greeks regarded this god as a physician, and called him Asclepios. The goddess of the triad is **Sechet**, who was also worshipped at Bubastis under the name of Bast, and whose symbol is a cat. Ptah, it will be seen, is a less distinct figure than either Osiris or Ra, and he very readily passes into combinations with other gods. Ptah-Sokari and Ptah-Sokar-Osiris are found much more frequently than Ptah alone.

These are the chief gods of the old kingdom—that is to say, of the first six dynasties. When we come to the great twelfth dynasty, after the gap in the monuments which extends from 2500-2000 B.C., we find that these gods have become faint and new gods have become supreme, namely, the local gods of Thebes and of the adjoining nomes. Of these, **Amon**, god of Thebes, has the most distinguished history, though **Chem**, the agricultural god of Coptos, and **Munt** of Hermonthis were originally as important. Amon, the hidden, *i.e.* the hidden force of nature, like Ptah, is seldom found alone; he is generally combined with some other god, especially with Ra. The gods of agriculture bow their heads by degrees before the sun-gods who tend to draw to themselves all Egyptian worship; rude country representations connected with the idea of fertility being discredited before the religion of the royal temples which was directed mainly to the god of light.

Was the Earliest Religion Monotheistic?—We have mentioned only some of the chief gods of Egypt, out of a countless number. These are the gods favoured by kings and city priesthoods, who, we cannot doubt, desired the religious elevation of the people. The gods they praised were of a nature to promote that end. It will be granted that the worship of the light-gods of Egyptian religion was fitted to lead the minds of the Egyptians to theism. In illustration of this statement extracts may be here given from hymns, which date as we have them from the eighteenth dynasty 1590 B.C., but which are probably much older.

To Horus

The gods recognise the universal lord. . . . He judges the world according to his will; heaven and earth are in subjection to him. He giveth his commands to men, to the generations present, past, and future; to Egyptians and to strangers. The circuit of the solar orb is under his direction; the winds, the waters, the wood of the plants, and all vegetables. A god of seeds, he giveth all herbs and the abundance of the soil. He affordeth plentifulness, and giveth it to all the earth. All men are in ecstasy, all hearts in sweetness, all bosoms in joy, every one in adoration. Every one glorifieth his goodness, his tenderness encircles our hearts, great is his love in all bosoms.

To Tehuti or Ptah

To him is due the work of the hands, the walking of the feet, the sight of the eyes, the hearing of the ears, the breathing of the nostrils, the courage of the heart, the vigour of the hand, activity in body and in mouth of all the gods and men, and of all living animals; intelligence and speech, whatever is in the heart and whatever is on the tongue.

To Ptah-tanen

O let us give glory to the god who hath raised up the sky and who causeth his disk to float over the bosom of Nut, who hath made the gods and men and all their generations, who hath made all lands and countries and the great sea, in his name of "Let-the-earth-be."

To Amon-ra

Hail to thee, maker of all beings, lord of law, father of the gods; maker of men, creator of beasts; lord of grains, making food for the beast of the field. . . . The one without a second. . . . king alone, single among the gods; of many names, unknown is their number.

There is a beautiful hymn addressed to the Nile, who is also conceived as the chief deity and the ruler, nourisher, and comforter of all creatures. From these hymns and others like them, important conclusions have been drawn as to the nature of the earliest Egyptian religion; namely, that those who wrote such pieces must have been acquainted with the one true god and addressed him under these various names, so that the true origin of Egyptian religion would be a primitive monotheism.

There are some texts indeed which seem to point even more strongly than those cited to the conclusion that Egyptian religion started from the belief in one supreme deity. Mr. Le Page Renouf quotes along with the passages above, one from a Turin papyrus, in which words are put into the mouth of the Almighty God, the self-existent, who made heaven and earth, the waters, the breaths of life, fire, the gods, men, animals, cattle, reptiles, birds, etc. This being speaks as follows:—

> I am the maker of the heaven and the earth. . . . It is I who have given to all the gods the soul which is within them. When I open my eyes there is light, when I close them there is darkness. I am Chepera in the morning, Ra at noon, Tum in the evening.

M. de la Rougé maintains that Egyptian religion, monotheistic at first, with a noble belief in the unity of the Supreme God and in His attributes as the Creator and Lawgiver of man, fell away from that position and grew more and more polytheistic. "It is more than 5000 years since in the valley of the Nile the hymn began to the unity of God and the immortality of the soul, and we find Egypt arrived in the last ages at the most unbridled Polytheism."

The sublimer part of Egyptian religion is demonstrably ancient, as Mr. Le Page Renouf says; yet we are not shut up to the conclusion that Egyptian religion as a whole is nothing but a backsliding and a failure. If we were obliged to regard that monotheism which Egypt had at first but failed to maintain, as a gift conferred from above, which human powers proved unequal to conserve, then the opening of the history of this religion would be indeed most melancholy. But though monotheism appeared in Egypt so early, there is no necessity to think that it was not attained by human powers. For all we know, it was not an early but a mature product of thought, and was reached after a long development. It is not impossible for the human mind, starting from the works of God, to rise by its own efforts to the belief in His invisible power and Godhead. The beginnings of this rise of thought may be witnessed among savages, and the Egyptians in their secluded valley had an opportunity such as no other nation had, to work out, as their civilisation grew up from rude beginnings to its unequalled splendour, a noble view of the Deity whose works they adored. The god ruling from his heaven of light over the great empire of a monarch who knew no equal in the world, possessing for his earthly abode a temple of unsurpassed magnificence, uniting perhaps under his sway districts long at war and extending his influence over remote continents as the armies of Egypt prospered, such a being drew to himself from his worshipping retinue of priests and nobles, the highest praise and adoration, was exalted far above all other powers in heaven and earth, and extolled even as the Creator and Ruler of all.

Monotheism is thus approached in thought, but only in a prophetic and anticipatory way; the circumstances of the country forbade its realisation as a general belief or as a working system. Even in the highest flights of those early thinkers, when they seem to be speaking of a god quite universal and supreme, it is a local deity that lies at the basis of their speculations, a being who has his temple in a certain place, who is symbolised in a certain animal, who has a local legend and a limited popular worship. These are the facts that clog the wings of Egyptian monotheistic speculation and bring it to the earth again. Pure monotheism accordingly, the belief in a god beside whom no other god exists, it might be hard to find in Egypt at all. The last extract given above comes nearest to it; but the last line of that extract cannot be called monotheistic.

An attempted religious reformation at the end of the eighteenth dynasty may be mentioned here, as it appears to have aimed at concentrating all the worship of Egypt on a single object. The object chosen, however, was a material one,—the sun's disk, Aten,—and though all Egyptian gods tended to become sun-gods, some sun-gods, no doubt, were better than others, and Aten was not the finest of them. King Chut-en-Aten, or Glory of the Sun-disk, the royal fanatic who made this attempt at unity, went great lengths to accomplish his object, but the attempt was a failure, and was abandoned after his death even by the members of his own family. What Chut-en-Aten tried to introduce perhaps came nearer true monotheism than anything that ever existed in Egypt. He made war on other gods and wished to establish one only god in the land, but this exclusiveness the Egyptians could not understand. The Egyptian believed in many gods, and while worshipping one god with fervour, by no means denied the existence or the power of others in other places. Even foreign deities were in his eyes real and potent beings, each in his own territory. It is henotheism, not monotheism, that we see in this most religious land; the worship of one god at a time while other gods are also believed to exist and act. The one god who is before the mind of the worshipper is exalted above the rest, and spoken of as if no other god required to be considered; but the worshipper does not dream as yet of questioning the existence of other gods, or feel himself debarred from worshipping them if he should visit their country.

Syncretism.—The hymns contain several other speculative positions about the gods (p. 51 *sq.*), and we may briefly mention these. Syncretism, as we saw, is very largely represented in Egyptian thought, and enters, indeed, into its very bone and marrow. In the ennead of a city the great gods may be arranged together after the fashion of a court where one or two rule over the rest; but in numberless passages we find the relations of gods adjusted in another way, by making them one. Ra "comes as" Tum, the god is known here under one name or aspect and there under another. The names of two deities being added together, a new deity is produced; and in later times these gods with double, treble, or multiple names are among the most important. Raharmachis and Amon-ra are national gods, and have left much evidence of themselves.

It is a little step from syncretism to **pantheism.** Let the gods once lose the individual character that keeps them separate from each other, and it is possible for one god, who grows strong and great enough, to swallow up all the rest, till they appear only as his forms. In the position which they occupied in Egypt the various gods could not disappear, their local connections kept them alive; but they were so like one another that one of them could be regarded as a form of another, and a multitude of them as forms of one. The god who did most in the way of swallowing up the rest was Ra, the great sun-god of Thebes. The Litany of Ra[1] represents that god as eternal and self-begotten, and sings in seventy-five successive verses seventy-five forms which he assumes; they are the forms of the gods

[1] *Records of the Past*, viii. 105.

and of all the great elements and parts of the world. The separate gods are reduced from the rank of independent potentates to shapes of Ra, and thus a kind of unity is set up in the populous Egyptian Pantheon. But Ra is not strong enough to get the better of these shapes, and to rule a sole monarch by his own right, in his own way. He is the god, but he is not an independent god; it is pantheism, not theism, to which he owes his exaltation. The one in Egypt cannot govern the many; the pure exaltation of Ra as a supreme and absolute god does not prevent the worship of a different being in each different town. The one sole god is for the priests alone, not for the people; and this belief in him does not even lead to attempts to root out the worship of animals, or to concentrate the service of the temples on him alone. And in the absence of such attempts we read the sentence condemning a religion which produced most noble fruits of thought, to grow worse and not better as time went on, and to pass away without bringing any permanent contribution to the development of the religion of the world.

Worship.—The Egyptian temple was constructed rather to afford the god a splendid residence among his people than to accommodate a large congregation at an act of worship. The temple was the public place of the community, its point of meeting (for the Egyptian town has no market-place), and its fortress when attacked (for the town is not fortified). But while the courts of the temple were open to the people, there was a holy place which only the priests might enter, where the sacred ark, the symbol of the god, remained, and where sacrifices were offered. The images about the temple were not placed there to be worshipped, but were votive offerings meant to provide the god with a body which he might enter when he chose. The obelisk is such a symbol or incorporation of the sun. On certain days the sacred objects and animals were taken in procession through the temple grounds, or made voyages on the lake belonging to the temple, or were even taken through the nome among the fields and dwellings of their people; and on these occasions representations took place symbolising the principal events in the history of the god. It was thus that the private individual came to know the god; it was a great festival and an occasion of the utmost joy when the divine protectors and benefactors of the nome, who generally remained in their splendid retirement, came forth to mingle for a brief space with the faithful community. The worship of the gods was in Egypt, as in every nation of the ancient world, a matter of state, not of individual concern. It is the chief branch of the public service; the state is under the direct rule of the gods; never was there a more absolute theocracy. The king is a child of the god,—a conception often treated in the most material way,—and being thus of more than human race, becomes himself the object of worship, and even offers sacrifice to himself. It is one of the king's chief cares to provide a stately dwelling for the god; the king himself offers sacrifice on the most important occasions. The god in his sacred ark goes with his people when they are at war and fights with them, so that every war is a holy war. The priests are public officials, and often exercise immense influence. The king institutes them into their functions; they are exempt, as we may read in Genesis, from public burdens; every function involving learning or art is in their hands. Framed in such institutions religion is not likely to have any free growth; the time is far distant here when men will form voluntary associations of their own for spiritual ends. Yet, no doubt, the lay Egyptian had a private religion of his own as well as his share in the great public acts he witnessed. Though the gods of Egypt are nearly all good, the evil power Set was much worshipped, and would be approached in private as well as in the public acts depicted on the monuments, by all who had anything to fear from him—that is to say, by all. Every one had to treat with kindness and respect the animal species sacred in his nome, and other sacred animals. The belief in magic was strong; hidden powers had to be reckoned with on manifold occasions; sickness was imputed to the agency of evil spirits, and treated by exorcism, by persons duly trained and learned in such arts. Lucky and unlucky days, and days suitable or unsuitable for particular undertakings, filled the calendar; the belief in amulets and charms was universal. Such things we expect to find among the people, even where religious thought has risen highest.

THE DOCTRINE OF THE OTHER LIFE

Most of our knowledge about ancient Egypt is drawn from the tombs. No other nation ever bestowed so much care on the dead as the Egyptians did, nor thought of the other world so much. The living had to prepare for his further existence after death, and the dead claimed from his successors on earth elaborate offices of piety. It is in this part of the religion that there is most growth, and this part of it in its ultimate form is best known.

1. **Treatment of the Dead.**—The doctrine of the other world takes its rise with the Egyptians in the belief common to all early races, which was described above (p. 30 *sq.*). The spirit still lives when the body dies, and it comes back to the body, and is affected by the treatment the body receives. To care for the dead is the first duty of the living, and a man must marry in order to have offspring who will pay him the necessary attention after his death. Various things are buried with the corpse for the use of the

spirit, and offerings are made to it from time to time afterwards. This is no more than the common primitive belief, but the Egyptians carried it out more fully in practice than any other people. They sought to make the body incorruptible, embalming it and restoring to it all its organs, so that the spirit should be able to discharge every function of life. They placed the mummy if possible in such a situation that it should never be disturbed to the end of time; the grave they called an eternal dwelling. They even instituted endowments to secure due offerings to the dead in all coming time.

Cultivated as this part of religion was in Egypt, it could not fail to assume a special character. For one thing, there is a variety of names for what survives of man after death; we hear of his heart, his soul, his shade, his luminosity; and in the later doctrine these are all combined and made parts of one theory; all the different parts of the man have to come together again after their dispersion at death before his person is complete. The principal term, however, is the "ka," image, or, as we say, genius, of the man, a non-substantial double of him which has journeys and adventures to make, and to which the offerings are addressed. The "ka" needs food, and regular gifts are made to it of all it can require; it needs guidance and instruction, and these can be conveyed to it by pictures and writings on the walls of the tomb or in the mummy-case; even its amusement and its need of society and of ministration can be to some extent met in this way. It is not peculiar to Egypt that the advantages of wealth and rank are continued after death, and that the rich can do much more, or cause much more to be done for his eternal welfare, than the poor. The king's mummy lies in a pyramid, where it will never be moved; that of the noble in a rock-tomb or a stately edifice or "mastaba"; the poor man has to be content with an inferior kind of embalming, and a tomb of tiles if he gets any at all; and no priest can be retained to pray for him.

2. **The Spirit in the Under-world.**—Before history opens, this common belief and practice in regard to the dead had come to be combined in Egypt with the worship of a solar deity; a step of immense importance, which added immeasurably to the pathos and the moral power of this kind of religion.

Milton says in *Lycidas*—

> So sinks the daystar in the ocean bed;
> And yet anon repairs his drooping head,
> And tricks his beams, and with new-spangled ore
> Flames in the forehead of the morning sky;
> So Lycidas sank low, but mounted high.

But what to Milton was a poetic imagination was to the early Egyptian a serious belief. If the sun was his god, he did not say like Wordsworth in his early period—

> Our fate how different from thine, blest star, in this,
> That no to-morrow shall our beams restore,

but he was convinced that the history of his god, who sank under the Western horizon, and after a period of darkness came back again to light and triumph, was an undoubted indication of what he himself had to look for after death. The mummy was carried across the Nile and deposited in the west land, which is also the under-world, to share in the repose and in the further progress of the dead. As the jackal pervades that region, the dead is left to the care of Anubis, the jackal-headed deity, who opens paths to him for further travel, and leads him into the presence of the gods. The under-world is elaborately portioned out into various parts and scenes, and manifold are the shapes of evil and mischief with which it is peopled.

On the other hand, it contains abundance of blessings, which the departed may secure if the proper means have been taken by himself and by his friends surviving him. The earthly life is there repeated with all its occupations and enjoyments, but free from fear and from decay.

The doctrine of the dead accompanying the sun-god to the under-world, and living under his protection, is very old in Egypt; we saw it in an early form in connection with the god Ra. It was in connection with Osiris, however, that it attained its widest diffusion; to the whole Egyptian people Osiris was the lord of the world below, with whom the departed were. The identification of the departed with Osiris was thorough and complete; he becomes Osiris, takes the name of the deity, and is known in the inscriptions as "Osiris N. N." Isis is his sister, Horus his defender, Anubis his herald and guide, and having shared the god's eclipse, he is also to share his triumph and revival.

3. **The Book of the Dead**, the most famous relic of Egyptian literature, is a collection of pieces many of which are very ancient, bearing on the passage of the soul through the under-world. The book has also been called the *Funeral Ritual*; a better translation of the title is, "Book of Goings Forth to Day." It is the soul's *vade mecum* for the under-world, and contains the forms the soul must have at command in order to ward off all the dangers of that region, and to secure an easy and happy passage through it. How the person is to be reconstructed, the different parts coming back to be built up again in one, how he is to know the spirits he meets, how he is to get the gates opened for him,—such are the subjects of various chapters; and the soul's success in its passage depends on its knowledge of these. The words they contain are not merely information, they have magic power to smooth

away obstacles and to open doors. Hence it is important for a man to have learned them when alive, and, to assist his memory, a few chapters are written on papyrus or linen, and the rolls placed with the mummy in its case, or they are written on the walls of the tomb. No other Egyptian work, in consequence, has been preserved in so many copies, but one roll contains one set of chapters and another another set.

Does the fate of the individual after death depend then entirely on magic; is it a question of how many of these formulæ he is able to remember, or how many his relatives have got written out for him? Do no doubts intrude on his mind lest, even if he has all the requisite knowledge at command, he himself should be found unworthy to live with the immortals? For the most part the *Book of the Dead* stands on the earlier position at which man never thinks of doubting the favour of his god, and trusts to overcome what is hostile by having his magic ready, not by having his heart pure. But in several chapters a deeper tone is heard. There is a form for having the stain rubbed away from the heart of the Osiris, and if there are abundant directions for outward purification, there are also directions for having his sins forgiven. In the great 125th chapter the deceased enters the Hall of the two Truths, and is separated from his sins after he has seen the faces of the gods. Here he stands before forty-two judges (compare the number of the nomes of Egypt) styled Lords of Truth, each of whom is there to judge of a particular sin, and to each he has to profess that he did not when on earth commit that sin. I have not stolen, he has to say; I have not played the hypocrite, I have not stolen the things of the gods, I have not made conspiracies, I have not blasphemed, I have not clipped the skins of the sacred beasts, I have not injured the gods, I have not calumniated the slave to his master; and so on. The line is not yet clearly drawn between moral and ritual or conventional offences; and moral duty is expressed in a negative form, and appears as a shackle, not as an inspiration. Yet the very great advance has been made here, that divine law watches not only over specially religious matters but over social life, and even over the thoughts of the individual heart. The gods enjoin on a man not only to offer sacrifice and to respect the sacred beasts, but also to do his duty as a citizen and as a neighbour, and to keep his own lips unpolluted and his own heart pure. It is to the same effect when we find that a man's justification depends on the state of his heart at death. His heart is weighed against the truth, and if it is found defective, he cannot live again; if it turns out well, then he is justified and goes to the fields of Aalu, the place of the blessed of Osiris.

CONCLUSION

This doctrine of the life to come, like the theistic doctrine the Egyptians at one time attained, might have seemed destined to lead to a pure spiritual faith, from which superstition should have disappeared. But in neither case is that result attained. The later history of Egyptian religion is that of the increase of magic, and of the rise of a priestly class absorbing to itself, as the older priests who were closely connected with the civil life of the nation had never done, all the functions of religion. Doctrine grows more pantheistic and more recondite, mysteries and symbols are multiplied, all to the increase of the influence of the priesthood, and to the infinite exercise of ingenuity in coming times. Popular religion, on the other hand, comes to be more taken up with such matters as charms and amulets and horoscopes; and while morals did not decline from the high level they had gained from the reign of the gods of light, the spirit of the nation lost vigour under the growth of religiosity at the expense of patriotism, and healthy reform grew more and more impossible. What of the religion of Egypt lived on in other lands which felt her influence, it is hard to say. The religious art of Egypt, and with it no doubt some tincture of the ideas it embodied, undoubtedly went northwards to Phenicia; and Greece owed to Phenicia, as we shall see, many a suggestion in religious matters. Long before Isis and Serapis were introduced in Rome in their own persons, the legend of Osiris had flourished in Greece under new names, and the Greek doctrine of the life to come, taught in the mysteries, has suggested to some scholars an Egyptian origin. To the Greeks and Romans this religion afforded an infinity of puzzles and mysteries; to the modern world it affords the greatest example of a religion the early promise of which was not fulfilled, the splendid moral aspirations of which were stifled amid the superstitions they were too weak to conquer.

Books Recommended

For general information Wilkinson's *Egyptians.* E. A. W. Budge, *History of Egypt*, vols. i.-viii., 1902-03. E. A. W. Budge, *The Mummy*; chapters on Egyptian funeral archæology, Cambridge, 1893. Flinders Petrie, *A History of Egypt*. The Histories of Antiquity of Duncker, Maspero, and especially Ed. Meyer. Erman, *Life in Ancient Egypt*, 1894. Maspero, *Manual of Egyptian Archæology*, Second Edition, 1895. Renouf's *Hibbert Lectures.* Tiele, *History of the Egyptian Religion*, translated by Ballingal. Wiedemann, *Ägyptische geschichte*, 1884-88; "Die Religion der alien Aegyptier," 1890; also "Egyptian Religion," in Hastings' *Bible Dictionary*, vol. v.

A. O. Lange, "Die Ägypter" in De la Saussaye. *Records of the Past*, First Series (1873-1881), vols. ii., iv., vi., viii., x., xii. Second Series, 1888-92, vol. ii.-vi.

Benson and Gourlay, *The Temple of Mut in Asher*, 1899.

PART III

THE SEMITIC GROUP

CHAPTER X

THE SEMITIC RELIGION

As used by the modern scholar, the term Semites or Semitic races includes the Arabs, the Hebrews, the Canaanites and Phenicians, the Syrians or Arameans, the Babylonians and the Assyrians. This enumeration differs from that of the tenth chapter of Genesis, where the children of Shem include Elam, or the dwellers in Susiana, and Lud or the Lydians, while the tribes who dwelt in Canaan before the Hebrews are placed in another and a lower division of the human family. The principle of the enumeration in Genesis is probably that of geographical neighbourhood; the modern principle is that of linguistic affinity. The peoples mentioned above spoke, or still speak, languages which belong to the same family of human speech. The inference from affinity of language to affinity of blood is in this case a strong one, so that the peoples using the Semitic tongues are considered to be of the same race. To the question, where the cradle of the Semitic race is to be sought, most scholars now answer that we must seek it in Arabia. From this isolated land the Semitic dispersion spread in every direction, till Semitic language and customs filled the earth from the south of Arabia to the north of Syria, and from the mountains of Iran to the Mediterranean, and far along the northern shores of Africa; of Babylonia and Assyria, where Semitic culture and religion assumed at the dawn of human history a very special and peculiar form we have already spoken. We have now to speak of Semitic religion as found in the lands bordering on the eastern Mediterranean in a more original form. The Semitic peoples outside of Babylonia founded no lasting empires, and showed no great aptitude for art or for literary style; but, in point of religion, they communicated to the world impulses of immeasurable force, which will act powerfully on the world as long as the Prophet is named or Christ preached.

It is possible to define to a certain extent the typical religion of the Semites. The Burnett lectures of the late lamented Professor Robertson Smith[1] profess to do this; a book in which great learning and bold speculation are remarkably combined, and which forms one of the most important contributions to the early history, not of Semitic religion only, but of early religion in general. The writer was keenly interested in the study of prehistoric man and of primitive institutions, and much of his book refers to an earlier period in the growth of religion than that of the formation of the Semitic type. On the question of the specific character of Semitic as distinguished from other religions, it is one of our principal authorities.

The Semitic races differ from the Indo-European, with whom alone we need compare them, in their greater intensity of disposition and a corresponding poverty of imagination. The Semite has a smaller range of ideas, but he applies them

[1] *Lectures on the Religion of the Semites.* First Series. The

more practically and more thoroughly. He has, indeed, an intensely practical turn, and does not touch philosophy except under an irresistible pressure of great practical ideas; while for plastic art he has no native inclination. From this it follows that the religious views he entertains appear to him less as ideas than as facts, which must be reckoned with to their full extent as other common facts of life must, and from which there is no escape. His religious convictions, therefore, are apt to be carried out to their utmost extent, even at the cost of great and painful sacrifices. Religion admits with the Semite of less compromise, and is less affected by fancy, than with the Aryan; it is, in fact, a more practical matter. The result proves to be that the Semitic mind brings religious ideas to bear on life and conduct with the greatest possible force; the substance is more, the form less, than is the case elsewhere.

When we ask for the common type of working Semitic religion, where are we to look for it? Not in Babylonia; the Babylonian religion is Semitic, but late Semitic; it has received the character of civilisation and empire. Nor need we look for it in the town life of Phenicia. It is in the seclusion of the Arabian peninsula that we find it, in the district, as we saw, now regarded as the cradle of the Semitic race, where life continues to this day little changed from what it was before the days of Abraham. There the type of society still exists with which scholars like Wellhausen and Smith consider the earliest Semitic religion to be connected. It is a society of nomad clans, which own no allegiance to any central authority, who have no king and do not yet form a nation. This is a stage of social growth which in every ancient people precedes the rise of the nation and of monarchy. The Hebrews are rising out of this stage when we first see them. Their neighbours the Moabites and Canaanites have already passed beyond it. But all these peoples alike have their root in a state of society when there was no large and orderly community, but only a multitude of small and restless tribes, when there was no written law, but only custom, and when there was no central authority to execute justice, but it was left to a man's fellow-clansmen to avenge his murder.

Now the religion of the clan, the ideas of which determine the character of later Semitic systems, may be briefly described as follows. Each clan has its own god, perhaps he was originally an animal, at any rate he is the father or ancestor of the clan, he is of the same blood with them, he belongs to them and to no other clan. So far the assertion that the Semites are naturally monotheists is true ; but it is also true of all primitive totemistic or clannish communities. A man is born into a community with such a divine head, and the worship of that god is the only one possible to him. Should he be expelled from his clan he is driven away from his god, [and he cannot obtain access into another clan except by a formal adoption as a stranger client. The link on the other hand between the god and his clansmen is of the strongest. He joins in all their enterprises, after being consulted on the subject, and having a sacrifice offered to him, which renews the union of the clansmen to him and to each other. Their wars are his wars ; when any of them is injured or slain he joins in their necessary acts of retaliation; it is a religious duty for each of them to be faithful to the others, and to keep up the tribal customs, of which the god approves.

Thus the Semites have as many gods as they have clans ; and these gods do not greatly differ from each other. As long, moreover, as the clans are at constant feud, no single god can grow very great. It is only when one clan conquers others, that a king-god can arise to rule over all alike as a monarch rules over his nobles and their provinces. But in this type of deity the genius of Semitic religion is already expressed. The god of the Semite is not a nature-power who bears the same aspect to all men, but a member of a particular clan, a person to whom the clansman occupies the same position of natural subordination as he does to his father or his chief. The god takes his name not from a part of nature but from a human relationship. He is "Baal," master or owner, he is "Adon," lord; in later circumstances he is "Melech," king. "El," mighty one, hero, is a more generic term; like our "God," it is applied to any divine being. These deities, it will be noticed, are all masculine; but it is not to be supposed that the Semites had no goddesses. Not to speak of the goddesses of Babylonia, mere doubles of the gods whose names they bore (p. 94), the earliest Semites are believed by several great scholars to have had a goddess but no god. The matriarchal state of society, in which the mother alone ruled the family, came before the patriarchal, and so the reign of the goddess came before that of the god. Each community had its own Al-lat, "The Lady," as she is called in Arabia, a strict and exacting lady not to be confounded with the licentious goddesses of later times; and in all Semitic lands traces of her early prevalence are found.[1] As the male god came to the front, the female became a less definite figure, till she was generally a mere counterpart of the male god, with little character of her own. With gods of this type there is little scope for mythology. The history of the god is that of the tribe; the gods are too little independent of their human clients to form a society by themselves, or to give rise to stories about their doings.

This is one side of the natural history of the Semitic gods; but that history has another side. The lands in which the Semites dwelt were full from the first of sacred spots; and we have to notice that the god of a clan is also the god of a certain piece of earth where he is supposed

[1] See Robertson Smith's *Kinship and Marriage in Early Arabia.*

to dwell, which is regarded as his property, and the fertility of which is ascribed to his beneficence. In the Bible we read of sacred trees, of sacred wells, of sacred stones or mounds, and of stones or pillars which were connected with sacrifice. In various Semitic lands there are also sacred streams and sacred caves. The Semites in fact had their share of the inheritance the whole world has derived from the earliest times, of prehistoric religious sites and objects. A spirit spoke in the rustling of the branches of the tree, counsel could be procured at the spring; wherever there appeared to be something mysterious in nature, a spirit was believed to dwell; and especially in woods and fertile spots, where wild beasts originally had their lair, a spirit was thought to reside, which was approached with fear. Many of these superstitions the various branches of the Semites long continued to hold;[1] but the race superseded in the main this world of spirits by a set of gods, and the magic addressed to spirits by religious observances addressed to gods. The genius or jinn haunting the thicket, who had no regular worshippers, but was an object of fear to all, and had to be propitiated or controlled by mysterious arts, gave way to the god of a clan, who took up his residence there, and received the regular worship of his clansmen; the stone became the symbol of a deity who had been asked and had consented to become identified with it for the purpose of the stated rites of the clan. In this way the clan gods became localised as the clans tended to acquire fixed settlements, and each sacred spot was occupied by the deity of the clan who dwelt around it. The view was held that each god was to be found at the spot where, on some marked occasion, he had given evidence of his power, and he who wished to enquire of that god

[1] The late Professor Ives Curtius in Professor read to the Basel Congress (1905, *Verhandlungen*, p. 154), on "Traces of Early Semitic Religion in Syria," gives details of local sanctuaries still resorted to in that country.

had to go there. It might happen that the god manifested his power at another spot to one of his dependents on a journey, as Jehovah did to Jacob at Bethel. Then that spot also was recognised as a holy one where communication could be had with the deity, and the apparatus of worship was erected there so that the intercourse might be suitably carried on, as Jacob is reported to have done. In time also it came to be thought that each god had his land which belonged to him, on which alone his worship was possible, and so the earth was parcelled out among a number of deities; and Naaman, who wishes to worship Jehovah in his Syrian home, carries off two mules' burden of Jehovah's soil, to make in the midst of Syria a little piece of the land of the God of Israel.

One circumstance remains to be mentioned which constitutes a marked difference between the Semitic and the Aryan religions. Aryan religion has its centre in the household; the hearth is its altar, and the gods of the domestic cult are the departed ancestors of the family. Semitic religion is without this cult; the hearth is not an altar; the religious community is not the family but the clan. The worship of ancestors, if, as there is reason to believe, it had once been practised by the Semites (the Arabs tied a camel to the grave of the dead chief), lost at a very early period all practical importance. While the early Semites believed in the continued existence of the departed, they thought of them as beings quite destitute of energy, as "shades laid in the ground," and did not worship them. The other world occupied, therefore, a very small space in Semitic thought. Religion confined itself to this life; after death, it was held, even religion came to an end. A man must enjoy the society of his god in this life; after death he could this part in no sacrifice, and could render to his god no thanks nor service.

From what has been said the character of sacrifice among the Semites is readily understood. Sacrifice is not domestic but takes place at the spot where the god is thought to reside, or where the symbol stands which represents him. Usually this was an upright monolith, such as is found in every part of the world, and the central act of the sacrifice consisted in applying the blood of the new-slain victim to this stone. The blood was thus brought near to the god, the clansmen also may have touched the blood at the same time; and the act meant that the god and the tribesmen, all coming into contact with the blood, which originally perhaps was that of the animal totem of the clan, declared that they were of the same blood, and renewed the bond which connected them with each other. A further feature of early Semitic sacrifice is also that the slaughter and the blood ceremony are succeeded by a banquet, at which the god is thought to sit at table with his clients, his share being exposed for him on the stone or altar. When he came to be believed to dwell aloft, his share was burned with fire so that the smell or finer essence of it might ascend to him. Many examples may be collected in the early historical books of the Old Testament of sacrifices which are at the same time social and festive occasions; in fact, in early Israel every act of slaughter was a sacrifice, and every sacrifice a banquet. The people dance and make merry before their god, of whose favour they have just become assured once more by the act of communion they have observed. The undertaking they have on hand is hallowed by his approval, so that they can boldly advance to it; the corporate spirit of the tribe is quickened by renewed contact with its head; all thoughts of care are far away; the religious act makes the worshippers simply and unaffectedly happy, if it does not even fill them with an orgiastic ecstasy.

This careless happiness, in connection with religious acts, is found also in Babylonian sacrifice. It is not, however, peculiar to the Semites, but is characteristic of the religion of the early world in general. Nor is it peculiar to this race that religion does not address the individual as such, but only as a member of his tribe, and that it provides small comfort for private sorrows or longings. The sad face is out of place in the presence of the god. Religion is essentially a happy thing; sin is not yet thought of, and if things go wrong, the tribe never entertains any doubt but that with proper sacrifices and promises the god will show them his favour again and renew their prosperity. All this is not specially Semitic, but simply early religion. What is specially Semitic is, to repeat that with which we set out, that gods are worshipped whose relations to their worshippers are borrowed from existing forms of society. The god is the father or the master or the champion, of the circle of worshippers; he is of their kindred, he is their greatest and strongest clansman, he belongs to them and to none but them. This, whether it is derived—as Professor Robertson Smith thinks—from the ideas of totemism or not, leads to a religion which is exclusive and intense, and cannot be trifled with. The god who is a man's master, and the head of his clan, stands in a more imperative position towards him than the god of the sky, or than a departed ancestor. He does not change with the seasons or the weather, nor is there any doubt as to his intentions and demands. Semitic religion, even at this stage, is a very real thing, and may easily, in favouring circumstances, become a force of overmastering energy.

Books Recommended

Hommel, *Die Semitischen Völker und Sprachen.*

"Semites," by M'Curdy, in Hastings' *Bible Dictionary*, vol. v.

CHAPTER XI

CANAANITES AND PHENICIANS

WHEN the Children of Israel crossed the Jordan and settled in Palestine, they found that country inhabited by a race of men who spoke the same language as themselves, and who were much further advanced than they in civilisation. The letters of El-Amarna which belong to this period show Syria to have been full of small theocratic states, all pervaded, though now under the power of Egypt, by Babylonian culture, each with a god and a settled worship of its own. The Israelites of a later time regarded the Canaanites with such disdain that they reckoned them (Genesis x. 6, 15) as belonging to an inferior race; but the two peoples belonged to the same race, and had many common ideas and practices. In religion they resembled each other, or Israel could never have been tempted so strongly, and for so long a period, to adopt the rites of the people they conquered.

The Israelites were not the only people who invaded the land of the Canaanites and stayed in it. Three such invasions took place: those of the Phenicians, of the Philistines, and of the Hebrews—the first and third being Semitic peoples, and perhaps the second also. The Philistines, settling on the south-eastern corner of the Mediterranean, had a Semitic religion, of which the fish-god Dagon, the Fly-Baal of Ekron, and the Ashtoreth, probably of Ascalon, are known figures. The Philistines, however, lost ultimately their separate character, and ceased to exist as an independent people. It will not be necessary for us to mention them again. The Phenicians, settling on the northern sea-board of Syria, where great trade routes to East and West converged, and where good harbours could be made, became a nation of merchants, and kept up active communication with the great kingdoms of the East, with Egypt, and with the islands and the distant shores of Western Europe. The carriers of the ancient world, they transmitted to Europe not only the spices and the fabrics but also the ideas and the practices of Asia, and rendered to the world the inestimable service of awaking the slumbering energies of the Aryan peoples to new life.

A short chapter may be devoted to the religion of the Canaanites and to that of the Phenicians, not because these were important in themselves, for in neither was there anything original or anything destined to survive, but because of the light they throw on other religions which were to have a great career. It was in conflict with the Canaanite religion that the faith of Israel first realised its true nature and was led to organise itself in a manner befitting its character. And from Phenicia both Israel and Greece accepted many a suggestion, both in external matters connected with worship and in matters of a deeper nature.

The religion of the Canaanites is well known to us from the Old Testament. It is such a system as we found that of the Semites to be, with certain peculiar developments, of which we have already seen something in our chapter on Babylonia. A local community recognises an invisible head, with whom it meets at the sacred spot, whom it regards as overlord or master, of whose favour it is in no doubt, and whom it serves with sacrifices and with lively manifestations of joy at certain fixed periods. The god is called **Baal**. This, however, is not a proper name but a title; it means lord, master, and the Baal may have a name of his own in addition: we hear of Baal Peor, the lord of Peor, and of many another. Baals are spoken of in the plural; we read in Judges ii. 11 and in other passages that the Israelites followed the Baals, that is the gods of the Canaanites. Each place has its own Baal, who is worshipped at the local sanctuary. The sanctuary is at an elevated spot outside the town or village, either on a natural eminence or on a mound artificially made for the purpose; these are the high places of the Old Testament; originally Canaanite places of worship, they drew to themselves also the worship of Israel. The apparatus of worship at these shrines is of a very simple nature. An upright stone represents the god; it is not a statue of him, being unhewn and having no resemblance to the human figure. He was supposed to come to the stone when meeting with his worshippers; and in the earliest times of Semitic religion this stone served the purpose of an altar: the gifts, which were not originally burned, were laid upon it, or the blood of the victim was applied to it. But besides the altar and the upright stone or *massebah* the Canaanite shrine had another piece of furniture. A massive tree-trunk, fixed in the ground and with some of its branches perhaps still remaining, represented the female deity who is the invariable companion of the Baal. This is the **Ashera** of Canaan, a word which in the Authorised Version is translated "grove," after an error of the Vulgate, but which in the Revised Version is rightly left untranslated. (Judges iii. 7, vi. 25; 2 Kings xxiii. 6, there is one in the Temple at Jerusalem; etc.) The word Ashera is in such passages the designation of the tree which stood to represent the goddess; whether it is ever the proper name of the goddess herself is doubtful. At any rate Ashera, like Baal, is not the name of one historic deity, but a name applied to the goddess of each place all over the country.

The character of Canaanite religion is clearly revealed in

its apparatus of worship. We saw that the Babylonians added to many of the gods of their country a female counterpart, turning the name of the god into a feminine form (p. 94, also p. 159). In Canaan we find that Semitic worship is addressed to pairs of deities; there is a god and a goddess at each shrine. While it would be wrong to regard this as the general type of Semitic religion,—our chapter on that subject points to a different conclusion, and the great gods of Phenicia, of Moab, and of Israel are solitary beings,—we must recognise that the worship of god and goddess was widespread in Semitic peoples. In Canaan it is not difficult to understand it. We have here the worship of an agricultural community; and as the Baal is the lord of the soil and the author of its fertility, who is entitled to receive the first-fruits, so the Ashera is the fertile matron who represents the principle of increase. The Old Testament leaves us in no doubt as to the kind of worship which was carried on at these shrines. The festivals were those of the farmers' calendar; the Baal is presented with the first-fruits of corn and wine and oil, in the midst of general feasting and boisterous merry-making. His consort, on the other hand, is served with rites applying in the most direct manner the principle she represents. The shrine has a staff of female attendants for this part of the service of religion. The rustic worship of Palestine thus shows us a side of the religion of Western Asia which we know from other sources to have been widely diffused. A female deity like the Babylonian Ishtar (p. 98), is served with impure rites in great cities as well as in country districts, and her worship spread westwards with other Eastern products. She is found as Baalit, as Mylitta,[1] as Astarte; the Greeks call her Aphrodite, and her horrid worship found entrance in various Greek cities.

[1] Herod. i. 199.

To the Israelites the worship of Canaan proved a great temptation (Numbers xxv.), but they gradually rose above it. The **Phenicians** also came to have gods of a much higher character, and of these also we must speak. The Phenicians were not original in their religion any more than in their art; their religion began with the ordinary Semitic notions as these had been applied by the older population in Syria, and they improved it by borrowing from various parts of the world with which they trafficked. So various were their borrowings that it is impossible to draw up a consistent system of their gods. One town has one set of gods, another town another, and the same deity wears different and even opposite characters in different places. All that can be done is to single out a few features which we can see to have been on the whole characteristic of Phenician religion, and to have enabled it to influence the worship of other peoples.

The Phenicians were very much in earnest about the maintenance of state and of religion. In their successive city-states of Sidon, Tyre, and Carthage, we see them exhibiting an intense devotion to the commonwealth, and very much under the influence of their priesthood. Semitic religion tends to grow more sombre and intense as it develops; and the Phenicians, while still holding the principle of a god and goddess, concentrate their worship more and more on a single divine figure, and come to regard that figure from a greater distance and with greater awe. The liberal and easy-going Baals and Asheras of agricultural life are not suited to the temple of a great commercial city; a figure of more dignity is wanted. And thus above the crowd of Baals there appears the **Moloch** or king, a much greater being and requiring a much statelier service. Moloch also is not originally a proper name; there are various Molochs or king-gods who rise above the Baals, and the individuals have special designations, as Melcarth, "king of the city." This type of deity occurs not with the Phenicians only, but with several other Syrian peoples about the same time. The Moloch of Sidon and Tyre is a being of the same character as the chief gods of Moab, Ammon, and Israel. He has to do not only with the blessings of agricultural life, but with state and government. He is the founder of a state; he is the inventor of navigation and of purple; he is the first king; when a colony is sent out, it goes with his approval, and he himself leads the expedition; he is the dread ruler whom none must disobey; the majesty, the power, and the enterprise of the state are all embodied in him. And as the king-god is far above the landlord-god in power, he is infinitely removed from him in character also. The chief gods of Sidon and Tyre have nothing luxurious or effeminate about them. They are strict and awful beings, and must not be incautiously approached. They retain their primitive character as sources of life, but they are destroyers of life as well. Pure and holy themselves, they require purity and holiness in all who draw near to them. Their priests are celibates, their priestesses virgins. They require sacrifices of a very different nature from those of the Baals, more costly and more dreadful. Human sacrifices appear to have been a regular feature of their worship: when the Israelites turn to the worship of Phenician gods, or when they copy Phenician practices, we hear of their "making their children pass through the fire"—that is, offering them up as burnt-sacrifices. The Moloch requires what is most costly as a sacrifice, or what will cause the strongest thrill of terror in his worship. Even the first-born child is not to be kept back from him (2 Kings xxiii. 10, Jerem. vii. 31, cf. Micah vi. 7).

So far the origin of the Phenician gods is simple

They are purely Semitic deities, formed on the pattern of human rulers and deriving their attributes from that character. When a state becomes highly organised before it is quite civilised in other respects, its religion is apt to be stern and cruel; of this various instances may be found in the history of religion, and the present is one of them. The Phenician gods were of such a character as to favour the survival of savage practices; the Semite, as we saw, is extremely matter-of-fact and practical in his religion, and a god who was a king would receive the same kind of offerings as the king of Sidon or of Tyre was accustomed to. A strict and dreadful religion thus survives beyond the savage state; pleasure is taken in trampling on natural feelings and in setting forth shocking spectacles at the bidding of the deity.

Astral Deities of Phenicia.—It is not possible to arrange in a system the remaining phenomena of Phenician religion. In the historical period the gods have another character besides that of being heads and rulers of communities. They are connected with the heavenly bodies. The chief god, whatever name he bears, El, Baal, Moloch, Rimmon, or Adonis, is always the sun. A sun-god may have come from Egypt or Babylon, but there is no reason why the Phenicians may not have had a sun-god from the first, whose character spread to their other deities. And in accordance with the tendency above spoken of, the sun-god has a consort. Sometimes his consort is the earth; and then we have a sensuous and immoral worship such as that of the Canaanites. Sometimes it is the moon; her name is Astarte or Ashtoreth, and she is a very different being from the Ashera of Canaan; the names are not the same, and the characters are opposite. Ashtoreth, like the primitive Semitic goddess (p. 159), is a chaste matron; she is represented robed and in stately attitude, and is a fit companion for the strict Moloch of the cities. Her worship is described to us by Jeremiah, in whose time the matrons of Jerusalem made cakes for her and poured out drink-offerings and burned incense to her as the "queen of heaven"; all this was done with the knowledge and co-operation of their husbands, so that the worship had nothing immoral about it. This strict goddess is not to be identified with Istar of Babylonia, although the names are alike. Istar is not a moon-goddess like Ashtoreth; in Babylonia, in fact, the moon is masculine, and the characters of the two goddesses are opposite. The Sidonian Astarte and the Canaanite Ashera represent two opposing types of female deity, both of which may possibly have their reflections in Greece—the latter in the lower forms of the worship of Aphrodite, and the former in the figures of such strict maiden goddesses as Artemis and Athene.

Another worship which prevailed in Phenicia should not be left unnoticed—that of the Cabiri. There were temples of the Cabiri in several of the towns; their worship, however, was secret, and little was known of it even in antiquity. We know at all events that the Cabiri were seven in number, and the number is thought to be connected, not with the seven planets, but with the seven heavenly spheres of early astronomy. They have a head called Eshmun, who is the god of the eighth or highest sphere. The Cabiri are beings of a moral character; they are not only mighty ones and creators, but they are the children of Sydyk—that is, of Righteousness; and they give counsel. It is here that the tendency to speculative exaltation of the deity appears in Phenicia; but there is little of it, and neither in this direction nor in that of morals was the religion destined to have any remarkable growth. The service of the gods was so closely identified with the service of the state,—for either the priest and the king were one, as in Israel after the exile, or nothing could be done without the priesthood,—that no independent religious development was possible. In a theocracy religion cannot grow, at least it cannot be openly acknowledged to do so; and the prophet and reformer finds every influence arrayed against him.

How greatly Israel was indebted to **Phenician art** is known to all. It was by artificers from Tyre that Solomon's royal buildings were planned and executed, when he had married a daughter of Egypt and was compelled to aim at some magnificence. A royal temple formed part of these buildings, and was necessarily erected according to the ideas which prevailed in the more advanced neighbouring kingdoms. It was from the same source that the Greeks a century or two later drew suggestions for their sacred architecture; and thus we find that the ground-plan of Solomon's temple and that of the Greek temple are closely similar. Both are to be traced ultimately to the model derived by the Phenicians from Egypt. And those who borrowed from Phenicia the form of their temple, borrowed many other things too. In the porch of Solomon's temple stood two great pillars of bronze, which were called Jachin and Boaz; they were simply the symbols which stood at the entrance to every Phenician temple of the sun-god worshipped there. The priests of Israel were dressed like those of Tyre and Sidon; they offered the same animals as sacrifices, they received the same dues for their maintenance. When so much apparatus was borrowed, it is no wonder that the gods of Phenicia were at times worshipped at Jerusalem. We see from this whole chapter that the religion of Israel was not so much apart from that of the other Syrian peoples as we have been wont to imagine. Even in his religion Israel owed something to his neighbours ; his religion came to be better than theirs, but it was the result of a movement in which they also had taken part.

Books Recommended

The Histories of Antiquity. E. Meyer, Duncker (see p. 101).

Tiele's *Egyptische en Mesopotamische Godsdiensten*. Book II. : Phenicia and Israel.

The Histories of Israel, especially Kuenen, *The Religion of Israel.*

F. Jeremias, in De la Saussaye, vol. i. p. 348-383.

CHAPTER XII

ISRAEL

IT is a circumstance of the greatest value for the science of religion that the Old Testament is so well known. That book is the most valuable literary storehouse we possess of the facts and ideas connected with the early religion of mankind; it is the best text-book of the earlier portion of our subject. In our chapters on primitive worship, as well as in that on the Semites, we have drawn largely from this source, and for the earlier stages of the religion of Israel we may refer to these chapters. We have now, however, to deal specially with the religion of the Old Testament, and to endeavour to show, as has been done in other cases, what was its specific character, and how its character determined its history. The story to be told in this chapter is, even apart from our special interest in it, as fascinating as any in this volume; it was through a mental movement of unparalleled grandeur, as well as through an outward history of tragic and entrancing interest, that the Jews came to possess the religion which was the desire of all nations, and the chief preparation for Christianity.

We have to begin, however, with repeating in this case what has been and will be the burden of our opening paragraphs in many chapters of this book, namely that the traditional ideas about the nature of this religion require to be corrected, and that its sacred books as they now stand do not accurately represent its history. The Old Testament literature has suffered in a high degree what seems to be the predestined fate of every set of sacred books. Old materials and new are mixed up together in it; many works have been revised by later editors, and so much changed, that laborious critical processes are necessary before they can be used by the historian. In forming his first impressions as to the relations the books bear to each other, and as to the purport of the whole, the reader is naturally guided by the order in which he finds them; but the order in which the sacred books of the Jews stand in the Old Testament was fixed from a peculiar point of view at a late age in Jewish history, and is in many respects quite unnatural and misleading. To come to particulars; the Old Testament as it stands suggests that the Law was the earliest product of Jewish literature, and that all the details of ritual, as well as of moral and social duty, were fixed for the Jews at the very outset of their history; and it suggests that the books of the prophets were written last. This, till quite recently, was generally believed to be the case, but by the labours of a series of illustrious scholars of the Old Testament the conclusion has been reached, which is now less and less disputed, that the earlier prophetic books come first in chronological order, and that the law, which is not all of one piece, but contains a number of codes of different periods, together with a collection of legends and traditions drawn from various quarters and subjected to editorial treatment, did not assume the form in which we have it till after the exile. The historical books, in which no doubt various ancient pieces are embodied, were written under the inspiration of prophetic ideas; and the latest books of all are those which stand in the centre of the Old Testament in the English Bible; the Psalter, which had been growing during a long period before it came to contain its present number of pieces, the books of morals and philosophy, and the book of Job. Daniel belongs to the period of the Maccabees. The historian, therefore, starts from the age of the prophets of the eighth century B.C. The writings of these great men afford a graphic picture of their time, and an entirely trustworthy account of the mental furniture Israel then possessed. From this fixed point the student is able to infer what happened to Israel in earlier times, and to judge of the spirit in which the early history of the people was afterwards written and edited. The history of Israel which the student arrives at after these critical processes differs, it is true, in very important respects from that which appears at first sight on the face of the Bible. But the same thing has occurred in the case of other nations. The sacred books of Persia also have to be turned outside in before they furnish the historian with an account he can accept. Even of the speeches of Mohammed the same is true. Those who undertake the task of codifying sacred literatures have to consider the purpose to which the books are to be put in the community, and to arrange them so as best to serve that purpose ; they do not ask, How must they be arranged so as to exhibit the true sequence of the history ?—that interest only arises much later—but, How will they best serve the needs of the community ? The order of books in sacred collections is, therefore, fixed by practical considerations, now of one kind and now of another, and not according to the requirements of the student of history. We now proceed to give the outline of the history of the religion of Israel as it appears in the light of recent critical investigation.

Israel consisted originally of a group of tribes, bound together by the memory of a great deliverance they had experienced in common, and of battles in which they had fought side by side. Accustomed to the free life of shepherds, they had been enslaved in Egypt and held to intolerable tasks; but they had made their escape in a wonderful manner under a leader who had known how to kindle them to heroic efforts by reminding them of their religious traditions. Under his leadership they had visited the Sinaitic peninsula after leaving Egypt, and had wandered in the regions to the north of Sinai, till at last they conquered territory to the east of Jordan, on which some of them settled, while others crossed the Jordan, and took up their abodes among the Canaanite tribes whom they found there.

The nation and the religion came into the world at the same time. Although the tribes retained their separate gods and religious observances, and families among them also had their own family cults, the bond by which they had been formed into a people and made capable of common action was stronger than these earlier ties; the God whom Moses proclaimed as their head inspired in them an enthusiasm and vigour unknown before. His name was Yahweh, and is said to have a metaphysical meaning, and to designate the god as more really existing than any other. This is doubted; what is certain is that Moses declared that Yahweh promised to be with the tribes, and that they took him for their God. Jehovah, to use the more familiar form of the name, was perhaps the God of the most powerful of the tribes, he was probably a nature-god, and connected with storms and thunder, and he had his seat at Mount Sinai. Thither the tribes repaired to hold a solemn meeting with him; from there he was afterwards represented as coming forth when about to do any mighty act for his people. He is thought of as a being who cannot be seen, since he dwells in clouds and darkness. He utters his voice in thunder and storm; he is possessed of irresistible energy which he unfolds in battle, and in which he causes his people to share when he goes before them to war. But he is also a god of counsel, and takes the greatest interest in the moral and social life of his people. His human representatives, aided by his spirit, settle disputes which are laid before them, and pronounce authoritative counsels on difficult matters. This kind of guidance is constantly going on, so that Jehovah is felt to be watching over the conduct of his people, and to be an effective helper and guide in their domestic concerns, which not every god attends to, as well as in their meetings with their enemies.

The Early Ritual was Simple.—In all this we have a very apt example of the advance which, as we saw in a former chapter, religion makes when it becomes national instead of merely tribal; when the great god of the nation takes his place above the gods of the tribes. In Israel, however, it is not the case that the national religion, when it appears, at once develops a higher style of worship, and draws attention to itself by greater pomp and deeper solemnity of form. The priestly legislation of Exodus and Leviticus, indeed, represents this as having been the case. Here the tribes have scarcely adopted the service of Jehovah, when an army of thousands of priests is called into being, for whose maintenance elaborate provision is made, and a splendid and highly-organised worship is arranged. This directory of worship, however, most scholars are agreed, never was in operation till after the exile: we see in it the worship which Ezra and his fellow-scribes aimed at introducing in the second temple at Jerusalem. The worship of the wilderness and of the early period of Israel in Canaan was of a very different nature. The leading features and principles of it differed little from what we have described in former parts of this book (pp. 65 *sq.*, 162). It was conducted according to custom rather than statute, and its leading characteristic was that it was a common meal at which the god was present along with his worshippers, and assurances were given that the good understanding still continued which bound the tribesmen to their god and each other. It was by the person of his god rather than by a more elaborate worship, or a more numerous priesthood, that Israel was distinguished from Moab and Ammon.

Contact with Canaanite Religion.—After being delivered out of Egypt by the power of Jehovah, and entering Canaan, Israel was placed in a position in which it is wonderful, indeed, that the national character and the national religion were not merged in those of the surrounding population. Bringing with them the few ideas and the scanty appliances of the wilderness, they found themselves dwelling amid a people whose civilisation was fully formed, and who possessed a comparatively elaborate worship. The tribes of Canaan spoke the same language, and were of the same race with themselves, but had advanced to the higher life of agriculture and of cities. Their worship was the same in principle as that of Israel, but it had a higher organisation. The land was studded with sacred places, the sanctity of which Israel could not deny, and which formed centres of pilgrimage and worship. The worship of the Canaanites was described in last chapter (pp. 165-67); the reader will remember the upright stone (masseba) representing the Baal, and the tree-trunk (ashera), if there was no living tree, representing the goddess. If all this or most of it was new to the Israelites, so was the sacred year which fixed the seasons of worship in Canaan. Minor festivals were fixed by the appearance of the new moon, or by the regular return of the seventh day (it is doubtful if the Sabbath was observed in the wilderness, it is connected with agriculture, and is scarcely compatible with pastoral life); greater ones by the epochs of the year, such as harvest and vintage. The worship connected with agriculture in the early world is of a noisy and frantic order; and where gods are worshipped who are connected with fertility, it is apt, as we saw, to be marked by sexual features.

Danger of Fusion.—The Israelites were naturally prompted to adopt what they could of the religion of the Canaanites. The old sacred places of the land, whether connected with their own ancestral traditions or not, they could not help adopting; it would have been strange, indeed, if, when they became agriculturists, they had not adopted the agricultural festivals; and if, as was natural, they regarded the Baal of the Canaanite as the lord of the land and the giver of its fertility, their thanks for the harvest would be addressed to him (Hosea ii. 8). Their worship of Jehovah could not be left poorer than that which their neighbours addressed to Baal; for it also they erected asheras and made use of standing stones, and of Jehovah also they had images. One of these, which was destroyed by Hezekiah was in the form of a serpent: in other places Jehovah was worshipped under the form of a bull. Where an image of him was kept, he could be consulted by means of lots or in other ways. The ark or chest which was kept at one of the more important shrines, represented him most fully; it was carried into battle, and he was thought to go with it.

Religious Conflict.—But the more developed worship thus paid to Jehovah after the settlement in Canaan, as it had not grown out of the religion of Jehovah did not truly express its spirit, and was felt by those who believed most thoroughly in the national god, to be a wrong way of serving him. If, moreover, the Israelites, who lived scattered and far apart from each other among the older inhabitants, went so far in adopting Canaanite practices, there was a danger that Israel would forget the faith which had made him a nation, and thus part entirely with his character and nationality. A contest thus arose, which continued during the whole of Israelite history down to the exile, between the few who cared for Jehovah only, and desired to see the principles of His religion carried out purely and without reserve, and the many who, while also professing to follow Jehovah, saw no harm in worshipping him as other gods were worshipped, or even in addressing other gods as well as him. This struggle is represented in the histories as if Israel had from time to time become entirely apostate from its own faith. But it is clear that Israel never forgot Jehovah so far as to be incapable of being called back to him. The call was generally a call to war. The people, having forgotten the true source of their strength, and so lost spirit and became a prey to their enemies, were summoned by one in whom the spirit of Jehovah was burning freshly, to follow him to battle against their enemies. The spirit of Jehovah, thus applied anew to the hearts of his people, did not fail of its effect. The wave of courage and of martial ardour spread from place to place, from tribe to tribe, and soon an army stood in the field which struck with the old vigour, and soon shook off the yoke of the oppressor. Jehovah thus proved Himself to be Jehovah Sebaoth, *i.e.*, in the most probable rendering of the phrase, the God of the armies of His people. A religion which proved itself in this way could never cease to be a power in the heart of the nation; even if the tribes, dispersing again after a victory, soon seemed to lose touch of each other, and to be sinking deeper than ever in the surrounding tide of Canaanite life, yet the faith, which was associated with all the highest moments of their past history, and was the secret of all their victories, could not die.

The Monarchy.—It was a great advance, however, in the history of the religion of Israel, when the judges or heroes who appeared, at distant intervals of time and in different parts of the country, to summon Israel to fight for freedom in the name of Jehovah, were succeeded by the monarchy. This was a step which those most zealous for the national faith warmly approved, and, indeed, themselves brought about; the monarchy was founded, in the case of the first two kings, on religious enthusiasm. The religion of Jehovah at once became the state religion, and a more satisfactory worship was formed at the court. The permanent union of the tribes under the monarchy soon showed Israel to be possessed of much greater force than could have been imagined, and within a century the people of Jehovah formed a considerable power, which was heard of in all ends of the earth. Instead of a set of scattered tribes they were now a homogeneous people, conscious of a great past and looking forward to a still greater future. As they passed rapidly from barbarism to civilisation, Jehovah shared their rise. His energy had always been undoubted, but he now put on in addition all the settled attributes of kingly power—he was a great god, and a great king, a just judge, a liberal friend—all his doings were wonderful. He had chosen Israel for his people, and by a series of mighty acts had guided and preserved them, and made them great. His people stood in a peculiar position in the world; with such a god they must rise higher still, there could be no limit to what He could do for them.

Religion not Centralised.—We must not, however, suppose that the rise of Jehovah to a great position, and the institution of his worship at the court, made any great or sudden change in the religious arrangements of the people at large. While the worship of the monarch went on at Gibeon or at Jerusalem, the great shrines at Bethel, at Dan, and at Beersheba were still frequented, and the sacred places throughout the land remained in honour. Stories indeed were told to show that they had been founded by the patriarchs for the worship of their god.

so that there need be no scruple in frequenting them. The worship of Baal and that of Jehovah went on at these places side by side, and neither could fail to be influenced by the other. Sacrifice was guided by more than one principle, on the one hand it was a common meal with the deity; and as Jehovah was thought to have his dwelling in Heaven, his part of the banquet was burned, so that it might ascend to him in the column of smoke. The sacrifice of agriculturists, however, naturally turns to the idea of presenting to the god, with joy and thankfulness, a part of the gifts, or the first or best part of the gifts, which, as lord of the soil, he has bestowed. The idea of propitiation or atonement does not enter into the ordinary sacrifices at this time. Jehovah in his sterner moods may demand more awful offerings. As we see from the story of Abraham offering up Isaac, it was thought that Jehovah might demand human sacrifice, and instances of such sacrifice actually occur in the records. Jephthah dedicates his daughter; after a war the best of the booty is offered to Jehovah, and Samuel hews Agag in pieces before him. But such occurrences lie quite apart from ordinary worship, which is of a joyful character and is accompanied by merry-making of various kinds. No fixed ritual prevailed throughout the country; the attempt to introduce uniformity came much later. Every one knew how to sacrifice, as the stories of Manoah and of Gideon show; it was by no means necessary that a priest should be present. The functions of the priest indeed were often connected with other matters than sacrifice, and might be of a humble description. Eli with a few attendants was the guardian of the ark which was the symbol of the presence of Jehovah. A young priest was engaged by Micah for ten pieces of silver yearly to take charge of his collection of idols. But the most important duty of the priesthood, and that on which their influence mainly depended, was that of consulting

Jehovah and ascertaining his will. This was done by some sacred object in the charge of the priest, and various objects are named (Ephod and Teraphim are images of deities; Urim and Thummim are the lots used on such occasions) which possessed this virtue. The priest also acted as a judge in matters brought to him for decision, and thus was in a position to form the unwritten law of the people, and to set up principles of conduct which came in course of time to be regarded as sacred. The priests' "torah" or law is the beginning of the Jewish legislation, and we see from the humane and kindly provisions of the earliest codes that this important function was discharged in no unworthy way. It was thus that Jehovah acted as the living lawgiver of his people, long before any written law existed. With his character as a warrior, a mighty lord, and a giver of rich gifts, he combines from the first that of one who watches over the conduct of his people, checks their excesses, and is willing and able to lead them on to better living. This fact will be of much importance when the mind of the people expands and seeks to understand more clearly his being and character.

The Prophets.—Israel, like other nations of antiquity, had, in addition to the priests who were professionally connected with religion, a class of men who were organs of the deity not on account of their position but by a special personal gift. The inspiration of Jehovah appeared in early times in somewhat crude forms. Bands of fervid devotees were seen, who produced in themselves by dance and song an ecstatic enthusiasm, in which they were thought to become the organs of the deity. These men lived in societies or guilds, which were found in Israel for several centuries. There were such prophets of Baal as well as of Jehovah, so that the phenomenon is not specifically Israelite. What we hear of them does not always give us a lofty idea of their character. They are found practising magical tricks, and when they prophesy they all say the same thing; sometimes they are willing to prophesy what a king wishes to hear.

The greater prophecy of Israel arose out of such beginnings as these. Israel was accustomed to expect to hear the will of Jehovah declared by a speaker of whom the spirit had laid hold, and among those who came forward to meet this expectation there appeared from time to time men of commanding insight and of great intensity of character. The name "seer" indicates the nature of this kind of prophecy. The seer is one to whom Jehovah communicates his intentions personally, perhaps without any steps having been taken on his part to place himself in the way of the god. He sees visions while awake and in his ordinary frame of mind, he also hears what others do not hear; and the vision and the message have reference to the future. Things are intimated which are shortly to come to pass, and they are things concerning the state or the monarchy: the fate of Israel is the burden of the prophet's intimation. Samuel's seeing led him to institute the monarchy under Saul. The prophet Abijah declared for the division of the kingdom into two; and his prophecy was not vain. Elijah foretold the downfall of the house of Omri, and Elisha saw to the accomplishment of that prediction. The prophets we see were a great power in public affairs, and were able in important crises to determine the course of the nation's history. Often the prophet stands quite alone, and in opposition to the court and apparently to the nation, and yet his words have a tendency to get themselves fulfilled; Jehovah's word does not return to him void. At other times the prophet seems to have many sympathisers among the nation, and to speak as the mouthpiece of the most earnest section of the community, the section most devoted to Jehovah; and in these cases it is less wonderful that his words come true. When, however, we speak of the prophets as a whole, the expression is a loose one; the prophets are not a party that always acts together, nor a school in which the leader is always sure of a following. A great voice sounds, perhaps once in a century or a half-century; and these voices represent the true tradition of Israelite religion, and develop it further. In the time of Elijah we notice that there is a puritan movement in Israel; a number of men are agreed together in detestation of the foreign worships which are practised at court, and are heartily agreed in wishing to bring back the good old ways and the pure worship of Jehovah only. And when Elijah speaks, he gives voice to this tendency; he claims that everything should be determined by religion; no considerations of state should for a moment stand in the way of the pure faith of Jehovah by which everything should be decided; and whatever stands in the way of this policy is dedicated to destruction. This, broadly speaking, is the keynote of Hebrew prophecy.

When we come to the canonical prophets, however, we feel that there is a great deal more in their teaching than the bare demand that everything must give way to the require ments of religion. A great change has taken place in their world of thought. It is no less than that a new god and a new religion have announced themselves in the thinking of these men. They do not say so; they are not aware of it, and yet it is so.

The Old Religion National.—The religion of Israel during the monarchy is, in the full sense of the term, a national one. From a cluster of tribes Israel has become a nation, and has begun to think of itself as a unity. It has its national history, its national rulers, as other nations have. In their nationality it cannot be denied that the Israelites had much to be proud of; nor did their rapid growth in wealth and power, which gave them several centuries of prosperity, tend to lessen that pride. Now as they have their own king, they have also their own god. Jehovah is the god of Israel; Israel is the people of Jehovah, on this they were all agreed. That Jehovah was their god did not prevent them from believing in the existence of other gods: Chemosh was the god of Moab, a being not very unlike Jehovah, the Baals were the old gods of Canaan. Jehovah, of course, was the greatest and strongest, and an Israelite should worship him, in Canaan at least; but there was no great harm if he worshipped other gods too, when it came in his way to do so. He might join in the worship of Baal in country places; and the king might, without doing any harm, set up the images of the gods of his wives beside the images of Jehovah in the capital, and if many of his subjects joined in these other worships, it was but natural. In this way a great variety of gods was in some reigns brought together from different countries.

Jehovah, however, was the special god of Israel, there could be no doubt of that; Israel was specially pledged to him; and he on his side was pledged to Israel, who was entitled to look to him for help in every emergency. Jehovah had no other people; he was entirely bound up with Israel, he must, if only for his own honour, come to the aid of his own people when they needed him. He never could permit Israel to suffer any fatal injury, such as deportation to a foreign country. Religious faith forbade the thought that such a thing was possible; if Israel was destroyed, where would Israel's religion be? It was utter impiety, therefore, to doubt that Israel was safe, that Jehovah watched over his own land and his own people, or that he would guard them from any fatal harm. If, on the other hand, as was too often the case, Israel had to submit to injury and insult from other peoples, there could be no doubt that Jehovah took notice of the fact, and that in due time he would set things right. It might be some time before his attention was sufficiently directed to the case; he might be waiting till more of the same kind of occurrences took place before he finally interposed; but the time would come, the "Day of the Lord" would arrive in due season, when the spoilers and insulters of Israel would be dealt with according to their deserts, and Israel set on high in full deliverance and peace.

Criticism of the Old Religion by the Prophets.—The prophets, impressed more deeply than the people by the moral character of Jehovah, and under the pressure of great national dangers and calamities, attained to views of God and of his ways so different from those current at the time as to appear, when first produced, most unpatriotic and even impious. In their character of seers they foresaw with clearness the terrible catastrophes which were about to burst upon their people. Amos prophesies that Israel will be carried away captive out of his land; Isaiah announces the same thing in the southern kingdom, and declares that only a remnant shall return. These men are in no doubt as to the impending political annihilation of Israel, and they set themselves to find some reason for an occurrence so portentous, so impossible to harmonise with ordinary religious faith. They account for it by a view of the nature of Jehovah far exalted above that of their people. He is punishing them for their iniquities, they say, he is so righteous that he must punish sin, and he must punish the sin of Israel his beloved people not less strictly, but more strictly than that of other peoples. As a husband whose wife has gone astray must subject her to discipline before he can receive her again to his favour, so Hosea, made a prophet by such a domestic affliction, contends that Jehovah cannot but deal strictly with Israel. This theory of the meaning of the impending calamities is supported by the prophets by those denunciations of the national sins which give so gloomy a complexion to their works. Among the national delinquencies the disorganisation and apparent wilfulness shown in worship have a prominent place. Worship is not what the service of Jehovah ought to be. Other beings than he are sought after; heathenish festivals are kept, the indecent practices of heathen worship are introduced into that of Jehovah: there is no seriousness, no dignity, no worthy order, in the acts of worship that are done. Any place does for them, and many of the places used are quite unfit, from their associations, for the service of Jehovah. They are celebrated more as wild orgies than as solemn approaches to the deity.

The interests of the prophets, however, do not centre in ritual. The worship of other gods than Jehovah, or the service of Jehovah in unfitting ways, they could not but denounce, but they have no positive instructions to give about worship. When the people have apparently given up the wrong worships, and are applying themselves with zeal to that of Jehovah, seeking his favour by austerities, or by costly offerings, the prophets are no less severe on this line of conduct. Every one is familiar with the passages, in which they apparently denounce sacrifice altogether as a thing God has never asked, and by which Israel cannot hope to win his favour. These passages do not prove that the prophets desired the entire discontinuance of sacrifice; they merely compare sacrifice with another line of duty which is said to be vastly more important. Not sacrifice but mercy, not sacrifice but to do justly, and love mercy, and walk humbly with God,—is the burden of these utterances. Even more than by the irregularities of worship, the prophets are shocked by the more directly moral shortcomings of their people. The people are accused of all the acts that are forbidden in the decalogue of Exodus xx., and of many offences not there named. Especially are the prophets indignant at the hardheartedness of the rich towards the poor, and at the frequent disregard of faith and truth; oppression and bribery, gluttony and other luxurious excesses, are frequently their mark. These most of all are the sins which have called down the divine judgments; these are the transgressions which make it impossible for Jehovah to turn away the punishment of Israel and of Judah. He is, above all things, a righteous god, who loves judgment and mercy, and a people which so manifestly fails to practise justice and mercy cannot continue to be his people; he must destroy them.

The prophets therefore **declare that Jehovah has decided on the rejection of his people.** This shows that they have advanced to a new conception of what Jehovah is. To them he is something more than the mere national deity indissolubly linked to the fortunes of his people, pledged to advance them in the world, and doomed when they fall to fall himself along with them. He is first of all a moral ruler; the maintenance and promotion of righteousness is far more to him than the prosperity of any single people, even of Israel. He loves Israel it is true; Israel is his son, whom he loves, the wife of his youth, the people of his covenant. But that makes it the more and not the less necessary that Israel should not be allowed to go on in iniquity. Jehovah can be no partisan of a people that does not walk according to his laws. Thus the prophets have arrived at a new conception of Jehovah's character, which necessarily unfits him, though they do not yet see this, for the *rôle* of a national god. They have identified him with the ideal of righteousness and mercy, and in so doing they have made the great step, at least in principle, from national to universal religion, from the religion that is bound up with the history of one particular people, and cannot pass beyond them, to the religion which is capable of being understood by all men, and fit to be preached to all men of whatever race.

Appearance of Universalism.—To the deeper view which they have gained of the character of Jehovah the prophets add a wider and higher view of his relation to the world, and to the various nations in it. They frankly state that Jehovah has relations to other nations than Israel. He might if he had chosen have taken some other race to be his people; they were all at his disposal and he regarded none of them as hostile. He is not dependent on Israel, and the inference is clear, that if he could have done without Israel at first, he could do without Israel still, were he driven to that. Israel is not indispensable to the continuance of the true religion. Jehovah indeed has a position far above that which Israelite national thought ascribed to him. He is lord not of one nation only, but of all the nations. He can use any of them as his instrument when and as he chooses. It is he who has brought each of them to its present seat, it is he who is directing their movements now. And for what end does he wield this mighty rule? He is governing the world not in the interests of one nation only, but in the interests of righteousness. He is guiding the destinies of nations so as to bring about an end which he has fixed, namely the establishment of a world-wide kingdom of truth. The day is indeed coming as the Israelites believed when he would hold a judgment over the world, only let Israel beware lest that day should be darkness and not light to them; it will bring about the punishment of sinners of whatever race. An end is to be made of sin both in Israel and in other nations, that a new world may begin. The position thus given to Jehovah is clearly one which lifts him high above the rank of a national deity. The prophets understand with growing clearness that Jehovah is the creator of the world, and the author of all the glories, both of the celestial and of the terrestrial frame. The Maker of the ends of the earth, and the Governor of all the nations, though he has chosen to reveal himself to one particular race, cannot be limited to them. The position of Monotheism has been attained. The earlier prophets speak of the gods of other nations as if they really existed, though for Israel Jehovah is the only god, but by degrees the advance is made to the position that these beings do not exist at all, and are simply "vanities" or "nothings." Instead of saying that Jehovah is the greatest among the gods, and that there is none like him, these preachers say that Jehovah alone is god, and that he is the author of all that exists and of all that takes place in the universe. A god has been unveiled whom all beings exist to glorify, and whom all the nations of the earth can confidently be summoned to praise.

Ethical Monotheism. — These results were reached gradually: there is a great difference between the teaching of Amos and that of Jeremiah. And it must be remembered that they were attained not as other monotheisms have been, by philosophical speculation, but by purely moral ways. It is because Jehovah is supremely just and holy, that he grows so great. The justice and holiness which are seen in him are the strongest of all; the world exists for nothing else but to realise them, and everything that stands opposed to them, whether in Israel or in any other nation, must go down before them. It is in this way that the conclusion is reached that Jehovah is the only God. The moral ideal must be one. The whole of the religion of the prophets is governed by moral considerations. God asks from man nothing but goodness; the true sacrifices are those of the heart and conduct. Man's intercourse with God is to be kept up as that of an affectionate human relationship, into which no motives either of force or of commerce enter.

Although God is so just and holy, he is perfectly placable, and ready to greet the approaches which are made to him. It is absurd to spend so much money and toil on sacrifice, when the happiest relations with God can be attained so much more simply. God forgives without any sacrifice; his love and his desire to meet with love surpass all that human relationships can show; his constancy is like that of the returning seasons, or of the stars. He yearns over Israel as a father over a wayward son, and will leave nothing undone that he can do to bring his son back to him. He will alter all his former plans to bring about that result. He will change man's nature, and give him a new heart, if nothing short of that will suffice; or he will change his own procedure entirely, and deal with man not by way of commandments, but by way of inspiration, placing his law in man's inward part, writing it in his heart, so that the great union of God and man may be attained, which he desires.

Individualism of the Prophetic Teaching.—Here we must pause to notice another great advance which the prophets have been led to make in religious knowledge. Their view of Jehovah as a purely moral being, and of man's relation to him as a moral relation, like that between two human beings who have to live together, such as a husband and wife or a father and son, makes religion less a matter for the people as a body, more a matter for the individual. When religion is carried on by public sacrifices and stately festivals and ceremonies, then it is the people as a whole that transacts with God, and the individual need feel no great weight of responsibility in the matter. But if God asks for love, if he says he does not care for sacrifice, but insists on love and devotion, and rather than not have it will work a miracle on man's nature, then the individual is addressed. Every one who has any love to offer feels himself appealed to. Only in his own heart can any one know whether or not God's desire is met; every one, therefore, who understands the appeal becomes personally responsible for the answer, and religion becomes a matter, not only between God and the people, but between God and the individual as well. Personal religion, therefore, makes its appearance among the Jews at this time. Jeremiah carries on dialogues with God; prayer is met with, as the outpouring, not of public needs alone, but of private feeling, the soul has learned that it is called to a life of its own with God, and not merely to a share in the life of the nation with him.

We have dwelt at some length on the ideas of the prophets; not at such length, indeed, as to satisfy any of those who love their writings, for we have thrown together in one view what belongs historically to different centuries, while to the personalities of the prophets, to their sublime certainty and their stupendous courage, we have given no attention. We have stated the outlines also of the great movement of thought in which advances of such transcendent importance were made in religion. They are advances which have not been lost, but which we still enjoy. If it is the gift of the Semitic race to bring the thought of God to bear on life with such direct practical force, as Aryan religion never by itself exerted, we must look with profound veneration on those Semitic thinkers who applied this great force in the service of a God, who has no other nature and property but that of justice and love. Religion thus became to them and to all they influenced an engine for the direct promotion of justice and love among men; and we do not think the less of the prophets that the harvest of which they sowed the seed could not be reaped in their day.

Prophecy Leads to no Immediate Reform.—The message of the prophets seems at first sight to have been delivered long before the world was ready for it. Even the practical measures which can be traced to their influence are far from being in accordance with their ideas. The causes of this we have already to some extent seen. The prophets were not practical reformers. The amendment they called for was one to be realised in individual lives rather than in public policy, and they do not bring forward schemes of reform which they urge the people as a whole to adopt; they rather fling great ideas upon the mind of their nation, and leave it to others to find out how practical effect may be given to their teaching. To the very end of the Jewish state the prophets and their sympathisers appear to be in a small minority of their nation. The people as a whole is unconverted, the worship of idols goes on, and so does the worship of other gods, even in the temple at Jerusalem. It has seemed to some great scholars that Israel, as a whole, was a heathen people up to the time of the exile, and still needed to be converted to the religion of Jehovah. Kuenen shows[1] in a convincing way that this is an exaggeration, and that people and prophets alike held the religion of Jehovah to be the true religion of Israel; but up to the exile that religion was not reformed in the way the prophets desired.

The Reforms.—Yet the word of Jehovah had not returned to him void even during this period. A considerable series of reforms are narrated in the histories, and attested by successive codes of law now embodied in the Pentateuch. These show that the prophetic ideas had gained for themselves a strong party among the people, and that in several reigns the court was under their influence. These reforms show progress in two directions. There is a growing desire to make the worship of Jehovah correspond to the exalted new conceptions of his character as a being of incomparable

[1] *Hibbert Lectures*, ii.

majesty and holiness; and there is, on the other hand, a rapid growth of moral sentiment; justice and kindness to others are placed more and more in the forefront of the divine requirements. We can do little more than name the passages where the details of these matters may be found. The **reforms of Hezekiah** (1 Kings xviii.) did not last long. He destroyed a celebrated image of Jehovah, a fate which other images may have shared, and he remodelled the worship of the holy places throughout Judah, so as to remove its more heathenish features, and concentrate it on Jehovah alone. Manasseh, Hezekiah's successor, pursued the opposite policy. In his reign a large collection of strange cults, some of them perhaps those of the individual tribes, were brought back into use; even the barbarous rite of human sacrifice was established at Jerusalem, and the worship of Jehovah became more intense and darker. The shadow of the Assyrian is upon Israel, and as generally happens in times of public anxiety, rites long disused are imagined to have a specially national character and a peculiar potency, and are fetched back from oblivion. The **reform of Josiah** (2 Kings xxii. xxiii.) was more thorough-going than that of Hezekiah. He made an end of all the unseemly worships his predecessor had encouraged at Jerusalem, so that nothing but the direct worship of Jehovah was left. The strongest step he took, however, was that he attempted to put an end altogether to the shrines at which local worship had hitherto been conducted, thus making a clean sweep of the idolatry of the rural districts. All this was done, we are told, in accordance with a law-book which had been found in the temple by certain high officials, and which, after duly consulting a prophetess about the matter, Josiah brought into operation, and solemnly pledged himself and his people to observe. We are in no doubt as to the nature of this book. The book of **Deuteronomy** prescribes just such reforms as Josiah carried out, and is generally allowed to have been the written law which was promulgated on this occasion. Now Deuteronomy, while incorporating no doubt many old laws, is in spirit and effect a work of the prophetic school. Its moral teaching and its exhortations to love Jehovah, and to be true to him alone, are quite in the manner of Jeremiah, who was living in the reign of Josiah. And the principal reform of Josiah, namely, the suppression of the local worships, and the concentration of all worship at the temple of Jersualem alone, stands in the forefront of the special laws in Deuteronomy. Those who aimed at the reform of religion, according to the ideas of the prophets, had thought this out. The worship of the one supreme God should take place, they had concluded, at one place only, and should be national in its character; the whole people should worship the one God at its capital. Provision was made that this should not imply the deprivation of the dwellers in country districts of the use of flesh meat. Formerly, every act of slaughter was a sacrifice, and it was only in connection with a sacrifice that this food could be enjoyed. But in future, animals may be slaughtered at a distance from Jersualem for food only, apart from any connection with sacrifice. The promulgation of Deuteronomy is an important epoch in the religion of Israel. That work is the first sacred book of Israel; from this time forward Israel knows the will of Jehovah, not only from the prophet's living voice, but from a book which is regarded as having divine authority. This principle once introduced could not fail to develop; to Deuteronomy other books were afterwards added as part of the same law, though in reality they superseded it, and it thus proved the nucleus of the whole Jewish canon.

Earlier Codes.—Deuteronomy was not the earliest law drawn up under prophetic influence. Leviticus xvii.-xxvi.

is recognised as being a code by itself, and is an earlier attempt in the same direction as Deuteronomy. The decalogue contained in Deuteronomy v., identical in the main with that of Exodus xx., is of earlier origin than Deuteronomy itself, but is also a prophetical work. It deals with ritual only to the extent of removing certain obstacles to a right worship of God, and places the chief weight of his requirements in the fulfilment of the natural duties. An earlier decalogue which deals principally with ritual, and which contains an early prophetic attempt to free the worship of Jehovah from heathen abuses, is found in Exodus xxxiv. 10-26. The oldest legislation of all is the code found in Exodus xx. 22 to xxiii. 33, which goes by the name of the Book of the Covenant. It belongs to the times of the early canonical prophets, and scarcely deals with ritual at all, but shows the just and humane spirit cultivated by the religion of Jehovah in an agricultural community.

The Exile.—The reformation of Josiah was quickly undone by his successor on the throne, and there was no further opportunity for a reform while the people remained in Palestine. But the exile did not cause the friends of reform to abandon their ideas. The prophets had foretold the exile, and had maintained that the religion of Israel would not be destroyed but rather would be saved by it, and the event proved that they were right in this point also. The exile cured the people definitely of idolatry, and gave them a strong grasp of the idea that they were a peculiar people, called to a work which no other people could accomplish or indeed understand, namely to hold aloft in the world, and for the benefit of the world, the true religion. This conviction forms the burden of the prophecy of **the Unknown prophet** of the exile (Isaiah xl.-lxvi.) He exalts still more highly than his predecessors the name and power of Jehovah. It is the Creator of the ends of the earth, to whom the nations, including even that great Babylon, are as a drop of the bucket, to be flung whither one will; it is he who has chosen Israel for his people and who now comforts Israel for the sorrows of the exile. In the great drama He is unfolding in the earth Israel has a principal part to play. Israel is called to make known to the nations who do not know him, the true God. It had been prophesied before that the heathen nations would come to Mount Zion to ask counsel of the God of Judah, and that Jehovah should become law-giver and judge over them. The Unknown enlarges on this theme with splendid imagery, and strives to persuade the people to make this cause their own, and to rise to the responsibility it involves. Israel is to be a prince, a leader and commander, of the peoples. The Gentiles are to come from far bringing their treasures and doing homage to the people of the true faith. If Israel as a whole is not fit as yet to discharge this duty for the world, yet there is an inner Israel, a faithful elect of the people who sympathise entirely with Jehovah's purposes and are entirely devoted to his will. This "Servant of Jehovah," at least, has risen to the height of his calling; Jehovah's spirit is in him. He will not fail nor be discouraged till the true religion is established in the earth. At another part of the prophecy the fate of the Servant is seen in darker colours. He is subject to ill-treatment and misrepresentation of all sorts; even when he is suffering for the sake of others he is derided and despised; nay, more,—he is called to suffer martyrdom, and die for sins not his own. But even so, the Servant will conquer in the end. He will know that his sufferings have not been in vain; he will be the means of leading many to righteousness and will be the instrument of Jehovah to bring in the true religion.

The Return. The Reform of Ezra.—Such utterances could not fail of effect on the nation to whom they were addressed, and when the Jews came back to Palestine they were undoubtedly inspired with a new sense of their peculiar national mission. They at once proceeded to show that they were to be a people apart from others, by separating themselves rigorously and even cruelly from entanglements with the surrounding population. They also at once set up the worship of Jehovah as the sole God who had his one shrine at Jerusalem. Their early experiences in Palestine were not encouraging. For a century they remained a struggling and poor community, and it might seem doubtful if they would prove strong enough to maintain their separate position, and to hold up their special testimony to the world. But at that time the Jews who had remained in Babylon came to their aid. These men had never ceased to labour along with their brethren in Palestine for the advancement of their nation; and in particular they had laboured earnestly at the problem of worship, and the result of their labours was a religious constitution so rigid in its ideas, so logically worked out in detail, and so skilfully incorporating and appropriating to itself all the past traditions and usages of the race that it might almost be said to be strong enough to stand by itself, and would certainly afford to the people, if they adopted it, the support and the discipline they needed. This constitution was introduced by Ezra, the priest and scribe, in the year 444 B.C., when he read in the ears of the people at Jerusalem (Nehemiah viii. ix.) the new law he had brought with him from Babylon fourteen years before, and had waited all that time to promulgate. The new law of this period was what is called the Priestly Code; it occupies the latter part of Exodus and a large part of Leviticus and Numbers; and the older writings are skilfully interwoven with it, but in general it may easily be distinguished by its tone from the work of earlier periods. Deuteronomy, the earliest law-book, is simply tacked on to it as if it were a part of the same code, though in reality it is often inconsistent with the later law. The result is the **Torah** or law, or, as we call it, the Pentateuch, or the five books of Moses (Moses being regarded by a convenient fiction as the source of all Jewish laws). This was thenceforward the law of the Jews.

The **Jewish religion,** of which this is the code, is generally distinguished from the religion of Israel which prevailed down to the exile; and several important new principles undoubtedly make their appearance at this point. This chapter may fittingly conclude with an enumeration first of the features of Jewish religious life connected with the law or the priestly system, and then of those features of it which lie outside that system.

1. The priestly religion is founded on a sentiment which forms but little part of the faith of early peoples, namely **the sense of sin.** The prophetic denunciations of Israel's backslidings have at last found entrance, and the people is found submitting to a system which implies that the whole of its past history was sinful and mistaken, and that there is a constant need for supplicating forgiveness. Every prayer begins with a long confession of national sin, in which the present generation also shares. "We have sinned with our fathers," they say. This view is spread over the historical books in the sweeping judgments passed on individual monarchs, on periods of the national life, and especially on the whole of the Northern Kingdom (cf. Nehemiah ix.). The old confidence in the presence of Jehovah with his people has now departed. The earlier Israelites never doubted that Jehovah was in the midst of them; that could be taken for granted except when events proved the contrary. But now Jehovah has grown greater and more awful, while the people have become painfully aware of their

deficiencies and cannot assume that he is with them, but must take steps to secure his presence. This is no doubt connected with the growing sense of an individual position and responsibility in religion. To the nation or the tribe it is natural to feel that its cause is just and that its God is with it; but the individual, thrown upon his own inner world for his alliances, is less apt to feel that confidence. Now the religion preached by the prophets is essentially one for the individual. Ezekiel especially felt himself responsible for the fate of individuals, and laboured to awaken his fellow-countrymen one by one to a sense of their danger and responsibility; he taught that each man had to see to his own salvation, that each man would receive the fruit of his own acts. All this tends to a deeper feeling and a more anxious mood in religion, and helps to explain how the sense of sin, on which religious progress at its higher stages depends so much, was fixed so strongly in the Jewish mind. That the Jews underwent a radical change in their disposition is proved by the fact that they submitted to the yoke of the law: for it may be questioned if any people ever sacrificed their natural liberty for the sake of their religion to such an extent as this people did.

2. The divine will is now received by the people in the shape of **a sacred book.** They cease to look for the living voice of prophecy, and come to think that God has given them in the Torah a perfect and complete revelation. The book takes the place of the prophet, and in time also to some extent of conscience. A man ceases to think for himself what is right and good, and only asks, What does the law say? It is true that a great part of the book is taken up with ritual, with which the ordinary individual has not much to do, but he also believes that the whole of his own duty is to be found there in it, as is no doubt the case. We see from the 119th Psalm how beautiful a form religion may assume

even under these terms, when the book in question is felt to be a spiritual treasure, and to speak the words of a living God; but the system of a book-religion has in it the germs of very different fruits. The sacred book is believed to be an exhaustive directory of conduct; but to make it apply to the various cases that arise in practical life it has to be interpreted, and deductions have to be drawn from it. It thus comes to give many a direction which does not appear on the surface. The secondary law, or "tradition," is thus founded, a system which calls for the services of a special class of students. The scribes, who interpret the law and apply it to life, obtain great influence and become the virtual rulers of the nation. While no doubt guided in the main by the noble spirit of their religion, they are led by their system into many absurdities, and their casuistry even becomes at times immoral. They afford the classical example of the results which flow from the doctrine of verbal inspiration, thoroughly worked out; and the life of the Jews under them becomes highly unnatural and artificial, and tends to occupy itself with the husk instead of the kernel of religion.

3. The principal part of the divine will, as expressed in the law, is that connected with sacrifice. **Sacrifice** occupies the central place in the book, and in the history it records. In this book the temple service, thinly disguised as the service of the tabernacle in the wilderness, is set forth as the great end and aim for which God created the world, settled the nations in it, and called Israel to be a people. The ritual which was observed down to the destruction of Jerusalem may be studied in Exodus and Leviticus. We read of orders and companies of priests who offer daily and other sacrifices according to a rule in which the smallest details are carefully arranged, sacrifices in which little of the old cheerful common meal now lingers, but which are

mostly of a purificatory or piacular character. The ritual of sacrifice would not appear to an outward observer to differ very much from that in use among the Greeks or Romans; the Jews certainly conducted it on a larger scale. What end precisely was aimed at in it, the Jew would have found it perhaps hard to say. It was done, he would say, because the law so ordered it, and the law must be obeyed even if one did not quite understand what was enjoined. The daily sacrifice removed the impurity of the temple staff, and enabled the people to be sure that the favour of the deity continued with them. Many sacrifices aimed at the removal of particular sins; thankfulness also was expressed in them, and other feelings may also have ascended with the smoke from the altar. To Jews living at a distance the sacrifice, which could be offered nowhere but at Jerusalem, was the chief symbol, the great mystery, of their faith.

4. The notion of **holiness** is closely connected with worship. Things and persons are holy which belong to Jehovah, and are withdrawn from common use. These it is dangerous to touch unwarily. Jehovah is an unapproachable being; the high priest may come into the innermost part of the temple, but only once a year, and no one else may come there; the priests may enter the Holy Place, but not the people. To speak lightly of the temple was a crime the Jews could not forgive. The Sabbath was the Lord's day; man must not attend on it to his own worldly concerns. The deity is surrounded with dread to an unparalleled extent; all that belongs to him is to be regarded with awe. Connected with the notion of holiness is that of purity. In the later Persian religion the distinction has always to be anxiously remembered by the believer between what belongs to the good spirit and what has fallen under the power of the evil spirit. The Jew, also, who is called to be holy and separate from other men, lives in constant dread lest he should touch something unclean,

and so forfeit his own purity. There are clean animals, and unclean ones which he must not eat; various washings of the hands and of domestic utensils are needed in order to keep up the state of purity; many trades involve contact with substances which make purity almost impossible. Above all, it is defiling to eat what a heathen has cooked, or to sit at the same table with heathens. Thus the Jew was confirmed in the belief of his own superiority to men of other races; and was prevented by many barriers from mingling with them, or even regarding them as brethren. His circumcision, his Sabbath, his laws of purity, his peculiarities of diet, the absolute impossibility of his eating along with Gentiles, kept him separate, and helped to nourish in him the spirit of haughtiness and exclusiveness. The accepted worshipper of Jehovah is, with the early prophets, the man who is morally sound, who has curbed his passions and his selfish impulses; with the later Jew that may still be the case, but there are also a number of indispensable preliminaries of which the prophets certainly did not dream. The man who would go up to the hill of Jehovah must be one who has not eaten shell-fish or pork, nor opened his shop on the Sabbath, nor touched a dead body, nor used a spoon handed to him by a Gentile without washing it. How all this unfitted the Jewish people to be a missionary of the pure religion, and how adverse the whole Levitical system was to the earnest apprehension of that religion no less than to its diffusion, the New Testament amply shows. But it kept the people separate from the world and constant to their faith amid even the greatest temptations and the severest persecutions, and so enabled them to preserve the precious treasure committed to them till the time should come when the world was to receive it from their hands.

Heathenish Elements of Judaism.—In the system we have sketched, in which the prophetic teaching was hardened into a ritual and a law, there are various elements which do not belong to an advanced stage of religious progress. While the sacrificial ritual, not outwardly exalted above heathenism, is to some extent redeemed by the motives which enter into it, the great system of clean and unclean rests on no rational basis, and resembles the set of taboos, which no one can explain, of a savage tribe; and the reduction of daily life under a set of minute and troublesome rules, shows the devotion more than the enlightenment of those who submitted to it. There was a necessity that the vessel should be so narrow and so hard which was to keep the wine of Jewish religion from being mixed with other liquids, but the vessel itself belongs to the rude and early world. In the Jewish religion of this time there are far different elements, which point forward and not backward, and in which the future course of religious progress is clearly anticipated. If his temple ritual was crude, and if his law pursued him into every one of his actions, the thoughts of the Jew were free; the truths which were unfolding their riches in his mind were sufficient compensation for much outward restraint, and the fair world of imagination was open to him in which the past clothed itself with legend and the future with splendid hopes.

Spiritual Elements.—The period after the exile is that of the composition of the **Psalms.** Many of these poems may have been written earlier; many were undoubtedly written at this time, and the belief gains ground that the Psalmist came after the prophet, and adopted for popular use the prophet's ideas. In the Psalter we hear the thrill of joy and triumph as the great truths of theism come to be grasped as certainties. The congregation now utters in song what, when the prophet first announced it, so few had courage to believe, that Jehovah is king, that he rules over the nations, that he is far above all the gods, nay, that there is no other God than he. The joy of having embraced this thought, of having escaped from all confusion with regard to the powers that rule the world, and of seeing all things in this splendid light, finds manifold expression. The believers delight themselves anew in the worship of Jehovah, and see fresh beauties in his courts, and in the service of him there; they delight in his word in connection with every part of their experience. They understand the world as they never did before, since it is his work, and praise the Creator as they follow the whole process of creation. New lights open to them on the history of their race, new solutions occur to them of the moral difficulties they have felt, as they saw the wicked prosper and the good cast down. There is very little about ritual in the Psalms; it is regarded chiefly as an offering of thanks and praise to Jehovah for his wonderful works, and for his mercies; and it is viewed ideally as an act of homage in which not only the immediate worshippers, but all nations on the earth may be conceived as taking part. On the other hand, the observance of Jehovah's moral requirements, and implicit trust in him while one seeks to do his will, is insisted on again and again, as the true method to please him, and to obtain his protection against all dangers. There are few moods of the religious life that are not represented in the Psalms: penitence, intellectual perplexity, domestic sorrow, feebleness, loneliness, the approach of death, the excitement of great events, the agony of persecution, quiet contemplation of nature, each has its word. The imprecations of some of the Psalms show a trait of the national character without which the picture would be incomplete. It may be in part extenuated by the consideration that in these Psalms it is the community that speaks, and that the enemy of the good cause deserves less forbearance than the private adversary. Whether the Psalms in general are to be conceived as uttered by the community rather than as private outpourings, is a question not yet decided. In either sense the Psalms have been used and are still used as the hymn-book of Christendom, as well as of the Jews; and it will always be a wonderful feature in the religion of Israel, that so soon after the truth of the one God was discovered by the prophets, it received a form of expression which has proved fitted for the use of every nation in the world.

The Jews after the exile are in possession of a **new form of religious association** which belongs to a high stage of growth. The temple worship is one in which the ordinary layman has no part, or only an occasional part to play. The priest does everything in it; even the singing of Psalms is done by choirs of priests. And the dweller in the country might rarely be a witness of these great solemnities. But we know that in the Maccabean period the country was covered with synagogues: with buildings, that is to say, where the surrounding population met on the Sabbath, and perhaps on other days as well, to join in common prayer, and to hear lessons of Scripture and exhortations. Some local religious meeting was necessary; an earnest people could not do without it, and the local sacrifices were now of the past. But the synagogue service marks a great advance in the religious position of the Jews. They can now meet without any act or sacrament which they have to do in common, to engage in purely intellectual religious exercises. The same advance, as we shall see, took place in Greece about the same time; what moral or religious furtherance they wanted, the earnest there began to seek from the lectures of philosophers. The synagogue, however, was a territorial institution; all the Jews in the neighbourhood came to it. It kept them acquainted with the law which otherwise they might have forgotten, and also with the writings of the prophets, which were regularly read, and thus strengthened the bonds which held all Jews together, in the past history and in the growing hopes, of their race.

The National Hopes.—Judaism becomes more and more, as befits a faith of which prophets are the principal exponents, a religion of hope. Debarred by their subjection under successive heathen powers from political activity, and keenly aware of their outward humiliation, the Jews turn to an ideal world in which they are free. The prophets had spoken of a judgment in which Jehovah would judge the whole world, of a happy time when Israel would be at peace from all his enemies, and God and people would dwell together in full communion; and when the land of Israel would become the religious capital of the world. They had added to their picture features even more ideal, and had declared that the conflicts of external nature would cease, the wild animals would grow tame and friendly, all physical as well as all moral evil would disappear. It was in this world, not in a remote region or in the land beyond death, that all this was to be realised. Jerusalem is the centre of the picture and the Jewish nation stands in the foreground of it as the chosen people of the God of all the world. Now these predictions, which with the prophets are vague and idealised, were taken by the Jews always more seriously and worked out in detail. After the prophet comes the apocalyptic writer, such as Daniel (the Apocalypse of the New Testament belongs to the same class of literature), who is able to give the exact course of the history which is to lead up to the final judgment, to fix its precise date, and to give many details of the ultimate state of affairs. These "revelations," which were written generally to comfort the Jews in their trials and to encourage them to steadfastness in persecution, were very popular. It is true that they nourished the national pride, and enabled the Jew to feel himself superior to a world in which he occupied outwardly no great position;

but on the other hand the hopes they fed were not necessarily unspiritual; at the Christian era we find it to be a mark of the most genuine piety that one should be "waiting for the redemption of Israel." At this period the national hope was occupied with the figure of a Messiah, a God-sent Deliverer, whose coming was to be the prelude to the establishment of the divine kingdom. We learn from the Gospels what various ideas were entertained by the Jews of the first century about this "coming one," and how little Jesus Christ was felt to answer to the common expectation.

A few words must be said of **Jewish beliefs concerning the other world.** While there are traces of an old ancestor-worship in the earlier parts of Jewish history, no belief of the kind had much importance in Israel. The Jews shared the general belief of the early world that the dead continued in a shadowy existence without any power for action. They have an under-world, Sheol, where the dead are; Isaiah has a magnificent description of the dead kings sitting on thrones together in Sheol and rising up to greet a newcomer who was a great potentate on earth, with the words "Art thou also become weak as we? Art thou become like unto us?" The dead are conceived as continuing in a weak and unsubstantial reflection of their former selves. They can be fetched up to the earth by magic arts to tell the future, but this was strictly forbidden at a very early time. The Psalms and other later books contain many plain denials that man has any continuance to look for after death. The religion of the Old Testament, as has often been said, is for this life. God's rewards are to be looked for before death; once gone to the grave one can no more enjoy God's bounty or give him thanks. God's kingdom of the future is also a kingdom of this world; Jerusalem is its capital, and nature is to be transformed for it. In the later period of Jewish history, however, the hope of the future which has been so entirely abandoned, which Job, for example, in an early chapter puts so peremptorily away from him, creates itself afresh in a new form. In the time of Christ the Jews believe, as a matter of course, that men will rise again. It has been contended that the Jews derived their later doctrine of a future life from their contact with Persia, but it is not necessary to account for it in this way. It arose naturally among the Jews in more ways than one. The individual believer like Job, entirely sure of his own innocence, and feeling that he was doomed to die of his disease without any vindication in this life, claimed that an opportunity should be found beyond the grave to pronounce the sentence which a just God could not omit to give. In Daniel xii. it is foretold that men of conspicuous virtue and men of conspicuous wickedness will have a resurrection — the former to share the glories of the kingdom from which as teachers and martyrs they could not be wanting, the latter to receive their punishment. And as prophets who have been long dead are expected to return to the earth, the gate of death is not so firmly closed as formerly and the belief in a future life easily became current.

Thus Judaism comes to be a religion full of contradictions, and could not as a whole pass to other nations. The temple and the synagogue represent opposite principles of worship. The Jew feels himself to be entrusted with a world-religion, and yet shuts himself up in such exclusiveness as to draw upon himself the hatred of all peoples, and to be charged in turn with hatred of the human race. A religion of faith and love consorts with a religion of rules and limitations. If the faith of Israel was to fulfil its mission to the world it was necessary that some one should come who could purge this threshing-floor, burning the chaff and gathering up the wheat to be the seed of the progress of mankind.

Books Recommended

The Books of the Old Testament, including the Apocrypha, in the Revised Version.

The Histories of Israel; Ewald, Kuenen, Wellhausen, Stade.

Robertson Smith's *The Old Testament in the Jewish Church*, and articles in the *Encyclopædia Britannica.*

Smend's *Alttestamentliche Religionsgeschichte.*

Stade, *Biblische Theologie des Alten Testaments*, 1905.

For a criticism of the critical historians the reader may consult *The Early Religion of Israel*, by Prof. James Robertson.

Prof. Valeton, *Die Israeliten*, in De la Saussaye.

Schurer, *History of the Jewish People in the Time of Christ*, 1885-90.

CHAPTER XIII

ISLAM

IN chronological order Islam stands last of all the great religions; it appeared six centuries after Christianity, and Christian ideas enter into it. It is, however, so essentially Semitic that it can only be understood aright if studied in connection with the group now occupying our attention. In Islam Semitic religion opens its arms to embrace mankind, and accomplishes, in a fashion, the destiny to which Judaism was invited, but which Judaism failed to realise till it was transformed in Christianity. In Islam Semitic religion is not transformed, but enters in its own stern and uncompromising character into the position of a universal faith.

This religion sprang up and entered on its career of conquest with startling suddenness, and even, some scholars hold, without any natural preparation for its coming in the country of its birth. The Arabs called the period before Islam the "time of ignorance"; in that period they considered their race had no history; the new religion, when it arose, had made a clean sweep of all that had gone before, and had caused a new world to begin. The labours of Arabic scholars have, however, done something to dispel the mists which hung over early Arabia, and it is possible both to give a much more satisfactory sketch than formerly of the earlier religion of the Arabs, and to discern to some extent the processes which had unconsciously been preparing for the advent of a higher and stronger faith.

Arabia before Mahomet.—The Arabs of the central peninsula in the times before Mahomet were not a nation but a set of tribes—mostly nomadic, but some of them settled in cities, who, while united by language, custom, and traditions, had no central government or organisation. The desert which they inhabited, as it admitted no cultivation, kept human life uniform and unprogressive; external influences penetrated slowly into this corner of the world, and society was still arranged as it had been for thousands of years. The strongest tie was that of blood. A man's fellow-tribesmen were bound to avenge his murder; and so one slaughter led to another, and from generation to generation the land was filled with a perpetual series of blood-feuds. Twice a year, however, a cessation of these feuds took place; a month came round in which there was a universal truce. Men who were enemies then made the same pilgrimage to a distant shrine; at such a time trade caravans could set out and travel in safety; and the great markets or festivals then took place, which, while based at first on religious ideas, had in most part ceased to have any religious character. Some of these markets were, at the time of Mahomet, national occasions: men of every tribe met and came to know each other there; the poetry which had been composed during the preceding months was publicly recited, so that the rise of a new poet was known to all Arabia; the news of all the tribes circulated, and foreign ideas and doctrines were also to be heard. In proportion as the face of nature was hard and forbidding, social life was bright and gay; wine, women, wit, and war provided the themes of poets and the ordinary aims of life.

The Old Religion.—It has generally been said that the Arabs before Islam were irreligious. They themselves contrasted the sternness of the new period with the gaiety of the old one. The truth is, as Wellhausen has admirably shown,[1] that the working religion of the country had become before the period of Islam entirely effete. Arab religion was based on the ideas and usages which have been described in chap. x. of this book; it is mainly from Arabia, indeed, that the original character of Semitic religion is known to us. Each tribe had its god, whom it regarded as a magnified master or ruler, and with whom it held communion by sacrifice, the blood being brought in contact with the god and the victim devoured by the tribesmen. The god is represented sometimes by a tree, generally by a stone; a piece of fertile land belongs to him, within which the plants and animals are sacred; the religious meeting can be held in no other spot. Hence the Arabs are said to be stone worshippers; but the phrase is an awkward one: what they worshipped was not the stone but a god connected with it. And the early gods of Arabia are a motley company; it is only in their relations to their worshippers and in the order of the worship paid them that they have some uniformity. The greatest and oldest deity of the Arabs is Allat or Alilat, "the Lady." Like the female deity found in all primitive Semitic religions, she is a stately and commanding lady. She is not the wife of a god, nor are unseemly ideas connected with her. She belongs to the early world in which motherhood was synonymous with rule, since the family had no male head; she has a character but no history: mythology has not gathered round her. Arabia has also certain nature-gods. The stellar deities are mostly female; there is a male sun-god Dusares. Heaven is worshipped by some, not the blue but the rainy heaven, which is a source of blessings. There are no gods belonging to the region under the

[1] *Reste Arabischen Heidenthums*, p. 188.

earth. The serpent is the only animal that receives worship.

But **the gods of Arabia** belong mostly to another class than that of nature-gods; or at least if they ever were connected with nature, they have parted with such associations. They are uncouth figures, with vague legends and miscellaneous attributes. One set of them is said to have been worshipped by the contemporaries of Noah; they are big men, and it is their property to drink milk. Hubal was the chief god of Mecca. It was his property to bring rain. Vadd was a great man, with two garments, and a sword and spear, bow and quiver. Jaghuth, "the Helper," was a portable god, not a stone probably, since he was carried into battle by his tribe, as the ark was by the Israelites. Another god is called "the Burner," no doubt from the sacrifices offered to him. Each tribe has its god or set of gods, and certain sacred objects connected with its gods. One god is found by those who kiss or rub a certain black stone, another in connection with a white stone, another with a tree. And of many of them there are images; the stone has some work done on it, or there is a wooden block roughly hewn. The "Caaba" is originally a black stone which is kissed or rubbed at Mecca. The name was given, however, to the cube-shaped building, in one of the walls of which the black stone had been fixed. In this building there stood in old days images of Abraham and Ishmael, each with divining arrows in his hand. Of such idols a large number existed in Mahomet's time, and were destroyed by him. In some cases the image had a house, and a person was needed to guard it; this functionary also kept some simple apparatus for casting lots or otherwise obtaining counsel from the deity, and oaths and vows were made before him, to which the deity became a witness.

To these beliefs of early Arabia must be added a

lively belief in **jinns**, spirits who are not gods, since the gods are above the earth but the jinn is compelled to haunt some part of the earth's surface. The jinns can assume any form they choose, and are often met with in the shape of serpents. Wellhausen surmises that the seraphs of the Jews are to be traced to some such origin. They infest desert places, and are nocturnal in their habits. What they do is often not observed till afterwards. They spy upon the gods, and may bring information from above to men whom they haunt or with whom they are in league. Of the magic of Arabia, the signs and omens drawn from birds, from dreams, and other occurrences, it is not necessary to speak; and we need only say, in concluding this rough sketch of the ideas of the early Arabs, that the belief in a life beyond was very faint; they set out food for the dead, whom they professed to think of as still existing, but the belief, if they entertained it, was perfunctory and had no influence.

Confusion of Worship.—At the period of Islam the worship of Arabia had fallen into great confusion. The gods were stationary, but the tribes wandered; and the consequence was that the wandering tribe left its shrine behind it to be cared for by its successors in that piece of country, and itself also, when it gained a new seat, succeeded to the guardianship of a new god. Thus, on the one hand, the worship of each shrine was constantly gathering new associations, as each tribe which had been there left behind it some new legend or practice; and on the other hand, pilgrimage became universal, since each tribe had to pay periodical visits to its gods whom it had left behind. At Mecca we read of hundreds of idols; a hundred tribes have left there something of their own. Thus Mecca became a sacred place for tribes far and near, and rose into national importance; and the same was the case to a less degree in other places also. But as this process went on, it inevitably led to the weakening of religion. The tie of blood, which was felt always, was a far stronger thing than the tie of a common worship for which the tribe had to go to another part of the country, and to come in contact with a multitude of other cults. Worship therefore became more and more a superstition: a thing, that is to say, whose real sacredness was in the past, and which was only kept up from pious habit; it did not supply the inspiration of ordinary life nor guide the more active minds among the people.

We have not yet spoken of Allah, who is understood to be the god *par excellence* of Arabia. But for this there is a good reason. Allah is not, like the other beings we have spoken of, a historical god, with a legend, a shrine, a tribe all to himself. He is not a historical personage, but an idea consolidated, no doubt at an early period, into a god. Wellhausen traces the rise of Allah for us in a most interesting way. The name, he shows, is not a proper name that belonged to one particular figure in the pantheon of Arabia; it is the title which the Arab conferred on his god, whatever the proper name of that being might be. Whatever god he worshipped, he called him Allah, Lord; and thus every Arabic god was Allah, as every head of a household has the name of "father" and every monarch that of "king." And as every tribal god was Allah, the thought arose, no doubt in very early times, of one god who was common to the tribes. Language paved the way for thought; while the tribal gods were still believed in and adored, this figure rose above them—a being who has no special worship of his own, who does not ask for it nor need it, but who yet fills, as none of the lesser beings does, the character of deity. Allah was the god of all the tribes; and as his figure grew in the mind of the country, it was inevitable that the worship of the historical gods should still further lose its importance, till only the women and children really cared for it. A monotheism of a grave and earnest kind thus made its way beside the old belief in many gods. Mahomet found that his fellow-countrymen did not really believe in the minor gods; when they were in danger or in urgent need of any blessing, it was to Allah that they called. The fall of the idols, when it came about, took place very easily; they were no longer needed. The Arabs had come to believe in a god who dwelt in heaven and was the creator of the world, who ordained man's life with an irreversible decree, by whom the bitter and the sweet, both the hitting of the mark and the missing it, were alike fixed. The moral character of Allah was not markedly in advance of that of his people. What a man gains by robbery he calls the gift of Allah, while what is gained by industry is called by another name. Yet Allah is also felt by some to keep them back from robbery; he powerfully upholds the moral standards which have been reached. He is the defender of strangers, the avenger of treason. His moral influence is negative, however, rather than positive. He does not inspire with ideals of goodness; but he holds back from evil. He is not a being who is ever likely to enter, like the God of the Jews, into intimate and affectionate relations with men; he is too abstract and has too little history to be capable of such unbending; his religion, when it comes to be fully formed, will be one of puritans and fanatics rather than of the meek and lowly. He is the one great instance of a god without any natural basis who has come to exercise rule. He is a god of whom reason can thoroughly approve—no absurd legends cling to him; he is from the first great, mighty, and moral; and he rules the world in righteousness by inflexible standards. This religion is coming to the surface even in the "time of ignorance."

Judaism and Christianity in Arabia.—The question has been much discussed whether the new religion of Arabia was due to contact with Judaism or with Christianity Both of these faiths were known in Arabia before the time of the Prophet. There was a large Jewish population at Medina, and synagogues existed in many other places; and there were Christians in Arabia, though their Christianity was that only of small sects and of lonely ascetics, and had failed to convert the country as a whole. To the Arabs the Jews were "the people of the Book," the book in the traditions of which they also had some share. Ignorant themselves for the most part of the arts of reading and writing, and divided among a multitude of petty worships which they were ceasing to respect, they looked up with envy to those whose faith had been fixed for so many ages in a literary standard. But while the Jews were respected in Arabia, they were far from popular. The qualities which have drawn down on them the bitter hatred of modern peoples among whom they dwell, acted there in the same way; their pride and exclusiveness, their keenness in business, their profession as money-lenders, made them detested in Arabia as in modern Germany. On the other hand, the ascetic view of life which the Christians represented had attractions even for some of the higher minds among the Arabs. A set of men called "Hanyfs" were well known in Mahomet's time, who were seeking for a better religion than the Arab worships afforded, and a better life than that of eternal feud. The meaning of the name is controverted; those to whom it was applied had not attached themselves to Judaism nor to Christianity; they were people in earnest about religion who had not reached any definite position. Even where, as with Mahomet himself, the facts of Judaism and of

Christianity were most inaccurately known, the view of God held in these religions and the moral standard they set up could not fail to exercise much influence. If in Arab thought itself a god like Allah was rising to definite personal character and to a position of great superiority over the old gods, then the inner movement was in the same direction as the influence of older religions from without, and the time was ripe for a new faith. It was not to be expected that a people like the Arabs should accept a religion which had its origin in another country, or which threatened like Christianity to bring to an end the old tribal system ; a new growth from within was needed, and this was ready to appear.

The beginnings of most religions are wrapt in obscurity ; but the rise of Islam is known to us with perfect certainty and in considerable detail. The only difficulties in the way of understanding it are of a psychological nature ; we have to account for the foundation of a religion which spread with lightning speed over many lands, and which still continues to spread, by one whose character was in some respects far from noble, and who was capable of stooping to compromise and to the darkest treachery in order to gain his ends. How a religion fitted for many races and many generations of men could be founded by a barbarian and by the aid of barbarous means—that is the problem of this religion. The materials for solving it lie open before us. The Koran is undoubtedly the authentic work of Mahomet himself: the chapters are arranged in a wrong order, and if they are read as they stand they do not tell any intelligible story ; but when placed, as has now been done by scholars, in the true historical order, they show the history of Mahomet's mind with great clearness. After the Koran came the traditions. From the immense volume of these the industry of the scholars of Islam as well as others has succeeded in sifting out what is most to be relied on. In no other case is the separation of the mythical from the historical element in the early traditions so easily made, and the religion comes into view in the full light of day.

Mahomet. Early Life.—Mahomet was born about 570 A.D., of a family belonging to the Mecca branch of the Coreish, a powerful tribe, who carried on a large caravan trade with Syria, and who were the guardians of the sanctuary which was the central point of Arabian religion. He entered therefore from his birth into the centre of the faith of his country. He was early left an orphan, and was brought up by relatives, who were kind to him but who were very poor. He had to make his living at an early age by herding sheep, an occupation which conduced in his case, as it has done in others, to contemplation and thought. In early manhood he entered the service of Khadija, a rich widow; and he made journeys in her affairs to Syria and Palestine, where he may have seen places famous in Jewish history and may also have come in contact with Christianity. At the age of twenty-five he married Khadija, who was fifteen years older than himself; the marriage was a happy one, and there were several children. He is described as a man of middle height, with a fair skin, a pleasant countenance, and pleasing manners; and he had proved his ability in business. Some years after his marriage he began to think deeply about religious subjects. He came into connection apparently with some of those Hanyfs or penitents, mentioned above, who, without being formed into a sect, were at one in seeking for a more satisfactory religious position. The religion to which they were feeling their way was a monotheism, a service of the one God of Abraham, but not that of Judaism with its exaltation of the Jewish race, nor that of Christianity, in which God had a Son for his companion. Submission to the one God was to them the essence of religion. "Islam" means submission, and the "Moslem" is the person who thus submits himself to the one sole God, whether he be Jew or Christian or neither. The Hanyfs also held the belief of the Christians in a coming judgment; and the effect of their beliefs on their lives was that they practised austerities and often retired from the world.

His Religious Impressions.—Mahomet at this part of his life began also to withdraw himself, and to go apart to lonely spots for meditation. What he meditated we see from his sayings and doings afterwards. The contrast between the pure religion of Allah, as held by the Hanyfs, and the popular religion of Mecca with which his birth connected him, with its trade associations, its idols, its unintelligible rites, was certainly a tremendous one; and if a judgment was impending over all but the believers in Allah, it was a terrible prospect. For many years, however, Mahomet was simply a Hanyf. He was one who had surrendered himself, with a tender and impressionable soul, to the divine will and guidance, and was filled with the sense of Allah's presence and power, and of his own accountability to him in the great and tremendous realities of life. In addition to this, however, we have to mention a circumstance which is generally thought to have had a determining influence in Mahomet's production of Islam. He had a peculiar temperament; mental excitement led in him to inner catastrophes which, whether they are classed under epilepsy or hysteria, caused him to see visions and to believe that certain words had been addressed to him by heavenly visitants. The new religious movement in Arabia had secured an adherent in whom its teachings would be felt with tremendous intensity, and would possibly break forth with irresistible force.

The Revelations.—Mahomet was forty years of age when the thoughts which had long been working within him burst into open expression. This took place by means of a vision.

An angel appeared to him as he slept on Mount Hira on one of his nightly wanderings, and held a scroll before him which he bade him read. He had not learned to read, but the angel insisted, and so he read; and what he read was the earliest revealed piece of the Koran (sura 96):—

> Read,[1] in the name of thy Lord who created, created man from a drop. Read, for thy Lord is the Most High, who hath taught by the pen, hath taught to man what he knew not. Nay, truly man walketh in delusion when he deemeth that he sufficeth for himself; to thy Lord they must all return.

All men, *i.e.*, however they may think, as the Arabs were given to think, that they need no help but that of their own right arm, must come before Allah's judgment and render an account to him: this is the doctrine by which Mahomet first appealed to his fellow-countrymen. It is a revelation. Allah teaches it by sending down a copy of what is written in the Book in heaven, the "mother of the Book" from which all revelations, Jewish, Christian, or Mahomet's own, are alike derived. Mahomet has thus begun to prophesy. The first outburst of revelation threw him into great agitation; he thought he was possessed by a jinn; and it tended to his further distress that an interval of two or three years elapsed before another vision took place. Then the vision came again. "Rise up and warn!" it said to him; "and thy Lord magnify, and thy garments purify, and abomination shun, and grant not favours to gain increase; and wait for thy Lord." The revelations now began to come in rapid succession, and Mahomet now believed in his own inspiration. In this conviction he never wavered afterwards; and there can be no doubt that the earlier revelations were felt by him as if they came from without and were dictated by a power

[1] Or, Preach!—loud reading or repetition being the mode of claiming attention for the divine word.

he could not resist. His fellow-countrymen naturally took another view; like other prophets, Mahomet was said to be mad and to be possessed by a spirit; and these accusations stung him, because he himself had at first apprehended something of the kind. The later pieces were of a different character; he had the power afterwards of producing a revelation to suit any situation which arose; but the contents of the earlier ones were not unworthy of being revelations, and such he felt them to be.

His Preaching.—He preached the new truth at first to those with whom he was intimate. It was not new but old; it was the religion of Abraham that he preached, that of the Book of which both Jews and Christians had counterparts; he did not think of founding a new religion. He called his own household and his relatives to submit themselves to Allah, the supreme Lord and the righteous Judge, before whose judgment they must soon stand. They were to put away heathen vices and to practise the duty of regular prayer, of giving alms without hoping for any advantage from it, and of temperance. After a time he is encouraged by new suras to preach publicly, and does so. The Meccans, however, do not listen to him. The prophet's preaching acquires by this opposition a sternness it did not possess at first, and he proceeds to attack the popular worship in a way fitted to stir up against him the bitterest hostility. The Meccans hear from him that the religion to which all Arabia flocks together, and without which they would do little trade, is not only a vanity but a thing abhorrent to Allah, and undoubtedly drawing down damnation on all who partake in it; and that their forefathers are unquestionably in hell. Such preaching could not be tolerated; Mahomet's friends are appealed to to stop his mouth, but in vain, and his fellow-tribesmen, though they do not believe in him, yet protect him, as the laws of kindred require.

Persecution.—Mahomet suffers as other prophets have done; he is ridiculed, misjudged, threatened. On the other hand he has his consolations; when depressed he receives encouraging messages from above. His enemies will perish; his cause will succeed; the day will come when men will flock to his doctrine in crowds. Persecution, however, is not without effect on him: on one occasion he attempted to compromise matters with idolatry; in a sura recited at the Caaba he allowed himself to use certain complimentary expressions about the three daughters of Allah, in whom the Meccans put their trust. The Meccans were much pleased with this, but Mahomet had to suffer the reproaches of the angel Gabriel after he went home, and the concession was erelong withdrawn. If, as appears likely, the compromise had been deliberately planned, a strange light is thrown on the nature of the revelations at a time not long after they had begun to flow. But there is no approach to compromise after this. The position of the prophet naturally grew worse after this display of weakness, and the persecution of the townsmen more embittered; for two years Mahomet and his followers were rigorously cut off from intercourse with their fellow-citizens. On the other hand the prophet's tone became harder and more sombre as he saw that no turning back was possible. Never were the terrors of hell preached with more intensity; it makes one's blood run cold to read the denunciations of the Mecca unbelievers, men personally known to the prophet, and to hear him forecast the words with which they will be bidden to take their place for ever in the fire. Personal irritation gives edge to the denunciations of fanaticism. Examples are sought in Jewish history of those who rejected prophets, Moses or Noah, and suffered a prompt and terrible judgment for so doing. The Meccans were little moved by such threats; they had no real belief in a future life, and scoffed at the idea of a resurrection of the body; and for this scepticism also parallels are found by the prophet in history, which show what fate the doubters may expect.

From reading the Koran we should judge Mahomet to have been a disagreeable fanatic; but he also possessed very different qualities. Those who knew him best were most devoted to him. His followers adhered to him with a faith which was proof against all persecutions; we find him even ordaining that slaves who are converts may dissemble their connection with him in order to avoid the cruel treatment it drew down on them. Such attachment could only have been inspired by a noble nature; his followers felt him to be indeed a teacher sent by Allah, and were enthusiastically convinced of the truth of his doctrine.

Trials. He decides to leave Mecca.—In spite of this his position was a precarious and trying one. His wife Khadija, to whom he had been most faithful, died; so did his most powerful protector. The cause, moreover, was not advancing at Mecca, and was not likely to do so; and Mahomet began to consider the propriety of transferring it to new ground. The first attempt to do so was not successful; at Taif, where he asked to be received and to be allowed to preach, he was rudely repulsed, so that he came back to Mecca in deep dejection. The new opening which he sought was, however, about to present itself in another quarter. Among the visitors to one of the feasts he met a company of pilgrims from Medina, who both addressed him with respect and showed that they understood his doctrines. Medina was well acquainted with Jewish ideas, and presented a more favourable soil for the prophet to work on; it is even suggested that the Arabs of Medina, having heard of the Jewish expectation of a Messiah, considered that it would be an advantage for them if the Messiah should be of their own race, and that

Mahomet might possibly be He. The transference of the cause to Medina was, however, brought about with great deliberation. Those who wished Mahomet to come preached his doctrine at Medina for a year, and with encouraging success. Pledges were given and repeated by his friends there, that they would have no god but Allah, that they would withhold their hands from what was not their own, that they would flee fornication, that they would not kill new-born infants, that they would shun slander, and that they would obey God's messenger as far as was reasonable:—these are the practical reforms which Islam at this time demanded. The result of these proceedings was that Mahomet advised his followers to go to Medina. He himself waited till nearly all had gone, and did not set out till a plot had been laid by his enemies the Coreish to assassinate him. The **Hegira** or flight took place on 16th June 622 A.D. The flight, not the birth of the prophet, forms the era of Mohammedan chronology, since it was from the moment of the flight that Islam entered on its victorious career.

Mahomet at Medina.—From this point onwards the prophet is seen in a different position and a different character. At Mecca he is a persecuted, struggling, and unsuccessful preacher, but at Medina he rapidly becomes the most powerful person in the commonwealth. He organises the service of religion, but he also gives new life to the community in other ways, terminating its feuds, uniting all its forces in the service of Allah, and by his decisions in the cases which are brought to him laying the foundation of a new jurisprudence. A pure theocracy was set up at Medina, and he as the prophet was its sole organ and administrator. In this capacity he displayed consummate ability. Alike in religious and in civil matters he showed the most perfect comprehension of his countrymen. He resorted freely to compromise in order to make his religion and policy suitable to the masses of his people and to secure their adhesion. In this way he soon secured for himself an absolute authority.

The new religion thus became the cement by which a strong commonwealth was formed out of elements formerly at variance. Mahomet's first care on reaching Medina was to organise the service of the faith. A place was built where the congregation could meet for prayer and exhortation; the prophet's house stood beside it, or rather the apartments of his wives, for he now had two, and was soon to have more. The mosque, which all over the world is the local habitation of Islam, may have been derived from the synagogue or the Christian church. The service which takes place in it is not a sacrifice, but consists of intellectual exercises which nourish in the hearers the spirit of the religion. In the Mosque of Medina Mahomet taught his converts the practices and duties which were required of them. He taught this with great precision, and himself set an example how each exercise was to be done; so that, as Wellhausen says, the mosque became the exercise ground where the people were drilled in the requirements of the new faith. "There the Moslems acquired the *esprit de corps* and the rigid discipline which distinguish their armies."

New Religious Union.—A new bond of union thus took the place of the old tie of blood, which had been by far the strongest in Arabia. Every Moslem regarded every other Moslem as his brother, even though belonging to a different tribe. The claims of religion came to supersede all others; all natural tastes, all family affections, were taught to yield to them. Within a few years of his coming to Medina Mahomet had forbidden the use of wine and the pursuit of art, and had imposed on all women who adhered to him the use of the veil. In every way the community was taught to regard itself as separated from the former life of the country and from all who did not share the new faith. It was represented as the duty of believers to fight against all unbelievers: in this way the universal prevalence of the religion was to be brought about. The courage of the faithful was stimulated by the promise of rich booty and by the assurance that those who fell in battle would go straight to the joys of Paradise; and the wars they waged acquired in consequence a relentless character which was new in Arabia. They were allowed to fight in the sacred month, in which ancient custom ordained a universal truce. They fought with a gloomy determination, and used their victories with a relentless cruelty, which excited the consternation and horror of all witnesses. They did not scruple, as other Arabs did, to fight against their kinsmen. "Islam has rent all bonds asunder, Islam has blotted out all treaties," they said, when reproached with their disregard of old understandings. The prophet himself was foremost in this unrelenting policy. Captives taken in battle were slaughtered; a whole tribe was massacred which had joined the enemy, and had surrendered after a siege in the hope of merciful treatment.

Breach with Judaism and Christianity.—As Mahomet thus freed himself, in spreading the faith of "the most merciful God," from all considerations of mercy and of honour, he also shook off, as his position grew strong, relations which might have proved embarrassing with other religions. In his earlier teaching he speaks of his own religion as being substantially the same as Judaism and Christianity. All three have "the Book"; the Koran is a continuation and supplement of the Jewish and Christian revelations, and he is only the last figure in the great line of prophets who had appeared in these religions. Like other founders, he did not at first intend to found a new religion, but only to bring to light again and restore to authority the original truths of these faiths, which had become obscured. His attitude at first, therefore, was friendly to both Jews and Christians, and his friendly feelings for the former were likely to be strengthened by the circumstances of his coming to Medina. Not long after his arrival, however, his attitude towards the Jews was changed. His followers had at first prayed with their faces turned in the direction of Jerusalem; but the prophet ordained that this should be altered, and that they should pray with their faces turned not towards Jerusalem but towards Mecca. This setting of a new "kiblah," as it is called, declared that Islam was a different religion from Judaism, and had an Arab not a Jewish centre. The hostility to the Jews, of which this was a symptom, grew more intense; quarrels were sought with them which ended in the utter annihilation of the Jewish power at Medina. From Christianity also Mahomet was careful to distinguish his religion. The Christians of Arabia were less tenacious of their faith than were the Jews, and easily accepted Islam, so that the hostility was not in this case so intense. The doctrines of the Trinity and of the Incarnation were of course denounced as intolerable blasphemies against the sole deity of Allah.

Domestic.—The history of Mahomet during the Medina period is taken up to some extent with the various marriages into which he entered, and with the scandals of his household. On several occasions he produced revelations to warrant a step in this connection which he felt to require justification, and the modern reader is forced to wonder how his credit survived some of those proceedings. While it is undoubtedly the case that he did much to improve the position of women in Arabia, the absence of any high ideal in this matter is very apparent.

Conquest of Mecca.—In giving his followers a new kiblah and bidding them turn their faces towards Mecca at their prayers, Mahomet declared that city to be the religious capital of Arabia. Though he had left Mecca in anger, he could not forget or ignore a city which held this place in his eyes. At first his thoughts of Mecca were those of vengeance; he had a score to settle with the Coreish, who had scorned and persecuted him, and had driven him forth. For several years there was war between Medina and the Coreish; the Moslems plundered the rich caravans of Mecca; in the great battle of Bedr (A.D. 623) Mahomet defeated his enemies and compelled them to respect and fear him; and they afterwards attacked and besieged him at Medina, with no decisive result. The next step was that Mahomet made use of the sacred month to attempt a pilgrimage to Mecca, from which he had been absent for six years (628); and though he was prevented from performing his devotions at the Caaba on this occasion, the Coreish found it good to make a treaty with him, thus recognising him as a potentate, and to promise that he should be allowed to make the pilgrimage on a future occasion. That pilgrimage took place; and so quickly was Mahomet's power increasing in the rest of Arabia that the Meccans began to feel that they could not long resist him. In the year 630 he moved against Mecca with a large army, and met with but faint opposition. Mecca fell into his hands. He used his victory nobly: only four persons were put to death. It was at once shown that no injury was to be done to the city. The old worship and its various ceremonies were preserved. All idols, of course, were destroyed, both those about the Caaba, of which there are said to have been one for each day in the year, and those in private houses.

Mecca made the Capital of Islam.—In fact Mecca gained new importance from this conquest. It was constituted by the irresistible power of Mahomet the central sanctuary of the true religion. A year after the victory Mahomet again visited Mecca, and performed the pilgrimage with all its rites in his own person, setting the correct pattern in every detail, which all pilgrims were to observe in all time coming. Those who wish to know what the rites of Mecca are, will find them graphically and minutely described in Captain Burton's *Pilgrimage to El-Medinah and Mecca;* that gallant officer was one of the three Europeans who, during the nineteenth century, assumed the disguise of pilgrims and took part in the observances. The kissing of the sacred black stone in the wall of the Caaba, the sevenfold circuit of the building, the drinking of the water of the well Zem-zem, the race from one hilltop to another in the neighbourhood of Mecca, the throwing of seven stones at a certain spot, and the sacrifice of an animal in a certain valley—these form a collection of rites each of which had probably a separate origin, and of some of which the original meaning can scarcely be made out.[1] This "block of heathenism" Mahomet made part of his religion. He could not have abolished it, and by adopting it in an improved form as a part of his own system he served himself heir to the national religious traditions, and acquired for his own religion the authority of a national faith. "This day have I appointed your religion unto you," are his words after fixing the forms of the pilgrimage, "and applied Islam for you to be your religion." Islam adopts the Mecca rites, and thereby becomes the national religion of Arabia. Hubal, the chief god of the Caaba, disappears; Allah becomes the sole god of the shrine. The legend that Abraham founded it is put in circulation, and it is thus connected with the supposed earliest Arabian religion, the religion before idolatry, the Islam before Islam. As

[1] See for this Wellhausen's *Reste arabischen Heidenthums*, pp. 64-98.

Paul appeals to the faith of Abraham as being a Christianity before Christ, so Mahomet claims the Caaba for the pure worship of Allah in primeval times. It is sacred henceforth to him alone. The rule was set up that no idolater should be admitted to the pilgrimage, and it thus lost its character as a heathen, and became instead a Moslem, institution.

Spread of Islam.—Mecca once converted, the rest of Arabia could not long remain outside. There was reluctance in various places to make the change which Mahomet now required of all his countrymen. But the penalty of refusing it was the prophet's wrath, with its terrible attendants, war and rapine, and none of the Arabs cared enough for their old gods to brave such terrors for their sake. The inhabitants of Taif endeavoured to make terms, so that the change might be less abrupt. Their ambassadors urged that fornication, usury, and the use of wine might be allowed them, but this could not be granted; the Taifites must accept the deprivations to which all the Moslems had agreed. Then they asked that their Rabba, their goddess, might be spared to them for three years, and as this was refused, for two years, a year, a month. But the only concession they could obtain was that they should not be obliged to destroy their goddess with their own hands. The ancient paganism, it will be seen, fell easily and without any tragedy.

Mahomet did not long survive the national acceptance of his religion; he died on 8th June 632. But he did not die without having opened up to his followers very wide views for the future of his cause, and started them on a career of religious war and conquest which was not soon to be arrested. From a comparatively early period of his career he had considered that Islam was destined to prevail not only in Arabia but in other lands. Starting with the idea that his revelation was only a later stage of that which had taken place in Judaism and Christianity, he had advanced to the position that the latter were false religions, and his own the only true one. Wherever he looked in the world he could see no true religion but his own; it must therefore take the place of all others. Accordingly he sent embassies from Medina to Heraclius the emperor of the East, to the king of Persia, to the governor of Egypt, and to other potentates, announcing himself to be the "Prophet of God," and calling upon them to give up their idolatrous worships and return to the religion of the one true God. These embassies had small effect; but Mahomet was prepared to take much more forcible measures in order to spread the faith. War against infidels being one of the standing duties of the faithful, various regulations were laid down for the treatment of captives and the disposal of booty in such wars. God, who is said in every verse to be forgiving and merciful, encourages the faithful in such passages to slay and rob, and to make concubines of women taken in sacred wars. At the moment of his death an expedition, not the first, was ready to start against the Greek power. It is in this guise that Islam assumes the *rôle* of a universal religion.

The Duties of the Moslem.—The missionary of Islam requires of his converts nothing very difficult either in the way of belief or in the way of action. His demands are brief and precise. They consist of the following five points:—1. The profession of belief in the unity of God and the mission of Mahomet. The formula runs: "There is no God but Allah, and Mahomet is the prophet of Allah." 2. Prayer. This consists of the repetition of a certain form of words at five separate times each day, the worshipper standing up with his face towards Mecca. The mosques are always open for prayer, and there is a special service on Friday, the day of the week chosen by Mahomet in contradistinction to the Jewish Sabbath and the Christian Sunday. 3. Almsgiving. This is done on a fixed scale, and the contributions were, in Mahomet's time, devoted to the support of war against infidels. 4. Fasting. This takes place during the month of Ramadan, and the fast is very strictly observed. 5. The Hagg or pilgrimage to Mecca.

The Koran is the sacred book of Islam. The name means "reading"; see p. 224. Like other sacred books, the Koran is arranged in such an order that he who reads it as it stands finds it very confused, and fails to grasp its historical meaning. The claim to divine inspiration is made in every chapter and every line of it; God himself is the speaker. But the divine oracles refer to very various matters. All sorts of legal decisions, military orders, injunctions about religious affairs, legends and speculations, have a place in it. Of prediction of the future, indeed, there is but one instance; the prophet disclaimed the power to work miracles, and held that no wonders beyond those of the splendid order of the universe are necessary to faith; and similarly he does not pose as foreteller, but as an organ of the divine will for the present. As the ruler of a theocracy, the leader of armies, the judge in many a civil case, the guardian of the manners of the people, the officiating minister in public worship, and, let it also be mentioned, the head of a very peculiar domestic establishment, he has a hundred matters of immediate concern to attend to; and when he has formed his decision on any of these matters, it takes its place in the Koran. The book thus produced is far from being an attractive one; even in the translation of Professor Palmer[1] it can afford pleasure to no reader. The translation, it is true, loses the poetry and music of the original, which are highly spoken of; but the main obstacle to reading the Koran is its want of

[1] *Sacred Books of the East*, vols. vi. and xi.

arrangement. The earliest suras (chapters ; literally courses of bricks) stand mostly towards the end of the collection ; the long ones in the beginning and middle are later, and many of them are composite : two or several chapters have been joined into one. When read in their historical order, the suras can be read with pleasure by the student as showing the growth of the prophet's ideas and of his cause. The earliest ones are short, poetical, and intense. These are the suras which threw the prophet into such excitement and distress that his hair turned white. They are full of the wonders of God in nature and in history, of fiery denunciation of idolatry, and of fearful threatenings. In later pieces we come to long legends taken chiefly from the Jewish Haggadah and the Christian Apocrypha, in which the prophet displays much ignorance of the commonest facts of the Bible history ; and as his power increases and his functions multiply, we come to the miscellaneous matters spoken of above. The style, at first poetic and exalted, becomes afterwards prosaic and diffuse ; it is not the inspired seer who speaks, but the statesman or the judge ; and the placing of these later utterances in the mouth of God could not deceive the original hearers. The Koran, like the Vedas and the Gathas and the Jewish Scriptures, was exalted in later stages of the religion to the highest conceivable honours ; and one of the greatest controversies of Islam raged round the question whether it had existed from eternity and was uncreated.

Islam a Universal Religion.—What is most remarkable about Islam is the rapidity of its growth. Mahomet begins life a poor and lowly herdsman, and at his death bequeaths to his successors a kingdom which he has formed, and which is shortly to prevail over all its neighbours. In the same way his doctrine, confined at first to a small circle and bitterly opposed, becomes within half a century the faith of his nation, and not only of his nation, but of many other lands. Within that brief space it has entered on the stage of a national religion, and has also passed beyond the national into the universal stage, at which only two other religions have arrived at all. The progress which Christianity took centuries to accomplish, Islam accomplished in so many decades. The title of a universal religion cannot be denied to it. The truth which it declared—the doctrine of the unity and the omnipotence of God, and of the responsibility of every human being to his Creator and Judge—is one which does not belong to any particular race of men, but to all men. The attitude of soul which is called Islam—that of implicit surrender to the great God, of entire acquiescence in his decrees and entire obedience to his will—is good for all. All should be called to take an earnest view of their life and to realise their deep responsibilities; and the idea expressed by the title given to God on every page of the Koran, "The Merciful and Compassionate," that God sympathises with the aspirations and efforts of his servants, and that they may look up to him with love as well as fear, is one which all can understand and feel helpful. Especially at the stage when the world is given up to idolatry, Islam may well rank as a universal religion; when each place has its idol, each nation its greater idols, religion divides instead of uniting, and the frivolous and senseless service of such petty deities prevents men from realising their solemn obligations to the great God before whom they are all alike, since he is the Governor and Judge of all. Islam is an admirable corrective of heathenism; it brings the scattered and bewildered worshippers of idols together in one lofty faith and one simple rule.

The weakness of Islam is that it is not progressive. Its ideas are bald and poor; it grew too fast; its doctrines and forms were stereotyped at the very outset of its career, and do not admit of change. Its morality is that of the stage at which men emerge from idolatry, and does not advance beyond that stage, so that it perpetuates institutions and customs which are a drag on civilisation. Mahomet's Paradise, in which the warrior is to be ministered to by beauteous houris (the number of whom is not mentioned), may not have been an immoral conception in his day; but it is so now, and apparently cannot be left behind. An admirable instrument for the discipline of populations at a low stage of culture, and well fitted to teach them a certain measure of self-restraint and piety, Islam cannot carry them on to the higher development of human life and thought. It is repressive of freedom, and the reason is that its doctrine is after all no more than negative. Allah is but a negation of other gods; there is no store of positive riches in his character, he does not sympathise with the manifold growth of human activity; the inspiration he affords is a negative inspiration, an impulse of hostility to what is over against him, not an impulse to strive after high and fair ideals. He remains eternally apart upon a frosty throne; his voice is heard, but he cannot condescend. He does not enter into humanity, and therefore he cannot render to humanity the highest services.

Books Recommended

The Life of Mahomet, by Sir W. Muir, 1858.

Mohammed, by Wellhausen, and "The Koran," by Nöldeke, in *Encyclopædia Britannica*, vol. xvi.

The Preliminary Discourse prefixed to Sale's *Koran;* and Professor Palmer's Introduction in *S. B. E.*, vol. vi.

Islam, by J. W. H. Stobart, in the "Non-Christian Religious Systems" Series of the S.P.C.K.

Der Islam, by Houtsma, in De la Saussaye.

Hughes, *A Dictionary of Islam* (1885, 1896).

Gell, *The Faith of Islam*, Second Edition, 1896.

PART IV

THE ARYAN GROUP

CHAPTER XIV

THE ARYAN RELIGION

THE science of language has placed it beyond dispute that the languages of the leading European peoples are genealogically related to each other, and that the languages of India and of Persia also belong to the same family of speech. The Indo-European languages, those, namely, of the higher race in India, and of the Persians, and those of the Greeks, Italians, Celts, Germans, Slavs, Letts, and Albanians, approach each other always more nearly as they are traced upwards. Sanscrit is not the source of these tongues but an older sister of the group; the mother language, which the facts prove to have at one time existed, was a highly-inflected speech, and is perhaps more nearly represented by Lettic than by Sanscrit; but it can now be known only by a study of the common features of its surviving children.

The fact that the peoples named above are related to each other in point of language led at once, when it was discovered, to the conclusion that they were also of the same race, and must have come originally from the same quarter of the world. Where, then, was the early home of the undivided Aryan[1] race, from which the swarms first issued which were to conquer and rule the various lands? At first it was found in the East; the fact that Indian civilisation was much earlier in time than that of any other Aryan people, naturally suggested this. Professor Max Müller described in a very poetical way how the European as well as the Indian must find in the East the cradle of his race. From the high tableland of Asia, it was held, the superior races came who were to rule nearly the whole of Europe, while another migration descended towards Persia and the plains of India.

The theory, however, which placed the home of the Aryans on the inhospitable steppes, the "high Pamere," of Asia, did not long command assent; and attempts were made to place that home elsewhere, in the valley of the Danube, on the south shores of the Baltic, or even in the Scandinavian peninsula. The conquest, it is argued, cannot have come from the East; it is much more probable that Aryan speech and custom originated in the West, where it has the larger number of representatives, and that it spread eastward. The more extreme step has also been taken of denying that the Aryans are related to each other at all in point of race. Unity of language, it is argued, is no proof of unity of race—a glance over the British Empire or even the British Islands is enough to show this. It is maintained, therefore, that the relationship of the Aryan peoples is not one of race but only of language and of culture; the word Aryan denotes no more than a certain type of speech, and of accompanying civilisation, which spread over all the peoples in question

[1] "Aryan" was the name of the conquering race of India. The title "Indo-European" tells us that the race now dwells in India and in Europe. "Indo-Germanic" describes the group by its Eastern, and what is supposed to be its principal Western, member.

at a very early time. Aryan language and civilisation laid hold of a number of races not otherwise related to each other.

The view, however, still prevails that the various lands where Aryan speech and culture prevail were settled from one centre. When society was in the nomadic stage, it may naturally be presumed that a superior civilisation which had established itself in any one quarter of the world would be carried by wandering hordes in various directions, and that the bearers of the new civilisation would become the conquerors and masters of the countries to which their wanderings led them. And there is now some agreement on the part of leading authorities as to the quarter of the world from which the migrations of the Aryans proceeded. In the Southern Steppes of Russia, in the great plains north of the Black Sea, the Caspian, and the Sea of Aral, there dwelt, we are told, in times far before the dawn of history, hordes rather than tribes of men, who, though they had originally spoken the same language, were coming to differ from each other in speech and culture. These hordes were peoples in the process of formation. It was natural to them to wander, and as each wandered farther from the centre, it came to differ more markedly from the common type. Some of these went southwards and eastwards to Persia and India; others went westward, to conquer and possess the countries of Europe.[1]

The Aryan question lies at the threshold of the history

[1] *Prehistoric Antiquities of the Aryan Peoples;* Schrader and Jevons (Griffin, 1890). This is the English of Schrader's *Sprachvergleichung und Urgeschichte.* Compare Dr. E. Meyer's *History of Antiquity,* vol. i. book vi. Dr. Isaac Taylor's *Origin of the Aryans* gives a compendious account of the question, concluding against the unity of the Aryans in point of race.

of each of the Aryan peoples, and has to be met in the study of each of the religions. It must be confessed that the world now knows less on this point than it thought it did a generation ago. The difference between the Semitic and the Aryan spirit is real and substantial, as will appear from the study of the Aryan religions, but it is more important as well as more possible to know these well in their individual character than to have a correct theory of their historical relation to each other. The student ought, however, to be informed as to the course of a deeply interesting enquiry.

The civilisation of the Aryans was primitive enough. The following is from Dr. Taylor:—

> The undivided Aryans were a pastoral people, who wandered with their herds as the Hebrew patriarchs wandered in Canaan. Dogs, cattle, and sheep had been domesticated, but not the pig, the horse, the goat, or the ass; and domestic poultry were unknown. The fibres of certain plants were plaited into mats, but wool was not woven, and the skins of beasts were scraped with stone knives, and sewed together into garments with sinews by the aid of needles of bone, wood, or stone.
>
> Their food consisted of flesh and milk, which was not yet made into cheese or butter. Mead, prepared from the honey of wild bees, was the only intoxicating drink, both beer and wine being unknown. Salt was unknown to the Asiatic branch of the Aryans, but its use had spread rapidly among the European branches of the race. In winter they lived in pits dug in the earth and roofed over with poles covered with turf, or plastered with cow dung. In summer they lived in rude waggons or in huts made of the branches of trees. Of metals, native copper may have been beaten into ornaments, but tools and weapons were mostly of stone. Bows were made of the wood of the yew, . . . trees were hollowed out for canoes by stone axes, aided by the use of fire.
>
> According to Hehn, the old or sick were killed, wives were obtained by purchase or capture, infants were exposed or killed.

After a time, with tillage, came the possession of property, and established custom grew slowly into law. Their religious ideas were based on magic and superstitious terrors, the powers of nature had as yet assumed no anthropomorphic forms, the great name of Dyaus, which afterwards came to mean God, signified only the bright sky. They counted on their fingers, but they had not attained to the idea of any number higher than one hundred.[1]

These sketches of the early Aryan certainly attest more vigour than refinement; and it takes some effort to realise that those who lived in this way had already made much progress, and that these early arts and institutions were full of promise. Savage as the early Aryan is, he is better than his neighbours, and has made a good start in the way of civilisation. His family arrangements, especially, are fitted to survive and to develop. The early domestic architecture of the Aryan countries, while it belongs to a much later period, yet gives good evidence that the patriarchal ideal of the family was part of the common inheritance. In every country they conquered the Aryans lived in large patriarchal households. The sons, with their wives and children, remained under their father's roof, the father being judge and priest of this domestic community. We can specify other features of the society connected with this type of household. As the family increases and becomes too large to dwell under one roof, another house is built, in which son or grandson, with his wife, founds a new family. Thus a group of families arises, all related to each other by blood, and in a position of equality, but looking to the original house as their centre. This type of society must have been carried to India by the Aryan invaders, who there set up patriarchal establishments in houses which are similar in arrangement to those of North Holland, of Iceland, or of early England. The men who lived in this way

[1] *Origin of the Aryans*, p. 188.

were not agriculturists, they were shepherds and huntsmen, and when they settled in a district they were wont to force the former dwellers in it to till the land for them as their inferiors.[1]

It is this type of civilisation which overspread the lands in early times, and by its coming created in most instances a new world. Some of the Aryan peoples made more rapid progress than others. They passed early into the age of metals, and appear before us at the dawn of history with fully-formed institutions, which bear the impress of patriarchal ideas. Others remained longer in the stone age, and only in historic times received the impulse which caused them to advance to the rank of nations. The arts and inventions which are found in many or in all of them are not necessarily a common inheritance from the undivided Aryan age. Many of them may have come into being in each of the lands independently, or one Aryan people may have borrowed them from another at a later time. Starting from the common stock of civilisation, the various races worked it out each in a way of its own, and often, as we shall see, with wonderful similarities.

Is it possible to give any description of the religion the Aryans had in common before they developed it in different ways in their various lands? We can no longer, following Mr. Max Müller, look to India to tell us what was the common Aryan religion. Indian religion, when we first become acquainted with it, has already grown into an elaborate priestly system, and is evidently at a much later stage of Aryan development than the rustic cults with which we have a good deal of acquaintance, in various European lands. If, however, we cannot follow the great German scholar in this, we gladly use his words on another aspect of the subject,

[1] See two recent works by Mr. G. L. Gomme, *The Village Community* and *Ethnology in Folklore*; also Hearn's *Aryan Household*.

when he is showing the etymological identity of the chiel god of the Aryan peoples.

In his *Lectures on the Science of Language*, vol. ii. p. 468, he tells us that "Zeus, the most sacred name in Greek mythology, is the same word as Dyaus in Sanscrit, Jovis or Ju in Jupiter in Latin, Tiw in Anglo-Saxon, preserved in Tiwsdæg, Tuesday, the day of the Eddic god Tyr; Zio in old High-German.

"This word was framed," he says, "once and once only; it was not borrowed by the Greeks from the Hindus, nor by the Romans and Germans from the Greeks. It must have existed before the ancestors of those primeval races became separate in language and religion; before they left their common pastures to migrate to the right hand and to the left. . . . Here, then, in this venerable word, we may look for some of the earliest religious thoughts of our race."[1]

In this instance etymology admittedly points out one of the principal features of the common Aryan religions. But if we hope that etymology will reveal to us many further instances of the same kind, and introduce us to the whole Pantheon of the Aryans, we shall be disappointed. There are one or two more cases of etymological agreement between the gods of India and those of Europe,[2] but the

[1] See also Mr. Müller's *Hibbert Lectures*, and his *Biographies of Words*.

[2] The principal are the following:—

1. Dyaus, god of the sky, see above.
2. Sans. Ushas, goddess of dawn; Gr. ἠώς; Lat. aurora; Lith. auszra; A.-S. eostra.
3. Sans. Agni, fire, god of fire; Lat. ignis; Lith. ugnis; O.-S. ogni.
4. Sans. Surya, sun; Lat. sol; Gr. ἠέλιος, also Σείριος; Cymr. seul.
5. Sans. Mâs, moon; Gr. μήνη; Lat. mena; Lith. menu.

Mars = Maruts, Manu = Minos = Mannus, Varuna = Ouranos, and other equations formerly brought forward, are not now relied on by etymologists.

agreement is in some of these cases no more than etymological. The Tiw or Tyr of the Teutonic mythology does not correspond in office or character with Zeus or Jupiter, though the names are etymologically akin. The agreement does not extend to all the religions in question, nor does it extend in any two religions to all their gods; most of the gods of Europe have no parallels in India. The evidence of etymology, therefore, tells us but little of that early religion of which we are in search. But if we consider the views and habits of the barbarous shepherd-huntsman, who is now seen to be the typical figure of common Aryanism, we need not seek long before we find something that was common to all the Aryan faiths. The patriarchal household has a religion which belongs to itself, and which is the working bond of union of its members. The hearth is its altar, because the forefathers of the house lie buried under it, or for another reason. These forefathers certainly are its gods. This hearth-cult has for its priest the father of the family, he in his turn will be gathered to his fathers if he has a legitimate son to do the last rites for him. No one but members of the family can partake in the domestic worship, all unconnected with the family by blood must be kept at a distance from these rites. This is not a religion in which the individual counts anything for his own sake, any more than totemism is; in both it is the community alone that serves the deity, in the one case, those acknowledging the same totem, in the second, those united by blood in the same family. In totemism the individual sacrifices himself to the tribe; here he is nothing apart from his family. Aryan piety is family religion pure and simple. It fosters sentiments which have been the strength of Aryan society in all lands. It makes family life a sacred thing, lends to all domestic ties the highest sanction, and causes the mere mention of "hearth and home" to be the strongest incentive to valour and self-denial. Even in the wild-beast ferocity with which early men defend their homes against the intrusion of strangers, the germs of lofty domestic and patriotic virtues may be seen. Thus ancestor-worship, which is a part of the very beginnings of human religion, is a more effective force among the Aryans than anywhere else. In Egypt and China that worship is a highly artificial thing, and has lost much of its original force. In Egypt it is the fortunes of the dead that are most thought of; in China the cult has been smoothed down and deprived, according to the character of the people, of its intenser motives. Among the Aryans it combines actively with strong family feeling, causing them to cling with an extreme tenacity to their own gods and their own worship.[1]

But those of whom we are speaking worshipped other gods besides those of the household. The second great characteristic of Aryan religion is its adoration of gods who are neither local nor tribal, but universal. Dyaus, the sky, the heaven-god, can be worshipped anywhere, so can the earth, so can the heavenly twins, who were objects of early Aryan religion, so can the sun and moon. Not that the Aryans always remembered that these beings were not local or tribal. The god of heaven could be the god of a particular place too, having a special name there; or he could be appropriated by a tribe who gave him a title as their own particular patron. Each family could have its own heaven-god as well as its own hearth-god. Nor are we to think that when they worshipped beings who could be found in every place, the Aryans overlooked the sacred

[1] The comparative absence of ancestor-worship among the Greeks leads Dr. Schrader to doubt whether their religion is Aryan. The Semites and the Greeks occupy the same position in this respect (see pp. 161, 288).

places, and the sacred objects worshipped formerly. They had themselves risen out of savagery, and still held many of the ideas of savages. Though they had a few great gods they could still believe in a large number of smaller ones. The tree, the stream, still had its spirit for them, the cave or the dark fissure its bad demon. And many a piece of magic did they practise, such as the rain-charm which would cause even the highest god to send what was needed. The world was well peopled with gods, and to keep on good terms with them all was, no doubt, a matter that required much attention and skill.

Other features which have been stated to be characteristic of Aryan religion are its non-priestly character, and the fact that its gods are generally arranged in a monarchical pantheon. But neither of these constitutes a specific difference of the kind we are in search of. All primitive religions are non-priestly; a religion becomes priestly at a certain stage of its growth, when it is organised separately from the state. The monarchical pantheon, too, such as that of Homer and of the Eddas, is an indication, not of the genius of a religion, but of its having reached the systematising stage, and of the political ideas according to which the system is drawn up. The Aryan religions, it is true, arrange their gods when the time comes to do so, after the pattern of an Aryan patriarchal establishment, the father at the head, his sons and daughters near him, the servants in attendance, the unorganised host of spirits, nymphs and elves, outside. But to know the original character of the religion it is less important to ask how the Pantheon is arranged, than what gods are worshipped, and how they are related to man. And the point which stands out clearly is that while Semitic religion is purely tribal and local, there is an element in Aryan religion which naturally transcends these limits. On Semitic ground the body with whom the god transacts is the tribe, the link is that of blood which connects all the members of the tribe with their divine head or ancestor. In Aryan religion also blood counts for much. The family altar is the seat of worship, and he who has been cast out of his own family cannot worship anywhere. The family gods are most thought of, no doubt, and exercise immense power in the ways we have mentioned. But the worship of which blood is the tie is not to the Aryan, as to the Semite, the whole of religion. There are beings aloft as well as beings on the earth and under the earth, and the worship of these beings is wider than the family. The family may address Heaven by a special private name, or at a particular spot, but Heaven itself was above all these titles and places. The spirits of the household made, as all the Semitic gods do, for separation, but the gods above made for union, and as any community grew, the upper gods, who were worshipped by all its members alike, became more lofty and more important. Thus we may agree with Mr. Gomme when he speaks (*Ethnology of Folklore*, p. 68) of the emancipation of the Aryans from the principle of local worship, and says that the rise of the conception of gods who could and did accompany the tribes wheresoever they travelled, was "the greatest triumph of the Aryan race."

Farther than this it may be dangerous to go in a field so full as yet of uncertainty. In all Aryan worships there are sacrifices of various kinds and degrees of importance. The horse sacrifice appears in several of the nations as one of distinction, but human sacrifice was most important of all, though in each of the Aryan lands commutations are made for it at a very early stage. The strife of Aryan with non-Aryan religions gave rise to many superstitions; after the conquest the gods of the latter often became the bad gods or demons of the former, the ministers of the defeated cult were regarded as sorcerers or witches, the dethroned gods made many an attempt to come back to their seats, and to revive disused practices. But a religion based, as we have seen the Aryan to be, in the family affections is destined to rise as civilisation advances. It will be found that the Aryan draws a less absolute distinction than the Semite between the human and the divine. To the Semite God is, broadly speaking, a master, or Lord, whose word is a command, in regard to whom man is a subject, a slave. To the Aryan the relation is a freer one. His god is more human, and art and imagination can do more in his service.

E. Siecke, *Die religion d. Indogermanen*, 1897.

C. F. Keary, *Outlines of Primitive Belief among the Indo-European Races*, 1882.

CHAPTER XV

THE TEUTONS

The Aryans in Europe.—There is more than one European people which before it was touched by Roman civilisation had remained for an indefinite period—a period to be measured probably rather by millenniums than by centuries —in the state of society described in last chapter (p. 244 *sq.*) as occurring when the Aryans dwelt among those whom they had conquered. In various lands alike we meet with the combination of the patriarchal household with the village, the combination of agricultural with pastoral life, to which the Aryans early settled down among non-Aryan populations. This type of society, which is the basis of feudalism, is recognised alike in India and in Germany. It stretches far back into the past, and may even be recognised in some quarters at the present day.

As with civilisation so with religion. The early faith of the Slavs, the Celts, and the Teutons is now generally regarded as best representing that of the Aryans. It was a religion in which rite and belief were indefinite and variable compared with those of the later Aryan faiths of India and of Southern Europe, there being neither a regular priesthood nor the use of writing to impart fixity to religious forms. The river, the fountain, and the aged oak, each had its legend and its observance of unknown antiquity. The pre-Aryan and the Aryan elements of religion acted and reacted on each other, the Aryan, no doubt, being the element of progress, but blending with the other in indistinguishable mixture. The spirits of ancestors lived in the belief and the practice of posterity; a thousand unseen agents in the sky, and in the earth, and under the earth were believed in and treated according to tradition, fed or flouted, bribed or exorcised, as occasion suggested. New gods appeared, or old ones were combined into new, or a god migrated from one province to another. Here also myths and rituals were formed by various processes. But a more constant growth of belief took place in connection with some gods as larger social organisms came into existence, village communities combining into tribes, tribes into nations. The great gods of heaven, whatever the history of their early growth, proved specially fitted to unite together clans and peoples. These beings received different names in different countries. Their early history, no doubt, was not the same in all, yet in each mythology there were figures and stories which occurred also in others, whether in consequence of parallel growth out of similar circumstances in each land, or from a process of borrowing at a later time, or from both, we need not try to decide.

We give a short account of the religion of the Germans. That of the Celts, which may be studied in the Hibbert Lectures of Professor Rhys,[1] or that of the Slavs (of which there is an excellent short summary by Mr. W. R. Morfill in *Religious Systems of the World*), would have equally well served the purpose of exhibiting an Aryan religion at a low stage of development, and held by a people not thoroughly compacted into a nation. The religion of the Teutons has the advantage for our study over these others, that it remained longer unsuppressed by Christianity, and in

[1] *Lectures on the Origin and Growth of Religion as illustrated by Celtic Heathendom.* 1886.

its Scandinavian branch put forth a vigorous original growth in comparatively recent times. The latest paganism which flourished in Europe, it is also the religion of our ancestors, on which the Christianity of the Northern lands was grafted, and many a survival of which may still be recognised in our own land. It therefore possesses for us even in itself considerable interest.

Of the ancient Germans, of the dwellers in the basins of the Rhine and the Danube, we have accounts by Cæsar and by Tacitus.[1] After this there is a dearth of information; the Christian missionaries to the Germans thought it their duty to cover the former beliefs and rites of their converts in oblivion, and abstained from giving information about them. What we know is drawn from Church writers. The Eddas belong to a much more developed stage of Teutonic life; they tell their own tale, which will be noticed in its turn.

The early Germans dwelt in scattered settlements surrounded by the great forests and marshes which then covered Central Europe. Every one has read the description of the brave and warlike people of whom the Romans justly stood so much in awe, and knows about their fierce blue eyes and their fair hair, their tall stature, their battle-cries and charges, their hardy habits and strict morals. As the Roman writers describe them, they are by no means savages. They do not live in towns, but migrate from one spot to another, the community cultivating the land it takes possession of, on a system of common ownership with rotation of occupants. The women did the hard work, Tacitus says; the men spent their time in the chase and in fighting. They had an organisation beyond that of the village, being arranged in what we may call hundreds and shires, each district having to furnish so many men for

[1] Cæsar, *B. Gall.* vi. 21. Tacitus, *Germania*.

war, electing its own heads and holding meetings for various purposes. Amidst these local and tribal divisions they did not forget that they were a nation different from other nations, and invasion found them a united people. The religious expression of this is to be found in the legend which represents the three great divisions of the nation as descended alike from the god Mannus, son of the earth-born Tuisco; hymns were sung to the latter as the father of the German race. It was by hymns that this people remembered things which were important.

The Early German Gods.—There is a national god, then; and other gods of whom Tacitus tells us are national too, not local or tribal. The tribes to the south of the Baltic worship Herthus, which, Tacitus says, is their name for Terra Mater, Mother Earth. The other gods he mentions are called by Roman names. They worship Mercury, he says, as their principal god; on certain days they worship him with human sacrifices. They also worship Mars and Hercules with animal victims; and a particular tribe, the Suevi, worship Isis. Cæsar says the Germans worship the sun, and Vulcan, and the moon. Tacitus mentions other German gods; the two statements are both true. Tacitus gives the German gods Roman names according to a common practice of antiquity, which has been the source of much confusion; we shall see afterwards how the Romans identified the gods of Greece also with those of Rome.

The equation which Tacitus gives of the German gods with Latin ones is still in daily use in the names of the days of the week. The Romans applied the names of the planets, which were the names of their own gods, to the days of the week as early as the first Christian century; and in Germany the days were called after the German gods supposed to answer to the Roman gods in question. Half Europe to this day calls the days of the week after the Roman, and the other half after the German gods. We give the Latin names with the modern French and over against them the English, in which the names of the German gods appear more clearly than in modern German :—

Dies Solis, the Sun's day = Sunday. (The French *Dimanche* is from *Dominicus*, the Lord's Day.)
Dies Lunæ (Lundi) = Monday or Moon's day.
Dies Martis (Mardi) = Tuesday, the day of Tiw or Ziu.
Dies Mercurii (Mercredi) = Wednesday, the day of Wodan.
Dies Jovis (Jeudi) = Thursday, the day of Thor. In German this is *Donnerstag*, the day of Donar = Thor.
Dies Veneris (Vendredi) = Friday, the day of Freya.
Dies Saturni retains the Latin god's name in our Saturday. (The French *Samedi* is derived from Sabbath.)

These Teutonic names for the days of the week are common to all the branches of Teutonic speech, and must have a high antiquity. They tell us what gods the Germans had in early times, and to what Roman gods these were believed to correspond; but it would be a vain endeavour to attempt to deduce from this, or indeed from any early information we possess on the subject, the origin and nature of these gods. From Grimm's laborious study of the question (*German Mythology*, vol. i.) we gather that it is a matter mainly of speculation what it was in Wodan that led the Romans to identify him with their Mercury. Thor, who is identified with Jupiter, was probably a sky-god, while Tiw or Ziu (whom etymology identifies with Zeus, not Mars) was a god of war, and Freya, like Venus, had to do with female beauty. We come to know more of these gods when we find them in the Eddas, but it is scarcely legitimate to fill in the South German gods of the first century from the North German gods of the same names of the eleventh or twelfth. We reserve, therefore, our description of the German gods till we come to the Northern mythology.

The Roman writers do not furnish any accurate idea of **the working religion of the Germans** of their day. Cæsar says they were not so much under the guidance of priests as the Gauls were, and that they were not greatly addicted to sacrifice; neither statement can be received without scrutiny. Tacitus idealises the untutored savage as Rousseau does, in order to rebuke the vices of a luxurious civilisation; but his statements of actual facts may be trusted. Knowledge recently acquired of early forest-cults disposes us to trust him when he speaks, as he does more than once, of the peculiar sacredness the Germans attached to woods and groves. He is idealising when he says, "They did not confine their gods in walls nor represent them under the likeness of men, being led thereto by considering the greatness of the heavenly beings." A few centuries later at least we find Christian bishops busy destroying temples of German heathenism and burning images found in them. Undoubtedly, however, the great sanctuary of a district was frequently, as he represents, in the recesses of a wood. Under a mighty tree a tribe would hold its meetings and sit in judgment and in council; and there were sacred groves in which no human foot might stray, where the god was supposed to dwell, where great sacrifices both of animal and of human victims took place, where the boughs were hung with the bones of former sacrifices which in war were carried forth at the head of the tribe as its sacred standards. This was done by the priests, who accompanied the host to battle, and were charged at such a time with the infliction of all necessary punishments, since they represented the god who was supposed to be personally present as commander. The priests had to work the auguries when consulted on matters of state; on private matters the paterfamilias might do this himself. The priests also had charge of the sacred white horses, by whose neighing the will of the deity became known. Several women are also mentioned as having enjoyed the reputation of sacred personages; and "even in their wives they considered that there was a certain holiness and inspiration."

To judge from Tacitus and from other writers of the first Christian centuries, there was little system in the religion of Germany in those days; the gods were not organised in a divine family, the priests were not a caste like the Druids of France and Britain, and religious practice was loose and variable. It must also be remembered that what foreign writers reported on the subject was connected rather with national and official cults than with popular local observances. Of the latter there was an abundant growth; a distinguished foreign writer might not know about it, but the evidence of it survives in various forms which are only now being seriously studied. To know the practical religion of early Germany we have to consult the village festival and legend (as has been done by Mannhardt in his *Wald- und Feld-kulte*), which, though now apparently meaningless, were once the serious religious observance and doctrine of the peasantry. The peasant carried his wishes and prayers to the familiar wishing-well, and presented offerings to the spirit of the well by throwing them into the water or hanging them on the surrounding trees. The fairy rather than far-off Wodan was looked to for good fortune; the rite of the fabulous village hero, with its quaint immemorial usages, roused more enthusiasm than the stately public ceremonial. Another side of the mind of early Germany is to be gathered from the heroic legends and the fairy tales, many of the elements of which, we are assured, were even then in existence. Were these legends formed by a process of degradation; did they begin with telling about the gods, and were they afterwards applied to heroes and princes and common men? Or was the process in the opposite direction from this; were the stories, first of all, those of human warriors, their wars and loves, and did they then become mixed up with solar and celestial ideas? Were the fairy tales originally stories of the gods, and did they by popular and familiar treatment fall below the dignity of their original themes till they came to be a debased and broken-down mythology? or were they at first stories about beasts and about clever tricks, such as savages love to tell, and did they rise to something more dignified, till in some of them we may trace the stories of the gods? It is not necessary that we should answer these questions, which carry us back to an earlier time than that with which we are concerned; but any one who knows the tales, and will try to realise the state of mind of those who received them not as fancy but as serious fact, will know something of the religion of early Germany; of the strange beings, fairies, dwarfs, magicians, talking animals, animated sun and moon and winds, by which the German believed himself to be surrounded.

Later German Religion.—In Southern Germany the introduction of Christianity early put an end to any development of Teutonic religion which might have taken place there. The old faith, however, still maintained itself in more Northern latitudes. It was brought to Britain by the German invaders, continued there till the seventh century, and was brought in again in a more Northern form by the Norsemen, who in their turn "gradually deserted Thor and Odin for the white Christ."[1] Bede tells hardly anything of the paganism which had been the religion of England a century before he wrote; in this he is like other Christian teachers who might have told but did not. But though it came to an end in England, Teutonic religion continued to prevail in the countries from which the invaders had come. In Frisia in

[1] Kingsley's *Hereward the Wake.*

the eighth century we hear of a goddess Hulda, a kind goddess, as her name implies, who sends increase to plants and is a patroness of fishing. A god called Fosete, or Forsete (Forseti in modern Icelandic=chairman), identified both with Odin and with Balder, was worshipped in Heligoland; he had a sacred well there, from which water had to be drawn in silence. There are temples, often in the middle of a wood, with priestly incumbents, and rich endowments, both of lands and treasure; and human sacrifice in various forms is said to have been in use. Idols are mentioned, even (at Upsala in Sweden) a trinity of idols; but this is what Church writers would naturally impute to heathens, and the statement is discredited. No Teutonic idol has survived; the loss to art may not be great, but such a relic would have settled the controversy.

Iceland.—Teutonic paganism reached its highest development in Iceland. Of this branch of it alone is there a literature, for many of the sagas are the fruit of a literary movement in Iceland anterior to the establishment of Christianity; and the historian Ari, who wrote within a century after that event, gives careful information of the earlier state of affairs. The reader of *Burnt Njal* sees that among the Icelanders life was short and precarious. With the spirit of adventure, which led them to be constantly setting out on warlike and piratical expeditions, they combined a strong tendency to local quarrels, which filled up their life at home with a constant series of blood-feuds. These latter are gone about in a methodical and business-like way; custom sanctions them, the meetings of the popular assembly do not seek to suppress or punish them if only they are conducted according to the rules. No public authority had as yet arisen to carry out the law between one household and another; the avenger has his recognised place and duty Society is patriarchal as in other Aryan communities; each family is a community of blood-kindred for mutual defence and also for worship. The leading cult of Icelandic religion was the domestic worship of ancestors, conducted by the head of the household. The dead were buried in knolls or burrows near the dwelling, and their spirits were thought to inhabit these places; they are said to "die into the hill." Altars are erected and sacrifices offered there; the blood of the victim poured out upon the ground is supposed to be enjoyed by them. These knolls became the sacred places of their district, and many a belief existed about these quiet neighbours and the help they afforded to the living. "Elves" they were called, and they were thought of as a cleanly and kindly race. The spirits of bad men, on the contrary, lived an uneasy life, as demons, and were the workers of mischief.

Along with this belief in the spirits of the dead as inhabiting the burial hill of the household, there is another conception, namely, that the dead go to a distant region of the unseen world. In Homer also these two conceptions are combined. The Icelandic burial rites are founded on the latter view. The "departed" is going on a long journey, and his friends escort him as far as they can; shoes are bound on his feet, the Hel-shoes, for Hel is the name of the region of the dead. Gifts are given to him; horses, male and female attendants, hawks and hounds, are burned with him on the pyre, and his wife voluntarily accompanies him; all these he is to have with him in the country beyond.

In addition to the domestic cult we have that of local objects; holy wells, waterfalls, groves, stones are worshipped. Mother Earth is called on, so is Thunder, so is Heaven. But besides these minor worships there is the public one, connected with a large tribe or with a king's court. A temple on the same plan as a large dwelling-house forms a place of meeting and of sacrifice, an asylum, and a place of oaths and covenants. On a table in front of the high seat stands the bowl which, filled with blood and along with certain sticks, forms a means of divination. A gold ring also lies there, which a man puts on when he is about to swear an oath, and which the priest puts on at meetings.

The priest has the duty of keeping up the building and property of the temple and of maintaining the sacrifices. At the latter various rites are done with the blood of victims, and those present feast on the flesh and drink toasts. The first cup is for Wodan, various other gods are celebrated, and there is a cup of remembrance for the departed. Sacrifices are offered for the crops, for victory, for any great object on which the community is bent. In this ritual there is no evidence of any idols. Though the Icelanders are not without art, the great gods have not yet perhaps assumed to their minds such definite figures as to be thus set forth: no Homer has placed them clear before the inward eye. The rites are bloody, the altar has ever anew to be made to shine with the blood of victims. Human sacrifices are only resorted to in times of great common danger, as a terrible last resort; the god to whom the human victim is devoted is moved by the bloodshed to avert his anger, or to make greater exertions for his people. Bloodshed forms the strongest of all bonds. To link themselves together in an indissoluble brotherhood, two friends mingle their blood on the ground and then each of them treads on it. The shedding of human blood at the launching of a ship or at the laying of the foundation of a building is also known. Savage and cruel as this religion is, there are signs that it is softening, and that some of its darker rites are beginning to admit of commutation. When Christianity approaches, the Icelanders feel that it must make a great change, and that some of the cruelties which they regard as the good old customs, will have to be laid aside. We hear of the stipulation being made that if they receive baptism they shall not be required to give up the removal of unpromising children nor the eating of horseflesh.

The Eddas, in which Scandinavian mythology reaches its ultimate form, seem to belong to a higher plane of human life than the religion we have described, and it has appeared to many scholars of late years that they cannot be regarded as a pure product of paganism, but are in great part influenced by Christianity both in matter and in sentiment. The older Edda, written in verse, is said to have been collected by Sæmund Sigfusson the learned, one of the early Christian priests of Iceland, who lived about the eleventh century. The other Edda is in prose; it is a collection made about two centuries later. The form given to the myths in these collections is due to the Skalds, who flourished in Iceland in the early Middle Ages; but the legends themselves are older. Nothing is known precisely about their origin or early diffusion.

The Eddas may be compared in many respects with the Homeric poems. As in the latter, the gods form a family, the members of which come together to a certain place for meetings, while individually they have their own adventures, their loves, their jealousies, their jokes, their tricks. In the Eddas too we find that the gods are not, strictly speaking, eternal; they succeeded an older race of gods, and their turn too may come to pass away. They are called Æsir, which is the plural of As. The etymology of this is uncertain; compare the Sanscrit Asura, said to mean the living or breathing one. The Æsir are spoken of in later times, not in the Eddas, as if they had been a race of warriors; they are said to have come in to Scandinavia and got the better of those who lived there before, because they worshipped a superior set of gods.[1] An historic

[1] See a similar statement about the Incas, p. 85.

reminiscence may lurk here. Before the Æsir there were giants, and the earth with all its parts is made of the body of one of these giants,[1] whom the new race superseded as governors of the world. But the giants are still there and their spirit is unchanged; there is a danger of their interfering to subvert the rule of their successors.

There are other cosmogonic myths besides that of the division of the giant Ymir. One is on this wise. Ere this world began, there was on one side Niflheim, the land of mist and cold, on the other side Muspelheim, the region of fire; between these two lay Ginnunga-gap, the north side of it frozen, the south side glowing hot, and life originated by the meeting, in one way or another, of the heat and cold. There are very primitive myths of the shaping of man out of two pieces of wood, of Night and Day as drivers of chariots and horses, of the sun and moon fleeing from wolves, and so on. A more poetic conception is the division of the world into Asgard, the garden of the Æsir; Midgard, the world of man; and Utgard, the world outside. In the first Odin has his seat Hlidskjalf; when he sits in it he can see and understand whatever is happening in any part of the broad world (is he the Sun, then?). The third region is generally called Jötunheim, the home of the giants, an icy region at the extreme part of the habitable world. A bridge exists from the dwelling of men to that of the gods; it is called Bifröst, and is the rainbow.

The gods have various places of meeting; but their principal seat is under a great tree, the ash. Yggdrasil[2] is a tree worthy of the gods; it is a world-tree; its roots extend to all the worlds; its branches spread even over heaven. Under it is the fountain Mimir, spring of wisdom, from which Odin drinks daily. Near it is the dwelling of the Norns, fates

[1] Compare "Purusha" in the *Rigveda*.

[2] Yggdrasill = Odin's horse = the gallows. Is it the cross?

or weird sisters, who establish laws and uphold them by their judgments, and allot to every man his span of life. They are named Urd the past, Verdandi the present, and Skuld the future. Daily do they water the ash from the spring to keep its leaves fresh, and help it to contend with its numerous foes, for a great serpent is continually gnawing at its root, and it has also other troubles. This myth of Yggdrasil is the apotheosis of Teutonic tree-worship, and is richly suggestive.[1]

The Gods of the Eddas.—We now come to the gods of the system. **Odin** is in the Eddas the founder of the world as now constituted. He has displaced the old formless race of gods, and is the leader of a new and vigorous race now ruling in their stead. The old scholars rationalised Odin into a chief who had led a migration from Asia to Norway in early times. He is the inventor of the art of writing by runes and the founder of poetry; thus he has the aspect of a culture-hero; that is to say, of a man of advanced views who, for the benefits he conferred on his people, was exalted first to a hero and then to a god. But the worship of Odin or Wodan is one of the earliest things we know about the German race. He is the god of the South-Germans from the very first. His earliest character is that of a storm-god. Whether his name is connected with the German *wüthen*, rage (Scot. *wud*) or with the Vedic Vata, who is a god of storm, he is from the first an impetuous being. The early myth of him is scarcely dead at this day; the peasant hears him rushing through the woods at night. That is the "wild hunt of Wodan," he says; the god is out with his followers, and woe to him who gets in his way! The early Germans thought of him as a kind being who fulfilled the wishes of men, and it was probably this side of his character that caused him to be identified with

[1] Carlyle in his *Heroes*, p. 18, draws out the spiritual significance of it and of Norse mythology generally.

Mercury. In the Eddic theology he is a patron of war, as becomes the chief god of a warlike people. He arranges battle and dispenses victory; the heroes who fall in battle he receives into his heavenly army; they live with him in Valhalla or Valhöll, the hall of choice. Odin chooses those who are to go there; he is assisted in this by the Valkyries or choice-maidens. Life in Valhalla is a constant round of fighting, the wounds of which are healed at once, and feasting, the materials for which are ever renewed. Odin, like other great gods, bears traces of low surroundings, as if he had once lived among savages. He can turn himself into an eagle or other animal to gain his object, and he has engaged in disreputable adventures. But he tends to improve, and the Eddas show him at his best. Here he is called the All-father, the Ruler of all, who gave man a soul that shall never perish; and we hear that he needs no food and takes no share himself in the feasts of the heroes. All the righteous shall be with him in Vingolf (the same as Valhalla), but the wicked shall go to Hel, the kingdom of Hel or Hela, the goddess of the under-world.

Thor or Donar, Thunder, is said to be the mightiest of the gods; he is identified, as we saw, with Jove, but he is a rougher and more primitive deity. He drives in a chariot drawn by two goats, and is possessed of three things which have wonderful properties. The first is the hammer Mjölnir, which the Frost- and Mountain-giants cannot resist when he throws it; the second is the belt of strength, which makes him twice as strong when he puts it on; and the third a pair of gauntlets with which he grasps his mallet. Many stories are told of his prowess, of his conflicts with the giants, who, however, give him a good deal of trouble with their cunning; and of his catching the Midgard serpent which surrounds the world at the bottom of the sea. Being a god of storm, he forms a connection with agriculture, and thus gains a more sedate aspect; he has also to do with marriage, and a hammer is used symbolically at Icelandic weddings. Thor is only half-brother to the other sons of Odin; his mother was Fiörgyn, the earth; the worships of Odin and Thor, originally distinct, seem to have been united at an early period.

The god **Tyr**, son of Odin by a giantess, is the Eddic figure of the German Tiw or Ziu, etymologically equivalent to Zeus or Jupiter, but identified by the Romans with Mars. His greatness belongs to early times; he was then a sword-god, and had an extensive worship in various parts of Europe. In the Eddas he has scarcely any character, and seldom takes a prominent part in the legend. **Loki**, by etymology a fire-god (Germ. *Löhe*, Scot. *lowe*),[1] is in one account the brother of Odin, in another his son by a giantess. His character is fitful; sometimes he acts a brotherly part by the gods and helps them out of their difficulties by clever devices, and sometimes he provides entertainment for them; but for the most part he is an embodiment of cunning and mischief; his course is downwards, he tends to become a being purely evil, setting himself heartlessly against the wishes of the other gods, and acting so as to imperil them and their world till they are obliged to cast him out of heaven. He is thus a kind of Lucifer or Satan, and like the Christian devil, his ultimate fate is to be bound till the end of the world shall arrive. **Baldur**, the son of Odin and Frigga, is the best and brightest of the gods. Like Apollo, he has to do with light, and no pollution can come near him; he has also to do with the administration of justice, and pronounces sentences

[1] The etymology is not perhaps correct, but it suggested itself and influenced the view taken of this god, in very early times.

which can never be reversed. **Heimdall** also is a light and gracious god; he is the warder of the Æsir, and stays near the bridge Bifröst. Of him it is told that he wants less sleep than a bird, sees a hundred miles off by night or day, and hears the grass grow on the ground and the wool on the sheep's back. **Bragi** is the god of poetry and eloquence, the best of all skalds.

Of the goddesses, **Frigga,** wife of Odin, stands first, an august matron of mysterious knowledge, whom even gods consult, and by whom men swear; she has also to do with marriage, and the childless appeal to her. Etymologically she is scarcely to be distinguished from **Freya,** wife of Odur, who, however, is lighter in character, and is rather a goddess of love. The goddesses in the Eddas are more shadowy figures than the gods; there are others, and an attempt is made to reckon up twelve of them to answer to the twelve chief gods, but their names are taken from the qualities they represent, and they have little reality.

The story of the **death of Baldur,** brought about by the evil mind of Loki in defiance of the whole divine family, sounds the note of tragedy in the divine family of the Eddas. The gods themselves suffer, and are unable to retrieve the misfortune which has come upon them. With one accord they try to get Baldur brought back from the under-world, but they are foiled by the same agency of evil which carried him off. With the death of Baldur the gods feel that their rule, which, we saw, had a beginning, and with it the world they govern, for the two are inseparably bound up with each other, is coming to an end. The gods perish in the ruin of the world; and this is well, for sin cleaves to them and to their house, and they are not fit to endure. **Ragnarök,** the twilight of the gods, comes on; the universe is burnt up in a mighty conflagration, and while there are abodes of bliss and abodes of misery where some survive, the universe as a whole is entirely changed, and a milder race of gods will rule over a better world.

If this mythology were found to be of native Scandinavian growth, it would prove that Teutonic religion was capable of lofty development, and would throw back an interesting light upon its previous history. Here, it has been maintained, we see the Teutonic faith rising towards monotheism. Odin has among his other titles that of All-father; he is rising above the other gods to a position of supremacy, which will fit him, if the process were allowed, as it was not, to advance somewhat further, to represent pure deity and to attract to himself an undivided reverence. Here also we find a religion which was formerly a rude intercourse between barbarous men and savage gods, clothing itself with an ideal element. As the Greeks found religion in beauty and the Romans in utility, so did the Germans find it at last in pathos. They attain to the conception of suffering deity; in Baldur a god falls victim to malice and wickedness, and the sorrow of his fall takes possession of the whole of heaven. Thus pain and sacrifice are hallowed for man by the history of the gods, and his intercourse with them leads him into heights and depths unknown before.

But the conviction is now establishing itself that this phase of Teutonic religion is borrowed from Christianity, which was then seriously menacing the existence of the old faith, and that it is the shadow of their approaching extinction by the new religion, which occasions among the Northern gods this feeling of sadness. They feel themselves falling from their position; they are to be gods no longer, but are to yield to the world-order, based on a deeper law than theirs, which called them into being and now is preparing their dismissal. Distinctly Christian ideas enter the old world of gods; the ideas of sin, of shows that they are abandoning their rule, and they acknowledge that their successors will be better than they have been.

Books Recommended

Grimm's *German Mythology*, translated by Stallybrass, 4 vols.

Grimm's *Fairy Tales.* Mr Lang writes an Introduction to the English translation in Bell's edition.

Mannhardt, *Germanische Mythen*, 1858, and *Wald- und Feld-kulte*, 1875, 77.

For the later Northern section, Vigfusson and Powell's *Corpus Poeticum Boreale*, especially the Excursus on Religion, i. 401.

Dasent, *Burnt Njal; or Life in Iceland at the end of the tenth century.* Mallet's *Northern Antiquities.*

Thorpe, *Northern Mythology.*

De la Saussaye, *The Religion of the Teutons*, 1902, the most comprehensive statement of the whole subject.

Ralston, *Songs of Russian People*, and *Russian Folk Tales.*

Simrock, *Handb. der deutschen Mythologie.*

CHAPTER XVI

GREECE

THE history of Europe begins in Greece. It is there that the Aryans in Europe first feel the touch of the arts and civilisation of the East, and are stirred up to new activities; and the life thus quickened in Greece transmitted its spark to Italy, and so to the whole of Europe.

People and Land.—There is no direct evidence that the Greeks came to their country from elsewhere; and the theory of a Græco-Italic period, in which the future inhabitants of Greece and Italy lived together somewhere to the north of both these countries and made common advances in civilisation, is now abandoned. There are, however, faint indications that the Greeks spread over their country from the north southwards. What people dwelt in it before them it is impossible to say; the Pelasgi and Leleges, whom they themselves conceived to have preceded them, left behind them no other trace than that belief. When first we descry this land in the faint dawn of history, it is tenanted by the people whose name it bears, touched only by the Thracians to the north, and the Illyrians to the west, these also being Aryan races. Though the Greeks are on both sides of the Egean, which seems from the earliest times to have connected rather than divided them, their centre of gravity is in the mainland of Hellas, including the Peloponnesus. In this country many a migration no doubt took place before the people was finally arranged in it; and some of these migrations are faintly known to history. When once the settlement had been accomplished, the nature of the country did much to fix the institutions of the people and the mutual relations of their various communities. Large tribes coming into the narrow valleys and sequestered coasts of Greece necessarily broke up into small cantons, each of which, though not cut off from intercourse with its neighbours, was free to develop by itself. The country is said by travellers to be the most beautiful in the world. The branch of the Aryans which settled in it may have brought scanty acquirements with them, but they brought great capacities. The Greeks had an unrivalled talent for doing what they saw others do, in a much better way, and so making it their own. They had an inborn disposition to what is reasonable. That they had a deep-seated inclination to what is harmonious and beautiful is proved by their first great work of art, their language. Of that language there were several dialects in the earliest times; the principal ones being the broad Doric of the peninsula and the colonies, and the softer Ionic of which the classical language is a branch. But the Greeks of all dialects could understand each other, and regarded as barbarians those without who spoke other tongues. Thus from the first this people was much divided, but was also held together by strong bonds.

Earliest Religion—Functional Deities.—The religion the Greeks brought with them to their country was undoubtedly that which we have discussed in our chapter on the Aryans. The primitive elements of Aryan religion all reappear in Greece; the combination of many small household worships with the supra-family worship of a great god or gods, the few great gods who are surrounded by a multitude of spirits, some of these also growing into gods, the recognition of spiritual presences in many a natural object, living or dead. All this we find in early Greece. The whole nation believes in Zeus; to all he is the Lord of heaven, the giver of rain, the fertiliser of mother earth, the supreme ruler in earth as well as in heaven, the father of the gods as well as of men. This is the first bond of unity in Greek religion. But every family, every village, every town has its own peculiar worship which is to be found nowhere else. That worship may be addressed to Zeus with a local title; each circle of men has its own particular Zeus, who is their protector and ruler; and thus Zeus has many forms and names. In each community there is also the worship of the goddess of the hearth (Hestia); each household has its own Hestia, and carries on the worship which in other Aryan peoples is connected with the memory of departed ancestors. But the family or the township has also other objects of worship. There are other gods besides Zeus who are connected with heaven, such as Apollo and Heracles. There are gods connected with each activity of the people. Artemis is goddess of hunting, Aphrodite of the peaceful life of nature and of gardens, and also of love. Poseidon, the sea-god, was also worshipped inland, and was perhaps originally a god of horses and oxen; Hephæstus was the god of workers in metal, Ares the god of battle These are in their origin what are called functional deities, that is to say, gods who are present in the function with which they are associated, and of which they constitute the ideal or sacred side, and who have no existence apart from it.

The gods of Greece in fact had their origin in that view of nature as animated in every part, which the Greeks shared with other branches of the Aryans, and with early man generally. Like the Latins, the Greeks at first saw a mystery, a spirit, in every part of life; each fountain had its nymph, each forest glade its dryad; and they felt the gods to be returning to fresh life when spring came with its flowers. Each of their own activities also had its unseen genius. Each enclosure for flocks had its Apollo, "him of the sheepfold," who protected the flock and the shepherd; and each boundary stone its Hermes, "him of the boundary," who also watched over flocks and took charge of marches and of paths.

Growth of Greek Gods.—Such beings, however, are something less than gods; and the Greeks, long before we know them, had made the step which the Romans scarcely made at all, from the spirit to the god, from the vague unseen power behind an object or an act, to the free being conceived with human attributes and feelings, who can be the patron of a community, and afford help in all its concerns. Not all the spirits rise into gods; it depends on circumstances which of them are selected for that advance; but the choice once made, their rise was rapid. As the gods grew into personality and definite character, though the function out of which they first sprang was not forgotten, other functions were added to them; and as a god grew in power and consideration, his worship was set up in new places, where other titles and attributes awaited him. The local god might be identified with the great god from a distance. The god of a powerful community, as Athene ("she of Athens"), might be adopted wherever the influence of that community extended; thus new gods arose and old ones took local form. When a change took place in the habits of the people, it was followed by a corresponding change in the character of their gods. When agriculture comes in, the gods have to take notice of it, the pastoral god turns agricultural, and even the huntress Artemis becomes an encourager of fertility. When navigation rises in importance, a number of the gods, Poseidon at their head, become sea-gods.

Stones, Animals, Trees.—In Greece the worship of the gods soon superseded that of objects not possessing any human character. Traces of such lower worships survive, it is true, in the later religion in great abundance, but they have no influence in its development; they only tell their story of the otherwise forgotten past. Stones were worshipped in early Greece. Not to speak of the cromlechs and dolmens, which are found there as in all parts of Asia and Europe, and the meaning of which is so little understood, stones were preserved as sacred objects in various places, even to late times, and no doubt had originally been worshipped. The god Hermes was represented in every period by a slab of stone set upright, a human head and other human features being indicated on it. Even in later Greece, boards or blocks of wood were in some places exhibited on rare occasions, which were the oldest images of the Artemis or the Aphrodite there adored. Though for the public eye splendid statues had taken the place of the goddess, the original image was still thought to have a sanctity all its own. We also notice that the gods of Greece are associated with animals. Zeus is a bull in Crete; he has also other transformations: Pan is a goat; Artemis is a bear in some provinces, elsewhere a doe. The Athene of the Acropolis is a serpent. Apollo is sometimes connected with the mouse. Along with these identifications of the gods with animals we may mention the animal emblems with which they are generally represented. The eagle is the bird of Zeus, the owl of Athene, the peacock of Hera, the dove of Aphrodite. In this connection we cannot help thinking of the sacred animals of the Egyptian nomes; and the question may be asked whether such animals must be taken to be in Greece also the signs of a primitive totemism?

Of the tree-worship of Greece much has been written of late. The oak was the sacred tree of Zeus; he must have been conceived as living in it; he gave oracles at Dodona by the rustling of the branches of the tree. Athene has the olive, Apollo the palm, and also the laurel.

After the introduction of agriculture rustic cults arose, in which the inhabitants of a village followed in sympathetic rites the fortunes of the gods who live in the life of the plants in summer and die with them in autumn. The god of the Semites is generally a changeless being, who himself conducts and orders the changes of the seasons, but in Greece we find gods whom man can accompany in the tragedy of their fall and the triumph of their rise. We shall see afterwards that the rustic worships of Demeter and Proserpine were brought forward at a critical period in Greek religion, to supply an element which was much required in it. These worships, similar, as Mr. Frazer suggests,[1] to those still kept up by our own peasantry, were doubtless of immemorial antiquity in Greece, though in the earlier period they are little heard of.

Thus the Greek gods grew up in the period before Greece was awakened to new thoughts by contact with foreign peoples. Many harsh and cruel rites were no doubt practised; human sacrifice, heard of even in later times in remote parts of the country, was not unknown, and practices were connected with the service of stern gods and goddesses which, though literature is silent about them, left their mark on custom. Zeus and one or two other gods are essentially moral, and some duties were strongly encouraged by religion, such as those of hospitality and strict regard for boundaries, of faithfulness to pledge, of respect for strangers. But many of the gods are too closely interwoven with external nature to be very decidedly moral powers; they are like the plants and animals, neither good nor bad but natural.

Greek Religion is Local.—What strikes us most strongly about this early Greek religion is its entire want of system and its local and disintegrated character. Every town, every family, has its own religion. There is no central authority.

[1] *Golden Bough*, vol. i. p. 356.

New gods are constantly springing up; the old ones are constantly receiving new titles and forming new unions with each other or with newer gods. The god of one place is in another only a hero; the same god is represented in different places in entirely different ways, and entirely different legends are attached to his name. Thus the Greeks have from the first a mythology singularly extensive and inconsistent, and their worship also varies in each place. There is no general religion, but only a multitude of local ones. In story and in rite old and new are mixed up together,—what is local and what is imported, what is savage in its nature and origin, and what is on the side of progress. This is a state of matters which lies in every land before the beginning of organised religion. Rites and legends are everywhere of local growth, and the attempt to frame the various rites and legends into a consistent ritual and a systematic account of the gods, comes later. In Greece, as Mr. Robertson Smith observes, the earlier state of matters continued longer and influenced the national faith more deeply than elsewhere. As the Greeks never succeeded in forming a central political system, so they never attained to unity in worship. No national temple arose, the priesthood of which had power to frame the national religion, to lay down rules for sacrifice, or to edit sacred texts. The Greeks were less than any other people under the sway of religious authority. While local practice was fixed, and custom and tradition declared plainly enough what was to be regarded as religious duty, belief was quite free to grow as circumstances or the growth of culture dictated. A religion in such a position, and among a people of lively imagination and specially gifted in the direction of art, must necessarily receive its forms rather from the artist than the priest.

Artistic Tendency.—Thus we can discern from the

first the direction which Greek religion must take. The Greeks shaped their gods earlier and more freely than other peoples, and went on shaping them till no further advance could be made in that way. Long before Homer they had been making their gods such as free men, and men endowed with a sense of beauty, could worship. They were not content to worship lifeless objects, but must have living beings. They were not content to worship beings without reason, they must worship reasonable beings. They were not inclined to regard the natural objects they worshipped with terror or self-prostration, but rather in a spirit of genial friendliness and sympathy as being something like themselves. And so they turned their gods into men. The anthropomorphising tendency, present as we have seen in other lands and at much earlier periods, present indeed wherever religion is a growing power, had freer play with them than with any other people. Thus the spirits of the fountain and the tree, and of every part of nature that was worshipped, took human form. At first, no doubt, the nymph was in the fountain, the dryad in the oak, but as time went on the human maiden cast off her mosses and her bark and leaves, and stood forth to imagination a being wholly human, dwelling beside the fountain or the tree. In the same way heaven becomes a great human father, the sea an earthshaking potentate drawn by dolphins over the waves, the sun a mighty archer, fire a lame craftsman (from the flickering of flame?) whose smithy is underground where the volcanoes are. And the figures once arrived at, it was no hard task to spin out their stories and their relations with each other, and to connect with them older tales, as taste or fancy suggested.

The thorough humanisation of the gods, the clothing of the gods in the highest types connected with free human society, is the first great contribution made by this gifted race to the progress of religion. Receiving from the earlier world the same kind of gods as other nations did, Greece proceeded to treat them in a way of her own, idealised and refined the parts of nature held divine, and ascribed to them not only, as all early races do, human motives and human passions, but also human beauty and wisdom and goodness. Whatever rude materials she received to work on, either from the earlier dwellers on Greek soil or from foreign lands, she made them her own by transfiguring them into ideal men and women. Thus the Greeks reached the position, which they taught the world first in immortal poetry and then in immortal plastic art, that man should not bow down to anything that is beneath him, and that nature can only become fit to be worshipped by being idealised and made human. An end was made to the dark imagination which was so apt to creep over all early religion, that deity and humanity may be different and opposite; that an object devoid of reason, an object or an animal admired not for its goodness but for something about it which man cannot understand, may be his god and have a claim to his allegiance. God and man are of the same nature, the Greeks found; to arrive at a true idea of a god we have to form, on the basis of the natural object where he is supposed to dwell, the image of an ideal man or woman. This was a great step, but in this conception of deity the Greeks also laid up for themselves, as we shall see, many difficulties.

Early Eastern Influences.—Our positive knowledge of Greek history begins about the middle of the second millennium B.C.; we have information of this period in the ruins of Mycenæ and Tiryns and other places. These remains attest a political condition widely different from that of the patriarchal settlements of the period when the Greeks were emerging from Aryan barbarism; very different also from the free city life which came afterwards. The recent excavations have brought to light the palaces of kings, built, it is evident, according to an Eastern type, and with arrangements for the burial and worship of dead potentates, not unlike those of the pyramids. The art is rude, but shows large forces to have been at the command of those who directed it. We have here, therefore, a state of matters such as that described in the Homeric poems, in which petty kings rule in many of the Greek towns, some of them being personages of great rank and power. The movement in civilisation attested by these remains is admitted to be due to an impulse from the East; but whether this impulse was imparted by the voyages of Phenician discoverers and merchants, or whether it came by land along the trade routes of Asia Minor and across the Egean, is uncertain. It is in any case traceable to North Syria, where in the early part of the second millennium B.C. Babylonian and Egyptian influences met and gave rise to some rude civilisation. Greece was not conquered from the East, but stirred to new life by the communication of Eastern ideas.

Greek religion was not much assisted, or indeed much modified in any way, by this movement. The worship of ancestors which went on in the palaces was not contrary to Greek sentiment, perhaps not even much more elaborate than that sentiment required. But this part of religion was not a growing thing in Greece; and the royal practices did not prevent it from dying gradually away in later times. That any god was imported into Greece at this time, is not proved. Where Greeks and Phenicians met, as in some of the islands, a Greek and an Eastern god might be identified; the worship of Aphrodite and that of Astarte were fused in this way in Cyprus, and Aphrodite may thus have acquired some new characteristics even in Greece. This is not certain. Perhaps the most important thing to notice in this connection is that the new type of society at the royal courts may have furnished a model for the arrangement of the heavenly family when that arrangement came to be made. The Eastern influence came to an end in time, and the pressure being removed, the monarchies crumbled away, the court worships were discontinued, and Greece was left free, after this awaking to fuller life, to pursue her own thoughts in her own fashion.

Homer was regarded by the Greeks who lived after him as the founder of their religion. Herodotus considers (ii. 53) that Homer and Hesiod lived four hundred years before his time, and that it was they who framed a theogony for the Greeks, gave names to the gods, assigned to them honours and arts, and declared their several forms. These writers accordingly formed a standard of religious belief; we know that their works were the basis of the education of the Greek, and they thus provided an early bond of national unity.

The Homeric poems are the outcome, whether we regard them as the work of one singer or of two, or of a whole school, of long processes of growth. The poetic art which makes them the delight of all mankind is not a first experiment, but the ripe result of an elaborate method. The stories and the wisdom they contain are brought together from many quarters by long accumulation. And in the same way the accounts they give of the gods individually and of their relations to each other are not thrown together at haphazard, but are the result of a work of unconscious art which must have been carried on for centuries before it issued in this form. Homer does not by any means repeat all the stories he knows about the gods. He passes over many local myths, especially those of the more repulsive order, which were known for centuries after, and undoubtedly existed in his day; only what is "worthy of a pious bard" does he reproduce. A pious bard, however, had considerable latitude; and the phrase does not represent all that Homer was. He was an entertainer of the public at royal courts, where a feast was incomplete without him (*Odyssey* viii.); he had to produce his songs at banquets or in the open air at festivals; what he gave had to be entertaining. This could not but influence his choice of materials even when the gods were his theme. He could not deal in what was most terrible about the gods, nor could he enter into speculations or mysteries, nor could he make use of a legend which, though it had point for the locality it belonged to, was not generally interesting. What was powerful and dramatic, what all men could understand, what was curious and piquant, what met the general sentiment, that he would be led to adopt and to work up into a telling form; he naturally sought after broad pictures, amusing conversations, simple and true emotions, curious incidents connected with well-known characters. Religion, it is plain, could not gain in depth and intensity from the treatment of such poets; many of the thoughts men had about the gods could not find expression in their lines. But, on the other hand, we have the fact that the Greeks accepted the Homeric representation of their religion as the standard one; not till it had existed for centuries were voices raised against it. And this is not strange. Homer took away nothing from the religion of any Greek; no local worship was in any way infringed upon by him; and on the other side he gave to the Greek world, whose belief consisted formerly in a multitude of disconnected or even inconsistent legends, a united system of gods, in which there was at that stage rest for the mind, and for the imagination an inexhaustible spring of ideal beauty.

The Homeric Gods.—What, then, is the religion of Homer? The gods are a set of beings not very unlike men;

they present a curious combination of human frailty with superhuman powers and virtues. To speak first of the physical side of their nature, the gods are far stronger than men, their frame is huger, their eye keener, their voice louder; like the sorcerer of savage times, they can assume other shapes to gain their ends, they can become invisible, or they can travel very swiftly through the air. Yet, on the other hand, they can be wounded when they strive even with men; accidents happen to them, they require to eat and drink. They eat, it is true, ambrosia, and drink nectar, which give immortality; and they have in their veins not human blood but divine ichor. It is the fact of their immortality that makes them different from men; it has happened that a man obtained immortality and became thereby a god. The line between gods and men may be crossed; in former times it was crossed more frequently. The gods entered into relations with mortals; many of the heroes are of divine extraction, and the gods are still interested in the royal houses they thus founded. But such unions do not take place in the poet's time. The world is growing less divine.

Homer, however, looks further back than this, and we find in him the belief, found also in India and in Iceland, that an older and more savage race of gods once ruled, whom the present dynasty conquered and dethroned. Of that older set was Kronos, the father of Zeus, and the Titans, who are now cast down to Tartarus, the nethermost region of all. The world known to men was apportioned at the beginning of the present age to the three sons of Kronos, Zeus obtaining the upper world, including heaven, which is at the top of Mount Olympus in Thessaly; Poseidon the sea, and Hades the under-world, above Tartarus, to which men go after death.

Zeus rules in Olympus. He presides there over those gods who are at present in power. He summons them to council, he sits at meals with them. They are a very human set of beings. They are moved by ordinary human motives; love and revenge, jealousy and anger, rule in their breasts. They do not act from eternal principles, but as men do, from sudden impulses or from the desire of temporary advantages for themselves or for their favourites. They even indulge in loose amours, and are brought into ridiculous situations. They laugh at each other; the stronger god hurls the weaker out of Olympus to the earth. Taking them together, we do not find the Olympians an impressive set of beings. Taking them, however, one by one, we judge of them quite differently. The individual gods represent lofty ideals and are not unworthy of worship. Whatever they were once, powers of nature, fetishes or men, whatever village legends they have brought with them from their native place, or whatever traits of savage life still cleave to them, to the poet they are the embodiments of various moral excellences. Zeus, father of gods and men, combines in his character the attributes of righteousness and of kindness; he is the founder of social order and the defender of suppliants, he possesses all wisdom. Hera is the matron of fully unfolded beauty and matchless dignity; Apollo is the faithful son who carries out his father's counsel; Athene is the warrior-maiden skilled in battle but equipped with every kind of skill, best counsellor and guide for the mortal whom she favours; Aphrodite is the goddess of love, in whose girdle are contained all charms; Ares is the impetuous warrior, Hermes the trusty messenger, of the heavenly circle, Hephæstus, the lame and awkward smith, is the artificer for the gods of all manner of cunning work in metal. Around and under the Olympians are many other deities; such as Hebe, the budding girl, and Ganymede, the youth born of human race but taken up to heaven for his beauty to minister to the gods at their banquets. Aphrodite is attended by the graces, Apollo by the Muses, and the world is not stripped by Homer of its local deities, although the chief deities now dwell aloft; mountains, rivers, caves and isles of ocean, all have their immortal occupants.

Worship in Homer.—The gods being of such a nature, what relations does man keep up with them, and how do they affect his life? Worship follows the simple practice of the early world. It is not priestly. There are priests, and they offer sacrifices regularly at the shrines of which they have charge, but the king can sacrifice, or the head of the house; and while one or two temples are mentioned in the *Iliad*, sacrifice may be offered anywhere. Temples first appear in Greece merely as shelters for images, but in the *Iliad* the god is generally worshipped not by means of an image but as himself directly present; the need of temples has not yet arisen. In the *Odyssey* temples of the gods are spoken of as buildings no town could be without, but this is less primitive. Sacrifice is a feast in which the god's portion of the viands is first offered to him, and the worshippers then eat and drink to their hearts' content. There is a detailed description of the proceedings in *Iliad* i. 456 *sqq*. Here after the feast there is music; "All day long worshipped they the god with music, singing the beautiful pæan to the Fardarter (Apollo); and his heart was glad to hear." "The gods appear manifest amongst us," we read in the seventh book of the *Odyssey*, "whensoever we offer glorious hecatombs, and they feast by our side, sitting at the same board." There is nothing of the nature of an expiation about such a sacrifice; it is simply the renewal of the bond between the god and those who look for his aid, when a new enterprise is about to be undertaken or a solemn engagement is entered on. Prayers are very simple. Thus prays the wounded Diomede to Athene (*Iliad* v. 115): "Hear me, daughter of ægis-bearing Zeus, unwearied maiden! If ever in kindly mood thou stoodest by my father in the heat of battle, even so be thou kind to me, Athene! Grant me to slay this man, and bring within my spear-cast him that took advantage to shoot me, and boasteth over me!"

As there are no bad gods, good and evil are considered to be sent by the same beings. Thus there is a great deal of uncertainty in men's relations to the gods. "All men need the gods," we read; the Homeric hero regards the companionship of a god as proper and necessary for his enterprises. But some trouble must be taken in order to secure their favour. They must not be neglected; their signs must be attended to; above all, a man must be reverent and must studiously practise moderation in his conduct and in his ways of thinking; else the gods may easily be offended or made jealous, and withdraw their countenance. And if they are to a certain extent capricious, there is another consideration which impairs confidence in them. They are not all-powerful. There is a point beyond which they cannot give a man any help. Each man has a fate or destiny, which the gods did not fix and with which they cannot interfere. When his hour comes, they must leave him to his doom; indeed they may even deceive him, and lead him into folly so that his fate shall overtake him. The punishment of crime, both in this world and afterwards, is committed to a special set of beings, the Erinnyes. The gods who are most worshipped do not exercise that function; they are not immovably identified with the moral order of the world, but frequently deviate from it themselves. In the *Odyssey*, it is true, we meet with a deeper feeling. Here Zeus is a kind of providence, in whom a man may trust when he does right, and to all whose dispensations it behoves him humbly to submit. A root of monotheism is present here, as in all the Aryan religions from the first, and in Greece it is destined to have a stately growth. The Homeric pantheon, however, as a whole, shows religion at a stage in which it is rather an external ornament to life than an inner inspiration. Perhaps there was never a set of real men who thought of the gods and addressed them according to the fashion of Homer. If such a religion ever actually existed, it was not a strong one. These gods, with their caprices and infirmities and their limited power, could never exercise any strong moral influence or rouse any passion in their worshippers. They are fair-weather gods; the religion is one of children, in whom conscience is not yet awake and the deeper spiritual needs have not yet appeared. What the mind of the Greek has done up to this stage is to discover that nature is not above him; the powers of nature are human to him; they are divine not because they are essentially different from himself, but because they are matchless ideals of his own qualities. It is a religion of free men. But the Greek has not yet discovered how different he himself is from all that is around him; that element of himself which is above nature will when he discovers it make such a religion as the Homeric for ever impossible to him.

Omens.—As the godhead is never far away from the Homeric Greek, and is an active being who takes an interest in human affairs, signs of his presence are not infrequent. The air is the scene of them; in the flight of birds, in sudden noises, the gods send messages; lightning is a sign from Zeus of approaching rain or hail, it may be of approaching war. There are rules for the interpretation of signs, which, however, are in many cases of doubtful significance. Dreams also are a favourite channel for divine communications, but they also may be interpreted wrongly. There are persons who have a special gift for knowing the divine will; the seer (μάντις) is enlightened by the deity not by an outward sign but inwardly; he hears the god's voice, and can declare the divine will directly. This gift may reside in a certain family, and may be attached to a certain spot, where a regular oracle is open for consultation. At Dodona we read that the Selloi or Helloi, a band or family of priests of ascetic habits, interpret the rustling of the sacred oak, and Agamemnon consults the Pythia, the Delphic priestess, before the Trojan war.

The State after Death.—With regard to the state after death, belief is not uniform in Homer. There are elaborate funeral rites which point to the assumption that the spirit of the hero is living somewhere and needs various things. But the life of the departed was not mapped out in Greece as it was in Egypt. The ritual of Mycenæ had little influence, for the funeral celebrations in Homer are very similar to those of other early Aryan peoples, and undoubtedly were not imported. What then is thought of the present existence of the hero? He has ceased to exist. The body is the man, the spirit when it has left the body has but a shadow-life, without any strength or hope; at the most it may revive a little at the taste of blood. But while the worship of the departed is seen from Homer to be decaying among the Greeks, imagination is seen to be occupied in more than one direction with the regions where they are, and to be asserting for them a more real and active existence than the old beliefs allowed. The subterranean kingdom of Hades (the "Invisible") is acquiring clearer shape. The punishments are described which certain great transgressors, such as Tantalus and Ixion, are there undergoing; and other details are also known. Of a different spirit is the conception of the Elysian plains in the far west, whither the hero is taken by the gods when he dies, and where there is no snow nor storm nor rain.

Homer was not the only poet who furnished the Greeks with a system of their gods; nor was his system everywhere accepted without demur. **Hesiod,** writing in the latter half of the eighth century B.C., gives a "theogony" or birth of the gods, which is also a genesis or origin of the world, for to the Greek mind the gods and the world came into existence together. He complains of those who on this subject have taught fictions which resemble truths, referring perhaps to Homer. His own system of the world is not a light and airy fabric but a laborious work, due no doubt to professional or priestly industry, in which the attempt is made to treat all the divine figures or half-figured spirits the Greeks knew, genealogically, and to give a complete enumeration of them. Myths are given, some of them of a horrible character, which do not occur in Homer. The battle of the gods with the Titans occupies a large part of the poem, and it concludes with a collection of stories showing the descent of heroes from alliances between gods and mortals. This work, as we saw, was considered, along with the Homeric poems, as a standard authority on the subject of the gods, and was appealed to even in the early Christian centuries as showing what the Greeks believed.

The Poets and the Working Religion.—The work of these poets proves that the Greeks in their days were anxious to arrive at clear and harmonious conceptions about the gods. The movement on which Homer and Hesiod set their seal, of fixing the characters and attributes of the various deities, must have been long going on; and it led, as we see, to different results in different places. That labour when accomplished endowed Greece with a new religion. The local rite still went on, which acknowledged no central authority and presented the spectacle of an infinite diversity. Each city carried on in grave and solemn fashion the traditional worship of its own gods, on whose favour its prosperity depended. The other gods of the Pantheon the city did not need to worship; and moreover local worship was addressed to a large extent to the Chthonian or earth-gods, as Demeter and Dionysus, of whom the epic poems know but little. The poets were of little assistance therefore to the working religion; but on the other hand the happy and beautiful deities of Homer found entrance wherever poetry was loved. This was a religion for all Greece; these gods were national; though some of them belonged originally to Æolia, they had become national by being enshrined in poetry which the whole nation regarded as its own. The Homeric conception of deity acted therefore on the whole Greek mind; all gods rose in rank by the example, a subject was set before the mind of the people, which the closely succeeding development of religious art shows to have been studied in the noblest way.

Rise of Religious Art.—The seventh century B.C. was a period of rapid development and of great prosperity in Greece. It was the age of colonisation; manufacture and trade were active, and though the Phenicians were not now in the Egean, Greeks sailed to the East and brought home with them many ideas. It was a time like the sixteenth century in Europe, when the world of geography was quickly opening out, and views and sentiments were also widening. Worship could not fail to share in the upward movement of such a period, and it is here that we find the appearance of the ideas in religious art which have made Greece the envy of the world. Architecture received a new impulse from Egypt and Babylon; dwellings were built, not for human rulers, as in the Mycenæan period, but for the gods. In country districts or small towns the wooden shed might still suffice to shelter the rude image, but in large towns, where the higher conception of the gods and the artistic impulse were both present in many minds, temples of more durable material were built. This came to be a universal practice; among the first tasks of a new colony was always that of erecting on a commanding site in the rising town, splendid temples to the gods of the mother city. The Greek temple is not a place to accommodate a large body of worshippers, but a dwelling for the god. It is of oblong shape, and is placed on a raised platform which is ascended by steps. It is generally surrounded by pillars, is roofed, and has a low gable at each end. The most important chamber in it is that containing the image of the god. From his dim chamber the god looks out to the east through the doorway facing him, which opens on the pillared portico in front. Here the worshipper stands when praying, his face turned westward to the god. As it was essential that the smoke of the sacrifice should ascend freely to heaven, the god's real dwelling, the altar stood outside. In some cases the roof was partly open, and the altar could stand under the sky in the *cella* of the god.

In the building and adornment of the temples Greek art found its highest exercise. The architecture of those specimens which can still be seen or described is of a dignity and beauty never before attained; the beings must have been lofty and reverend indeed for whom such dwellings were formed. The gable spaces and the flat surfaces between the tops of the pillars and the roof gave opportunity for sculpture; and the archæologist traces on these metopes (spaces between the beam-ends under the roof) and friezes, the progress of Greek sculpture from a rude stage to that in which the sculptor has gained complete mastery over his material, and can give an imposing representation of a myth, or place on the marble a complete religious procession of brave men and fair women. The images of the gods to be placed in the temples called forth the artist's highest skill; even when the rude old god was retained, a fine work of art could also find place. It is the ideal gods of poetry that are coming to be worshipped; the conception of the poet is expressed in marble. Sculpture, however, came to its highest point in Greece somewhat later than architecture. And offerings were made to the temples of just such rare and costly things as men loved then and love still to store up in their houses,—bowls and cups wrought curiously in precious metals, statues and tapestries and all kinds of treasure.

Festivals and Games.—The temple for which so much was done, formed the centre of the city where it stood. In it the town deposited its treasure and its documents; there oaths and agreements were ratified. There also at certain times, such as the annual festival of the god or the anniversary of some happy event in the history of the town,—and as time went on such occasions tended to multiply,—the town kept holiday. Women escaped from their monotonous confinement and joined the procession to the holy place, perhaps carrying a new dress for the deity. A sacrifice was offered, the god received his share of the victim or victims, and the worshippers feasted on what remained. But before this part of the proceedings arrived there was a pause, which was filled up with various exercises all connected with the act of worship, but tending also in a high degree to the delight of those taking part in it. Dancing formed a part of every rite, accompanied of course with music, and consisting not of a careless exercise of the limbs, but of a measured and carefully trained set of movements expressive of the emotions connected with the occasion. This part of the religious act is obviously capable of great expansion. We find the art of poetry also making its contributions to religious art; poems are recited bearing on the history of the god. The sacrifice is followed by contests of various kinds; the singers compete for a prize, and athletic sports also take place, the competitors for which have long been in training for them. The winners are crowned with a wreath or branch of the plant sacred to the god. The games of Greece, which thus arose out of acts of worship, and some of which became so famous and attracted competitors from every Greek-speaking land, are a notable sign of the spirit of Greek piety. There is no asceticism in Greek religion; the god is represented as a beautiful human person, and his worshippers appear before him naked, in the fulness of their youthful beauty and of their well-trained vigour, and offer him their strength and skill in highest exercise;—the whole city, or a crowd much larger than the city, rejoicing in the spectacle.

Thus does Greek religion enlist in its service all the arts, and increase as they increase. At this period irrational manifestations of piety tend to disappear, human sacrifice and the worship of animals are heard of afterwards only in remote quarters. The religion which now prevails is a bright and happy self-identification with a being conceived as a type of human beauty and excellence, by being as far as possible beautiful oneself, creating beautiful objects, composing beautiful verse, training the body to its highest pitch of strength and agility, and displaying its powers in manly contests. This conception of religion, for a short time realised in Greece, still haunts the mind as a vision which once seen can never be forgotten. No one whose eyes have opened to that vision can regard any religious acts in which the effort after harmony and beauty forms no part, as other than degraded and unworthy.

Zeus and Apollo.—It is impossible here to enter specially on the worship of the individual gods. Two of the gods, however, the same who even in Homer stand above the level of the rest, still maintain that superiority. Zeus draws to himself more and more all the attributes of pure deity; his name comes more and more to stand simply for "God," as if there were no other. He is the father of gods and men; goodness and love are natural to him. He is the supreme Ruler and Disposer, whose word is fate and whose ways pious thought feels called to justify; but he is also the Saviour, to whom every one may appeal. He is the source of all wisdom; all revelations come from him. The other god who occupies a marked position is Apollo, the god of light and the prophet of his father Zeus. His oracle at Delphi was the most important in Greece; it was held to be the centre of the earth, and was a meeting-place for Greeks from every quarter. His priests exercised through the oracle a great influence on Greek life, and as their god required strict purity and truthfulness and was the inspirer of every kind of art and of none but noble purposes, the worship of Apollo is one of the highest forms of Greek religion.

Change of the Greek Spirit in the Sixth Century B.C.—But the time was at hand when the worship of the gods of the poets was to prove, in spite of all that art had done for it, inadequate to meet the spiritual needs of Greece. Civilisation advances in the sixth century B.C. with immense rapidity; the Greeks, no longer prompted by any foreign influence, quickly learn to exercise their own powers, and to apply them in new directions. Life grows richer and deeper, new modes of sentiment appear, the nation grows more conscious of its unity, and at the same time the individual learns to value himself more highly and to assert himself more strongly. On one side thought awakes to an independent career and traditional beliefs are subjected to criticism; on the other spiritual needs are felt which the old worship does not satisfy, and for which religion has to find new outlets.

It is far beyond our scope to deal with the religious movements of a people thus passing into the self-conscious stage, and unfolding with unparalleled freshness and power all the various activities of the human mind. We can only point out a few of the lines of development which become prominent at this period. And firstly we notice the rise of *rationalism*, that is of the impulse to criticise belief and to ask for that element in it which approves itself to the reflecting mind. Reason asserts its right to judge of tradition; the doubter suggests emendations in the legend, the piously inclined turn their attention to those parts only which are capable of lofty treatment. This tendency is fatal to polytheism. As reason knows not gods but only God, the gods can only hold their place on condition that they are what God must be, and so they all tend to become alike in their character; attention is turned most of all to Zeus, the highest god, and when others are worshipped, it is as his prophets or delegates. The poets of the fifth century reflect the conviction which all the higher minds of their country were now coming to hold, that the world is under the rule of one god. From this they are led to take up the questions of theodicy or of the principles of the divine government. Æschylus and Sophocles, writing perhaps about the same time as the author of the Book of Job, are full of problems of this nature. Why is Prometheus, though the noblest benefactor of the human race, doomed to undergo such sufferings? Why does a curse cleave to a certain house, evil producing evil from generation to generation? What is the relation between the divine laws which are written in the hearts of all men, and human laws which sometimes contradict these older ones? Thus to the educated Greeks of the fifth century the old religion had in its essence passed away. With unexampled rapidity had the journey here been traced which India made more slowly, which Egypt made at a very early period, but was not able to maintain, and which every people starting from polytheism must make if their religion is to prosper.

New Religious Feeling; the Mysteries.—But the conscience as well as the mind of Greece awakes at this period, and Greek religion becomes inspired with a deeper feeling. The simple objectivity of the Homeric spirit is gone in which man could frankly worship beings like himself and not very far above himself. God at this time is growing greater and more awful, and man, less certain of himself, is beginning to feel a new sense of mystery and of shortcoming. Whether it was due to the anxiety and depression felt in Greece during the century before the Persian wars, or to foreign influences, or mainly to the natural growth of the Greek mind itself, religious phenomena of a new kind now appear. Sacrifices are heard of, which are not merely social reunions with the deity, but are intended to expiate some guilt or to remove some pollution. The sense of sin has arisen, which the Homeric world knows not, and gives a new colour to man's converse with the deity. Another new feature is the rise into prominence of cults in which man feels himself taken possession of and inspired by his god. Some of these belonged to Asia Minor, the great centre of worships accompanied with ecstasy and frenzy, but some were of native growth. In these the common man found a satisfaction which the stately ceremonial of the temples did not afford. The official religion had grown cold and distant; but in the worship of Demeter or Dionysus, as afterwards of the Phrygian Cybele, the "Great Mother" whom the Romans imported, the least educated could feel the joy of enthusiasm and of self-forgetting under the influence of the god, and could be closely identified with the object of worship by performing acts in which the experience of the god was symbolically repeated.

The rapid rise of the worships of Demeter and Dionysus thus furnishes an instance of the law that a religion of intellect and of art is apt to be confronted, even when it appears to have overcome all obstacles, by a religion of feeling, in which all the fair progress that was made appears to be entirely set at naught. When the worship of Zeus, Apollo, and Athene was coming to its highest splendour, these cults began to spread rapidly. They were originally peasant rites of unknown antiquity in Attica and Bœotia, in which, after the manner of rustic festivals, the coming of spring or the dying of the year were celebrated amid jest and song, and with certain prescribed actions in which the fortune of the god, corresponding to the season, was dramatically set forth. In spring Demeter, the mother goddess, received her daughter Persephone, who had left her for the winter; or in autumn Dionysus, the god of vegetation, was defeated by his enemies and driven away or torn in pieces. These worships, when developed and forming a prominent part of Greek religion, were called "mysteries," not because the knowledge of them was confined to few, but because some parts of them were transacted in deep silence, and were the objects of such awe and reverence that they were not spoken of. No one, moreover, could assist at these rites without being solemnly initiated after a period of probation and purification. Of the Eleusinian mysteries at least, which were the most widely diffused and which formed part of the state religion of Athens, ancient writers agree in their report that the course of training before admission was powerfully elevating and solemnising, so that the period of initiation was the highest point of the religious life. It was a condition that the candidate should be pure in heart and not conscious of any crime. There was apparently no doctrinal instruction ; everything was to be inferred from the spectacle. The mind was kept in a state of intense and devout expectation, knowledge and insight growing, it was held, as the time of admission came near. Before the final act there came a period of fasting, then a march from Athens to Eleusis along the sacred way, which was studded with shrines ; then a search for the lost goddess in the dark of a moonless night on the plains of Eleusis, and then at last admission to the brightly-lighted building. Here all the arts were enlisted to furnish a spectacle of unparalleled magnificence, during which the candidate was allowed to touch and kiss certain sacred objects of a simple nature, and repeated a solemn formula at his admission.

By partaking in these rites a man was believed to part with his former sins, to form a special union with the deity, in whose nature he was made to partake, and to be started on a career in which he could not fail to grow morally better. It is easy to see the immense superiority of this worship to the official rites of the temples. The great point is that a new principle of religious association is here introduced. The tie which binds the worshipper to his god and to his fellow-worshippers is no longer that of blood or of common political interests, but the higher one of a common spiritual experience. All Greeks were eligible for initiation at Eleusis. A man was not born into this circle, but entered it of his own free will and by means of voluntary effort and self-denial. A community of a higher order thus makes its appearance in Greek history, in which the limits of race and of locality are overstepped, and each is connected with the rest, because all have turned of their own voluntary motion to the same ideal centre. The analogies between the community formed on the mysteries and the Christian Church are too obvious to need to be insisted on. The adversaries of Christianity asserted that in the mysteries all the truths and the whole morality of that religion were to be found.

Religion and Philosophy.—But while the mysteries met to some extent the craving for a closer union with deity, another need which had long been growing in the Greek mind was to be satisfied in a very different manner. The Greek religion we have described had very little to offer in the way of doctrine. There are no sacred books in it, there is no theology, there is no religious instruction. When the mind of Greece awoke to intellectual life, and the demand was made for an explanation of the world, and for a view of the origin of things which should explain man to himself, the Greek religion was manifestly little fitted to meet such a demand. But man has everywhere looked to religion to do him this service, and a religion which is incapable of rendering it, or which like Buddhism explicitly refuses to take up the task, stands in a perilous position. If the shrine has no doctrine enabling man to understand the origin and the connection of things, he will seek such a doctrine elsewhere, and religion will have no control over it. Another alternative is that of Buddhism where in default of such a doctrine man is condemned to subside into intellectual apathy.

This, however, could never be the case with the Greeks, and their fate in this respect proved different from that of any other people. After their intellectual awakening took place, and when they had begun to seek in every direction for a first principle of all things, never doubting that the world was a system of reason, but trying one key after another to unlock its secret, we find that religion itself became aware of the need of the times, and that the attempt was made, late in the day but with deep earnestness and great ability, to construct out of the myths a reasoned account of the origin of things. This was the aim of the Orphic poets. Orpheus, the mythical singer of Thrace, who charmed men and beasts with his songs on earth, had descended into Hades to fetch back his wife, who had been taken from him, and had beheld the secrets of the underworld. The school which was named after him dealt with the deepest problems, and sought to explain both the nature of the gods and the destiny of the human soul. It insisted strongly on the power and sole headship of Zeus, in whom Greek religion had possessed from Homer downwards a figure fitted for a monotheistic position. "Zeus is the head, Zeus the middle, from Zeus are all things made. He is male and female, he is the foundation of the earth and of the starry heaven, the breath in all, the strength of fire, the root of the sea, sun, and moon. Zeus is the king, the progenitor of all things." The god Dionysus also is placed by the Orphic writers at the head of the whole process of creation. The myth of his dismemberment and of the scattering of his ashes over the whole world is made to symbolise the great thought of the connection of all things with the same source of life. Descriptions were also given, answering to the growing sense of personal responsibility, of the abodes of Hades and of the fate of souls there, and of the metempsychoses through which the soul must pass. This teaching had an influence which it is difficult to measure; it acted on the tragedians in their magnificent attempts to reform the beliefs of their country by making them moral; it is to be traced in Plato, it also found expression in the mysteries. In its own development it gave rise to a new phenomenon in Greek religion, that of itinerant preachers who went about appealing to individuals to take thought for the salvation of their souls, and also, strange to say, offering private charms and spells to put them on the right way of salvation.

But Greek religion was not thus to be reformed. It was not from the priests that the growth of the higher faith of Greece was to proceed, but from the philosophers. While much of the teaching of the philosophers was apparently negative and destructive of faith,—for Greece had her religious sceptics who turned the shafts of ridicule on existing beliefs, her Agnostics who considered that nothing certain could be affirmed about the gods, and even her secularists who held religion to be a mere invention of priests and rulers for their own purposes,—the course of Greek philosophy was, on the whole, constructive, even in matters of faith, and laboured to provide religion with a stable foundation in thought. In this great movement of the human mind the thinkers of Greece—Socrates, Plato, Aristotle, to name no more—were working at the same problem which occupied the prophets of Israel, and building up the rule of one God, a Being supremely wise and good, source of all beauty, and the worker of all that is wrought in the universe, in place of the many fickle and weak deities who formerly bore sway. In many ways the schools of Greece were the forerunners of Christianity. As the Jews, carried far from their temple, form a new principle of religious association and learn to meet for the service of God, without any sacrifice, in pious mental exercises, so the Greeks, for whom their temples could do so little, form little communities of earnest seekers after truth under some teacher. The philosopher's discourse is held by students of the early Christianity of the West, to be the model on which the Christian sermon was formed. Some of the schools even developed a true pastoral activity, exercising an oversight of their members, and seeking to mould their moral life and habits according to the dictates of true wisdom.

Thus there arose on Greek soil, after the temples had grown cold, what may truly be called a second Greek religion. It took possession of the Roman world, and was, when Christianity appeared, the prevailing form of religion among the more educated. Both in its outward forms of association, in its doctrine of God, which went through later developments very similar to those of Judaism, and in its concentration of thought on ethical problems and on the moral life of the individual, it powerfully prepared for Christianity. It was not a religion, for it had neither any historical root nor any belief and practice definite enough for the guidance of the common people. Yet Christianity could not have conquered the world without it.

Books Recommended

E. Meyer, *Geschichte des Alterthums*, vol. ii., contains the first attempt to deal with Greek religion in the manner now required.

The Histories of Greece of Grote, Curtius, Abbott, and Holm.

Roscher, *Lexikon der griechischen, a Römischen Mythologie.*

Dyer, *The Gods of Greece.*

Gardner and Jevons, *Manual of Greek Antiquities*, 1895.

L. R. Farnell, *The Cults of the Greek States*, 1896-1907.

Nägelsbach, *die Homerische Theologie.*

Williamowitz, *Homerische Untersuchungen.*

G. Anrich, *das Antike Mysterienwesen.*

Rohde, *Psyche*, 1891.

L. Campbell's Gifford Lectures on *Religion in Greek Literature*, 1898.

E. Caird, *The Evolution of Theology in the Greek Philosophers*, 1904.

Holwerda, in De la Saussaye, Third Edition.

Ramsay on "Religion of Greece and Asia Minor" in Hastings' *Bible Dictionary.*

CHAPTER XVII

THE RELIGION OF ROME

THE Romans themselves at a certain period in their history identified their own gods with those of Greece, and borrowed largely both from Greek ritual and Greek mythology, so that they came to the conclusion that the Roman and the Greek religions were essentially the same. To the early Christian writers the religions of Greece and Rome form one system; and the world has retained the impression that there was one old pagan religion which assumed certain local differences in the two countries, but was substantially the same in both.

Roman Religion was different from Greek.—Now the fact is that while Greek religion conquered Rome, Italy had an older religion of its own, which was not annihilated by the more brilliant newcomer, but remained beside it and never entered into entire fusion with it. The Romans were not a thinking so much as an organising race; in politics they were far ahead of the rest of the world, but in thought and imagination they were children; and so it happened that they borrowed ideas and usages from neighbours on this side and on that, and organised the whole into a system they could use, the organism being their own, but only little of the contents.

We must therefore inquire, in the first place, as to the religion the Romans had before they came under the influence of Greek ideas. Their earliest religion is to be traced in the calendar of their sacred year, in the lists of gods preserved for us in the writings of the fathers, and in numberless usages and institutions descended from early times.

The sacred year of early Rome is that of an agricultural community. The festivals have to do with sowing and reaping and storing corn, with vintage, with flocks and herds, with wolves, with spirits of the woods, with boundaries, with fountains, with changes of the sun and of the moon. There are festivals of domestic life, of the household fire, and of the spirits of the storeroom, of the spirits of the departed, and of the household ghosts. There are also festivals connected with warlike matters, some connected with the river and the harbour at its mouth, and some having to do with the arts of a simple population. The calendar, taken by itself, would create the impression that the community using it began with agriculture and added to it afterwards various other activities; there is nothing in it to contradict the supposition that Roman religion had its beginnings in the fields and in the woods.

The earliest gods of Rome also agree with this. They are, however, a very peculiar set of gods. Leaving the great gods in the meantime, we notice two of the agricultural deities; there is a **Saturnus,** god of sowing, and a **Terminus,** god of boundaries. These are what are called functional deities, such as we met with in Greece, p. 272 *sq.*; they take their name from the act or province over which they preside. Saturnus means one who has to do with sowing; Terminus is a boundary pure and simple. The god then, in these examples, is not a great being who has come to have these functions placed under him as well as others. He and the particular function belong together; he owes all his deity to it. Now these are only examples; the same is found to be the case with all or nearly all the distinctively Roman gods; they are, broadly speaking, all functional beings. Each bears the name of an object or a process; and on the other hand there is no object and no act which has not its god. It is astounding to observe how far the principle of the division of labour is carried among these beings. **Silvanus** is the god of the wood, **Lympha** of the stream, each wood and each stream having its own Silvanus or Lympha. Seia has to do with the corn before it sprouts, Segetia with corn when shot up, Tutilina with corn stored in the granary, Nodotus has for his care the knots in the straw. There is a god Door, a goddess Hinge, a god Threshold. Each act in opening infancy has its god or goddess. The child has Cunina when lying in the cradle, Statina when he stands, Edula when he eats, Locutius when he begins to speak, Adeona when he makes for his mother, Abeona when he leaves her; forty-three such gods of childhood have been counted. Pilumnus, god of the pestle, and Diverra, goddess of the broom, may close our small sample of the limitless crowd.

It is usually said about these multitudinous petty deities that the Roman was very religious, and saw in every act and everything for which he had a name, something mysterious and supernatural. The Greek, it is said, sees things on his own level, and adds to them a god who is human; it is by the human spirit that he interprets them. The Roman, on the contrary, sees things as mysteries and fills them with gods who are not human. That is true; but the question to be asked about these Roman gods is, to what stage of religious development do they belong: do they prove a primitive or an advanced stage of religious thought? It has been observed that these names of gods are all epithets, or adjectives; and it has been supposed that there was originally a noun belonging to them, that they were all epithets of one great deity, or, as some are masculine and some feminine, of a great male and a great female deity. The noun fell out of use, it is supposed, but was still present to the mind of the Roman, and thus his regiments of divine names are not really designations of different persons, but titles of the same person, supposed to be present alike in all these numberless manifestations. But it is not easy to conceive how if primitive Italy had reached the conception of the unity of deity, that deity became so remarkably subdivided, nor how his own proper name and character were lost. It is much more natural to suppose that the petty gods of Rome were all the deities the early Latins had, and were worshipped for their own sake. They represent the stage of thought called Animism (see p. 39) when every part of nature is thought to have its spirit, and the number of invisible beings is liable to be multiplied indefinitely. While other Aryan races had passed beyond this stage when we first know them, and advanced to the belief in great gods ruling great provinces of nature, the Latins, whose mind was organising rather than productive, made this advance more slowly, and instead of making it organised the spiritual world of animism with a thoroughness nowhere else equalled.[1] They had, therefore, no gods properly so called, but only a host of spirits. Even the beings they possessed, who afterwards became great gods, were at first no more than functional spirits. **Janus**, afterwards one of the chief deities of Rome, is originally the "spirit of opening"; an abstraction capable of great multiplication; a Janus could be invoked for each act of that kind. **Vesta** is the spirit of the hearth; each household had its Vesta, both in early and in later times. **Juno** is not one but many: as each man had his genius, a spiritual self accompanying or guarding him, so each woman

[1] See on this Mr. Jevons's preface to Plutarch's *Romane Questions* (Nutt, 1892); which deserves to be published in a more accessible form.

had—not her genius, but her Juno. There were many Vestas, many Junos; and it is only later that the great goddess arises, who may be looked to from every quarter. Others of the great gods of later Rome have a similar early history. **Mars** was at first the spirit which made the corn grow; **Diana** was a tree-spirit, **Jovis** or Diovis himself, though his name connects him with the Greek Zeus and the Sanscrit Dyaus, and though he is afterwards, like these, the god of the sky, was originally in Latin a spirit of wine, and was worshipped, the Jovis of each village or each farm, at the wine-feast in April when the first cask was broached. Thus the gods of the Latins are not beings who have an independent existence and features of their own; they are limited each to the particular object or process from which he derives his character, and have no realm beyond it. And the same is true of the family and house-gods, whose worship formed perhaps the principal part of the working religion of the Roman. The **Lares** represent the departed ancestors of the family; they dwell near the spot in the house where they were buried, and still preside over the household as they did in life. They are worshipped daily with prayers and offerings of food and drink; the family adore in them not so much the dead individuals, though their masks hang on the wall, as the abstraction of its own family continuity. The **Penates** or spirits of the store-chamber are worshipped along with the Lares, they represent the continuity of the family fortune. A more general name for the departed is the **Manes**, the kind ones; they are thought of as living below the earth; it is not individuals who are worshipped at their festivals, but the dead in the abstract, the former upholders of the family or of the people.

The character of **Roman worship** is determined by the nature of its objects. As each of the gods has his basis in a material object or action, there can be no need of any images of them; where the object or the act is, there is the god, his character is expressed in it and not to be expressed otherwise. Nor could such gods require any temples. And what need of priests for them, when every one who knew their names (a great deal depended on that) could place himself in contact with them as soon as he saw the object or took in hand the action behind which they stood? Nor can many stories be told about gods like these,—the Romans have no mythology. The beings they worship are not persons but abstractions. They have just enough character to be male or female, but they cannot move about or act independently of their natural basis; they cannot marry, nor breed scandal, nor make war. Nor can there be any motive for identifying with such beings a great man who has died; where there are no true gods, there cannot be any demi-gods or heroes. Only a very limited power can possibly be put forth by such beings; all they can do is to give or to withhold prosperity, each in the narrow section of affairs he has to do with.

The aim of worship where such a set of beings is concerned, is to get hold of the spirit or god connected with the act one has in view, and so to deal with him as to avert his disfavour, which the Roman always apprehended, and gain his concurrence. The house-gods are beings possessing a stated cult, but outside the house-cult the worshipper has to face the question at each emergency which god he ought to address. He might choose the wrong one, which would make his act of worship vain. If he names the god correctly he will have a hold on him; in a case of uncertainty, therefore, he names a number of gods, in the hope that one of them will be the right one; or he invokes them all. "Whether thou be god or goddess" he will further say, if he is in doubt on that point, "or by whatever name thou desirest to be called." Each god has his proper style and title, and it is vain to approach him without these; lists of the various gods and of their correct styles were therefore drawn up in very early times to serve as guides to the subject. The Latin word "indigito," to point out, from "digitus" a finger, is the term used of addressing a god; the lists of deities with their proper appellations were called "indigitamenta"; and the gods named in them "Dii indigetes." The act of worship is grave and formal; it has to be done with precision and in strict accordance with the rules; silence is commanded; the sacrificer repeats the prayer proper for the occasion after some one who knows it by rote; the worshippers veil their heads. In this the Roman ritual is markedly different from the Greek. Mommsen says the Greek prayed bare-headed, because his prayer was contemplation, looking at and to the gods; and the Roman with head covered, because his prayer was an exercise of thought; and in this he sees a characteristic indication of the difference between the two religions. A more modern interpretation of the Roman practice is that it arose from the fear that the worshipper might see the god whom he has just summoned by name, which would be dangerous. If any mistake is made in worship, the act is vain and has to be done over again.

The Great Gods.—The foregoing is the logic of the system on which the Roman religion, as distinguished from the foreign elements afterwards added to it, was based; the religion, however, does not come into view historically till it has begun to rise above such a worship of abstractions or of petty spirits, towards a worship of gods. It was apparently by the growth of larger social organisms that the Latin tribes advanced to the worship of greater gods. While the family religions continued to the end, the tribe had, as in the case of other early peoples, a larger religion than the family, and a union of tribes produced a religion on a still greater scale. The history of early Rome consists of a succession of such fusions of tribes into a larger political whole. When history opens, "Rome is a fully-formed and united city"; but Rome is made up of several tribes, which maintain many separate institutions. The religion of after times bears witness to these successive unions. "Deus Fidius" the god of good faith, is the sacred impersonation of an alliance. **Mars** and **Quirinus** are precisely similar to each other, and each has a flamen, or blower of the sacrificial flame, and a staff of twelve salii or dancers. Mars is the Roman, Quirinus the Sabine deity; and we see that the two tribes had, before they were united, very similar worships, which were both kept up after the union. The feriae Latinae, or Latin festival, celebrated on Mons Albanus, is common to the Latin tribes and commemorates their union. Jovis rises into importance with the growth of city life; he comes to be called father Jovis, Jupiter; there are many Jupiters but the **Jupiter** of the city of Rome is the greatest and best of all; he bears the title of **Optimus Maximus.** He rises above Mars, in earlier times the first Roman god, after whom the first month of the year was called, before the month of Janus and the month of Februus, the purifier, were added to it. Janus, the great state-god of opening, was the only one of whom there was a representation; Mars was represented symbolically by a spear, but Janus was figured as a man with two faces. Vesta, the hearth-goddess of the state, was of course a great deity with a very important worship.

Here we must mention a side of Roman religion which no doubt has its roots far back in prehistoric darkness, but which could scarcely be organised as we find it till the greater gods had risen to some degree of power. It was believed that the gods were constantly making signs to men, especially in occurrences which take place in the air, such as thunder and lightning, and the flight of birds, but also in many other ways. Some of the signs were simple, so that any one could tell if they were lucky or the reverse, but some were not to be interpreted except by men possessing a special knowledge of the subject. And such men might be asked by an individual or by the state when about to enter on any undertaking, to seek a sign from heaven concerning that business. This became with the Romans a great and important act, and those who had it in their hands exercised great power.

Sacred Persons.—The priest in the earliest times was, in the domestic religion, the pater-familias, in that of the tribe, which was but an extended household, the head of the leading family, and in the city, which was constituted after the same model, the king. Religion was the principal part of the service of the state; the king as such had to offer sacrifice, to cause the gods to be consulted, to prosecute and judge and punish those who had violated the laws and came under the anger of the gods. But as the state grew larger, various offices were set up to relieve the king of part of these duties; when new worships were added to the old ones, the care of them was in some cases committed to a special person or college; and these priesthoods and sacred guilds of early Rome maintained their place in the constitution for many centuries, and carried on this part of the public service long after the words they spoke and the acts they did had become meaningless. Beginning with the sacred persons attached to special cults, we have, first, three flamens, one of Mars, one of Quirinus, and one of Jovis (fl. Martialis, Quirinalis, Dialis). Mars and Quirinus have their dancers, as we mentioned above. Other flamens of lower rank were afterwards instituted for the separate worships of the tribes. Very old are the "fratres arvales," field-brothers, who served the creative goddess (Dea Dia) in the country in the month of May, with a view to a good growing summer, dancing to her and addressing hymns to her which may be read now but cannot be understood, and were unintelligible to the Romans themselves. The Luperci (wolf-men) held a shepherd's festival in the month of February, sacrificing goats and dogs to some rustic deity, and running naked through the streets afterwards, striking those they met with thongs cut from the hides of the victims. The six vestal virgins are well known, who had charge of keeping up the fire of Vesta, the house-fire of the state. They devoted their whole lives to this office, and enjoyed great respect. These priesthoods and corporations, instituted to secure the continuance of special cults, are not of a nature to foster a priestly type of religion. Nor were those other religious offices of a nature to do so, which were not attached to special cults but served the more general purpose of assisting and advising the state in matters connected with religion. First among these comes the office of pontifex, a word which is variously interpreted, either as "bridge-maker,"—that being a very important and solemn proceeding,—or as leader in a religious procession. There were originally five pontifices, and the number was afterwards raised to fifteen. They exercised a great variety of functions, and had a general oversight of all religious matters, both public and domestic. They were experts in ritual and in canon law; they advised the state as to the proper sacrifices to be offered for the public, and, when consulted, would also direct the private individual. Funerals, marriages, and other domestic occurrences into which religious considerations entered, were under their charge; and on the occurrence of portents and omens it was their duty to indicate the steps to be taken in order to find out what the gods wished to signify. They had charge of the calendar, and had to fix what days were proper for carrying on the business of the courts (*dies fasti*), and they were the authorities on the forms of legal process. The chief pontiff is called the "judge and arbiter of things divine and human," and the college had manifestly a very strong position. The same is true of the *augurs* or experts in signs and omens. Though they did not consult the gods about public undertakings until the magistrate or the general asked them to do so, they had power to stop proceedings of which they disapproved; and this at certain periods of Roman history they very frequently did. In Cicero's treatise on Divination a great deal of interesting matter may be found on this subject. Another sacred college of somewhat later date is that of the men, at first three in number, afterwards fifteen, who acted as expounders of the sacred Sibylline books, which King Tarquin purchased from the old woman or Sibyl, of Cumae.

Roman Religion Legal rather than Priestly.—While some of these priestly colleges exercised large powers, these powers were always regarded not as inherent but deputed. The sacred offices were not hereditary but elective; no course of training was necessary to qualify for them; men were chosen for them by the state as for any other public office, and those who became priests did not cease to be citizens but continued to sit in the Senate, and, as it might happen, to hold other offices at the same time. The growth of a priestly caste was thus effectively prevented; religion was precluded from having any free development of its own, and kept in the position of an instrument for the furtherance of ends of state. There is no great religion in which ritual is so much, doctrine and enthusiasm so little. All these priests and colleges exist for no end but to carry out with strict exactitude the ritual usage which is deemed necessary to keep on good terms with the gods. They have no doctrine to teach, no fervour to communicate, they do not even tell any stories. Punctiliousness and anxiety attend all their proceedings. To the Roman, Ihne says, "religion turns out to be the fear lest the gods should punish them for neglect; any unusual occurrence may be a sign that the gods are withdrawing their co-operation from the state, and this must be looked into, and the due expiations used if judged necessary." Ritual must always be carried out with the utmost precision; it is not the goodwill of the worshipper but his exactitude that counts. He may even cheat the gods of their due if he is formally correct in his observance. For example, if the auspices (the signs derived from birds) were unfavourable, they could be repeated till a better result was obtained.

What we have described is the religion of Rome in its original form, before it accepted foreign modifications. Its gods are spirits of the woods and fields, of the market, of the foray, of the treaty, of all the aspects, in fact, which life had borne to the tribes of Central Italy, especially to the Latins and the Sabines who combined to form the state of Rome. These gods form no family and have no history, they do not, like the gods of Greece, lay hold of the imagination, nor, like those of Germany, of the affections. They are only dimly known; but they are powerful, and it is necessary to reckon with them; and the only relations which can be kept up with such beings are those of business and of law. It follows that this religion is one of constraint and not of inspiration. In this it agrees with the Roman character, which is much more inclined to order than to freedom, to law than to art. The word religion has here its origin; its primary meaning is restraint or check, since the chief feeling with which the Roman regarded his gods was that of anxiety. Not that the gods were bad; Vediovis, the bad counterpart of Jovis, is a vanishing figure,—but they were ill-known, and might have cause to be angry. Worship, therefore, the practical cultivation of the friendship of the gods, swallows up here the other elements of religion as a whole. Religion does not free the forces of human nature to realise themselves in spontaneous activity, but enchains them to the punctilious service of a non-human authority. Everything exciting is kept at a distance, and men are trained in obedience and scrupulousness and self-denial. They produce no beautiful works of art, and have hardly any stories to delight in; but they are reverent and conscientious; private feeling is sacrificed with an austere satisfaction to the public interest, and they accordingly build up a great power. Living in an atmosphere of magic, where unseen dangers lurk on every side, and there is virtue in words and forms correctly used to avert these dangers, the Roman develops to perfection one side of religion. To its inspirations and enthusiasms and hidden consolation he is a stranger; but he knows it better than others as a conservative and regulating force, which checks passion, calls for wary and orderly conduct, and causes the individual to subordinate himself to the community.

Changes introduced from without. — The Roman religion had, properly speaking, no development. What it might have become had it been left to unfold itself without interference from without, we can only guess; but it was early brought under the influence of more highly developed religions, and it proved to have so little power of resisting innovations that it speedily parted with much of its own native character. The Romans were not unconscious that their religion was an imperfect one; they never claimed, when they were conquering the world, that their religion was the only true one, or had any mission to prevail over others. They were tolerant from the first of the religions of other peoples. The gods of other peoples they always believed to be real beings, with whom it was well for them also to be on good terms. If everything in the world had its spirit, these gods also were the spirits of their own countries and nations; the very notion of deity which the Romans entertained prevented them from having any exclusive belief in their own gods and from denying the right of the gods of others.[1] When therefore they came in contact with foreign religions, they were not protected by any profound conviction of the truth of their own, and were exposed to the full force of the new ideas. The new religions came to them along with the culture of peoples much further advanced in art and in thought than they were themselves; at each such contact, therefore, they felt the foreigner to be superior to themselves in intellectual matters; and wherever this happens the less highly gifted race is likely to change in its religion as well as in other things. We have to note the changes which were produced by such external influences.

In the first place, Rome borrowed from **Etruria.** Etruscan religion was both more developed and more savage than that of Rome. Human sacrifice was an acknowledged feature of it; divination was carried to absurd lengths, one great branch of it consisting in the prediction of the future from the appearance of the entrails of slaughtered animals. Etruria had a hell with regular torments for the departed; in Rome the belief in a future life was much less definite. On the other hand, Etruria had deities who were something more than abstractions; there was a circle of twelve gods, who held meetings on high, and regulated the affairs of the world. Above them was a power, little defined, to which the gods were subject, a kind of fate. Greek influence, so notably apparent in Etruscan art, is present, too, we see, in Etruscan religion; it is through this somewhat dark passage that Greek religious ideas first came to Rome. Under this influence

[1] Cf. Celsus in Origen, *Contra Celsum*, vii. 68.

various innovations took place at Rome. Before the end of the monarchy the Romans had begun to build houses for their gods, after being for 170 years, we are told, without any such arrangement. The Roman "templum" was not originally a building, but a space marked off, according to the rules of augury, for the observation of signs. A part of the sky was also marked off for such "observation" and "contemplation." On such a holy site, on the Capitoline hill, there was founded by the earlier Tarquin the temple of Jupiter which always continued to be the principal site of Roman religion. Its architecture was Tuscan; and it contained not only a cella or holy place for the image of Jupiter Optimus Maximus, but also a cella for Juno and one for Minerva. The latter was both an Etruscan and a Roman deity, the goddess of memory. Art was thus enlisted in the service of the gods; the divine figures acquired a reality and distinctness quite wanting to the earlier divine abstractions; and a new notion of deity was presented to the Roman mind. Other temples followed, to Jupiter under other names than that which he had in the Capitol, and to other deities. That of Faith was a very early one. It was a rule in temple-building that the image in the cella faced the west, so that the worshipper, praying towards it, faced the east. Here also the Roman custom is a departure from the Greek; for in Greek temples it is the rule that the image faces the east, and the worshipper the west. The Roman orientation of sacred buildings has passed into the practice of the Christian Church. From Etruria the Romans also derived a great addition to the rules of divination; but the more childish parts of Etruscan divination were regarded at Rome as superstitious, though private persons might frequently resort to them.

Greek Gods in Rome.—While Greek ideas thus came indirectly from the north, the south of the peninsula was becoming more and more Greek, and the gods and temples of Hellas, established first at the sea-ports and colonies, gradually came to Rome. This movement is connected with the Sibylline books which were acquired by the last of the kings. These books were brought to Rome from the Greek town of Cumae; they were written in Greek, and contained oracles which were ascribed to an old Greek prophetess. They were consulted in grave emergencies of state through the officials who had charge of them, and what they generally prescribed was that a god should be sent for from Greece, and his worship set up in Rome. Many foreign worships were thus imported. First came Apollo, disguised under the Latin name of Aperta, "opener," for the books contained many of his oracles; he was received and worshipped as a god of purification, since the state was in need of that process at the time, as well as of prophecy. In the year 496 B.C. came in the same way Demeter, Persephone, and Dionysus, identified with the old Latin Ceres, Libera, and Liber; and, a century later, Heracles, identified with the Latin Hercules. In the year 291, on the occurrence of a plague, Asclepios, in Latin Aesculapius, was brought from Epidauros; and when the crisis of the contest with Hannibal was at hand (204 B.C.) Cybele, the great mother of the gods, was fetched from Pessinus in Phrygia. The people of that town generously handed over to the Roman ambassadors the field-stone which was their image of the goddess, and her journey to Rome had the desired effect, in the expulsion of Hannibal from Italy. The Venus of Mount Eryx in Sicily arrived in Rome about the same time; a goddess combining the characters of Aphrodite and Astarte, and quite different from the simple old Roman Venus, who was a goddess of Spring, and presided over gardens.

The process, of which these are the outward landmarks, went on during the whole period of the Republic, and resulted in the substitution of what may be called with Mommsen the Græco-Roman, for the old Roman religion. The change was a very profound one. Not only were some new gods added to the old ones, not only did Greek art come to be employed in Roman temples, not only were new rites introduced, such as the *lectisternium*, in which couches were arranged, each with the image of a god and that of a goddess, and tables spread to regale the recumbent deities. The very notion of deity was changed; the Greek god, represented by an image in human form and moving freely in the upper world, was substituted for the Latin god who was the unseen side of an act or process or quality, from which he had his name, and apart from which he was not. The following is a list of the principal Roman gods and of the Greek ones with whom they were identified:—Jupiter (Zeus), Juno (Hera), Neptunus (Poseidon), Minerva (Athene), Mars (Ares), Venus (Aphrodite), Diana (Artemis), Vulcanus (Hephaestus), Vesta (Hestia), Mercurius (Hermes), Ceres (Demeter). The identifications are by no means accurate; Jupiter and Vesta, as we have seen, are the only two Roman gods who are really identical with Greek gods, the other equations are founded on accidental resemblances, and are more arbitrary than real. The result of them was, however, that the Romans forgot to a large extent their own gods, and got Greek ones instead. With the divine figures they took over the mythology of Greece, and thus the gods came to be well known with all their weaknesses, instead of as before surrounded with mystery and awe. The worship founded on the earlier conception of the deity, and kept up with unwavering regularity, was inapplicable to these new gods, and inevitably lost all its reality. This is not the only cause, but it is one of the chief causes which prepared for the fearful spectacle presented by Roman religion at the end of the Republic, when men of learning and distinction officiated as the heads of a religion in which they had no belief, and which they scoffed at in their writings.

Among the worships which came to Rome from the East there were several which are not of Greek, but of Oriental origin. The worship of Cybele belongs to Asia Minor, though it had spread over Greece; that of Dionysus also came to Greece from Asia. The practice of both these cults was accompanied by excitement and self-abandonment on the part of the worshippers; and they formed a great contrast to the staid and formal worship of the Romans, the only admissible passion in which was a calm passion for correctness. The worship of Cybele was carried on by eunuchs, it had noisy processions, and depended on begging for its support. When the Romans brought it to their city, they ordained that Roman citizens should not fill leading offices in it; but it flourished so strongly, among the numerous foreigners in the capital and among the poor, as to show that it met a great want there. The worship of Bacchus had to be suppressed by the state; it was carried on at nocturnal meetings, which even citizens attended, and it led to all kinds of irregularities. As the subject of this chapter is not the religions of Rome, but the Roman religion, we do not here review the numerous foreign worships which were brought to the capital from every part of the Empire, and made Rome, towards the close of the Republic, the residence of the gods of every nation. The Romans as we saw were not led by any convictions of their own to deny the truth of foreign religions; and their policy as rulers also inclined them to tolerate all worships which did not offend against civil order. In the provinces it was the rule not to interfere with local religion; at Rome the authorities recognised not the imported religion itself, of which the state did not feel called to judge, but the association practising it, which received permission to do so. The worship was then protected by the state—it became a *religio licita.* Amid the meeting of all the gods and the clashing of all the creeds which were thus brought about at Rome, the Roman religion itself maintained its place, not as a doctrine which any one believed, for the very priests and augurs laughed at the rites and ceremonies they carried on, but as a ritual which was bound up with the whole past history of Rome, and believed to be necessary for the welfare of the state as well as for the satisfaction of the common people. In the atmosphere of discussion and of far-reaching scepticism which then prevailed it was not to be expected that faith could again find any strong support in the historical religion of Rome. The Emperor Augustus made a serious attempt to reform and revive religion. He selected the domestic worship of the Lares as the most living part of the old system, and ordained that the two Lares should be worshipped along with the genius of the emperor, and that Rome should be divided into districts, each with its temple of this strange trinity; while in the provinces each district was to support a worship of Rome and of the Emperor in addition to its existing cults. Temples were rebuilt at Rome, new ones were raised, sacred offices were filled which had been vacant, religious games were instituted to carry the Roman mind back to the sacred past. Livy and Virgil treated the past from a religious point of view, showing the sacred mission of the Roman race, and exhibiting the valour and piety of the founders of the state. If the Roman religion could be revived these were the proper means to do it. But the religion of the future was not to be prepared in this way.

Books Recommended

The sections on religion in Mommsen's *History of Rome.*
Ramsay's *Roman Antiquities.*
Wissowa, *Religion und Cultur der Römer.*
Holwerda, in De la Saussaye.
For the period of the Empire, Boissier's *La Religion Romaine.*

CHAPTER XVIII

THE RELIGIONS OF INDIA

I. *The Vedic Religion*

NO contrast could well be greater than that between the German religion and that of India. In the one case we have a people full of vigour, but not yet civilised; in the other a people of high organisation and culture, but deficient in vigour; the former religion is one of action, the latter one of speculation. From the original Aryan faith, to which that of the Teutons most closely approximates, Indian religion is removed by two great steps. First we have as a variety of Aryan faith the Indo-Iranian religion, that of the undivided ancestors of Persians and Indians alike, in the dim period antecedent to the Aryan settlement of India. Of this religion, the common mother of those of Persia and of India, we shall give some sketch after we have made acquaintance with the gods of India, at the beginning of our Persian chapter. Indian religion is a variety of Indo-Iranian, which is a variety of the Aryan type. Neither its genealogy nor its character entitles it to be taken as a typical example of the Aryan religions. Chronologically it is the earliest of them, inasmuch as its books are the oldest sacred literature of Aryan faith; but in point of development it is not an early but an advanced product. The absorbing interest it offers to the student of our science is due to the fact that it presents in an unbroken sequence a growth of religious thought, which, beginning with simple conceptions and advancing to a great priestly ritual, can be seen to pass into mysticism and asceticism, and thence to the rejection of all gods and rites, and a system of salvation by individual good conduct. Nowhere else can the progress of religion through what we might call its seven ages of life be seen so clearly, nor the logical connection of these ages with each other be recognised so unmistakably. The present chapter deals with the infancy and lusty youth of the religion as seen in Vedism; the later stages of Brahmanism and Buddhism will be spoken of in subsequent chapters.

1. **The Rigveda.**—The Vedic religion takes its name from the Rigveda, the oldest portion of Indian literature, and the earliest literary document of Aryan religion. Of four vedas or collections of hymns, the Rigveda is the oldest and most interesting. It contains a set of hymns which, with much more of their early religious literature, the Hindus ascribed to direct divine revelation, but which we know to have been written by men who claimed no special inspiration. Most of them date from the time when the Aryans, having made good their entry in India, but without by any means altogether subduing the former inhabitants, were dwelling in the Punjaub. The religion of the hymns is a strongly national one. The Aryans appeal to their gods to help them against the races, afterwards driven to the south and to the sea coasts, who differ from themselves in colour, in physiognomy, in language, in manners, and in religion. Nor are these conquerors by any means an uncultivated people; they had long been using metals; they built houses,—a number together in a village; they lived principally by keeping cattle, but also by tillage, and by hunting. They drank Sura, a kind of brandy, and Soma, a kind of strong ale, of which we shall hear more. They

were, as a rule, monogamous, the wife occupying a high position in the household, and assisting her husband in offering the domestic sacrifice. At the head of each state was a king, as among the Greeks of Homer; he was not, however, an absolute monarch; his people met in council and controlled him. The king himself offered sacrifice for his tribe in his own house,—there were no temples,—but he was frequently assisted by a man or several men of special learning in such rites.

The hymns of the Rigveda were written for use at sacrifices. The sacrifice consists of food and drink of which the god who is addressed is invited to come and partake, or which are conveyed to the gods seated on their heavenly thrones, by means of fire. Soma, the intoxicating juice of the soma plant, is an invariable feature of the banquets in these hymns; the solid part consists of butter, milk, rice or cakes; but animals were also killed, and the horse-sacrifice was a specially important one. The hymn also is an essential part of the rite; the sacrifice would have no virtue without it. It consists of praise and prayer. The deity is extolled for the exploits he has done, for his strength, for his beauty, for his wisdom or his goodness, he is invoked again and again to partake of what has been provided for him, and in return he is asked to send the worshipper food or cows, guidance or protection, or whatever the latter is in want of.

The Vedic Gods.—And who are the gods who receive this worship? They are parts of nature or celestial phenomena, more or less personified. Worship is directed now to one divine being, now to another; each has a story which is dwelt on and a number of functions belonging to him, for the sake of which he is extolled and sought after; each god, that is to say, has his myth. In this set of gods the myths are so clear that we can identify with perfect confidence each of the gods with that part of Nature from which he arose.

M. Barth classifies the Vedic gods according to the degree in which they have become detached from their natural basis. There are two which are not so detached at all. **Agni**, who is one of the chief deities of the Rigveda, is fire, and **Soma**, the deity to whom all the hymns of the ninth book are addressed, is simply the juice of the soma-plant, the liquid part of every sacrifice. Agni is not any particular fire, but fire as a cosmic principle, born in heaven, born also daily at the sacrifice by the rubbing together of two pieces of wood, his parents whom he consumes. He is a priest carrying the offerings of men up to the gods, but he was a priest at the first sacrifice, the primeval heavenly sacrifice, before he had come down to men. He is also the guest and household friend of man, a kindly and familiar being. But he pervades all nature, and all growth and energy are due to him. Soma, also inseparably connected with all sacrifice, who strengthens the gods and makes them immortal, is likewise a universal principle; he too came at first from heaven, and he too is at work all through the world. There are stories of his first production among the gods, and of the first effects of his appearance; he is the nourisher of plants, he gives inspiration to the poet and fervour to prayer. Along with Agni he kindled the sun and the stars.

In other gods there is a nearer approach to a human figure, and the physical side is not so obtrusive. **Indra** is most frequently invoked of all the gods, and may be called the national god of this period. He is described as a chieftain standing in a chariot drawn by two horses. He waged a great battle, but still wages it constantly, against the monsters of heat and drought, Vrittra, the coverer, and Ahi the dragon, for the deliverance of the cows, the heavenly waters, kept by them in captivity. The contest between the god and the demon goes on for ever. Indra is also the giver of good things of every kind, he keeps the heavenly bodies in their places, he is the author and preserver of all life, the inspirer of all noble thoughts and the answerer of pious prayers, the rewarder of all who trust in him, and the forgiver of the penitent. It is good to sacrifice to him and to offer him soma in abundance; for it strengthens him to take up afresh his conflicts and labours as the champion of man. Indra is surrounded by the **Maruts**, the storm-gods, who are separately invoked in many hymns. They drive through the sky with splendour and with mighty music, and bring rain to the parched earth. Their father is **Rudra**, also a god of storms, the handsomest of all the gods, and, in spite of his thunderbolts, a helpful and kindly being. Wherever he sees evil done, he hurls his spear to smite the evil-doer, but he is also a healer of both physical and moral evils, and the best of all physicians. Of the same order of deities are **Vata** or **Vayu**, the wind, and **Parjanya**, the rain-storm. But the loftiest of all the Vedic gods is **Varuna**, the great serene luminous heaven. The hymns addressed to him are comparatively few, but among them are those which rise to the highest moral and religious level. In language recalling that of the psalmists and prophets of the Bible, they exalt Varuna as the creator of the world and of heaven and the stars, as the omniscient defender of the good and avenger of all evil, as just and holy, and yet full of compassion, so that the conscience-stricken suppliant is encouraged to turn to him.

We here give a few extracts from hymns addressed to some of the gods we have spoken of. The versions are those of Dr. John Muir. A metrical version can scarcely represent the hymns with the accuracy the scholar would desire, but, on the other hand, a literal translation such as that of Professor Max Müller in vol. xxxii. of the Sacred Books of the East, gives a less true idea of the spirit of the pieces, and is less fitted at least for a work like this.

To Indra

Thou, Indra oft of old hast quaffed
With keen delight, our Soma draught.
All gods delicious Soma love;
But thou, all other gods above.
Thy mother knew how well this juice
Was fitted for her infant's use,
Into a cup she crushed the sap
Which thou didst sip upon her lap;
Yes, Indra, on thy natal morn,
The very hour that thou wast born,
Thou didst those jovial tastes display,
Which still survive in strength to-day.
And once, thou prince of genial souls,
Men say thou drained'st thirty bowls.
To thee the Soma draughts proceed,
As streamlets to the lake they feed,
Or rivers to the ocean speed.
Our cup is foaming to the brim
With Soma pressed to sound of hymn.
Come, drink, thy utmost craving slake,
Like thirsty stag in forest lake,
Or bull that roams in arid waste,
And burns the cooling brook to taste.
Indulge thy taste, and quaff at will;
Drink, drink again, profusely swill.

Another to Indra

And thou dost view with special grace,
The fair complexioned Aryan race,
Who own the gods, their laws obey,
And pious homage duly pay.
Thou giv'st us horses, cattle, gold,
As thou didst give our sires of old.
Thou sweep'st away the dark-skinned brood,

Inhuman, lawless, senseless, rude,
Who know not Indra, hate his friends,
And spoil the race which he defends.
Chase far away, the robbers, chase,
Slay those barbarians black and base.
And save us, Indra, from the spite
Of sprites that haunt us in the night,
Our rites disturb by contact vile,
Our hallowed offerings defile.
Preserve us, friend, dispel our fears,
And let us live a hundred years.
And when our earthly course we've run,
And gained the region of the Sun,
Then let us live in ceaseless glee,
Sweet Soma quaffing there with thee.

To Agni

Great Agni, though thine essence be but one,
Thy forms are three; as fire thou blazest here,
As lightning flashest in the atmosphere,
In heaven thou flamest as the golden sun.

It was in heaven thou hadst thy primal birth,
But thence of yore a holy sage benign,
Conveyed thee down on human hearths to shine,
And thou abid'st a denizen of earth.

Sprung from the mystic pair by priestly hands,
In wedlock joined, forth flashes Agni bright;
But—O ye heaven and earth I tell you right—
The unnatural child devours the parent brands.

To Varuna

The mighty lord on high our deeds, as if at hand, espies;
The gods know all men do, though men would fain their acts disguise.
Whoever stands, whoever moves, or steals from place to place,

Or hides him in his secret cell,—the gods his movements trace.
Wherever two together plot, and deem they are alone
King Varuna is there, a third, and all their schemes are known.
This earth is his, to him belong those vast and boundless skies ;
Both seas within him rest, and yet in that small pool he lies.
Whoever far beyond the sky should think his way to wing,
He could not there elude the grasp of Varuna the king.
His spies, descending from the skies, glide all this world around,
Their thousand eyes all-scanning sweep to earth's remotest bound.
Whate'er exists in heaven and earth, whate'er beyond the skies,
Before the eyes of Varuna, the king, unfolded lies.
The ceaseless winkings all he counts of every mortal's eyes,
He wields this universal frame as gamester throws his dice.
Those knotted nooses which thou fling'st, O god, the bad to snare,
All liars let them overtake, but all the truthful spare.

Varuna, the all-embracing sky, is also in many hymns a solar deity. There are also other solar deities ; **Mitra** who is frequently invoked along with Varuna ; **Surya, Savitri, Vishnu,** and **Pushan,** are all gods of this class. Each of these has some attributes or some story of his own. Surya keeps his eye on men and reports their failings to Varuna and Mitra. Savitri, the quickener, raises all things from sleep in the morning with his long arms of gold, and covers them with sleep in the evening. Vishnu, the active, traverses the universe with three strides. Pushan is a shepherd who loses none of his flock ; a guide also, both in the journeys of this world and in the last journey. A number of the principal gods have the common title of **Adityas** or children of **Aditi,** immensity, a being too vast and undetermined to be clearly represented. We should also mention **Ushas,** the dawn, a goddess whom the sun-god is daily chasing ; the **Asvins** or two heavenly charioteers, who daily make the circuit of the heavens ; **Tvashtri,** the smith who made the thunderbolt of Indra ; the **Ribhus,** artificers who were once men and have been admitted to the society of the gods.

Yama is the god of the dead, he first traversed the road to the country beyond, and now he rules over it, and comforts with substantial joys the spirits guided there by Agni (this points to cremation which was frequent but not universal) or by Pushan. There the Pitris or fathers sit at the same tables with the gods, and are eternally happy. **Brahmanaspati,** lord of prayer, is a god of another type, a personification of the act of ritual, and his presence in the Vedas, beside the elemental deities, shows how early speculation had begun.

To what Stage does this Religion belong?—Our sketch of this system is necessarily brief; we have now to inquire as to the place it occupies in the religious growth of India. It is held, on the one hand, that it is a primitive religious product, that it shows us some of the very first efforts men made to have a religion; while on the other hand it is held that the Vedic hymns and the Vedic system are sacerdotal, and are due to an advanced organisation of worship and to a special set of men who were much in advance of their age.

1. **It is Primitive.**—Mr. Max Müller[1] says that "the sacred books of India offer the same advantages . . . for the study of the origin and growth of religion . . . which Sanscrit has offered for the study of the origin and growth of human speech." Dr. Muir[2] claims that the Vedic hymns illustrate the natural workings of the human mind in the period of its infancy. In the Vedas, these writers consider, we are able to watch the process by which the earliest men rose to the belief in gods, and the naïve and simple methods by which man's first intercourse with gods was carried on. The undoubted antiquity of these pieces favours this view; the Rigveda is admitted on all hands to be the earliest part of Indian literature, and many of the hymns were written

[1] *Origin of Religion*, p. 135. [2] *Sanscrit Texts*, vol. v. p. 4.

about 1500 B.C.[1] The pure and simple nature of the Vedic religion may also appear to favour this view. It is a religion singularly free from the lower elements of man's early faith. Savage legends and especially immoral stories of the gods are markedly absent from the hymns; they are also free from the element of magic and fetishism; the gods are great beings, and religion consists in intercourse with these great beings. Now the later religious literature of India, the brahmanas or commentaries on the Rigveda and the other, later Vedas, contain a variety of legends and a religion by no means free from magic. It may be maintained therefore that the pure religion of the Aryans afterwards became contaminated by contact with the lower religion of the tribes the Aryans had conquered. It was from the Dravidian and Kolarian aborigines, we are told, that Indian religion took its later corruptions. The Vedic religion has no idols, it has no dark descriptions of hell, the caste system on which later Brahmanism was based is absent from it, it has no demons to be guarded against, and no bad deities. The doctrine of metempsychosis is not found here, except perhaps in germ. The immolation of the widow on the funeral pile of her husband is not sanctioned by the Vedas, and of ancestor-worship only a few traces are found. All these, it may be held, are later corruptions. The Vedic religion is a bright and happy system, and the primitive beliefs of mankind, less changed by the Indians than they were elsewhere, are here to be seen; the hymns show the kind of faith to which a strong and happy race of men naturally came, as their minds began to open to the wonders of the world they lived in, the faith of "primitive shepherds praising their gods as they lead their flocks to the pasture." The Indians had preserved, longer than other peoples, the gift of recognising

[1] According to Mr. Max Müller the Mantra or hymn period is to be placed 1000-800 B.C.; but other scholars place it earlier.

deity in nature; and the primitive beliefs of mankind survive here in something like their first integrity, while elsewhere they were broken up and confused.

2. It is Advanced.—On the other hand, it is urged that the society in which the hymns arose was not a primitive one, but one considerably advanced both in arts and institutions. The Rishis (seers), who composed them, belonged to families who cultivated such an art; and the hymns were no artless outpourings of childlike emotion, but were written on an elaborate metrical system for a definite purpose, namely, to form part of great acts of worship. As for the absence from them of savage myths and of immoral stories of the gods, this fact does not prove that such things were not known to the people at the time, but only that the poets did not put them in their hymns. Mr. Lang has collected the savage myths, similar to those of other peoples in various parts of the world, which are found in Indian literature of a later date, and has also shown that the hymns themselves were not quite ignorant of some of them. The Indians knew the myth of the marriage of heaven and earth, with the consequent birth of the gods. They had the story of the deluge. They had the still more primitive story of the raising up of the earth from the bottom of the sea. They had various myths of old conflicts of the gods, and of the production of the earth and all the men in it from the dissection of an immense prototypal human monster. Men were of different castes, they held, because they came from different portions of Purusha's body when it was cut up. Many stories are to be found in Indian literature which when found elsewhere are judged to be products of savage imagination, and the fact that the Rigveda ignores some of them and refines others, simply shows that the authors of that collection were on a higher level than their people in point of cultivation and of piety, as the psalmists and the prophets of Israel were in advance of theirs. We are led, accordingly, towards the conclusion that during the period when the hymns were written those who took charge of the development of worship in India were seeking to draw away attention from the more superstitious and childish elements of religion, and to bring to the front the pure and lofty intercourse man could have with the good gods. Bad gods are not cultivated; if there are foolish stories about the gods, they are not repeated, everything dark and terrible, as well as everything irrational, is removed from the working religion. Ancestor-worship is not encouraged; family rites continued, but the worship was wider than the family, and was not restricted to particular places. The ideas connected with sacrifice are not indeed very lofty. Sacrifice is, in the first place, barter. Gifts are provided for the gods, that they may give in their turn. In the second place it is a social function in which the god and the worshipper both take part. The food, and especially the soma, strengthens the god, and man and god are thereby drawn into close sympathy. But in the third place sacrifice was a piece of magic. The mere accurate performance of the rite had a mystic efficacy. It was believed to help to uphold the order of the world; without it the gods would grow weak, the ordinances of nature would fail, and man would relapse to the state of savagery. The gods themselves first sacrificed; from sacrifice they themselves were born, so that sacrifice is an essential principle of the universe, was so in the beginning, and must always be so. The Vedic leaders of religion, therefore, were not merely champions of enlightenment in religion; they were also ritualists, the rite was to them an end in itself; the proper performance of sacrifice was their principal object. This side of their work had, as we shall see, grave consequences. But the Rigveda did a great work for India in cultivating gods who were moral, and to whom man was drawn by higher than selfish motives. Gods who are just and who watch man's conduct, and do not fail to reward him according to his deeds, must quicken the conscience of those who believe in them, and gods who are able to help the weak and to forgive the penitent must make their people also merciful. In all the aberrations of Indian religion the high moral standard set by the Vedic gods is never lost sight of.

Where a plurality of gods is believed in, these gods must stand in some relation to each other; and it is of importance to notice **how the gods of the Veda are arranged.** We can see here very clearly how unstable a thing polytheism is. The position of the gods is constantly changing with reference to each other. We find Agni addressed as if he were undoubtedly supreme; he dwells in the highest heavens, he generates the gods, he ordains the order of the universe; but then we find Indra spoken of in the same way, and Varuna, and Mitra, and others. Then we find pairs of gods addressed together. Indra and Agni are frequently so treated; so are Varuna and Mitra. There is no supreme god, or rather, each god is supreme in turn; the poet wants a god capable of being exalted in every way, and does so exalt the god he has before him. In this way a Monotheism is reached; the mind recognises a god to whom unlimited adoration can be paid. But it is a monotheism, as M. Barth well puts it, the titular god of which is always changing; and Mr. Max Müller gives to this partial monotheism the name of Kathenotheism; that is, the worship of one god at a time without any denial that other gods exist and are worthy of adoration. Now this form of religion, in which several gods are worshipped, each of whom in turn is regarded as supreme, is not peculiar to India; we have met with it already, we shall meet with it again. But in India a peculiar way was found out of the difficulty. The Indian gods were too little defined, too little personal, too much alike, to maintain their separate personalities with great tenacity; nor did they lend themselves to a monarchical form of pantheon; no one of them was sufficiently marked out from the rest or above the rest, to rule permanently over them. Yet the sense of unity in Indian religion is very strong; from the first the Indian mind is seeking a way to adjust the claims of the various gods, and view them all as one. An early idea which makes in this direction is that of **Rita**, the order, not specially connected with any one god, which rules both in the physical and the moral world, and with which all beings have to reckon. Philosophy is busy from the first with the Vedic gods; the impulse to good conduct and that to mysticism are equally innate in this religion. We can see, even in the Rigveda, that India is to solve the problem of its many gods not in the way of Monotheism, by making one god rule over the others, but in the way of Pantheism, by making all the gods modes or manifestations of one being. "Agni is all the Gods" we read here. And a religion which arranges its objects of worship in this way will not be a religion of action, but of speculation and of resignation.

Books Recommended

S. B. E. vol. xxxii. Vedic Hymns. xlvi. Hymns to Agni.

Muir's *Sanscrit Texts.*

M. Müller's *Hibbert Lectures.*

Monier Williams, *Indian Wisdom; Hinduism* in "Non-Christian Religious Systems" (S.P.C.K.)

Kaegi, *The Rigveda, the oldest literature of the Indians*, 1886.

Barth, *The Religions of India*, in Trübner's Oriental Series.

Herrmann Oldenberg, *Die Religion der Veda*, 1894.

Bergaigne, *La Religion Védique*, 3 vols., 1878-83.

E. Hardy, *Die Vedisch Brahmanische Periode der Religion des alten Indiens.*

Lehmann, in De la Saussaye.

CHAPTER XIX

INDIA

II. *Brahmanism*

THE period in which the songs were collected by the Aryans dwelling in the Punjaub was succeeded by a period of wars and troubles, after which the successful race is found to have spread further towards the East, and to have settled on the Ganges and its tributaries. Along with this change of position a great change has also taken place in the spirit of the people, a change which is strikingly seen in their religion. The priesthood has come to occupy the position of a separate class to an extent not formerly the case, and all the phenomena are apparent which are generally found associated with a hierocracy or rule of priests. The early religious writings have been formed into a sacred canon: there is an active production of new works which explain the old ones; the sacrifices grow more elaborate and new virtues are attributed to them; and along with this hardening and formalising of the outward parts of religion there is a religious speculation of great volume and of great freedom of character.

The Caste System: The Brahmans.—The key to the whole movement is to be found in the new position of the priesthood, or in the establishment at this period, of the system of caste. Though this system is only once mentioned in the Rigveda, and that in a hymn of late date, scholars find traces of it in the arrangement of the hymns, and as it is found in Persia, the Indians probably had it before they entered India. It may even, it is judged, be traceable to the division of ranks among the primitive Aryan families. Teutonic as well as Indian legends are found explaining how mankind were divided from the first into different classes. But the primitive differences of rank must have had a great development before they took shape in the rigid caste system of India. This system appears to be organised with a view expressly to the exaltation of the priesthood, and must have been the result of a struggle between the priests and the warrior or ruling classes. The priests have made themselves indispensable in nearly all religious acts. Their very title shows this. While *Brahman*, as the name of a god, means primarily growth, and later, devotion or prayer, *brahmana* (neut.) signifies the ritual texts according to which worship is performed, and *brahman* (mas.) is the name of those who use such texts, and comes to stand for the highest caste of Indian society. Without the brahman there can be no satisfactory worship, because there can be no security that any rite is performed correctly; and a rite which is not performed correctly has no efficacy. Religion, therefore, is in the hands of this caste, whose sacredness is hereditary, and cannot be acquired in any other way than by birth. The members of that caste and they alone are qualified to superintend religious observances, and without them the intercourse between man and the gods cannot be kept up. From his birth the Brahman is a being of superior holiness; he is destined for higher ends than other men, and the distinction between him and them must be manifested in all his acts and habits throughout his life. He is the natural lord of all the classes.

If the highest caste is strictly defined, so also are the others. The second caste is that of the **Kshatriyas**, warriors or rulers, the third that of the **Vaisyas** or farmers. These three have rank, they are the twice-born classes (their second birth answers to confirmation, and takes place when a young man is invested with the sacred thread). The **Sudras** are the fourth and lowest class; no duty is assigned to them in the law books but that of serving meekly the other castes. It has been thought that the Sudras represent the conquered aborigines, the three classes of rank belonging to the Aryan invaders, but this is open to question.

The student of religion has to fix his attention on the Brahmans, who have secured themselves in the position of the leading caste. We speak first of the literary movement in which they were concerned, then of the sacrifices they conducted, and of their gods. We shall then say something of the practical operation of their religion as a rule of life, and lastly we shall come to the speculative work of their period, which is not, however, to be set down to them alone.

1. **The Growth of the Sacred Literature.** — The Vedas rose in sacredness after the age which produced them passed away. A few centuries after they were written they were not generally intelligible; they needed interpretation, but at the same time the doctrine of their inspiration rose higher and higher. The brahmans had both to interpret the words of the old hymns and to explain how, when used at the sacrifice, they produced the effect ascribed to them. This led to the production of the earliest Indian prose, the brahmanas or ritual treatises. Primarily intended to be directories of worship for the priests, these works were enriched with all sorts of ideas about the sacrifices, their origin, and their effects; points in the ritual are explained in them by mythological stories which we should not otherwise know, and we see from them that many

superstitions, to which the Vedas gave no encouragement, yet lived among the people. Each Samhita, or collection of hymns, had its Brahmana, and some of the collections had several. These works, though transcending in dreariness most directories of worship, are yet of great value for the light they throw on the history of Indian manners and ideas, as well as on that of mythology. And as it happened among the Jews in their later period so it happened here ;—the sanctity of the text was extended to the commentary, the brahmana also was held to be god-given and inspired, and by some was even more highly esteemed than the hymns themselves. A third class of inspired writings consists of the Upanishads, or speculative treatises, of which we shall speak later. The "Veda" in the larger sense is made up of these three bodies of compositions mantras, brahmanas, and upanishads These three belong to revelation or "S'ruti," *i.e.* hearing ; what is contained in these is to be regarded as having been heard by inspired men from a higher source. The counterpart of Sruti is "smriti," *i.e.* recollection, tradition. This embraces the Sutras or works dealing with ceremonial in the way of short rules gathered from the older literature, with the exposition of the Vedas, with domestic rites and conventional usages. The law books, the epics, and the Puranas, or ancient legendary histories, also belong to this class.

The doctrine of the Vedas, of their sacredness and of their virtues, played a great part in Indian thought. They were revered not as a written word, for they were not written but handed down by memory,—the Brahman still knows his sacred literature by heart,—but as hymns possessing supernatural powers and of far higher than human origin. They were raised to the rank of a divinity, they were said to have had to do with the creation of the world, or to have been among the first created beings. The value of the study of them was not to be exaggerated; he who engages in it, we hear, offers a complete sacrifice, obtains for himself the world which does not pass away, and becomes united with Brahma. The class of men who had installed themselves as the authorised interpreters of the hymns, had evidently taken up a very strong position.

2. **Sacrifice.**—Indian ritual is an immense subject. In the Vedic period there were several orders of sacrifice—the hymns of the Rigveda have to do with the Soma-sacrifice alone—and several kinds of priests, and it stands to reason that an elaborate ritual derived from a distant age and cherished by a priestly caste which was growing in power, could not quickly change. In spite of the considerable amount of materials accessible in the Brahmanas and Sutras, a history of Indian sacrifice as a whole has still to be written.

It is characteristic of early Indian sacrifice that it is not confined to a temple or to any sacred spot, and that it does not require any image of the deity. Instructions are always given for choosing and preparing a place for the rite, and for erecting an altar; a place had to be prepared on each occasion. The gods were asked to come, or were thought to be seated in heaven looking on; the sacrifice is in the open air. While the celebration proceeded according to a certain ritual, it lay with the worshippers to fix to what god or gods the sacrifice should be addressed. There was not one ritual for Agni and another for Indra, but the same would serve for either or for both. The sacrifices of which we hear in the Brahmanas are domestic rites; they are offered by the heads of the household, who invite ancestors also to be present. A Brahman is present to direct those who sacrifice and the inferior priests who assist them, and the benefits of the act extended to all the dependants of the household. The time was determined by natural seasons or by household events. Some sacrifices were greater than others, the more elaborate ones requiring several days, months, or even years for their celebration. Among the kinds of offerings which might be made we find that of man enumerated; human sacrifice, however, if it had prevailed in earlier times, had now grown obsolete.

The rise of the Brahmans into a caste changed the character of the sacrifice by making its due celebration depend more on special knowledge, and by increasing its elaborate mystery. Once the hymn was recognised as an essential element of such an act, the person who could interpret the hymn and explain its effects acquired great importance. And when the explanation of all the various features of the sacrifice was once begun, a wide door was opened to minute ingenuity. It is astonishing to what trifles these priestly directories descend, what explanations are brought from every part of earth and heaven of the most trivial circumstances, and what sacredness is found in the very blades of grass around the altar. Now the effect of such a treatment of ritual is inevitably that the rite itself, the outward mechanical performance, comes to be regarded as important, and that the ethical and religious end which was originally aimed at, is lost sight of. The priest and those he acts for are so intent on the minutiæ of their celebration that they forget about the god it is intended for. And as they are quite convinced that the sacrifice, if offered with perfect correctness and with nothing left out, must produce its effect, the sacrifice itself comes to appear as the agent of the desired blessing; the god grows less but the sacrifice grows more. This process, which may be observed wherever ritualism exists, was carried in the period of Brahmanism to its utmost length. In this period the old gods lost the strong hold they had before over the people's mind; men ceased to look for their gods to the sky or to the tempest, and began to look instead to the long ceremonies of the priest or to the hymn he chanted at the altar, or to the austerities he practised. Gods of a new type now make their appearance. As in the Vedic period we saw that Brahmanaspati, lord of prayer, had a place beside Indra and Varuna, so now we see that the supreme deity is named **Brahma.** The prayer connected with the sacrifice has given its name to the ruler of the universe. Other names for the supreme are also found to be making their way to general use, as the old historical and mythological gods fall into the background, and an abstract divine unity is sought after. **Prajapati,** lord of creatures, who is little heard of in the hymns, is frequently invoked as the head of all the gods, and a triad of gods is heard of, consisting of Agni, Vayu, Surya, fire, the air, the sun, and summing up the divine energies. The attributes of the gods are personified, and a set of pale abstractions is thus added to the Pantheon ; and spirits and goblins not heard of in the hymns, though not therefore necessarily unknown in the former period, make their appearance. These are, perhaps, the gods of the aborigines, who thus revenge themselves, as the religion of the invaders which at first suppressed them loses its earlier vigour. The strong gods retire and weak gods, many and shadowy, and bad as well as good, are worshipped. The Asuras were formerly the gods generally, now they are evil beings with whom the good gods have to contend.

3. **Practical Life.**—We possess very complete pictures of Indian life and manners in the period of Brahmanism. Of the codes of ancient sages by which Hindu society was supposed to be governed many are extant to us ; and in Mr. Max Müller's *Sacred Books of the East* the English reader may make himself acquainted with several of these. The most famous and the longest, is the laws of Manu, a mythical

progenitor of mankind. In the form in which we have it this work dates probably from the second century A.D., but the body of the work is much older. Originally a local collection of rules, it extended its authority gradually over the entire Hindu population of India. With other collections, also of local origin, it represents to us the condition of Indian society after the caste system became fixed; but much of the law thus handed down to us must have had its origin in prehistoric times.

The law of Manu hinges on the superiority of the Brahman over the other castes. The Brahmans form the centre of the state and really control everything; but their life, in turn, is framed in strict rules, and their whole history and actions are laid down for them to the last detail from the moment of their birth. The life of the Brahman is divided into four periods. For a quarter of his life he was a student living with a teacher and learning from him the sacred knowledge of the Vedas. Every act of study begins with the so-called Savitri-verse, "Let us meditate on that excellent glory of the divine Vivifier. May he enlighten our understandings." This prayer, with the mystic syllable, Om (thought to have to do with the three gods of a triad, but probably the original meaning is Yes, an abstract all-embracing yes, in which nothing but pure being is affirmed) is repeated at every return to study, and also with great frequency at other times. The teacher is more to the student than his father, and is to be treated with the greatest deference and courtesy; these years are a training in gentle and seemly conduct as well as in law. His student days completed, the Brahman offers his first sacrifice, marries, and becomes a householder. Little is said of earning a living; the Brahman is not to be worldly, but he is to be independent if he can. He is, however, allowed to beg if in want. But more stress is laid on the continued pursuit of knowledge, and on the domestic sacrifices to gods and manes which are to be his daily care. After he has brought up a son to take charge of his house and goods, the third stage of his life is reached; he may retire from the world and become a recluse, giving himself to contemplation and austerities. The fourth stage is that of the ascetic, *bhikku* or *sannyasin*, the aged man who having given up all possessions, all human society, and the practice of all rites, and subsisting only on alms, seeks to purge his heart of all desire and to become united by deep meditation with the supreme soul, thus attaining union with Brahma and final liberation. In this section of the laws of Manu an ideal of moral perfection is set forth, which is not demanded at the earlier stages of life.

"*Let him not desire to die; let him not desire to live; let him wait for his time as a servant for the payment of his wages.*

"*Let him patiently bear hard words, let him not insult anybody, nor become anybody's enemy for the sake of this perishable body. Against an angry man let him not in return show anger; let him bless when he is cursed.*"

He is to be sedulously careful not to injure any living creature, he is to meditate on the supreme soul which is present in all organisms, both the highest and the lowest. He is to give up all attachments, and in this way, as his body decays, he enters even here into a state of perfect freedom and repose and union with the great spirit.

Such ideas prove that the mind of Brahmanism was not occupied with sacrifices alone. Manu speaks of the superintendence of sacrifices as only one of several careers which the Brahman might choose; and if he might with equal right devote himself to study or to self-discipline, we see that another side of religion than that directing itself to external gods or occupying itself with outward acts, was pressing itself forward. The inner world of the mind is growing larger as the outward gods grow shadowy; it is being found that salvation may be reached by inward efforts as well as by outward rites, that the search for wisdom and the work of self-conquest, and a union with the deity which is quite apart from any offering or from any form of worship, also lead to salvation. It is objected to the ethics of Manu that the ideal they set up is not an active but a suffering one; the ascetic is placed on a higher platform than the householder, men are encouraged to withdraw from the performance of their duties in the family and in society, and to devote themselves to an aim which, however lofty, is personal and, so far, selfish. It is certainly a weakness in the religion that it has no higher aim than this to set before its most eager minds. Apart from this, life is regulated in a way we cannot but admire. Amid the mass of trivialities and formalities in which every action is involved there breathes a grave humane and gentle spirit, and a sound practical morality, and the ordinary household of the Brahman may have been a scene of activity and cheerfulness. The Sudra, however, is spoken of everywhere as a being whose degradation can never be removed, and to touch whom is to be defiled. Those who belonged to no caste were in a still worse plight and lived in the greatest misery.

4 **Philosophy.**—We have seen how both in the ritual system they administered and in the ideal they formed of the highest good, the Brahmans were led forward from the old ground of the Vedic nature-worship to a more inward and subjective religious attitude. The exaltation of Brahma, the power of prayer, to be the supreme god, was an advance from an external deity to a deity both external and present in man's own experience; and the appearance of a new way of salvation, though only permitted at first to the world-weary ascetic, in which inner contemplation and absorption

could lead to the highest consummation of life, also showed that a new form of religion was at hand. In the philosophy of the Brahmanic period, the transition is made from the service of gods external to man, by the mechanism of rites, to the acknowledgment of a divine being with whom man feels himself to be inwardly akin and to whom he draws near by his own spiritual effort. In this movement, to which we learn that members of the lay aristocracy and even women of intellectual distinction made important contributions, and which may have appeared in its beginnings as a sceptical revolt against their own system, the Brahmans yet took part, and the works in which the record of it is contained became a part of revelation. The "Upanishads" or "communicated doctrines," form the third branch of the sacred knowledge, and much of this literature belongs to the period before Buddhism. These books are read still by the educated Hindu as part of scripture, and the philosophy of them is a part of his religion. We can only point out the principal terms and notions of that philosophy.

Seeking to escape from the confusion of many gods the Indian mind is looking out even from the Vedic period for some means to conceive of them all as one. In the earliest period each reigned in turn as the supreme; a god is supreme not because he is essentially the greatest of the gods, but because circumstances have brought him to the front. This is Henotheism. Then we have attempts to sum them all up in one expression. Prajapati, lord of creatures, Visvakarman, maker of all things, represent such attempts. Then we have as the supreme, Brahma, the power of prayer,[1] a being of a different character from all his predecessors. Brahma is an intellectual deity. He is a thinker, a knower, he is the "Mahan Atma" or great spirit, which sits in unbroken calm above the change and dis-

[1] On the etymology of Brahma see Mr. Max Müller's *Hibbert Lectures*, p. 366.

traction of the universe. In rendering Mahan Atma by great spirit, however, we are anticipating. Atma, originally breath or life, comes, afterwards, to mean the person, the self when all that is accidental is removed from it, the essential, innermost self. Now Brahma is the great self, the inmost essence of all things, which was before them, and is unaffected by their changes. But man also has an atma, a self; it may be very small and lodge in a part of the body where it cannot be detected, but it is there, and the small atma is the same as the great one. By what physiological doctrines this is upheld, cannot here be traced; but the notion of the atma, the great form of which in Brahma is identical with its small form in man, lies at the basis of Brahmanic thought.

In Brahma one god has been reached, but he has been reached by thinking away from him everything concrete. All predicates are unsuitable to him, as any predicate implies a limitation; he can only be described in negatives, or in questionable metaphors. He is meant to satisfy the religious craving for a being quite free from any imperfection and entirely supreme—and it is the penalty of this that he has no clear outline or character. And how indeed is he to be related to the world? This world of change and decay, of disappointment and sorrow, what has the perfect being to do with that? Did he make it, and is he responsible for it? The answer to this in Hindu thought is that the world is due to **Maya**, illusion. It was due to an aberration in Brahma, which is represented in various ways, that the transition was made from the one to the many, and this error has been productive of all that has been suffered on the earth. Or else it is held that it was not Brahma who became subject to illusion, but that the illusion resides in man's views and thoughts about the world; and if a man could free himself from the meshes of Maya by recognising that the world is an illusion, and that nothing exists but Brahma only, then he would have done something for his own emancipation, the Brahma in him would be free from illusion, and he would also have done something, though little, for the salvation of the world from its great error.

That the whole world-process is nothing but an illusion, a confused and troubled dream passing over the mind of Brahma, who himself alone is real, this is the cardinal doctrine of Brahmanism, from which Buddhism also, as we shall see, sets out. The world is really nothing but an apparent world; and the true wisdom, the only salvation consists in knowing this, and in living a life in accordance with that knowledge. The wise man should regard a world which he knows to be illusion, with complete indifference; it can do nothing to him, he can do nothing for it; it affects him only with an ineradicable regret that it exists at all, and with a longing for its disappearance. The practical outcome of the state of matters which he recognises is firstly negative, that he must not allow the world to influence him at all, and, secondly, positive, that he must strive to be united with Brahma. The negative task is performed by withdrawing the mind from all particular things, and letting it be filled with the general, the absolute alone; and similarly by forbidding the desires to fasten on any worldly objects, by extinguishing desire and ceasing to be affected in any way by worldly things. The positive task is performed by means of a mental process which we cannot here describe, but by which the mind returns to the self that is within and realises it as it is, cleared from all particular thoughts and affections. These exercises cannot be called moral; where all is illusion morality disappears. There is no good, no evil, no effort to promote the good and lessen the evil. It is not because the world is bad that it is condemned, but because it exists. The energy which in other faiths is devoted to a moral struggle, is here poured into the ascetic discipline by which the individual looks to escape altogether from the world as it is. There are no good works, what is good is to abstain from all works; there is no benevolence further than that the mind must be kept clear of all that confuses or degrades; the salvation of the individual alone is sought after; there is no desire to spread the light and save others, since few are capable of that knowledge of the illusive nature of all things by which alone salvation is possible.

This, it is plain, could never be a popular religion. Brahma, the abstract one, does not appeal to the imagination; he could not drive out the popular nature-gods with their definite myths and attributes. Nor could a religion spread among the people, which regarded the social and the domestic state as inferior, and could only be practised by one who had left his home and family. The hermits and ascetics, and begging monks may form the religious aristocracy; but a teaching of a different nature was necessary for the people. And we find, in fact, two religions prevailing in India in the period of Brahmanism; that which we have described, for the enlightened who escapes in it from all law, all creed, all ritual, whose whole religion more than any other which ever flourished in the world is within the mind;[1] and on the other hand, a religion in which outward gods are worshipped, an outward law enforced which is counted sacred because a god or gods inspired it, and in which superstitions gathered from all quarters find shelter. The higher religion by no means killed the lower one, as we see in India to this day. On the contrary, the withdrawal of the higher religion of the country to a region whither the people could not follow, left the religion of the people to sink into a degradation unknown before. One doctrine must here be noticed. The belief in transmigration

[1] "From the standpoint of unity with Brahma, the gods are no-gods, the Vedas no-Vedas."

which Buddhism received from the religion it found existing in India, does not belong to the higher thought of Brahmanism described in this section; the atman or self, which is identical with the supreme self, belongs to quite a different order of thought from the soul which was formerly in some one else, is now in me, and may yet come to be in many another being. The doctrine is thought to have been an importation into India about the time we are speaking of. It admits of being made a powerful deterrent from vice and incentive to virtue. If my present sufferings are due not to my acts, but to the acts of the person in whom my soul dwelt before, it is possible for me so to act that my soul's future existence may be better and not worse than this one, and that it shall not sink but rise in the order of beings, and draw nearer to its final deliverance. Of this we shall hear more in connection with Buddhism.

The further development of Indian religion, apart from Buddhism, is in two directions. There is a philosophical movement, in which the Brahmanic ideas on God, the world, the soul and its changes, are further worked out, and which leads to the six schools of Hindu philosophy. On the other hand, the gods have their history. Brahma remains the great god, but as his character is so undefined he is little worshipped. Indra, the old national god, yields to Vishnu, the old sun-god of the three steps (heaven, the air, the earth), who becomes the favourite deity. The stern and destructive S'iva is a new figure, and seems to be partly an adaptation of a god of the savage aborigines: his worship is the most fanatical. These three, the Creator, the Upholder, and the Destroyer, form the Trimurti, or divine trinity of India,—a trinity arrived at not by unfolding the riches of the one great god, but by compounding the claims of three gods who were rivals. The doctrine of incarnation is also found here. Vishnu has ten avatars or incarnations in human form; he comes down to the earth when there is a special reason for his interference. In these avatars, specially in Krishna, the dark god, whose exploits as a hero are told in the great epic the Mahabharata, the need is to some extent met, of which both Buddhism and Christianity lay hold, of a divine figure who is not too far away from man, and who can be regarded with personal affection.

Books Recommended

Most of the books mentioned at the end of last chapter deal also with Brahmanism.

Of the Brahmanic literature given in the Sacred Books of the East, the following may be mentioned:—

- Vols. i. and xv. Upanishads.
- Vols. ii. and xiv. Sacred Laws of the Aryas.
- Vol. vii. The Institutes of Vishnu.
- Vols. xii., xxvi., and xli. The Satapatha-Brahmana (Sacrificial Rituals).
- Vol. xxv. Manu.
- Vols. xxix., and xxx. Grihya-Sutras (Domestic Ceremonies).
- Vol. xxxiv. Vedic Hymns. xlvi. Hymns to Agni.
- Vols. xlii.-xliv. Hymns of the Atharva-Veda.
- Vols. xxxiv., xxxviii., xlviii. Vedanta Sutras.

Muir's *Sanscrit Texts*.

Weber, *Indische Skizzen*.

Haug, *Aitareya Brahmana*.

CHAPTER XX

INDIA

III. *Buddhism*

IN Buddhism the great movement of Indian religion works itself out to its ultimate conclusion and reaches a stage beyond which there can be no advance. Here we have a religion, if such it may be called, without a god, without prayer, without priesthood or worship; a religion which owes its great success, not to its theology, nor to its ritual, since it has neither, but to its moral sentiment and to its external organisation. Originating in the centre of India, and giving practical form to Indian ideas, it spread rapidly and widely both in the country of its birth and in neighbouring lands. It is now extinct in India, yet it numbers more adherents than any other religion. It has been divided since the Christian era into two great branches. Southern Buddhism is the religion of Ceylon, of Burmah, and of Siam; while Northern Buddhism extends over Tibet, China, and Japan, and the islands of Java and Sumatra.

The Literature.—These two branches of Buddhism have different literary traditions, though some works are common to both; and these literatures, differing from each other in language, also differ widely in contents and in spirit. The southern tradition, composed in Pali, the literary language of Ceylon, has recently been opened up to scholars, and has greatly changed their views of the origin and the true nature of this religion. The Canon of Southern Buddhism, which we might call the Pali Bible, is a literature about twice as large as the Bible of Europe, although if the repetitions in it were removed, it would be somewhat smaller than the Bible. It consists of three Pitakas, baskets or collections. The first is the Vinaya Pitaka, dealing with discipline, but including the Mahavagga, a history of the first beginnings of the order as the founder gathered it around him. The second is the Sutta Pitaka or collection of teachings. It contains the earliest account of the later life of the founder, books of meditation and devotion, collections of sayings by the Master, poems, fairy tales, and fables, stories about Buddhist saints, and so on. The third collection, the Abidhamma, contains speculations and discussions on various subjects. Much of these materials is not peculiar to Buddhism, there is much pre-Buddhistic speculation, and there are many stories which are not peculiar even to India. Along with all this, however, the books give us the earliest accounts of the life and of the death of the founder, and contain a representation written a century after his death, of what he was considered to have taught. The founder himself wrote nothing; but the work of composing books about him and his doctrine began early, and much of the canon is considered, especially by English scholars, to have been in existence during the first Buddhist century.[1] For many centuries they were preserved by memory alone.

[1] The Buddhist literature given in the Sacred Books of the East is as follows:

Vol. x. The Dhammapada, containing the quintessence of Buddhist morality, and the Sutta-nipata, giving teachings of Buddha on religion.

Vol. xi. Buddhist Suttas. Religious, moral, and philosophical discourses. Vol. xlix. Buddhist Mahayana Sutras.

Vol. xiii. Vinaya Texts. The Patimokha or order of discipline, and

Was there a Personal Founder?—Senart in his *Essai sur la légende du Buddha*, and Kern in his *Het Buddhisme in Indie*, both hold that we have here to do with a sun-myth, and interpret the various features of the legend in a very ingenious way in accordance with that theory. This view has made few converts. Many incidents in the story are natural, and appear to be due to a real tradition; there is literary evidence of the early existence of the books, and the religion can be best understood if regarded as the work of a real personality of commanding greatness.[1]

Scholars, however, are agreed as to the difficulty of drawing the line between what is history and what is legend. Even in the early Pali accounts the hero has become a

the beginning of the Mahavagga, containing an account of the opening of the ministry of the founder.

Vol. xvii. Vinaya Texts ii. Mahavagga continued. Kullavagga or discipline as established by the Master.

Vol. xx. Kullavagga continued.

Vols. xxii., xlv. contain Suttas of the religion of the Jainas.

Vols. xxxv., xxxvi. Questions of King Milinda.

[1] Recent archæological discoveries, of which an account is given by Mr. Rhys Davids in the *Century Magazine*, April 1902, place it beyond doubt that the Buddha really existed, and that pious offices were paid to his ashes after his cremation by the members of his own clan as well as by others. Inscriptions brought to light in 1898 show that the Sakhya clan of which he was a member, dwelt at the time of his death in what is now a frontier district of Nepal. Three years before that event they were driven from their old capital Kapilavastu; but they formed a new one fifteen miles further south, just beyond the present frontier of Nepal, and there they erected a *stupa* or massive stone cairn, to guard the portion of the ashes of the Buddha which was committed to their keeping.

religious figure, he wears titles which lift him above mankind, and he has supernatural powers at his command. A laborious critical process must be undertaken, comparing the various narratives with each other and testing them in other ways, before the real history can be regarded as made out beyond question. The slight sketch of the story which we give does not aim at such critical correctness; we merely indicate the outline of a narrative which is one of the principal sources of the strength of the religion.

The Story of the Founder.—The founder's family name was Gautama, and by that name he was commonly known during his lifetime. The personal name given him as a child was Siddartha. Those who wished after his death to speak of him with reverence called him Sakya-Muni, the sage of the Sakyas. These were a tribe who dwelt, at the period of the story, *i.e.* half a millennium before Christ, in the country to the north of the sacred Ganges, a few days' journey from the city of Benares. Gautama's father, Suddhodana, was rajah (chief) of the Sakyas; his residence was Kapilavastu, near Oude. The future sage thus belonged to the Kshatriya class, and was brought up in a position of rank and ease. We hear little of his youth; he had been married ten years, and his wife, whom he loved, had just brought him a son, when, at the age of twenty-nine, he suddenly and secretly left his home to devote himself to the religious life. He was led to this step by witnessing various painful sights which caused him vividly to realise the suffering which accompanies all existence, and made him scorn a life of luxury. It was a time when many were seeking a better way, and when a superior mind naturally turned to that retirement and absorption in which it was believed that the key to life's pains and mysteries was to be found. In the "Great Renunciation," as this act is called, there is nothing we cannot understand. This lofty act, however, was followed by a temptation; Mara, the spirit of evil, urged him, but urged him in vain, to give up the purpose he had formed. He then attached himself to Brahmanic ascetics, from whom he learned their philosophy; and after this he devoted himself for six years to a life of fasting and penance, the Brahmanic method for drawing nearer the goal of the religious life. After this period he gave up his fasting, not having profited by it as he had expected, and returned to an ordinary diet. This change cost him the adhesion of five disciples who had become attached to him, and had been filled with wonder at his mortifications. But the loss was a small one compared with the gain which was at hand. After a second great spiritual struggle and a renewal of the temptation, he at last reached that which he had long been seeking. Seated under a *ficus religiosa*, the tree afterwards called the tree of knowledge, or the Bo-tree, he rose in contemplation above all his temptations and doubts till he beheld at length the true nature of things. From this moment he was Buddha, Enlightened; he had the key of truth, and for himself he was assured that sorrow and evil had lost all hold on him. His doctrine had dawned in his mind. He had discovered the cause of the sorrow which is so closely intertwined in man's life, and had divined the way in which sorrow might be overcome. The method had been found by which one could escape from the unending succession of new lives, all painful, to which, according to the general belief of the time, men were condemned. The words placed in the mouth of the founder when he attained to Buddhahood tell their own tale. "Looking for the Maker of this tabernacle, I have to run through a course of many births so long as I do not find him; and painful is birth again and again. But now, Maker of the tabernacle, thou hast been seen; thou shalt not make up this tabernacle again. All thy rafters are broken ; thy ridge-pole is sundered ; the mind, approaching the eternal, has attained to the extinction of all desires."[1]

The great discovery being made, and duly pondered and realised, the question arose, What was to be done with it? The Buddha shrinks from the work of preaching it to others. Brahma himself is brought into the story to encourage him to make his secret known to others, and to assure him that many will receive it with great joy. The Blessed One consents, and thus replies: "Wide open is the gate of the Immortal to all who have ears to hear; let them send forth faith to meet it. The teaching is sweet and good; because I despaired of the task, I spake not to men before."[2] He turns his steps, guided by his own supernatural knowledge, to the city of Benares, to seek the five monks who had formerly abandoned him. On his way thither he meets a naked ascetic who asks the reason of his cheerful mien; he answers that he has overcome all foes, has reached emancipation by the destruction of desire, and has obtained Nirvana. "To found the kingdom of Truth I go to the city of the Kasis (Benares); I will beat the drum of the Immortal in the darkness of this world." The account which follows of the opening of the "kingdom of righteousness" presents many analogies to the early stages of other spiritual movements. The founder, immovably sure of himself and of his doctrines, goes from place to place, spending the rainy season in town, and preaching everywhere. It is at Benares that the "wheel of the law" is first set in motion; there the first sermon was preached. The circumstances are also narrated under which other sermons were delivered, details being given as to time, place, the persons who heard them, the incidents which occasioned them. His converts at first are few and their names are recorded, but by degrees they become more

[1] Dhammapada, *S. B. E.* x. 42. [2] Mahavagga, *S. B. E.* xiii. 88.

numerous. The more devoted of them become members of his order, Bhikkus (for Bhikshus), mendicants; they forsake domestic life, shave their heads, adopt the yellow dress and the alms-bowl. They also are sent out to preach. "Go ye, O Bhikkus, and wander, for the welfare of many, out of compassion for the world, for the gain and for the welfare of gods and men. Let not two of you go the same way. Preach, O Bhikkus, the doctrine which is glorious in the beginning, glorious in the middle, glorious in the end, in the spirit, and in the letter; proclaim a consummate, perfect, and pure life of holiness. There are beings whose mental eyes are covered with scarcely any dust, but if the doctrine is not preached to them they cannot attain salvation." The incidents narrated in this part of the story are mostly connected with persons seeking admission to the order, or persons requiring to be convinced; the doctrine and its spread are everything. That spread takes place, as it is desired by the Buddha, chiefly among the higher classes of society; a great triumph is reached when Bimbisara, king of Magadha, becomes a patron of the order, and some accounts tell of the conversion of the Buddha's own father and mother. The work of the mission is of a peaceful nature; the Buddha lives on good terms with the Brahmans and with other teachers and their pupils. The only formidable opposition he had to meet arose within the order. His cousin Dewadatta, who had become a monk, wished to found a new order with much stricter rules than those of the original one. The Buddha refused to attach importance, as was proposed, to matters of clothes and food, or living in the open air; to do so would have made his movement narrower and less universal than he desired.

The beginning of the ministry is told in some detail, but of a long period of the life only a few scattered incidents are given. There is a detailed account of the three last months of the life. The Buddha is now eighty years of age, and in the Maha-paranibbana Sutta[1] the tale of his migrations and preachings is carried on according to the same scheme as in the accounts of his early days. During the rainy season, however, when he has reached the age of eighty, he has an illness, and sees he cannot live long. This he tells his monks, exhorting them with urgency to be true to the teaching and the order, and to shed the light abroad. His end is hastened by a meal of pork set before him by a goldsmith, a man of low caste, who hospitably entertained him. After this his face shines with a heavenly radiance, and as the end approaches many heavenly signs appear. The Buddha is fully conscious that he is about to leave the world, and that his death is an event of supreme interest to the heavenly powers, whom he believes to be thronging around to watch his last hours. He is solicitous, however, to soothe the grief of his friends, large numbers of whom also are around him, and to give them such counsels and such incentives to a faithful upholding of the cause as he yet may. They ask about his obsequies, and he claims that the remains of such an one as he is, of a Tathagata, "one who has attained perfection," should be treated as men treat the remains of a king of kings. He recognises the kindness of Ananda, his most intimate disciple, and tries to comfort him by encouraging him to be earnest in effort, so that he too may soon be free from evils. He directs his disciples generally not to mourn too much at his removal as if they were being deserted. The truths which he has set forth, and the rules of the order he has laid down for them, are to be their teacher after he is gone. He asks if any of them has any doubt or misgiving as to the Buddha, or the truth, or the faith, or the way. If so, they are to inquire freely, so that they may not reproach themselves afterwards for not having consulted

[1] *S. B. E.* vol. xl.

him while still among them. The brethren, however, are silent, though addressed again and again in the same way. In the whole assembly there is not one who has any doubt or misgiving. Even the most backward of these brethren has become converted (lit. "entered into the current"); he is no longer liable to be born to a state of suffering, but is assured of eternal salvation.

"Then the Blessed One addressed the brethren and said, 'Behold now, brethren, I exhort you,' saying, 'Decay is inherent in all things that have come into being. Work out your salvation with diligence!'

"This was the last word of the Tathagata!"

His death or Nirvana forms the era of Buddhist chronology, and the date has now been approximately fixed with some certainty; it took place somewhere in the decade 482-472 B.C.

Is Buddhism a Revolt against Brahmanism?—Before proceeding to discuss the religion to which this somewhat monkish narrative forms the preface, it is necessary to say a few words on the relation which that religion is now supposed to hold to the general history of Indian piety. It was customary, till recently, to regard Buddha as a great reformer, and his religion as a great revolt against that which it found prevailing in India. He is credited with having preached atheism as a reaction against the burdensome worship of too many gods, with having instituted a great social movement consisting in the abolition of caste, with having openly denied the authority of the Vedas, till then unchallenged, and with having rebuked the pride of Brahmanism by making his order of mendicants the representatives of his religion. None of these assertions can now be upheld. Instead of having been a tremendous reaction against Brahmanism it is seen that Buddhism was the natural outgrowth of that system. The closer knowledge of both, gained by the opening up of the sacred books of India, tends to show that much that was formerly thought distinctive of Buddhism was in reality inherited from Brahmanism. We saw in dealing with the earlier form of Indian religion that a form of piety had been struck out in it which made the ascetic independent of sacrifice, priesthood, even of the gods, all save the one God who is in all things. In that phase of Indian religion the authority of the Vedas had already been impugned, an inner discipline had taken the place of outward worship, the saint had learned to forsake the world. This turn of religious thought produced all the phenomena of Buddhism before the period of Gautama. The sannyasin (*vide sup.*, p. 344) of Brahmanism is also called bhikku, mendicant; the rules of the older ascetics are closely similar to those of the Buddhist monk; their very outfit, their cloak and alms-bowl, are the same.

A circumstance which shows very clearly how far Buddhism was from bearing the character of a revolt, is the occurrence at the same time and in the same district of India of another movement of a very similar nature. **Jainism** is an Indian religion so like Buddhism as to have been considered by many to be a sect of the latter. It also has an order of monks with robes and with a rule like those of the Buddhist fraternity. It also has a human founder on whom many of the same titles are conferred as on Gautama, and who is afterwards deified and worshipped. Mahavira, the founder of Jainism is, like Gautama, the son of a royal house; and the Jainist and the Buddhist legend have many features in common. Was the legend of Mahavira, then, a sectarian version of the legend of Gautama, did no such person exist, at least as the founder of a religious body? So it was formerly considered; but it has now been discovered that the Buddhist scriptures themselves bear witness to the actual existence of Mahavira in the lifetime of Gautama, who once had an encounter with him and confuted him. It appears then that two similar movements were going on close together at the same time. They were independent of each other; the two rules differ in important particulars. Jainism carries to a much greater length than Buddhism the "ahimsa," or prohibition of the destruction of life; the Jainists practise austerities which Buddhism discards, and in the philosophies of the two systems there are far-reaching discrepancies. On the other hand, both Buddhism and Jainism borrow from Brahmanism most of their practices and institutions; both are developments of the way of salvation struck out not by Brahmans alone, but by men of other castes and other views, when faith in the old national gods was growing dim.

We now proceed to discuss **the Buddhist system,** taking it as it appears in the early books, which tell us at least what was believed in the fourth century B.C. to have been the ideas and intentions of the founder. The following is the formula in which the convert expressed his desire to be admitted to the order: "I take shelter in the Buddha, I take shelter in the Dhamma (doctrine), I take shelter in the Samgha (order)."

1. **The Buddha.**—This confession of faith is directed to a triad of which the Buddha is the first member. Now the title Buddha was not invented by Buddhism, but belongs to earlier Indian thought, which held that from time to time, in a specially favoured age, an Enlightened One and Enlightener, an omniscient and perfect teacher, visited the world. Of these there had been in former ages twenty-four, and the followers of Gautama held him to be the twenty-fifth, but not the last. The application to Gautama of this title removed him, to the believer, from the ranks of ordinary men, and was the signal for a constantly increasing exalta-

tion of his person. In adhering to the Buddha, therefore, the convert is not bowing to a mere man, but to one in whom a new type of deity is on the way to be realised. He is a man; there is a record of his human life, in which he made a great renunciation, abandoning, out of compassion for men's sufferings, a position of lordly ease for that of the mendicant. In this way he is a saviour not too exalted for the pious heart to love and follow. Having found out in his own experience the way of peace, and opened up that way for others, he is a pattern and an encouragement as well as a lawgiver to the earnest soul; and the personal relation which may thus be enjoyed with the founder is one great secret of the success of the religion. On the other hand, he is more than a man. The belief grew up very early that he was not born in the ordinary way, but that his birth had been his own voluntary act, and that his great renunciation consisted in his choosing, out of compassion for men, to enter human life and to bear the burden of its sufferings. In this way a religion which originally had no gods and no worship began to supply itself with these. Some scholars hold that it was among the lay community, among men not thoroughly initiated into Buddhist thought, and failing to find in the new faith what their former religions had afforded, that the deification of the Buddha and the worship of him began; it may certainly be doubted whether the religion could have lived long or spread far if these deficiencies had not been early supplied.

2. **The Doctrine.**—The life of the founder gives us the key to his doctrine. We see at once that that doctrine was not negative but positive and constructive. Neither was it socially of a revolutionary character, nor did it deny any part of the existing religion. We never read that Gautama's teaching was assailed by the Brahmans as unsound; it was centuries after his death that antagonism broke out between

the order and the upholders of other systems. Nor again did the teaching put forward a new philosophy. On certain points which we shall notice there is a development of thought in it; but this was not obtruded.

In fact **the doctrine is** not a speculation at all, but **a way of salvation** which is preached for its own sake, and carefully guarded from being mixed up with speculative or religious controversy. The Buddha is one who has found out a new way to be saved, and he comes forward to preach what he has discovered, and that alone. Other matters he leaves as they are. "All his discourses savour of redemption as all the sea is salt." Other men may draw inferences as to the relation his doctrine bears to the position of the Brahmans, or to the sacrifices, or to existing beliefs; he does not draw these inferences, he feels no need to do so.

The doctrine professes to be an answer to a definite problem—the problem of pain. It is the most characteristic thing about both the founder and the doctrine, that they start from the universal existence of pain, to seek a remedy for it; they are inspired therefore from the first by a dark view of human life, and by the sentiment of compassion. It was the impression made on the young prince, of the general prevalence of suffering, that drove him forth from the palace to be a sannyasin or devotee. In a striking sermon he uses the figure of fire to indicate how universal is the rule of pain in all parts of nature and of human life. "All is burning; the eye is burning, and all it looks on, and all it remembers of what it has seen"; so it is with each of the senses, so also with the mind. The fire is that of passion, of malice, of illusion, of birth, of age, of death, of pain, despondency, and despair. But the nature of the complaint from which man suffers, and also the remedy for it, are described most clearly in the "**Four Noble Truths**" set forth in the opening sermon at Benares. In these memorable utterances the teacher expresses himself according to the rules of the medical art, first setting forth the nature of the disease, then its cause, then how it takes end, and lastly, the means to be adopted in order that it may do so.

1. The Noble Truth of *Suffering*. Birth is suffering, decay is suffering, illness is suffering, death is suffering. Presence of objects we hate is suffering, separation from objects we love is suffering, not to obtain what we desire is suffering. Briefly, the fivefold clinging to existence is suffering.

2. The Noble Truth of the *Cause of Suffering*. Thirst that leads to rebirth, accompanied by pleasure and lust, finding its delight here and there. This thirst is threefold, namely, thirst for pleasure, thirst for existence, thirst for prosperity.

3. The Noble Truth of the *Cessation of Suffering*. It ceases with the complete cessation of this thirst, a cessation which consists in the absence of every passion, with the abandoning of this thirst, with the deliverance from it, with the destruction of desire.

4. The Noble Truth of the *Path which leads to the Cessation of Suffering*. The holy eightfold Path; that is to say, Right Belief, Right Aspiration, Right Speech, Right Conduct, Right Means of Livelihood, Right Endeavour, Right Memory, Right Meditation.

In these statements there are some things which we can readily understand, but also some things which are not so easy. It is a thought with which Christians are familiar, that desire is the parent of all sorts of pain and disappointment, that the assertion of the self, the putting forward of personal wishes and claims, involves suffering. And we read in the Gospels that the way to escape from such suffering is to cease from desire, no longer to be anxious about what this world can give us or take from us, and not to lay up treasures. Buddhist doctrine has its moral basis in the perception of the vanity of all human effort and desire, and in the conviction that the true riches for man cannot consist in any of those goods to which the heart naturally clings. Where that perception does not exist, where the first of the Noble Truths is not accepted as beyond all question, Buddhism can have no hold. So far the doctrine is easy to follow. But in the second of the Truths we find that the cause of suffering is sought in the history of the human person as Indian thought conceives it. Man suffers because he has been born again, has suffered a rebirth, and the cause of his rebirth is the thirst which has been felt or even nourished in a previous existence. The thought that suffering is due to desire is not presented simply, as it is in our Gospels, but in connection with a doctrine of man's life and of the connection of one generation with another, which is quite strange to us, but apart from which primitive Buddhism held that its doctrine of suffering could not be understood. The Buddha, after discovering the doctrine, is at first in doubt whether or not he will preach it; and the cause of his doubt is that he is not sure if men will be able to understand the law of causality and the chain of existence, on which he himself meditated a whole night after his enlightenment, and his discovery of which he regards as a great part of his achievement. This **chain of causation** is stated in a long series of asserted processes, in which the connection between one generation and another, and the transmission from life to life of the melancholy heritage of desire and sorrow, is obscurely and enigmatically traced. The beginning of all is ignorance (of the four truths); from ignorance proceed the "samkharas" or forms of production, from these in turn consciousness, the senses, contact, sensation, thirst, and so on to birth and the miseries of life. Suffering is destroyed by tracing this sequence over again in a negative way, so that, the first member of it being destroyed, each subsequent member is destroyed in turn.

It is no wonder that the founder doubted whether this doctrine of causation would be generally understood; for it is in fact an attempt to reconcile two opposite views of the nature of the human person. In the first place we find in early Buddhism the thought that there is no such thing as a self in the human being; a man is made up of various bundles of attributes and sensations called *skandhas*, but he himself is none of these. There is no persistent substratum of a self under these activities and forms, any more than there is a carriage in addition to the wheels, shafts, nails, etc., of which a carriage is composed. The Buddhist is called on to give up the belief in a permanent ego; only where the various parts come together is the man there. This is the well-known denial of the soul in this religion; the soul is nothing but the "name and form" of a chance collocation of elements. It is hard to know where this doctrine came from; Kern says it is derived from the science of dissection, others compare it with the doctrine of Heraclitus, taught about the same time in Greece, that all things are in constant flux, nothing permanent. The last words of the Master assert that decay is universal; and the doctrine of the skandhas is a corollary from that principle; if all the elements of which the human person is made up are in process of decay, then the self cannot be a substantial and persistent thing. That doctrine, however, does not go well together with the belief in the universality and inexorableness of suffering. If there is no self, must not consciousness come to an end when the elements fall asunder which chance has brought together, and must not the hour of death be also the hour of complete emancipation? This, however, it was impossible to hold in India at the time of Gautama; the belief in transmigration was too firmly fixed, he never thought of disputing it. That belief indeed is what chiefly makes the suffering of the world so lamentable. To Indian eyes the pain actually in the world was magnified a hundred-fold by the dark imagination of its connection with the past and with the future. What a man suffered was the result of acts done in many former lives, all spent in the vain misery of desire; and the sad prospect was extended before him that death would not end his pains, but that he would be born again and again to suffer ever anew so long as desire continued. But if this is the case, then the soul would seem to be a durable and persistent thing which is able to go through many lives and much suffering without being brought to an end. On the theory of transmigration the soul is not a mere shadow-name of an aggregation of qualities, but the one durable thing which survives when all that is accidental and temporary falls away from it. The doctrine of the Skandhas and that of transmigration are thus opposed, and the doctrine of the *nidanas* or the chain of causation is the bridge which satisfied Gautama's own mind, but which he was doubtful about presenting to others, to bring them into harmony. He aimed at showing by his catalogue of these obscure processes how the actions done in a life set up a tendency to a corresponding existence in another life which begins after the former one ends. Though there is no soul to be transmitted, the moral effects of former lives are transmitted to their successors.

The essential doctrine of the Buddha, however, is determined by the belief in transmigration. His cry of triumph at the time of his enlightenment is to the effect that the long series of suffering existences through which he has passed has now come to an end, and that he will not be born again. And what he preaches with constant iteration is the misery of this awful succession of births to renewal of suffering, and the infinite blessedness of escaping from this cycle. The disciple, when converted, is to be able to say: "Hell is destroyed for me, and rebirth as an animal or a ghost or in any place of woe. I am converted, I am no longer liable to be reborn in a state of suffering, and am assured of eternal salvation."

Now it rests with a man's own acts to end his sufferings. The chain of causation which ends with suffering begins with ignorance. The ignorance which is meant is that of the four noble truths, of the way of salvation. Let a man cease from ignorance, let him accept the Noble Truths and the insight they convey into the cause of suffering, then by ceasing to thirst, or to burn, or in our own language by turning his mind away from all desire, believing that what he does will be effective for his salvation, he sets up a chain of causation in an opposite direction, and having destroyed ignorance he may rest assured that he has destroyed suffering too and is in the right way. The burden he has inherited he will not need to carry any farther but will, when he dies, lay down for ever.

When we look at **the fourth Noble Truth**, which tells what a man has to do in order to obtain this salvation, we are at first surprised. After the deep earnestness with which the nature of the disease and the cause and cure of the disease have been stated, we expect that stronger practical measures will be asked for than these eight forms of moderation. Christianity speaks of cutting off the right hand, plucking out the right eye, in order to cut off desire: and the Brahmanic method of union with the Deity was, as we have seen, that of the most extreme self-mortification united with contemplation. This Brahmanic method, the *yoga* by which the devotee sought to escape from all the accidents of being and to make himself one with the great Self, the Buddha had tried for six years; but he had given it up for a year when the hour of his enlightenment struck, and he explicitly condemns for others the path he had found unprofitable for himself. It is one of two extremes, both to be avoided,

"The one extreme is a life devoted to pleasures and lusts; this is degrading, sensual, vulgar, profitless; the other is a life given to mortifications; this is painful, ignoble, and profitless. By avoiding these two extremes the Tathagata has gained the knowledge of the Middle Path, which leads to insight, wisdom, calm, to Nirvana." The way, therefore, to escape from the Karma, the moral retribution which works inexorably in one life the result stored up in previous lives, is that of a careful and unintermitted self-discipline, which does not run to extremes, but practises, with perfectly clear purpose and self-possession, the needful virtues mentioned in the fourth of the Noble Truths. What are these? There is to be—

1. Right belief, without superstition or delusion.
2. Right aspiration, after such things as the thoughtful and earnest man sets store by.
3. Right speech, speech that is friendly and sincere.
4. Right conduct conduct that is peaceable, honourable, and pure.
5. Right means of livelihood, *i.e.* a pursuit which does not involve the taking or injuring of life.
6. Right endeavour, *i.e.* self-restraint and watchfulness.
7. Right memory, *i.e.* presence of mind, not forgetting at any time what one ought to remember; and
8. Right meditation, *i.e.* earnest occupation with the riddles of life.

This is the path; there are four stages of it—

1. The stage of him who has entered the path.
2. The stage of him whc has yet to return once to life.
3. The stage of him who returns not again, but may be born again as a superior being; and
4. The stage of the worthy, holy one, the *Arahat*, who is free from desire for existence, and also from pride and self-righteousness, and who is saved and has obtained holiness, even in this life.

An **Arahat** is not equal to a Buddha; the former is himself saved, but the perfect Buddha is able by his perfect knowledge to save others. Of Buddhas, however, there are not many. One becomes an Arahat by a life of strenuous and untiring discipline. Ten fetters are to be broken by which a man is kept from freedom; self-deception is one of them, trust in sacrifice another, and the list embraces both sensual and intellectual weaknesses. One must watch and be sober; every act, however trivial, is to be done with full self-consciousness and earnestness. One must remember that he is engaged in a great and a hard work, and must resolutely "swim upstream," estimating at its proper value every affection and temptation that would hold him back. The body is to be contemned, and all natural ties; emotion is to be uprooted from the heart, so that the proper state of entire calm and undisturbedness may be maintained. Then one is an Arahat, a true Brahman. This manner of life requires withdrawal from the world; the true salvation can only be attained by him who has left his home for the houseless life. But Buddhism has also a general moral code for those who have not taken this step; the keeping of it will not save them directly; from the life they are now leading that is impossible, but it is a beginning; it will make it easier for them to become Arahats and attain salvation in some future existence. For all it is good to be free from desire; as all desire contains in itself a germ of death, there is no approach to salvation except in this direction.

Buddhist Morality.—Towards fellow-men Buddhist morality is based on the notion of the equality of all; respect is to be paid to all living beings. The five rules of righteousness which are binding on all followers of the Buddha are:

1. Not to kill any living being.
2. Not to take that which is not given.

3. To refrain from adultery.
4. To speak no untruth.
5. To abstain from all intoxicating liquors.

To these are added five more for members of the order, who are also required to refrain from all sexual intercourse, viz.:

1. Not to eat after mid-day.
2. Not to be present at dancing, singing, music, or plays.
3. Not to use wreaths, scents, ointments, or personal ornaments.
4. Not to use a high or a broad bed.
5. To possess no silver or gold.

These commandments, like those of the Decalogue, are negative in form; but in the Buddhist scriptures a positive moral ideal is inculcated on all, which is grave and attractive in its character, and is sustained by a strong though quiet enthusiasm. We find here a delicate conscientiousness as to the relations to be cultivated with one's fellow-men; the widest toleration is enjoined, a toleration extending to all beings, to all opinions. Hatred is to be repaid by love, life is to be filled with kindness and compassion. The Dhammapada and the Sutta-nipata deserve to be read by all who care for the unseen riches of the soul. By their simple earnestness, their quaint use of parable and metaphor, and their mingling of the homeliest things with the highest truths, these books take rank among the most impressive of the religious books of the world. We give only a few jewels from this treasury.

From the Dhammapada.—Earnestness is the path of immortality (Nirvana), thoughtlessness the path of death. Those who are in earnest do not die, those who are thoughtless are as if dead already.

All that we are is the result of what we have thought; it is founded on what we have thought, it is made up of what we have thought. If a man speaks or acts with a pure thought, happiness follows him, like a shadow that never leaves him.

By oneself evil is done, by oneself one suffers; by oneself evil is left undone, by oneself one is purified. Purity and impurity belong to oneself; no one can purify another.

From the Sutta-nipata.—To live in a suitable country, to have done good deeds in a former existence, and a thorough study of oneself, this is the highest blessing.

As a mother at the risk of her life watches over her own child, her only child, so also let every one cultivate a boundless friendly mind towards all beings.

A Bhikku who has turned away from desire and attachment, and is possessed of understanding in this world, has already gone to the immortal place, the unchangeable state of Nirvana.

Nirvana.—Our account of the doctrine would appear incomplete if we did not attempt to answer the question, What is Nirvana? It is, as the last extract shows, the state of salvation in Buddhism. As we have seen, it is the condition of the man who has escaped from the series of re-births, and will never be born again. It is attained even in this life by the Arahat, in whom all desire and restlessness have come to an end. On the other hand, it is said of such an one that he enters Nirvana when he dies, as if it were a state not of this life, but of the period beyond. Thus it has been much debated whether the Buddhist (or rather Indian, for the notion is not peculiar to Buddhism) Nirvana is extinction, annihilation, of which the quenching of desire in this life is the prelude, or if it is a state of negative or quiescent blessedness, on which the saint can enter here and now, but which is only made perfect when he dies. But there are two Nirvanas;—that of entire passionlessness attained in this life, and the consummate Nirvana entered at death. The saint does not need to wait for death for his redemption, nor must he hasten his death in order to enjoy it fully; Buddha, by example and by precept, forbids any such anticipation. Death seals that which was already won, there is no return from the Nirvana of death to any further life. This, however, does not amount to an assertion that the dead Arahat has no life or knowledge in the beyond; he is freed from desire, but whether his consciousness is altogether extinguished, Buddhism does not decide, and regards as a vain speculation.

No Gods.—We shall speak afterwards of this view of redemption, which is the key to the nature of the Buddhist religion. We remark here that it is a redemption man achieves by his own efforts, without any outward prop or aid. In this system there is no occasion for any priests or sacrifices, for any prayers, or for any gods. There is no ritual, because there is no object of worship, there is no sin in the sense of offending a higher being. The gods are denied not because of any speculative doubt of their existence, but because in that inner world of moral effort which man has come to feel so supremely real and important, they have no part to play. As all the gods faded away in Indian speculation before Brahma, so Brahma's own turn has come to fade away. The Buddhist speaks of the gods as if they existed, and he makes no attack on the sacrifices; but no living god fills his heart. The Buddha is greater than all the gods; his teaching is for the benefit of gods as well as men. But the Buddha is not an object of worship. If the Buddhist can be said to worship any higher power, it is the moral order which never fails to reward men according to the deeds done in this or former existences. That is for him a real and tremendous, though impersonal power, and in contemplating it he may be said to worship after a fashion. But he has no aid to look for from any power in heaven or earth in working out his salvation. Buddhism is the most autosoteric of all religions; it declares more uncompromisingly than any other, that man must save himself by his own efforts, and that no one can possibly stand in his place or relieve him of any part of his great task. All that any one, even the Buddha, can do for another, is to enlighten him, to open his eyes to the true knowledge, and show him the narrow path on which he must thenceforth walk.

3. **The Order.**—There were monks before Buddhism. That religion made its appearance when Indian thought was at the stage of growth at which monastic communities may be expected to arise. When religion has ceased to be regarded as the affair of the nation or the tribe, and is cherished as the affair of the individual, when the mind turns from the sacrifices and ritual of public religion to cultivate relations with a power known chiefly in the heart and soul, and when religious duty has thus come to be recognised as a boundless and all-embracing thing, not a service the hands and feet can discharge, but the effort, never ending, still beginning, to make the whole personality with all its acts and aims conform to the ideal, then it is that men who are living for religion seek for such aid as they can give each other, and find it in an order and a discipline. The rules of the Buddhist Samgha or order are extant, and so are the rules of the contemporary Jainist fraternity. The Samgha resembled the Franciscan more than the other great Christian orders. The Bhikku on joining it abandoned his family and property, assumed the yellow robe and other scanty properties of the character, and lived thenceforth by begging, and in strict subjection to the rules, in which every detail of his food, his clothing, his residence, and his daily walk and conversation, were laid down. The two great objects of the society were mutual help in the religious life and the preaching of the doctrine. Under the first head come the frequent meetings

of monks and the confessions they make to each other according to a fixed form. There is no vow of obedience; the monk obeys the law, not the human authority. In preaching they are to go one by one, and they are to preach to all. To all who would hear it was the gate open to this salvation. Here the Buddhist neglect of caste comes in. Buddhism makes no general or formal declaration of the equality of all men, nor is there any attack on the Brahman caste or any exaltation of the lower castes. The order drew its recruits at first from the ranks of the Brahmans. But the impelling motive of the new religion was compassion, and genuine compassion is not to be restrained in artificial limits. The salvation preached was fitted for all men. The disease to be cured was one from which all suffer, and the cure was one which all could at least begin to lay hold of. Thus Buddhism was fitted to break through the barriers of caste, and to gather into one religious community men of all castes alike. In the community, it was held, these distinctions disappeared. Not birth but conduct there made the true Brahman. The universalist tendency of the religion also fitted it to spread to other lands. It was not limited by anything in its teaching to the soil of India, nor to the territory of any particular set of gods. So wide indeed is its toleration, that a man may embrace it without giving up the faith in which he lived before. One can add it without incongruity to one's former beliefs and practices. The believer in Shang-ti can be a Buddhist as well as the believer in Brahma.[1] The absence of any hierarchy or centralised organisation enabled it to spread freely, and the very meagreness of its doctrine, and its freedom from ritual, were also in its favour.

Buddhism made Popular.—Buddhism proved able to spread over many lands because it was so simple, and

[1] Millions of Buddhists in China and Japan are also adherents of the other religions of these countries.

in its essence so moral and so broadly human. But, like other faiths which have spread to many lands, it assumed very different forms in different countries, and the later form is often very different from the early simplicity. Even at the outset it was not free from a strong infusion of magic; the Arahat, like the Brahmanic ascetic before him, was believed to obtain influence over the gods by his virtues, and thus a claim to supernatural power is brought in, which agrees but ill with the ethical doctrine. The religion, which at first ignored the gods and bade each man trust to his own efforts for his highest good, became, ere long, what a popular religion at the stage of progress prevailing at that time necessarily was, namely, a worship of superior beings and a method of obtaining benefits from them. The national gods were discarded, but the deification of the founder early furnished a being who could be worshipped Legend grew luxuriantly round his birth and early career; and he obtained the rank of the greatest of all the gods. Former Buddhas who had lived in former ages still lived as gods; and the divine family, being once founded, admitted of various additions; even a popular deity, such as Indra, could be joined to the growing circle. The chief scenes of the life of the founder became holy places and objects of pilgrimage, where relics were exposed for adoration. The growth of legend and of magic proceeded more rapidly, and went to greater lengths, in Northern than in Southern Buddhism; but in the land of its birth, too, Buddhism proved unable to serve as a working religion without additions and modifications entirely foreign to its true character. The profession of Buddhism was combined even with the savage worship of the non-Aryan tribes; Siva was identified with Buddha and then worshipped instead of him, as also was Vishnu, and the perversion and degradation of the religion prepared for its expulsion from the country of its birth. That expulsion was probably brought about more immediately by the advance of Mohammedanism in India, and took place in the period of the early Middle Ages. We cannot speak here of the strange guise Buddhism has assumed in the north of India, notably in Tibet. The Lamaism of that country, with its perpetual living incarnation of the divine Buddha in a succession of human representatives, its hierarchical church strongly resembling in many of its features the Church of Rome, and the prayer-flags and wheels for the mechanical discharge of religious acts, have long been the wonder of the world.

Conclusion.—It is not from what Buddhism is now in any of the countries where it flourishes, and where it has votaries who profess other religions also, that we can judge of what it really is, or estimate its value as a product of the human mind. It is to early Buddhism that we must look for this. What are we to judge of this religion without gods, and based on the assertion that all life is suffering, and that the chief good is altogether to escape from life? It is not true to characterise it as a religion in which there is no joy, and which deliberately refuses to have anything to do with joy. The Arahat, in whom desire is vanquished, and who has no further birth to anticipate, is filled with a deep joy and triumph as of a victor who has conquered every foe; and those who are less advanced in the path yet have their share in this enthusiasm, and are inspired by it to continue the struggle. Still Buddhism is a sad religion. It arrives in India when the Deity there believed in has deserted the world, and tells man he is alone in it. There is no one to help him, no one to assure him that the good cause in a wider sense—a cause extending beyond his own personal life—is destined to succeed; there is no upholder of any moral order beyond that which works itself out in each individual experience. The result is that the believer does not trouble himself about the world, but only about his own personal salvation. This religion is not a social force, it aims not at a Kingdom of God to be built up by the united efforts of multitudes of the faithful, but only at saving individual souls, which in the act of being saved are removed beyond all activity and all contact with the world. Buddhism, therefore, is not a power which makes actively for civilisation. It is a powerful agent for the taming of passion and the prevention of vagrant and lawless desires, it tends, therefore, towards peace. But it offers no stimulus to the realisation of the riches which are given to man in his own nature: it checks rather than fosters enterprise, it favours a dull conformity to rule rather than the free cultivation of various gifts. Its ideal is to empty life of everything active and positive, rather than to concentrate energy on a strong purpose. It does not train the affections to virtuous and harmonious action, but denies to them all action and consigns them to extinction. This condemnation it has incurred by parting with that highest stimulus to human virtue and endeavour, which lies in the belief in a living God. By so doing it ceased to fulfil the office of a religion for men, and though, for historical purposes, we may class it among the religions of the world, a system which leaves its adherents free not to worship at all, or to find satisfaction for their spiritual instincts in the worship of beings whom it regards with indifference, comes short of the notion of religion, and is not properly entitled to that name.

Books Recommended

Monier Williams, *Buddhism, in its connection with Brahmanism and Hinduism, and in its contrast with Christianity*, 1889.

Rhys Davids, *Buddhism* (S.P.C.K).

Oldenberg's *Buddha, his Life, his Doctrine and his Order*, 1882 (Third German Edition, 1897).

Spence Hardy, *Manual of Buddhism*, 1860.

E. Hardy, *Der Buddhismus*.

CHAPTER XXI

PERSIA

THE Aryans who entered India to become its dominant race came from Central Asia, and left behind them there other tribes of Aryan culture. These tribes remained in what is called Iran, in the lands, that is to say, between the Indus, the Caspian Sea, the Black Sea, and the Persian Gulf. It is from this region, a part of which bore in ancient times the name of Ariana, that the word "Aryan" is derived. The languages of this territory are akin to Sanscrit; and there is ample evidence that before the Indian invasion the progenitors of the Indians and those of the Iranians dwelt together there, and enjoyed a common civilisation. If the civilisation was the same the religion also was the same. How the Indo-Iranian religion was developed in India, we have seen. At first a worship of active and militant deities, it became by degrees a religion of a passive type, in which a suffering, acquiescent, and brooding humanity presented to heaven its needs and problems, and received a corresponding answer. The Aryans who remained in Iran retained their active and practical disposition. While by no means wanting in sensitiveness and flexibility of mind, they were less given to speculation and more to a robust morality than their Indian kinsmen. It has to be noted that while the religion of India has not influenced Europe in any manifest degree until the present century, that of Persia has contributed in a marked way to form the world of thought in which we dwell.

Sources.—The views generally current about the ancient religion of Persia are derived from late Greek writers, whose accounts will be noticed at the end of this chapter. A truer knowledge is now possible, since the sacred books of the religion are now open to the world. They were only obtained from the Parsis, who keep up their ancient religion on the soil of India, during last century, and the study of them has been very laborious and difficult, and has given rise to great controversies which are not yet settled. These ancient books are furnished with Eastern translations and commentaries. Is the Western scholar to place himself under the guidance of these, which no doubt are part of the historical tradition of the religion, or may he claim that he is himself in as good a position as the Oriental commentator for understanding the original meaning of the texts; and will he best interpret them by comparing them with the Vedas? What is their age; in which of the lands of Iran were they written; was any part of them written by Zoroaster, or is Zoroaster to be regarded as an historical personage at all? On all these questions and on many others, scholars are not yet agreed; and while so much is uncertain about the books, there must also be great uncertainty about the history and the very nature of the religion. In what follows we are guided mainly by the scholars who have taken charge of the volumes connected with Persia in the "Sacred Books of the East."[1] In the last of these volumes (xxxi.) a new clue is given to the subject, of which we shall gladly avail ourselves.

The sacred books of Persia are known by the name of "**Zend-Avesta,**" which is an incorrect expression; we ought

[1] Zend-Avesta, *S. B E.*, vols. iv. xxiii. xxxi.

to say Avesta and Zend. "Avesta," like the kindred word "Veda," signifies knowledge, and the word "Zend" denotes here not the language of that name, but the "commentary" afterwards added to the original knowledge or text. The commentary is not written in the Zend language, but in Pahlavi or Persian. The Avesta, which is written in the older Zend, the sacred language of Persia, is, like other Bibles, a collection of books written in different ages, and even, it may be, in different lands. The books were brought together into one only at some period after the Christian era. The later legends as to the supernatural communication to Zoroaster of the earlier books need not detain us; we must notice, however, that the preserved books of Persian religion are held to be no more than the scanty ruins of an extensive literature. The Avesta consisted originally of 21 Nosks or books, and most of these were destroyed by Alexander when he invaded the East; only one Nosk was preserved entire. As we have it, the Avesta is a liturgical work, it contains some legends and some ancient hymns, as well as a good deal of law, but its prevailing character is that of a service-book, and it is to this that its partial preservation both at the invasion of Alexander, and at that of the Mohammedans in a later century, is probably due. It consists of three parts. The oldest is the Yasna, a collection of liturgies, which admit and indeed invite comparison with those of early Christianity: along with these are found the Gathas or hymns, the only part of the Avesta composed in verse, and written in an older dialect. The Visperad is a collection of litanies for the sacrifice; and the Vendidad is a code of early law, but contains also various religious legends. Besides these works, which constitute the Avesta proper, there is the Khorda (or small) Avesta containing devotions for various times of the day, for the days of the month, and for the religious year; these are for the use not of the priests alone but of all the faithful, and many of them are still so used.

The Contents of the Zend-Avesta are Composite.—In these works the student soon observes that he has before him not one religious system only but several. In one place we find a worship of one god, as if there were no others to be considered; some of the litanies on the other hand contain lengthy and elaborate lists of objects of worship. In some parts the religion is personal and immediate; in others it is priestly. Parsism is often called fire-worship, and the elements of earth and water also obtain extreme sanctity in it, but of this also there is in the oldest books little trace. The variety in the literature no doubt reflects a variety in the religion of Iran. Iran in fact had not one religion but several, and thus the problem is to trace how these successively entered into contact with Mazdeism or Zoroastrianism, which is the religion most native to Iran, and were embodied in it. The different religions belonged to a certain extent to different provinces. We know that Persia, the conqueror of Media, was conquered in turn by the Median religion; we also know that the religion of the Persian kings as read in their inscriptions[1] does not correspond to any of the religious positions held in the Avesta. The Magi, from whom also the religion as a whole derives one of its names, belonged to Media and passed from there to greater power in Iran as a whole. From the Scythians on the north and from Babylonia on the south, ideas and practices were imported; and in these and other ways, forms of religion arose as different from the faith of Zoroaster as later forms of Christianity from the simplicity of Christ, yet looking to him as their founder and the giver of their law.

Zoroaster.—We begin with the teaching of Zoroaster. Dr. E. Meyer in his *Geschichte des Alterthums*, vol. i., and

[1] *Records of the Past*, i. 107.

Mr. Darmesteter in his admirable introduction to the Avesta (*S. B. E.* vol. iv.) both treat Zoroaster as a mythical personage, a figure-head of the official class of the religion, who give currency to their edicts under his name. Weighty authorities may, however, be quoted for the historical reality of Zoroaster, and what appears to us most important of all, the editor of the Gathas, in the *S. B. E.* vol. xxxi., departing from his collaborateur, Mr. Darmesteter, has treated these hymns, which give an account of the founder's acts and experiences when first proclaiming the true doctrine, in such a way as to produce on the mind of the reader the strongest impression of the historical reality of the prophet and of his mission. They introduce us to a religious movement actually in progress in the poet's time, a movement in which a pure and lofty faith is struggling to establish itself against prevailing superstitions. The doctrine placed in the mouth of the reformer is that which is most central in Persian religion; and only by such deep earnestness and devotion as is here ascribed to him, could it have attained that position. We start, then, with Zoroaster and his work; and first of all we ask what was his date, where did he live, and what kind of religion did he find existing in his country?

The date of Zoroaster or Zarathustra — the former is the Greek, the latter the old Iranian form of the name, contracted in Persian to Zardusht—can only be fixed very approximately. He stands at the very beginning of the Avesta literature, and the developments in religion to which that literature testifies must have occupied a long period. On the other hand no one proposes to place Zarathustra before the departure of the Indian Aryans from the Indo-Iranian stock. From such vague data he may be assigned perhaps to somewhere about 1400 B.C. As to his province, there is considerable agreement among scholars that his doctrine spread from the east of Iran westwards; and though tradition gives him a birthplace in Media, his mission lay nearer to India, in Bactria.

Primitive Religion of Iran.—He did not preach to men unacquainted with religion. Many of the religious ideas and figures of the Vedas occur also in Persia, and by the study of these it is possible to form certain inferences as to the mental history of Persia before Zarathustra. Mithra the sun-god belongs to Persia as well as India. The heaven-god known in India as Varuna grew into the principal deity of Persia. A fire-god, wind- and rain-gods, and the serpent hostile to man, on whom these made war, are common to both countries. The institution of sacrifice, in which the deities are served with offerings and with hymns, is markedly alike in both countries. In both alike sacrifice is at first the affair not of a priesthood but of laymen, especially of princes, and is not confined to temples but is performed in the open air, on a spot judged to be suitable. The most imposing sacrifice is that of the horse, and an offering of constant occurrence is that of the intoxicating liquor, in India Soma, in Persia by a recognised transliteration Homa, which is itself viewed as a cosmic principle of life, and addressed as a deity. And in both countries alike the view of sacrifice prevails in early times, that the gods come to it to take their part in a banquet which their worshippers share with them, and that they are strengthened and encouraged by it.

These similarities, and others which might be mentioned, show that the religion of India and that of Persia started from a common stock of ideas and usages. A further circumstance of great importance shows not only the original identity of the two systems, but also perhaps how they came to diverge from each other. Two generic titles for deities occur in India. The first of these—*deva*, is said to signify the bright or shining one, the second—

asura, the living one. Now these titles are also found in Persia; but the use of the terms is different in the two countries. In India both are at first titles for deity, but by degrees, while "deva" continues to denote the gods who are worshipped, "asura" assumes a less favourable meaning, until at length it comes to stand for a second order of beings, inferior to the devas, and including such powers as are malignant and hostile. In Persia the fortunes of the two words are reversed. *Ahura* becomes the god *par excellence*, the supreme god; while "deva," the title which in India remained in honour, is in the Avesta that of evil gods who are not to be worshipped. In this some scholars consider that we may hear the watchwords of the conflict which led to the separation of the two religions; there was a schism between the followers of the Ahuras and those of the Devas, which led to the entire separation of the two parties. This is the latest form of the old view which makes Zoroastrianism the outcome of a religious conflict, of a reaction against the gods afterwards worshipped in India. There is no direct evidence of such a conflict, and the difference we have described may be due to the natural development of the Indo-Iranian religion in different sets of circumstances and among different peoples. Zarathustra in the Gathas finds the antithesis fully formed between the good and the evil deities; he appeals to his countrymen on that matter as one which he does not need to teach them, but with which they have long been familiar. In speaking of his date this has to be remembered.

We proceed now to describe from **the Gathas** the work and teaching of Zarathustra. The Gathas are poems written in metres which occur also in the Vedas, and intended, like the Indian hymns, to be used in worship. The account which they furnish of the mission and the teaching of the sage are thus clothed in a poetical dress, and do not narrate bare facts as they occurred, but the facts as interpreted and treated for religious use. They are in the mouth of Zarathustra himself; he writes them for use at sacrifice, and remembering how they are to be rendered, he sometimes puts in the mouth of the celebrants the words, "Zarathustra and we." These words do not prove that the hymns are not by him. As explained by Dr. Mills, the hymns are seen to be very fully charged with meaning and with sentiment. Uncouth and inartistic in expression, and demanding an immense amount of patience and ingenuity to trace their connection of thought, they surprise the reader when once he seizes their meaning, by the depth and spirituality of their contents, and force him to acknowledge that they are a worthy document of the birth of a great religion.

The Call of Zarathustra.—The hymns give a vivid picture of that early world in which the prophet lived. It was a world distracted with conflict. On one side there is an agricultural community bent on industry, and, like the Hindus, even at this day, valuing as most sacred the cattle which forms their chief substance. On the other hand, there are men who dwell on the outskirts between the tilled land and the wilderness, who are constantly making raids on the farms, driving off and killing the cattle for sacrifice and for food, and ruining the fields by destroying the irrigating works on which their fertility depends. And there is a religious difference as well as a difference in culture between these two sets of people. The agriculturists are worshippers of Ahura; the contemners of the cattle worship beings called in the Gathas "daevas." This schism was not of Zarathustra's making, he found it going on, and being a priest was entitled to come forward and seek to guide others with regard to it. Such is the situation which the hymns present to us. We will try to state the substance of some of those hymns. The naked words of them, even when we are sure of the correctness of the translation, are barely intelligible without lengthy commentary; and on the other hand, no short statement in modern terms can convey the force and solemnity of these struggling utterances. As we are dealing with the original revelation of Zarathustra, the source of the Persian religion, we shall give the story with some degree of detail.

The first hymn in the arrangement presented to us in *S. B. E.* deals with what we may term the call of Zarathustra. It sums up in a poetic and dramatic form the religious result of the movement which led him to come forward.

The "Soul of the Kine" first speaks; it is the impersonation of the agricultural community, to whom their cattle are most sacred. She raises a complaint to Ahura and Asha (the righteousness which is an attribute of Ahura, and like his other attributes often appears as an independent person) of the insolence and high-handed devastation and robbery she has to suffer. "For whom did ye fashion me," she says; "wherefore was I made?" She appeals to the Immortals for instruction in tillage with a view to security and welfare.

Ahura then speaks and asks Asha what guardian has been appointed for the kine to lead and to defend her; and Asha answers that no one, himself free from passion and violence, could be found who was capable of being an adequate guardian. The causes of these evils lie at the roots of the constitution of things, and therefore those seeking success in any enterprise must approach Ahura himself and not any subordinate being.

Zarathustra speaks, and confirms the utterances of Asha; it is in Ahura himself that he and the kine place their confidence; to his will they submit themselves; the doubts and questions arising from their outward insecurity, they refer to him.

Ahura speaks and answers his own question. It is true that no lord of the kine is to be found, who in himself is quite equal to that position, but he appoints Zarathustra as head to the agricultural community.

A chorus speaks, consisting of a company of the faithful supposed to be present, or of the Ameshospends, the personified attributes of Ahura, and praise the Lord for his bounty and for the wisdom he makes known; but asks whom he has endowed with the Good Mind, or, as we might say, the Holy Spirit, to make known to mortals his doctrine. The call of Zarathustra, intimated in the foregoing verse, is overlooked, as if it were impossible that such a one as he could undertake the office. Ahura replies, repeating his commission to Zarathustra, here called also by his family name of Spitama, and promising to establish him and make him successful in his work.

The Soul of the Kine speaks, lamenting still that no adequate lord has been assigned her. Zarathustra is a feeble and pusillanimous man, not one of royal state who is able to bring his purpose to effect. The Ameshospends join in the cry for the true lord to appear.

Zarathustra then speaks, accepting the mission in an address to Ahura, whom he entreats to send his blessings of peace and happiness, since none but he can give them, and to set up in the minds of the disciples of the cause that joy and that kingdom which, though it first comes inwardly, yet brings with it also all outward blessings. For himself also he prays that the Good Mind and the Sovereign Power (another of the attributes) of the Lord may hasten to come to him and strengthen him for his mission.

This poetical rendering of the call of Zarathustra is free both from miraculous embellishment and from undue exaltation of the person of the prophet, and forms a great contrast to later statements in the Avesta, where the prophet is placed in secret conclave with Ahura, asking him questions and receiving detailed replies which at once rank as revelation. In the Gathas, allowing for the theological and poetic form, everything is human and natural. We are strongly reminded of the accounts of the calls of prophets in the Old Testament —there is the same choice by the deity of an apparently weak instrument to accomplish a work urgently called for by the times, the same sense of insufficiency on the part of the prophet, but the same absolute confidence on his part in the power of the deity, and hence the same absolute assurance, once the mission is accepted, that the cause which he has been called to carry forward must succeed. In many of the following Gathas the same parallel is strongly impressed on the mind of the reader. The sense of weakness is expressed again and again—the prophet has no victorious career, but is exposed to much gainsaying, which he feels acutely. Yet he never doubts that his god is with him, and is working for him. To him he commits his doubts and fears, of his goodness he is joyfully assured, and his aid he expects with confidence. He is entirely devoted to Ahura and his cause, and offers himself up with his whole powers to work out the divine will. He will teach, he says, as long as he is able, till he has brought all the living to believe. He is conscious of a divine power working in him. Nothing in himself, he is strong by the divine grace which Ahura sends him: his words have efficacy to keep the fiends at a distance, and to advance in men's minds the divine kingdom; like St. Paul he feels his message to be to some a savour of life unto life, to others a savour of death unto death.

The Doctrine.—And what is the message he proclaims? It is a philosophy of the origin of the world, but a philosophy the acceptance of which involves immediate and strenuous action. The distracted condition of the world before him requires to be explained, so that a remedy for it may be found; and Zarathustra prays, when he is about to bring forward his doctrine, that Ahura would help him to explain how the material world arose. The explanation when it appears is not quite new, it has been shaping itself already in the mind of his people, but he sets it forth as a dogma, and draws from it at once all its practical consequences. In the third hymn of the first Gatha he solemnly brings forward his doctrine before the people, and appeals to them, not as a people, but as individuals, each for himself, with a full sense of his responsibility, to consider it, and adopt it, and act upon it. It is the doctrine of dualism, not in the fully developed later form in which two personal potentates divide the universe between them from the first, but as yet in a form more speculative and vague. There are two primeval principles, spirits, things, as is well known—the expression is indefinite—the counterparts of each other, independent in their action, a better and a worse, and Zarathustra calls on his audience to choose between them, and not to choose as do the evildoers. The world, as it is, was made by the joint action of the two principles, and they also fixed the alternative fates of men, for the wicked, Hell—the worst life; and for the holy, Heaven—the best mental state. After the creation was accomplished, the two principles drew off from each other, the evil one making choice of evil and of evil works, and the bounteous spirit choosing righteousness, making his strong seat in heaven, and taking for his own those who do good and who believe in him. The Daevas and their followers are incapable of making a just choice between the good and the evil; they have surrendered themselves from the outset to the "Worst Mind," the demon of fury, and to all evil works. (There are vague suggestions here of a temptation and a fall, but only of the evil spirits and their followers.) From this point onwards the world is filled with a great struggle. On the one side is Ahura, the only god worshipped by name in the Gathas. Ahura is a heaven-god, he is, in fact, the bright heaven, and then the good and beneficent being who dwells in brightness. In the hymns he is losing his definite character and becoming an abstraction, a god of dogmatics rather than of history. He is the good principle personified, and as becomes a god of such transcendent character, he does not act directly, but through his satellites. His attributes personified, do his bidding, aid the saints in spiritual ways, and prepare for the better order of things. On the other hand are the Daevas with the demon of wrath, who propagate everywhere lies and mischief, and heap up vengeance for themselves against the final judgment. For the good there is nothing better than to aid,—for they can aid, in bringing on the renovation, dwelling with Ahura even now, and by his attributes which work in them as well as in him, reinforcing the righteous order, and preparing themselves to dwell where wisdom has her home. In the end the Demon of the Lie will be rendered harmless and delivered up to Righteousness as a captive.

Inconsistencies.—As it happens in every such reform, the new teaching is not quite consistent with itself; old views are taken up into the new teaching, although they do not harmonise with it; the spiritual way of looking at things alternates with a more worldly way. The following are some examples of this:—The great doctrine of Heaven and Hell as inner states, as being simply the best and the worst state of mind, is clearly announced; but the traditional view of future abodes of happiness and misery also appears. The Kinvat-bridge is mentioned several times in the Gathas, over which Iran conceived that the individual had to pass after death. If he was righteous the bridge bore him safely over to the sacred mountain, where the good lived again; if he was wicked, he fell off the bridge and found himself in the place of torment. It is another inconsistency that Zarathustra expects, on the one hand, to convert the world by his preaching, while on the other hand his sense of the antagonism between the good and the evil spirits and their followers often hurries him into violent methods. One hymn concludes with a summons to his adherents to fall on the unbelievers with the halberd, and he is constantly predicting their sudden overthrow. Along with this, we may mention that he sought to ally himself with powerful families for the sake of the support they would bring the cause. The name of Vishtaspa, king we know not of what realm, is always associated with the prophet as that of his royal patron; other influential friends are also mentioned. Another point, in which we notice accommodation to existing usage, is that of sacrifice. The Gathas have several noble passages describing the true sacrifice man has to offer to God for His goodness, as consisting simply in the offering of self, in the devotion to the deity of all a man is, and all he can do. At the same time Zarathustra has not a word to say in disparagement of the sacrifice of victims. He prays for guidance in this part of religious duty; he desires to have everything connected with sacrifice done in the best way and with the most effective hymns. Thus the spiritual life is not left to stand alone. There is a personal walk with God, our piety is said to be God's daughter in us, his righteousness is working in us and moulding us for his purposes; both will and deed of the good man are attributed to Him, and the processes are described with true insight by which the soul is sanctified and wedded to her task and her true destiny; but at the same time there is an intent looking to that sacred Fire which is an outward representative of deity; there is the offering of victims, even of horses, when the prophet's mind is bent on war (the Homa-offering does not occur, and we may suppose the prophet rejected this service of the deity by intoxication); there is the smiting of the demons with prayer, and imprecations, similar to those in the Psalms, against adversaries of the cause.

It is no proof of unspirituality that the welfare of the Kine, with whose wail the call of the prophet began, is steadily kept in view during his mission. The agriculturists are on the side of the righteous being, good and ever-better tillage is a means of pleasing him; it is his will that the kine should be freed from alarms and should prosper; and he may be appealed to to give lessons with a view to that end. The doctrine passes far beyond its first occasion; yet the occasion which called for it is never lost sight of.

The Gathas, taken alone, tell us hardly anything of the religion in which Zarathustra's fellow-countrymen believed. They believed undoubtedly in many gods; in those parts of the Avesta which come next to the hymns in time, polytheism is in full force. That Zarathustra only speaks of one god, Ahura (though he also speaks of "the Immortals" generally), may be due to the limited extent and special purpose of the hymns, but it may also be taken as an indication that the prophet did not needlessly interfere with the beliefs of his people: content to preach the doctrine with which he was charged, and which was to him the sum and substance of all religion, he, like several other religious founders, stirred up no strife he could avoid. The doctrine he preached was not unprepared for in the mind of his country, and continued to be the leading feature of Persian religion in subsequent periods.

It is a momentous step in religious progress, which the prophet of Iran calls on his countrymen to take. We notice the main features of the advance.

1. **Man is Called to Judge between the Gods.**—Zarathustra, like Elijah, puts before his people the choice between two worships. Various distinctions between the two cases might be drawn. In the Scripture case Baal is not a bad god, but simply the wrong god for Israel to worship. In the case of our reformer the difference between the two worships is a deeper one. The individual is to choose his god, he is to declare of his own motion that one god is better than others, and that no worship whatever is to be paid to these others. This was a new departure in antiquity; the early world loved to think of many gods, all alike divine and worshipful, each race or clan having its god whom it naturally served, or each part of the earth being portioned out to a divine lord of its own. Neither Greece nor Rome ever thought of making the individual man the arbiter among the unseen beings whom he knew, and requiring him to decide which of them he should consider divine, and which he should disown. In the case before us, moreover, the choice is to be made on moral grounds. Men are called to judge of the character of the beings who are called gods, they are told that there is no necessity to acknowledge those of whom they disapprove, they are emancipated from the fear of hurtful and evil beings. There is war in heaven, and men are encouraged to take part in that war, and to cast off allegiance to such powers as do not make for righteousness. How there came to be such strife among the gods, and how it became necessary that men should judge of it, we have no clear information; we only know that the momentous step was called for and was taken.

The belief, however, remains even after the decision that there are unseen evil beings, who had influence in forming the constitution of things, and who have influence still over the government of the world. The position taken up is not monotheism. The good god is not sole creator or sole governor of the world, he is a limited being ; from the outset he has only in part got his own way, and he has adversaries in the very constitution of things, whom he cannot get rid of. Persian thought is dualistic ; the conception of an Evil Creator and Governor co-ordinate with the good one differentiates it from the thought of India, which always tends to a principle of unity.

2. In the second place, **this religion is essentially intolerant** and persecuting. Having chosen his side in the great war which divides the universe, man can only prosecute that war with all his force ; he must regard the Daevas and their followers as his enemies, and try to weaken and extinguish them. The general feeling of the ancient world about differences in religion was that all religions were equally legitimate, each on its own soil. The Jews, we know, shocked the Greeks and Romans greatly by denying this, and maintaining that there was only one true religion, namely, their own, and that all the others were worships of gods false and vain. But the Persians came before the Jews in this ; the Gathas preach persecution, and the insults offered by Persian kings in later times to the religions of Egypt and Greece were no doubt justified by their convictions. In Persia, as in Israel, religion had come to entertain the notion of false gods. And a religion which entertains that notion must be exclusive. Those who have refused to worship beings hitherto deemed gods, on the ground that they ought not to be worshipped and are not truly gods, cannot but desire to bring the worship of such beings entirely to an end, and to make the worship of the true God prevail instead, by rude or by gentle means, as the stage of civilisation may in each case suggest.

Growth of Mazdeism.—After the Gathas proper we have other hymns written in the Gathic dialect, from which the history of the religion after its foundation may be to some extent inferred.[1] These show that the Zarathustrian religion was regarded, after the departure of the founder, as a great divine institution, and was worked out on the lines he had laid down. The forms of it became of course more fixed. The god it serves is now called "Ahura Mazda," "the All-Knowing Lord" (the name is afterwards contracted into the Greek Oromazdes, the Persian Hormazd; and the religion is called from it Mazdeism); he is still implored for spiritual blessings both for this and for the future life, and for furtherance in agriculture. There is, however, a tendency to address prayer not only to Ahura himself but to beings connected with him. As if the mind wearied of dwelling on the one supreme, the Bountiful Immortals are associated with him, the parts of his holy creation are invoked, the fire which is most closely identified with him, the stars which are his body, the waters, the earth, all good animals and plants. The kine's soul receives sacrifice, and not only the kine's soul which we have met before, but the souls of "just men and holy women," the **Fravashis** or spirits not only of the departed but of the living also, the service of which continues and increases henceforward in Persian religion. These are invented deities and have a shadowy character; but gods of more substance, and more historical reality also came into view at this point. Zarathustra becomes a god, the hymns themselves are adored; the Homa-offering reappears, Mithra is often coupled with Ahura, other old gods creep back and are mentioned along with the moral abstractions, which also increase in number; in one passage there are said to be thirty-three objects of worship, a number which also occurs in India.

Organisation of the Heavenly Beings.—With all this

[1] Yasna Haptanghaiti, *S. B. E.* xxxi. pp. 218 *sqq.*, and others following.

multiplication there is, as we shall see, no compromise of the supreme claims of Ahura. In some of the hymns, all beings, all attributes, all places, and all times of a sacred nature are heaped indiscriminately together, in interminable catalogues. But this apparent confusion is corrected by a remarkable tendency to organisation. The Persian religion ultimately came to have a very simple and very striking theology; and that theology was made up by transforming the abstractions in which the founder dealt, into persons, and arranging them after the pattern of Oriental society. In the later Yasnas (liturgies) a figure rises into view which the Gathas do not mention; that of Angra Mainyu, later Ahriman, the Bad Spirit. In this counterpart of Spenta Mainyu, the Good Spirit (who is not at first identified with Ahura, but proceeds from him), the demons obtain a personal head, and the dualism which appears in all nature and all human society is thus brought to a personal expression. Ahura and Ahriman confront each other as the good power and the evil. Both alike had part in making the world what it is. In every part of the world, and in all that is felt and done they are at strife. Ahura, to quote Mr. Darmesteter, is all light, truth, goodness, and knowledge; Angra Mainyu is all darkness, falsehood, wickedness, and ignorance. Whatever the good spirit makes, the evil spirit mars; he opposes every creation of Ahura's with a plague of his own, it is he who mixed poison with plants, smoke with fire, sin with man, and death with life.

The Attributes of Ahura.—Each of these beings has his retinue. That of Ahura was formed first; it consists of his attributes. Even in the hymns the attributes are regarded as persons, inseparable companions of Ahura; appeals are made to one or another of them, according as the worshipper seeks help from one side or the other of the divine being. By a process which frequently occurs in religious thought, they afterwards come to be more formally arranged and defined; there are six of them, and each is charged with a province of the divine economy. They are as follows:

Vohu Mano (Bahman) Good Mind; he is the head and the guardian of the living creation of Ahura.

Asha Vahista (Ardibehesht), Excellent Holiness: he is the genius of fire.

Kshathra Vairya (Shahrevar), Perfect Sovereignty; he is the lord of metals.

Spenta Armaiti (Spendarmat) divine piety, conceived as female, the goddess of the earth.

Haurvatat (Khordat) health.

Ameretat (Amerdat) immortality.

The last two are a pair, and have charge conjointly of waters and of trees.

Ahura is himself one of these spirits; thus there are seven supreme spirits.

Retinue of Ahriman.—Angra Mainyu on his part comes to have a corresponding retinue of six daevas, each being the evil counterpart of one of the good spirits. Evil Mind, Sickness, and Decay are the names of some of them. The whole spiritual world is ranged on the side of the good or of the evil deity. The **Izatas** (Izeds) or angels consist of gods of immemorial worship in Iran, some of whom are the same as gods worshipped in India; but the title also applies to gods, heavenly and earthly, of later creation, so that the class is a very wide and elastic one. It comprises some beings who have been reduced by the operation of the new ideas from the first to the second rank of deities, such as Verethragna, who corresponds to the Vedic Indra, and Mithra, the sun-god. These now appear in the same rank as gods of the newer style, such as Sraosha, Obedience, and survivals of early superstition, such as the "Curse of the wise," a very powerful Ized. Zarathustra himself belongs to this class of deities, a miscellaneous one indeed. Another class of sacred beings of world-wide extent is that of the Fravashis spoken of above. If the good spirits are many and various, so are the evil. Of these are the great demon-serpent Azhi who plays a great part in Persian mythology, as Vrittra does in Indian. Aeshma, later Asmodeus, may be named; he is one of the Drvants, or storm-fiends. Gahi, an unfaithful goddess, has fallen to a demon of unchastity; the Pairikas (Peris) are female tempters; the Yatu are demons connected with sorcery.

The firm organisation of these hosts of spiritual beings, and the sense of a great conflict in which they are all engaged from the greatest to the least of them, preserve Mazdeism from the weakness and absurdity which are apt to creep over religion when the population of the upper and the nether regions is unduly multiplied. The faithful never forget Ahura in favour of the minor deities, nor do they forget that morals and industry are the chief ends of religion, and that in cultivating these they hasten the coming of the kingdom. The following is the formula, the "Praise of Holiness," with which every act of worship begins in the Yasts[1] (liturgies of the Izeds):

> May Ahura Mazda be rejoiced!
> Holiness is the best of all good!
> I confess myself a worshipper of Mazda, a follower of Zarathustra, one who hates the daevas and obeys the laws of Ahura.

Ancient Testimonies to the Persian Religion.—It is at this stage, while it is still in a state of vigour, that we hear of the Persian religion from various quarters in ancient records. The chapters in the latter half of Isaiah, which so vigorously denounce idolatry, hail the approach of Cyrus towards Babylon, and claim unity of religion between him and the Jews (Isaiah xliv. 28 *sq.*). He is the shepherd who is to

[1] *S. B. E.* vol. xxiii.

lead Jehovah's people back to their own land, and to cause their temple to be rebuilt. And this claim that the Jewish and the Persian religions were the same, that the Jews and the Persians were alike worshippers of the one true God, while all the surrounding nations were polytheists and idolaters. was admitted on the side of Persia. After his conquest of Babylon, Cyrus at once permitted the exiles to return to their own land. The Persian monarchs of the following century, Darius and Artaxerxes, continued to take a friendly interest in the worship of Jehovah, whom they apparently regarded as a form of their own god, "the God of heaven," Hormazd (Ezra vii. 21). They accordingly took measures for the rebuilding of the temple at Jerusalem, and for the introduction there of the new religious constitution which had been prepared at Babylon. This could not have happened if the religion of the Persian kings had not been a pure service of one god,[1] and the other information we have on the subject shows that the Mazdeism of Persia at this period was a very elevated form of the religion. The inscriptions of Darius do not mention the spread of the worships of Mitra and Anahita, which, however, make their appearance in the later inscriptions of Artaxerxes; in none of them is Ahriman spoken of. This, of course, does not prove that he was not believed in; when the Jewish prophet proclaims that Jehovah makes both light and darkness, that he both wounds and heals, there may be a reference to Persian dualism. Yet Mazdeism was capable of appearing, and did appear to the foreigner, as a lofty worship of a god of light and goodness. The same impression is produced by the descriptions of the Greek writers. Herodotus (i. 131, 132) writes as follows; he is a contemporary of Ezra: "The following statements as to the customs of the Persians is to

[1] These two religions, Kuenen says, were more like each other than any other two religions of antiquity.—*Religion of Israel*, iii. 33.

be relied on. They do not fashion images of the gods, nor build temples, nor altars—they consider it wrong to do so, and count it a proof of folly; their reason for this being, as I think, that they do not believe the gods to be beings of the same nature with men as the Greeks do. They are accustomed to offer sacrifices to Zeus on the summits of mountains; they call the whole circle of heaven Zeus. They sacrifice also to the sun, and the moon, and the earth, and to fire, and to water, and to the winds. These are the ancient parts of their ritual, but they have added the worship of the Queen of heaven, Aphrodite; it was from the Assyrians and the Arabs that they acquired this. The Assyrian name for Aphrodite is Mylitta, the Arabs call her Alilat, the Persians, Anahita.[1] Such being their gods the Persians sacrifice to them on this wise. They have no altar, and do not use fire in sacrifice, nor do they have libations nor flutes, nor wreaths nor barley. He who wishes to sacrifice takes his victim to a clean spot and there calls on the deity, his turban wreathed, as a rule, with myrtle. He does not think of praying for benefits for himself individually in connection with his sacrifice; he prays for the welfare of the Persian people and king; he himself is one of the Persian people. He then cuts up the victim, boils the pieces and spreads them out on the softest grass he can find—if possible, on clover. This done, one of the Magians who has come to assist, sings a theogony,[2] as they call the accompanying hymn; no sacrifice is allowed to be offered without one of the Magi being present. After a short pause the sacrificer takes up the pieces of flesh and does with them whatever he likes."

In other passages Herodotus tells us of the extreme

[1] Herodotus says Mitra; but this is a mistake, whether of the father of history or of a transcriber.

[2] One of the Yashts in praise of the particular deity.

sanctity attributed by the Persians to waters, to fire, and to the sun. He also tells us that they regarded lying as the worst possible offence, and next to it falling into debt, since the debtor is tempted to tell lies.

Plutarch writes as follows, quoting from an earlier Greek writer of the third century B.C: "Zoroaster the Magician,[1] who was 5000 years before the war of Troy, named the good god Oromazes and the other Arimonius. . . . Oromazes is engendered of the clearest and purest light, Arimonius of deep darkness; and they war one upon another. The former of these created six other gods (here follow the Amshaspands), but the latter produceth as many other in number, of adverse operation to the former. . . . There will come a time when this Arimonius, who brings into the world plague and famine, shall of necessity be rooted out and utterly destroyed for ever . . . then shall men be all in happy estate, they shall need no more food, nor cast any shadow from them; and that god who hath effected all this shall repose himself for a time, and rest in quiet."

The Vendidad: Laws of Purity.—These extracts show the growth of certain ideas which we have not noticed before. The dualism is being worked out more in detail, other gods are coming in, and the doctrine of the sanctity of the elements has made its appearance. That doctrine is the basis of a new set of ideas and practices which we have now to consider, those namely which are contained in the Vendidad, one of the later works of the Persian canon. To pass from the Gathas to the Vendidad is like passing from Isaiah to Leviticus, and the laws of purity of Persian religion bear a strong analogy to those of Judaism. The Vendidad[2] is composed principally of laws and rules designed to direct the faithful in the great task of maintaining their ritual purity. The whole of

[1] Holland's translation.

[2] *S. B. E.* vol. iv.

life is dominated in this work by the ideas of purity and defilement; the great business of life is to avoid impurity, and when it is contracted to remove it in the correct manner as quickly as possible. Purity here is not primarily sanitary or even moral; though such considerations were no doubt indirectly present. Impure is what belongs to the bad spirit, whether because he created it, as he did certain noxious animals, or because he has established a hold on it as he does on men at death. A man is impure, not because he has exposed himself to the infection of disease, not because he has contracted a stain on his conscience, but because he has touched something of which a Daeva has possession, and so has come under the influence of that Daeva. Purification, therefore, and the act of healing consist of exorcisms of various kinds. This notion of purity plays a great part in other old religions also; it is here that we see its original meaning most clearly. Another great feature of the doctrine of purity in the Vendidad is that the elements, fire, earth, and water, are holy, and to defile them in any way is the most grievous of sins. As everything which leaves the body is unclean, a man must not blow up a fire with his breath, and bathing with a view to cleanliness is not to be thought of. The disposal of the dead was a matter of immense difficulty, since corpses, being unclean, could be committed neither to Fire nor to the Earth. They are ordered to be exposed naked on a building constructed for that purpose on high ground, so that birds of prey may devour them; and a great part of the Vendidad is taken up with directions for purification, after a death has taken place, of the persons who were in the house, of the house itself, of those who carried the corpse, and of the road they travelled, etc.

How this Doctrine Entered Mazdeism.—This system was not in force in the time of Darius and Artaxerxes, (when the dead were buried or, as in the case of Crœsus, burned) though the ideas were appearing at that period on which, it is founded ; and it is plain that it has no necessary or vital connection with the religion of Zarathustra. But in later Mazdeism there are many such importations. This religion, in its course from east to west, came in contact with beliefs and usages with which, though foreign to its own nature, it yet came to terms. Mazdeism is not originally a markedly priestly religion; it is thought that it became so when planted in Media. No doubt there were germs in the early Iranian religion of a priestly system. Zarathustra himself was a priest and was favourable to due religious observances. But it is quite contrary to his spirit that life should be governed entirely by ritual law. It was in Media that this came to be the case. The name of Magi, originally perhaps that of a tribe, became in Media the name of the priesthood, and so furnished an additional title for Mazdeism. It is to this stage of the religion that the priestly legislation of the Vendidad, with all its puritanical regulation of life, is to be ascribed. (The practice of exposing the bodies of the dead to be devoured by birds of prey is probably of Scythian origin.) In this period also, remote from the origin of the religion, we find a new view of Zarathustra himself and of his revelation. In the earlier sources Zarathustra composes his hymns in a natural manner; he is not an absolute lawgiver, but depends on princes for the carrying out of his views. In the later works the revelation takes place in a series of private interviews between Ahura and Zarathustra; the prophet puts questions to the god, and the god dictates in reply sentences which are at once promulgated as sacred laws. Mazdeism, like other religions, has its wooden age, its verbal inspiration, and its priestly code.

To trace the lines by which the influence of the religion

of Persia asserted itself in the wider world would be a large enterprise: only a few indications can be given here. One great service which that religion did to the world was undoubtedly that it had sympathy with the Jews, and enabled Jewish monotheism to take a fresh start on its way to become a religion for mankind. Mazdeism itself had a tinge of universalism; Zarathustra expected his religion to spread beyond his own land, and it did spread over all the provinces of Iran. It never became a world-religion, but it might have done so had it not become swathed and choked in Magism, or had any new movement arisen in it to assert the supremacy of its purely human over its artificial elements. But Ahura himself, perhaps, was too abstract and philosophic a god to inspire missionary ardour; it needed a being more firmly rooted in history, a god who had done more to prove the energy and intensity of his nature, and, further, a god more undoubtedly omnipotent than Ahura, to establish a universal rule.

The interesting inquiry remains, how far the Jewish religion was modified by its contact with the Persian. The laws of purity in the Jewish priestly code find a close parallel in the Vendidad; but with the Israelites the notion of religious purity existed, and was worked out in considerable detail, as we see from Deuteronomy, before the exile, and therefore long before the period of the Vendidad. The belief in the resurrection, found among the Jews after the exile, and not before it, has been maintained by many to be a loan from Persia, where the belief in future reward and punishment was a settled thing from the time of Zarathustra. But the Jews do not appear to have grasped this belief all at once or fully formed. They arrived at it gradually, many Old Testament scholars affirm, and by spiritual inferences timidly put forth at first, from their own religious consciousness. A belief which the Jewish religion was capable of producing of itself need not, without clearer evidence than we possess, be regarded as borrowed. We are not on much surer ground when we come to ask whether the angels and demons of Judaism are connected with those of Persia. This belief also arises naturally in Judaism, where God came to be thought of as very high and very inaccessible, and intermediate beings were therefore needed. Some of the figures of the Jewish spirit-world are, no doubt, due to Persia; the Ashmodeus of the book of Tobit is a Persian figure. Later Judaism is like Parsism in arranging the heavenly beings in a hierarchy, and assigning to the chief angels special functions in the administration of God's kingdom, and still more so when the upper hierarchy is confronted by a lower one with a great adversary and father of lies at its head. But this takes place long after the Persian contact.

The Persian deities had, as a rule, too little legend to enable them to be received in other countries. Ahura does not travel. Anaitis is thought to have passed into Greece, changing her name to Aphrodite, but also to the severer Artemis; but she is perhaps not original in Persia. The Persian god best known in other lands was Mithra, the sun-god and god of wisdom. He was a favourite with the Roman armies in the early empire, and representations of him as a hero in the act of slaying a bull in a cave have been found in many lands. There were also mysteries connected with him, in which the candidates had to pass through a great series of trials and hardships. Persia influenced Europe and the west of Asia at the same period in another way. Manicheism, a system which was one of the three great universal religions of that time, and had a worship and a priesthood and a sacred literature of its own, was founded by a native of Persia. He laboured at a distance from his own country, and the doctrines he propounded came more from Chaldea than from Persia, and consisted of great histories, like those of the Gnostics, of the doings and sufferings of cosmic and other persons; a great struggle between the powers of light and those of darkness was one of its principal features. The worship of this church was spiritual; its morals were in theory of the purest and most ascetic kind, being founded on a principle of dualism in the material world, and requiring much self-denial and long fasts. The higher virtue of the system was not, however, required of the ordinary member. Later Parsism, both in Iran and in India, has shown a disposition to cast off dualism, and to become, both philosophically and practically, a monistic system.

Books Recommended

S. B. E. vols. iv., xxiii. (Darmesteter); xxxi. (Mills). *The Zendavesta*, vols. v., xviii., xxiv., xxxvii., xlvii. Pahlavi Texts (E. W. West).

The Histories of Antiquity of Duncker, Maspero, and Ed. Meyer.

Haug's *Essays on the Sacred Language, Writings, and Religion of the Parsis*. Second Edition, 1878.

F. Windischmann, *Zoroastr. Studien*, 1863.

Geldner, "Zoroaster," in *Encyclopædia Britannica*; "Zoroastrianism," in *Encyclopædia Bibl.*

Mills, *A Study of the Five Zarathustrian Gathas*, 1892-94.

Lehmann, in De la Saussaye.

Dadhabai Naoroji, *The Parsee Religion*.

PART V

CHAPTER XXII

CHRISTIANITY

THE writer is aware that in offering a chapter on Christianity at the conclusion of this work, he attempts a difficult task. If treated at all, Christianity must be dealt with in the same way as the other religions, and no assumptions must be made for it which were not made for them. And a view of our own religion written, not from the standpoint of the faith and love we feel towards it but of scientific accuracy, must appear to many pious Christians to be cold and meagre. But, on the other hand, Christianity is the key of the arch we have been building, the consummating member of the development we have sought to trace, and to withhold any estimate of its character would be to leave our work most imperfect. It seems better, therefore, that some hints at least should be offered on this part of the subject. Christianity cannot indeed be dealt with in the same proportion as the other religions; that would far exceed our space. But some views are offered regarding its essential nature, which the writer believes to be so firmly founded in fact that even those who are not Christians cannot deny them, and thus to afford a valid criterion for the comparison of Christianity with other faiths.

In the chapter on the religion of Israel we saw how the prophets before and during the exile began to cherish the idea of a new relation between God and man, which would not depend on sacrifice nor be confined to Israel. God, they declared, was preparing a new age, in which He would receive man to more intimate communion than before; and man would be guided in the right path, not by covenants and laws, but by the constant inspiration of a present deity. The new religion would be one which all nations could share. Jerusalem, the seat of the true faith, would attract all eyes; all would turn to her because of the Lord her God.

But, alas, instead of growing broader to realise its universal destiny, the religion of Israel grew narrower after the exile, and seemed to forget the prospects thus opened up to it. Judaism, though immeasurably enriched in its inner consciousness by the teaching of the prophets, maintained its earlier semi-heathenish forms of worship, only surrounding them with new stateliness and new significance; and clothed itself in a hard shell of public ritual and personal observance. The Jews separated themselves rigorously from the world, and cultivated an exclusive pride; as if their religion had been given them for themselves alone, and not for mankind. Under the Maccabees they displayed the most heroic courage and tenacity, in maintaining their own beliefs and rites amid the flood of Hellenism which at one time almost swept them away. That they carried their nationality unimpaired through this period is one of the most wonderful achievements of the Jewish race. In the succeeding period, however, many signs appeared showing that their religion was losing energy. The rule of the priests and scribes extended more and more over the whole of life, tradition and observance grew more and more extensive, but the moral judgment lost its elasticity. The sense of the divine presence grew faint, and multitudes of spirits filled the air instead, oppressing human life with a sense of vague anxiety. As political independence was lost, the people became less happy and more easily excited. But while formalism held increasing sway over their actions, imagination was free, and surrounded both the past history of Israel and its future triumphs with manifold embellishments.

In such a condition was the religion of the Jews when Jesus appeared in Palestine and created a new order of things. Christianity was at first a movement within Judaism. Like all the religions which trace their history to personal founders, it grew from very small beginnings; but its doctrine was of such a nature, that if circumstances favoured, it could not fail to spread beyond Judaism, to men of other lands and other tongues.

The doctrine consisted primarily in a declaration that that great religious consummation, the kingdom of God, which the prophets had foretold, which was regarded by the fellow-countrymen of Jesus as a far-off hope, and which had just been heralded by John the Baptist as being immediately at hand, had actually taken place. The perfect state was announced to have arrived, and to be a thing not of the future but of the present. The long-expected intercourse of God and man on new terms of perfect agreement and sympathy, had come into operation; any one who chose could assure himself of the fact. The title by which Jesus described the intimate relationship of man and God which he announced, sufficiently shows its character. God is the Father in heaven; men are His children, and all that men have to do is to realise that this is so, to enter the circle and begin to live with God on such terms. The great God seeks to have every one living with Him as his child; and religion is no more, no less, than this communion. Father and child dwell together in perfect love and confidence; no outward regulations are needed for their intercourse, no bargains, no traditions, no ritual, no pilgrimage, no sacrifice. The intercourse can be carried on by any one, anywhere. It is not a matter of apparatus, but a purely moral affair, an affair of love. The Father knows all about the child, is able to give him all he needs, even before he asks it; is willing to forgive his sins when he repents of them; is anxious above all to reinforce his efforts after goodness. The child knows that the Father is always near him, carries every need and wish to Him in prayer, even though knowing that He is aware of them beforehand; regards all that happens, either good or ill, as sent by Him for the best ends, and seeks in every case to know his will and to submit to it sweetly, and execute it faithfully.

Nothing could be simpler, or deeper, or broader. Religion is here presented free from all local or accidental or obscuring elements; religion itself is here revealed. Accepted in this form, it does for man all that it can. The relation between God and man is made purely moral; the link is not that of race, nor does it consist in anything external. The individual—every individual who will pause to hear—is assured that there exists between God and him a natural sympathy, and is urged to allow that sympathy to have its way. It is easy to see what effect such a belief must have. The individual, bidden to seek the principle of union with God not in any external circumstance or arrangement, but in his own heart, becomes conscious of an inner freedom from all artificial restraints. He finds in his own heart the secret of happiness, and is raised above all fears and irritations; and hence the forces of his nature are encouraged to unfold themselves freely. He sees clearly what as a human person he is called to be and to do, and feels a new energy to realise his ideals. As God has come down to him, he is lifted up to God; a divine power has entered his life, which is able to do all things in him and for him.

It may be said that what we have described are the effects of religious inspiration generally, and may take place in connection with any faith. But the divine impulse communicated to mankind in Christianity differs from that of any other religion in two important respects. In the first place, the God who here enters into union with man possesses full reality and a character of the utmost energy. It is Jehovah with whom we have to do here, changed, indeed, but still the same; a God of real and irresistible power, on whom speculation has not laid its weakening hand. The union of man with God is not secured by making God abstract and vague, nor is his infinite kindness and forgivingness purchased at the expense of his intensity and awfulness. With Jesus, God is still the power who has actual control over everything that goes on, and who is able to do even what appears to be most impossible. He is a God of strict justice and holiness; though He is so kind, his judgments have not ceased, but are still impending over guilty men and a guilty people. It is He who can cast both soul and body into hell. It is a God of such energy, such zeal, who yet offers Himself as the willing benefactor and defender, and the loving guide and helper of the humblest of his human creatures. In the second place, the terms of the union here formed between God and man are such as can be found nowhere else. The deity inspires man not to any particular kind of acts, not to sacrifices, nor to withdrawal from the world, but inspires him simply to realise himself. Man is assured of the sympathy of this great God, and is then left in freedom as to the mode in which he should serve Him. No rules are prescribed; human life is not pressed into an artificial mould, as is the case in so many great religions; no preference is accorded to any one pursuit over others. This religion is not a yoke to coerce men and to make them less, but an inspiration capable of entering into every kind of life, and of making men greater and better in whatever occupation. Even religious duties are left to form themselves naturally; all that is insisted on is that the child shall have living and real intercourse with the Father. Prayer is necessary, and so is the practice of good works; the child must keep in sympathy with the Father by doing as He does. Further than this, the forms of the religious life are not prescribed. With regard to morals, it is the same. The moral life is to build itself up freely from within; goodness is not to be a matter of rule, but the spontaneous and happy development of a principle which lives and speaks deep in the centre of the heart. Jesus is not a lawgiver, save in a metaphorical sense: the law which he sets up is nothing more than that which every man, when he turns away from all that is artificial, can find in his own breast.

It is one feature of the spontaneity and spirituality of the religion of Jesus, that it has no constitution. Jesus regarded himself as the founder not of a new religion, but only of an inner circle of more devoted believers inside the old religion of his country; he did not therefore feel called to draw up rules for a new faith, and the result of this is that the mechanism of the religion is of later growth. The authority of the founder can be appealed to for a direct and constant intercourse with God as of a child with his father, and for the conduct of men towards each other, which such intercourse with God necessarily implies, but for hardly anything more. Here, as in no other historical religion, man is free.

The religion of Jesus, therefore, is one of love alone. The divine nature consists in love, and the impulse which religion communicates, is simply that which proceeds from being loved and loving. And a religion of love finds the way, as no other can, to make man free, to unseal his energies, and to lead him upwards to the best life. The appearance of such a religion forms the most momentous epoch of human history. He who brought it forward must occupy a unique position in the estimation of mankind. It can never be superseded.

It is no doubt the case that the doctrine of Jesus was not in all respects new. The ideas of the prophets live again in him; his followers have always found many of the Jewish Psalms to be perfectly suited to their experience. Jesus lived in the faith of Israel, and considered that he had come only to make that faith better understood, and to free it from improper accretions. What was new was his own person. His great work was that he embodied his teaching in a life which expressed it perfectly. It is far short of the truth to say that there was no inconsistency between what he taught and his own conduct. His life is a demonstration, in every detail, of the effects of his religion; all flows with the utmost simplicity, and even as a matter of necessity, out of the truth he taught. What he preached was, in fact, himself; he was himself living in the kingdom of God, to which he called others to come; he knew in his own experience what it was to live as a child with the Father in heaven, and to view all persons, all things, all duties, in the light of that intercourse. All his acts and words flowed from the same spring in his own inner experience. In no other way could his life shape itself than as it did, and he saw with perfect clearness what men must be, and on what terms they must live together when God and they were as Father and children to each other. What he thus knew he lived, as if no laws but those of the kingdom of heaven had any authority for him, and so he presented the world with that living embodiment of the true religion, which has been the main strength of Christianity. Jesus announces a new union of God with man, a union in which he himself is the first to rejoice, but which all may share along with him; and hence his person counts for more in his religion than that of any other religious founder in his, and necessarily becomes an object of faith to all who enter the communion. The doctrine does not produce its specific effect apart from the person of Jesus. Because in him alone they know the truth which brings them peace, his followers regard him, in a way which has no parallel in any other religion, as their Saviour.

But this name is given to him by his followers, as it is claimed by himself, for another reason also. Jesus was more than a teacher. He felt a power to be present in him which was able to supply all needs and to comfort all sorrows; he did not shrink from summoning all who were weary and heavy laden to come to him, nor from undertaking to give them rest. Keenly alive to the sufferings of others, and able to perceive even those sufferings of which they were not themselves conscious, he felt it to be his mission to deal with the sadder side of human life, he was a physician sent to the sick, a shepherd seeking the lost sheep. It was among the poor and the sick, and even among the outcasts of society, in whom the sense of need was strongest, that he felt himself most at home and most able to fulfil his calling. Thus the motive of compassion enters strongly into all he said and did; but the compassion is not hopeless in this case as in the similar case of Gautama (pp. 356, 363), nor is the cure recommended for the ills of humanity that of withdrawal from mankind or of forgetfulness. Here there is a belief in God. The compassion from which the religion flows is not as in the case of Gautama, that of a preacher who has ceased to trust in any heavenly power; it is announced as existing first of all in the heart of God Himself. God can do all things, and in his yearning pity for his children has sent his representative to assure them of his sympathy and to comfort them in their sorrows. With Jesus therefore no evil is so great as not to admit of a positive cure; he feels the remedy of all human ills to be present in his own heart, and so he appears as the Messiah, not such a Messiah as his countrymen looked for, but as the true Messiah, in whom all human wants are met, and all human hopes fulfilled. The cure which he announces for all ills consists in devotion to the will of the Father in heaven. To give oneself unreservedly to the labour of realising the purposes of the heavenly Father in one's own heart and in the world, is to rise above all cares and sorrows; enthusiasm in the Father's service is the sovereign remedy. To one who believes in the Father, and seeks to live as his child, no despair is possible. To be engaged in his business is at all times the highest happiness, and his kingdom is assuredly coming, though man has still the privilege of working for it,—the kingdom in which all darkness and evil will be put away.

We have indicated the chief points which in a scientific comparison of Christianity with other religions appear to constitute its distinctive character; and we have sought to make our statement such as the reasonable adherent of other religions will feel to be warranted. The points are these. Christianity is a religion of freedom, it is a system of inner inspiration more than of external law or system, it is embodied in the living person of its founder, in which alone it can be truly seen; and the founder is one who is living himself in the relation to God to which he calls men to come, and feels himself called and sent to be the Saviour of men.

It is impossible in this work to treat Christianity on the same scale as the other religions; but the question of its universalism must necessarily receive attention. Jesus himself did not expressly say that his religion was for all men. It was his immediate aim to bring about the renewal of the faith of his countrymen, and to give it a more spiritual character; and some of his followers considered that he had aimed at nothing more than this. But he formed a circle of disciples and adherents, which afterwards came to be the Christian Church, and he attached no ritual condition whatever, to membership in that community. Nay, more; by his repudiation of the Jewish system of tradition he showed that the Jewish laws of ritual purity were not binding upon his disciples, and the further inference could readily be drawn, that one could enter the Kingdom without being a Jew at all. The strong missionary impulse of the infant religion brought it very early in contact with Gentile life, and the question soon arose, whether those who refused to become Jews could yet claim a share in the Messiah. It was the task of the Apostle Paul to work out the theory of the universalism of Christianity, and after some conflict the principle was recognised that in the Church all racial differences disappear; "in Christ there is neither Jew nor Greek." This controversy once settled—and a few years sufficed to settle it—the new religion was free to spread in all directions. It spread rapidly; the gospel was very simple and imposed no burdensome conditions, and it soon proved itself to be capable of striking root in any country. The Apostle Paul was the first great theologian of the Church; but his doctrine, as will happen in such a case, does not in all points spring out of the nature of the religion itself. The Pauline theology is an attempt to reconcile the facts of Christianity and especially that great stumbling-block to the Jews, the death of the Messiah, with the requirements of Jewish thought. Instead of seeing in the death of Christ, as the older apostles at first did, a perplexing enigma, St. Paul saw in it the principal manifestation of the compassion of the Saviour, and the great purpose for which he had come into the world. He concentrated attention on Christ's death and made the cross rather than the doctrine of the Messiah the burden of his teaching. To understand Paul we must distinguish between his religion and his theology. His religious position is essentially the same as that of Jesus himself; with him, too, the new religion is that of father and child, and of the consequences which inevitably flow from such a union. But the movement of thought which began at the moment of the crucifixion, the concentration of Christian faith and love on the person of the Saviour, was now complete. The figure of the Crucified with its powerful tragic attraction, and with its deep lessons of conquest by self-surrender, of life by dying, remained from St. Paul onwards, in the centre of the faith.

The world of the early centuries was in great need of a religion, and Christianity supplied the place which was vacant. Brought in contact, in the great ocean of the Roman Empire where all currents met, with religions and philosophies of every kind, it proved best suited to the task of supplying an inspiration for life, uniting together different classes of men and schools of thought. But in the wide arena of the Empire it received as well as gave, and in its encounters with strange rites and doctrines it also put on many a strange aspect. It became the heir of the thoughts and aspirations of a hundred empires; all the pious sentiments that flowed together from every quarter of the world helped to enrich its doctrine, and to make it the great reservoir it is of all the tendencies and views, even those most contrary to each other, which are connected with religion. Its institutions are of diverse origin. From the Jews it received its earliest Bible, for the Christians had at first no sacred books but those of the old covenant, and its weekly festival, though the day was changed. Its God was the God of the Old Testament, and its Saviour was the Messiah of Jewish prophecy, so that it was a continuation of the Jewish religion, and the attempts which were made by early Gnostics to dissolve this tie were soon forgotten.

From Greece it received much. The world it had to conquer was Greek, and the conquest could only take place by an accommodation to Greek thought and to Greek ways. In the end of chapter xvi. we spoke of the second Greek religion which arose under the influence of philosophy, and found its way wherever Greek culture spread. In this great movement, Christianity found a preparation for its coming in the Greek world, without which its spread must have been much more doubtful. In the Graeco-Roman religion the advances which appear in Christianity are already prefigured. Thought has been busy in building up a great doctrine of God, such a God as human reason can arrive at, a Being infinitely wise and good, who is the first cause and the hidden ground of all things, the sum of all wisdom, beauty, and goodness, and in whom all men alike may trust. Greek thought also found much occupation in the attempt to reach a true account of man's moral nature and destiny. Both in theory and in practice many an attempt was made to build up the ideal life of man, and thus many minds were prepared for a religion which places the riches of the inner life above all others. The Greek philosopher's school was a semi-religious union, the central point of which was, as is the case with Christianity also, not outward sacrifice but mental activity. It is not wonderful therefore if Christian institutions were assimilated to some extent to the Greek schools. It has recently been shown that the celebration of the Eucharist came very early to bear a close resemblance to that of a Greek mystery, and that there is an unbroken line of connection between the discourse of the Greek philosopher and the Christian Sermon. In some of the Greek schools pastoral visitation was practised, and the preacher kept up an oversight of the moral conduct of his adherents. While Christianity certainly had vigour enough to shape its own institutions, and may even be seen to be doing so in some of the books of the New Testament, the agreement between Greek and Christian practices amounts to something more than coincidence.

It was towards the end of the second century that the alliance between Christianity and the Greek world was finally ratified. Till then belief and practice were determined mainly by custom and tradition ; but now these were to give way to definite laws and settled institutions. There came to full development, about the period we have mentioned, a highly-organised system of church government, a canon of sacred books of Christian origin, and a creed in which the beliefs of Christians were drawn together in one statement. It cannot be denied that the elaborate external forms with which the religion of Jesus was thus invested went far to change its spirit also. But this happens to every religion which reaches the stage of organising itself in order to continue in the world and to rule permanently in human thought and in human society. No external forms can adequately express living religious ideas ; and yet there must be external forms in order that religious ideas may be perpetuated. The ministers of the new truth inevitably rise in dignity till they grow into a hierarchy. That truth inevitably seeks to establish itself as scientifically true, and with the aid of the ruling philosophical tendency of the day clothes itself in a view of the universe and in a creed. Thus the essence of Christianity came to consist not in loving the Master and following him in faith and love, but in upholding the authority of the Church, receiving her sacraments, and believing various metaphysical and transcendental statements. Here also a hard shell is formed round the spiritual kernel of the religion which, if it is fitted to preserve the latter in rude and stormy times, is also fitted to confuse and also apt to conceal it.

In each of the countries to which it came, Christianity adopted what it could of the religion formerly existing there. The old religions of these lands were not all alike, and hence it came to pass that as the language of Rome was transformed in various ways, and passed into the different yet cognate tongues of the Romance nations, so the religion of the Empire, combining with various forms of heathenism, passed into several national religions, the differences of which are at least as conspicuous as their similarity. In Italy Christianity appears to be a system of local deities, each village worshipping its own Madonna or saint. In Holland worship consists almost entirely of preaching. In other countries the ritual and the intellectual elements of religion are blended in varying proportions; and the former heathenism of each land is also to be traced in many a popular observance and belief. So great is the variety of the religions of Europe, not to mention that of the negroes or the Shakers of America, that many have doubted whether they ought all to be considered as branches of one faith, or whether they would not more fitly be regarded as so many national religions which have all alike connected themselves with Christianity. Against this there is to be urged in the first place that as a matter of history they are all undoubtedly offshoots of the religion of Jesus. It may also be urged that wherever the name of Jesus is named, his ideas must to some extent be present, however much they are obscured and prevented from operating by lower modes of view. The Christianity of no country ought to be judged by the attitude of its most ignorant or even of its average adherents; and in every land where Christianity prevails, an influence connected with religion is at work, which makes for the emancipation and elevation of the human person, and for the awakening of the manifold energies of human nature. This, as we saw, is the immediate and native tendency of the religion of Jesus; it opens the prison doors to them that are bound; it communicates by its inner encouragement an energy which makes the infirm forget their weaknesses, it fills the heart with hope and opens up new views of what man can do and can become. It is this that makes it the one truly universal religion. Islam, it is true, has also proved its power to live in many lands, and Buddhism has spread over half of Asia. But Buddhism is not a full religion, it does not tend to action but to passivity, and affords no help to progress. Islam, on the other hand, is a yoke rather than an inspiration; it is inwardly hostile to freedom, and is incapable of aiding in higher moral development. Christianity has a message to which men become always more willing to respond as they rise in the scale of civilisation; it has proved its power to enter into the lives of various nations, and to adapt itself to their circumstances and guide their aspirations without humiliating them. A religion which identifies itself, as Christianity does, with the cause of freedom in every land, and tends to unite all men in one great brotherhood under the loving God who is the Father of all alike, is surely the desire of all nations, and is destined to be the faith of all mankind.

CHAPTER XXIII

CONCLUSION

IT will not be expected that the result of the great movement traced in the chapters of this work can be summed up in a few words. We set out with a definition of our subject which we said could only be fully verified after religion had accomplished its growth and had fully unfolded its nature. We also set out with the assumption that all the religion of the world is one, and that it exhibits a development which is in the main continuous, from the most elementary to the highest stages. We shall not now attempt to justify by argument that definition or that assumption. The history which we have sought to place before the reader must itself be the proof of them. All that can be done in bringing this work to a close is to point out one great line of development, which may be recognised more or less distinctly in the growth of each religion, and may therefore be held to be characteristic of religion as a whole. No doubt the growth of religion, as of other human activities, has many sides and aspects, but perhaps it may be possible to specify the central line of growth in which the explanation of all the subsidiary and parallel forward movements is to be found.

It was stated in our first chapter that religion is the expression of human needs with reference to higher beings who are supposed to be capable of fulfilling men's desires, and it was also stated as an inference from this, that the growth of human needs is the cause of religious change and progress. If this is true, then the key to the progress of religion is to be found in the successive emergence in human experience of higher and still higher needs. If we can discover the order in which higher aspirations successively emerge in the growth of humanity, then we shall possess the chief clue to the course of religious advance. Now while there is infinite variety in the needs and desires of men, every land and each nation having ideals all its own, we can yet discern, on a broad view of human progress, an advance from lower to higher needs which is common to the human race, and manifests itself in the history of each nation. Three successive conditions of human life stand out before us as markedly distinct, and as occurring wherever civilisation continues to advance. The first is that in which material needs are all-absorbing ; the second that in which freedom from material needs has been to some extent attained, and the highest aspirations are directed to the safety and advancement of the nation in which men find themselves united and secure ; and the third is that in which the individual realises his own value apart from the state, and develops a personal ideal which is thenceforward his chief end. To these three stages of human existence three types of religion correspond, and the growth of religion consists in the main in its passage from the lower to the higher of these stages.

The religion of the tribe belongs to that stage of man's existence in which his energies are entirely occupied in the struggle against nature and against other tribes. The conditions of his life do not allow his higher faculties to grow, and while he is not without many glimpses and anticipations of higher things, his religion, as a whole, is a mass of childish fancies and of fixed traditions which he cannot explain, but does not venture to criticise or change. His gods are petty and capricious beings, and his modes of influencing them, though used with zeal and fervour, have little to do with reason or with taste or with morality. It is in this kind of religion that magic of all sorts is at home.

The advance from the religion of the tribe to that of the nation was briefly described above (p. 79, *sqq.*). The leading classes of the state at least, having gained some measure of security and leisure, ideas of a nobler order spring up in their minds. The service of the great gods of the state is organised with befitting dignity and splendour; the best minds contribute to it all they can in the way of art, of poetry, of purified legend, of stately ceremonial. Patriotism and religion are one, the offices of worship are upheld by the whole power of the state, and the gods speak with new authority to the spirit of the worshipper. Now it is that great religious systems arise, so powerful, so highly organised, so splendidly adorned, and surrounded with such venerable traditions, that they seem to be destined for eternity. The priesthood becomes a very powerful class, and acquires a personal holiness which marks out its members as different from other men; the sacrifices acquire the character of divine mysteries, every detail of which, even the most trivial, has a sacred meaning; religious books are compiled or written, which by and by are regarded as inspired, and as possessing absolute authority. It is to be observed that the older style of religion is not at once driven out by the growth of the new, but continues to flourish beside it and under its shadow. The tribes of whom the nation is composed still cherish and adore their own special deities. That older worship is often thought to bring blessings which the new worship of the state does not command, and many a piece of ancient magic, many a practice which has no connection with the state religion, still goes on, especially among those who are not cultivated enough to appreciate the nobler faith which has arisen.

This, however, does not keep the national faith from growing in riches and consistency; and religion appears, as this growth proceeds, to have attained the highest degree of power and authority at which it can possibly arrive. Commanding as it does all the resources of the nation, enriched by all that can be brought to it of material or intellectual riches, placed in a position of absolute exaltation and inviolableness, to what further conquests can it still look forward? Yet when a national religion appears to be most firmly established, the forces are most certainly at work which must ere long lead to a far-reaching change. While the national worship has been growing up to its highest splendours, the lives of the citizens have also been growing richer and deeper, and the individual soul has become aware of wants and longings which cannot be satisfied in the national temple. The further progress of religion is apt to appear as a revolt against the system which has grown so strong. The individual sets out to seek a consistent intellectual view, and so figures as a sceptic. He aims at a higher moral law than that of the priestly system, and is accused of undermining public morality. He feels a new call to personal goodness, a new need for personal atonement with the ideal holiness which he has learned to apprehend; and as the public ritual does not meet these needs, he seeks for new religious associations and perhaps appears to preach a doctrine contrary to patriotism, as it is subversive of the established religion of his country, and to be wilfully destroying what his countrymen revere, and wilfully breaking through old ties and obligations. Thus the individualist stage of religion succeeds the national. But the individualist stage is also, in part at least, the universal stage. What the thinking mind and the pious heart seeks and cannot find in the national worship, is a religion free as the seeker himself has become free, from all that is unreasonable and artificial, a religion therefore in which every thinking mind and every pious heart can have a share. What is gained by individuals in this direction is capable, therefore, if circumstances favour, of proving an acquisition not only for the individual reformer or his nation, but for all men. But as the rise of national religion does not bring to an end the ruder worships of the tribes, which still go on beside it, so neither does the rise of individualism, even in its purest form, bring to an end the national worship. In the long run this may follow, but it does not take place at once. All three forms of religion go on together; the religion of magic, that of stately public sacrifices and ceremonials, and that of intellectual effort and pious meditation and prayer. Each no doubt influences to some extent the others, and is influenced by them in turn.

The movement thus indicated from tribal to national, and from national to individual and to universal religion, is the central development of religion, and all the minor developments which might be traced, as that of sacrifice from rude to spiritual forms, of the functions of the sacred class, of the morality dictated by religion at its various stages, or of the literature connected with piety, may be explained by reference to this one. This movement has taken place in every nation; we have seen something of it in each of our chapters. In some nations it has been early arrested, so that no important contribution has there been brought to the general religion of mankind, in others it has run its full course, and like a great river has arrived at the ocean at last, to mingle its waters with those of other mighty streams.

The story of the growth of the world's religion has

therefore to be told in a number of parallel narratives, each dealing with the experience of a separate nation. There can scarcely be any general history of the religion of the world, in addition to those special histories. Some epochs, it is true, stand out as having witnessed simultaneous religious movements in many lands, as if the mind of the whole human race had then been passing through the same crisis of thought. The sixth century B.C. is the age of Confucius and of Laotsze in China, of Gautama in India, of Jeremiah, Ezekiel and the Unknown Prophet of the Exile, of Pythagoras, Heraclitus, and Xenophanes, and also of the rise into prominence of the Greek mysteries. Widely different as the movements are which thus took place contemporaneously in these lands, we may discern in all of them alike the tendency to plant religion in the mind and heart, and to create a deeper union than the old external one, a union based on common intellectual effort and spiritual sympathy. The period immediately before and after the Christian era might also appear to be one in which the mind of the world as a whole made a great step forward. The union of many nations under the sway of Rome, and the universal diffusion of the Greek language as a means of general communication, made men conscious at this time as they had never been before, of the unity of mankind in spite of all differences of race and speech. A philosophy also was popular at this time which was cosmopolitan in its character, and occupied itself with the great problems, which are the same for all, of man's relation to the gods and of his moral duty. If we add to this the combination which took place at Rome and wherever different races met, of various rites and creeds, we see that the age was one singularly disposed to the breaking down of artificial barriers between men, and singularly fitted to promote the growth of a belief in which men of all nations might unite and feel themselves to be brethren.

In these two periods we may recognise important steps in that great Education of the Human Race which the Apostle Paul refers to in a bold philosophy of history (Galat. iv.), and which later thinkers have striven to set forth in detail. After the long servitude of mankind to irrational practices and to gods who were no gods, there comes first the period when men recognise that the true God is to be found not merely outside them but within their hearts and minds, and then the period when they find that the true God is the same to all men, that they are all children of the same Father. But while these general movements of the human mind may be acknowledged, the education of the human race proceeds for the most part in nations. As each nation has to elaborate its own art, its own literature, its own system of law, so each nation has to perfect its own religion. Even after a universal faith has appeared, religion does not cease to be a national thing. Each people moulds the universal religion which it has adopted into a special form, continues by means of it the rites and traditions of the past, and expresses through it its own national character and aspirations. Each nation as well as each individual must necessarily have a faith specially its own, arising out of its own character and experience and in great part incommunicable to others. No two nations could possibly exchange religions.

But on the other hand every nation contains within itself forms of religion which differ from each other as widely as those of two separate nations. It has been said that no religious belief or usage which has once lived can ever be destroyed; and the proof of this may be witnessed in every nation. Even after that religion has come which has its main seat in the heart and soul, the ruder forms of piety live on, and even at times aggressively assert themselves. If there are classes for whom the struggle against material hardships still continues, no lofty religion can be attained by them any more than by savage tribes. As the conditions of their life forbid the growth of their higher faculties, their religion cannot be one of thought or of refinement, but must be one which promises palpable benefits or an escape from immediate dangers. At a somewhat higher stage is the class of those who, while partly escaped from the struggle against want, have not yet fully realised themselves as thinking and spiritual beings, and to whom the benefits of religion still lie outside, rather than in the inner life. When the benefits of religion are thus conceived, its processes must be of a mechanical nature. Hence the various systems of apparatus for connecting the worshipper with a source of good distant from him in time or space, and for fetching as it were from another region, with certainty and accuracy, needed supplies of grace.

The further development of religion in a community so mixed must depend on the progressive education and elevation of the people. As more and more of them are freed first from distracting wants and cares, and then from sordid and materialistic views, their spiritual nature will expand. The need for God Himself rather than for his gifts, will arise and increase in their hearts, and they will grow capable of that highest religion which is the life of the soul with God; they will feel its beauty and will drink of the deep springs which it contains, of strength and peace.

To attain this true religion the human race has had to travel far and to make many experiments. Many temples were built and fell to ruin before the true temple of the soul was reached in which, as each finds what he as an individual requires, there is also room for all mankind. Even after this highest religion has been made known to men, it has often been obscured and lost, and many a struggle has been needed to vindicate its claims and help it to retain its rightful place. But with growing experience the world becomes more assured that the simplest and broadest religion ever preached upon this earth is also the best and the truest, and that in maintaining Christianity as at first preached, and applying it in every needed direction, lies the hope of the future of mankind. To those who agree in this conclusion the history of the religion of the world, full of errors and of grievous failures as it has been seen to be, cannot appear to have been a vain and purposeless excursion in a land of shadows. Not without a divine call, and not without divine guidance did man set out so early, and persevere so constantly in spite of all his disappointments, in the search for God.

INDEX

2 F

THE END

OUTLINES OF ENGLISH LITERATURE

By William Renton, Lecturer to the Scottish Universities. 12mo, with Diagrams, $1.00 *net.*

Contents: First Period [600–1600], pages 9–112: I. The Old English Metric and Chronicle [600–1350], *a.* Anglo-Saxon; *b.* Anglo-Norman—II. The Renascence [1350–1500]—III. The Reformation [1550–1600]—IV. The Romantic Drama [1550–1650]. Second Period [1600–1900], pages 132-232—V. The Serious Age [1600–1700]—VI. The Age of Gaiety [1650–1750]—VII. The Sententious Age [1700–1800]—VIII. The Sympathetic Age [1800–1900]—Appendix: Literature of America [1600–1900]—Index: Conspectus of British and American Poetry.

The general arrangement of the book and valuable diagrams showing the division of literature according to ages and characteristics combine to make this manual especially fitted to use in the class-room.

Criticism is supplemented by exposition, with extracts to exhibit the fashion of a period, or the style of a master. The number of authors indicates the importance of a period, and intrinsic power the importance of an author. American literature is considered as a part of the whole, but a brief summary of its history and general characteristics is also given.

THE PHILOSOPHY OF THE BEAUTIFUL

By William Knight, Professor of Philosophy in the University of St. Andrews. In two parts. 12mo, each $1.00 *net.*

(Part I. Its History.) Contents: Introductory—Prehistoric Origins—Oriental Art and Speculation—The Philosophy of Greece—The Neoplatonists—The Græco-Roman Period—Mediævalism—The Philosophy of Germany—of France—of Italy—of Holland—of Britain—of America.

(Part II. Its Theory and Its Relation to the Arts.) Contents: I. Prolegomena—II. The Nature of Beauty—III. The Ideal and the Real—IV. Inadequate or Partial Theories of Beauty—V. Suggestions towards a more Complete Theory of Beauty—VI. Art, Its Nature and Functions—VII. The Correlation of the Arts—VIII. Poetry, *a.* Definitions and Distinctions; *b.* Theories of Poetry; *c.* A Suggestion; *d.* The Origin of Poetry—IX. Music, *a.* Its Nature and Essence; *b.* The Alliance of Music with Poetry and the other Arts; *c.* The Origin of Music—X. Architecture—XI. Sculpture—XII. Painting—XIII. Dancing—Appendix A: Russian Aesthetic—Appendix B: Danish Aesthetic.

THE STUDY OF ANIMAL LIFE

By J. ARTHUR THOMSON, M.A., F.R.S.E., University of Edinburgh. 12mo, Illustrated, $1.50 *net.*

CONTENTS: Part I. THE EVERYDAY LIFE OF ANIMALS. The Wealth of Life—The Webb of Life—The Struggle—Shifts for a Living—Social Life—Domestic Life—Industries. Part II. THE POWERS OF LIFE. Vitality—The Divided Labors of the Body—Instinct. Part III. THE FORMS OF ANIMAL LIFE. Elements of Structure—Life History—Past History—The Simplest Animals—Backboneless Animals—Backboned Animals. Part IV. THE EVOLUTION OF ANIMAL LIFE. Evidences of Evolution—Evolution Theories—Habits and Surroundings—Heredity. Appendix I. Animal Life and Ours. Appendix II. "Best Books" on Animal Life.

Prof. J. H. COMSTOCK, *Leland Stanford, Junior, University.*—"I have read it with great delight. It is an admirable work, giving a true view of the existing state and tendencies of zoology; and it possesses the rare merit of being an elementary work, written from the standpoint of the most advanced thought, and in a manner to be understood by the beginning student."

THE FRENCH REVOLUTION

By CHARLES E. MALLET, Balliol College, Oxford. 12mo, $1.00 *net.*

This book has a special value to students and readers who do not own the great works of such writers as De Tocqueville, Taine, Michelet, and Von Sybel. Mr. Mallet presents economic and political aspects of society before the Revolution; attempts to explain why the Revolution came; why the men who made it failed to attain the liberty they so ardently desired, or to found the new order which they hoped to see in France; by what arts and accidents, owing to what deeper causes, an inconspicuous minority gradually grew into a victorious party; how external circumstances kept the revolutionary fever up, and forced the Revolution forward. History offers no problem of more surpassing interest and none more perplexing or obscure.

GREECE IN THE AGE OF PERICLES

By ARTHUR J. GRANT of King's College, Cambridge. 12mo, with Illustrations, $1.25 *net.*

CONTENTS: I. The Essentials of Greek Civilization—II. The Religion of the Greeks—III. Sparta—IV. The Earlier History of Athens—V. The Rivalry of Athens and Sparta—VI. Civil Wars in Greece—VII. The Athenian Democracy—VIII. Pericles: His Policy and his Friends—IX. Society in Greece—X. The Peloponnesian War to the Death of Pericles—XI. The Peloponnesian War—XII. Thought and Art in Athens.

THE REALM OF NATURE

An Outline of Physiography. By HUGH ROBERT MILL, D.Sc. Edin.; Fellow of the Royal Society of Edinburgh; Oxford Lecturer. Maps and 68 Illustrations. 12mo, $1.50 *net.*

CONTENTS: Story of Nature—Substance of Nature—Power of Nature—The Earth a Spinning Ball—The Earth a Planet—The Solar System and Universe—The Atmosphere—Atmospheric Phenomena—Climates—The Hydrosphere—Bed of the Oceans—Crust of the Earth—Action of Water on Land—Record of the Rocks—Continental Area—Life and Living Creatures—Man in Nature—Appendices—Index.

Prof. W. M. DAVIS, *of Harvard.*—"An excellent book, clear, comprehensive, and remarkably accurate. . . . One who reaches a good understanding of the book may regard himself as having made a real advance in his education towards an appreciation of nature."

Prof. JAMES D. DANA, *Yale.*—"Evidently prepared by one who understood his subject."

JOURNAL OF EDUCATION.—"It should not only be read, but owned by every teacher."

THE ELEMENTS OF ETHICS

An Introduction to Moral Philosophy. By J. H. MUIRHEAD, M.A., Royal Holloway College, England. 12mo, $1.00 *net.*

CONTENTS: Book I. The Science of Ethics: Problems of, Can there be a Science of, Scope of the Science—Book II. Moral Judgment: Object of, Standard of, Moral Law—Book III. Theories of the End. As Pleasure, as Self-sacrifice, Evolutionary Hedonism—Book IV. The End as Good: As Common Good, Forms of the Good—Book V. Moral Progress: Standard as Relative, as Progressive, as Ideal—Bibliography.

THE ACADEMY, *London.*—"There is no other introduction which can be recommended."

Prof. J. A. QUARLES, *Washington and Lee University.*—"I am pleased with Muirhead's 'Elements of Ethics.' It seems fresh, bright, thoughtful, stimulating. I shall use it probably next year."

Prof. J. STEARNS, *University of Wisconsin.*—"An admirably clear presentation and criticism of the teachings of the chief schools of thought upon the leading points of ethical theory."

Prof. GEORGE S. FULLERTON, *University of Penn.*—"I find the book very clear, simple, and forcible, and I shall take pleasure in recommending it to my students."

THE FINE ARTS

By G. Baldwin Brown, Professor of Fine Arts in the University of Edinburgh. 12mo, with Illustrations, $1.00 *net.*

Contents: Part I.— Art as the Expression of Popular Feelings and Ideals :—The Beginnings of Art—The Festival in its Relation to the Form and Spirit of Classical Art—Mediæval Florence and her Painters. Part II.—The Formal Conditions of Artistic Expression :—Some Elements of Effect in the Arts of Form—The Work of Art as Significant—The Work of Art as Beautiful. Part III.—The Arts of Form :—Architectural Beauty in Relation to Construction—The Conventions of Sculpture—Painting Old and New.

Yale Art School, New Haven, Conn.

Messrs. Charles Scribner's Sons,

Gentlemen :—As a text-book for the study of the "Fine Arts," there is nothing in the literature of the subject that answers the requirements as this little book.

The originality of Professor Brown's work is apparent. Out of a wide familiarity with the classical literature of the subject he has sifted the essential truths. And of the modern writers on æsthetics he knows and digests everything from Winkelmann to Whistler. But what distinguishes this book from others and gives it a special value is the treatment of the "Fine Arts" from their technical side. This is especially evident in his chapter on painting, which contains many suggestions of value to the young artist and amateur.

Respectfully yours, JOHN H. NIEMEYER.

THE LITERATURE OF FRANCE

By H. G. Keene, Hon. M.A. Oxon. 12mo, $1.00 *net.*

Contents: Introduction—The Age of Infancy (*a.* Birth)—The Age of Infancy (*b.* Growth)—The Age of Adolescence (Sixteenth Century)—The Age of Glory, Part I. Poetry, etc.—The Age of Glory, Part II. Prose—The Age of Reason, Part I.—The Age of Reason, Part II.—The Age of "Nature"—Sources of Modern French Literary Art: Poetry—Sources of Prose Fiction—Appendix—Index.

Edward S. Joynes, *Professor of Modern Languages, South Carolina College.*—"My first impressions are fully confirmed. The book is interesting and able. It would be difficult to compress into equal compass a more satisfactory or suggestive view of so great a subject. As an introductory text for schools and colleges or private readers I have seen nothing so good. The book deserves, and I hope will receive, a wide welcome."

THE USE AND ABUSE OF MONEY

By Dr. W. CUNNINGHAM, Cambridge. 12mo, $1.00 *net.*

A popular treatise, and the headings, Social Problems, Practical Questions, and Personal Duty, give a broad view of the scope of the book. The subject is Capital in its relation to Social Progress, and personal responsibility enters into the questions raised. The volume contains a syllabus of subjects and a list of books for reference.

THE PHYSIOLOGY OF THE SENSES

By JOHN MCKENDRICK, Professor of Physiology in the University of Glasgow, and Dr. SNODGRASS, Physiological Laboratory, Glasgow. 127 Illustrations. 12mo, 340 pages, $1.50 *net.*

The aim of this book is to give an account of the functions of the organs of sense as found in man and the higher animals. Simple experiments are suggested by which any one may test the statements for himself, and the book has been so written as to be readily understood by those who have not made physiology a special study. It will be found a suitable preparation for entering upon the questions that underlie physiological psychology. Excellent illustrations abound.

ENGLISH COLONIZATION AND EMPIRE

By ALFRED CALDECOTT, St. John's College, Cambridge. 12mo, with Maps and Diagrams, $1.00 *net.*

The diffusion of European, and, more particularly, of English, civilization is the subject of this book. The treatment of this great theme covers the origin and the historical, political, economical and ethnological development of the English colonies. There is thus spread before the reader a bird's-eye view of the colonies, great and small, from their origin until the present time, with a summary of the wars and other great events which have occurred in the progress of this colonizing work, and with a careful examination of some of the most important questions, economical, commercial, and political, which now affect the relation of the colonies and the parent nation.

THE JACOBEAN POETS

By EDMUND GOSSE, Hon. M.A., Trinity College, Cambridge. 12mo, $1.00 *net.*

This little volume is an attempt to direct critical attention to all that was notable in English poetry from 1603-1625. It is the first book to concentrate attention on the poetry produced during the reign of James I. Many writers appear here for the first time in a book of this nature. The aim has been to find unfamiliar beauties rather than to reprint for the thousandth time what is already familiar.

LOGIC, INDUCTIVE AND DEDUCTIVE

By WILLIAM MINTO, M.A., Hon. LL.D., St. Andrews, Late Professor of Logic in the University of Aberdeen. With Diagrams. 385 pages. 12mo, $1.25 *net.*

FROM THE PREFACE.—"In this little treatise two things are attempted. One of them is to put the study of logical formulæ on a historical basis. The other, which might at first appear inconsistent with this, is to increase the power of Logic as a practical discipline. The main purpose of this practical science, or scientific art, is conceived to be the organization of reason against error, and error in its various kinds is made the basis of the division of the subject. To carry out this practical aim along with the historical one is not hopeless, because throughout its long history Logic has been a practical science; and, as I have tried to show at some length in introductory chapters, has concerned itself at different periods with the risks of error peculiar to each."

CHAPTERS IN MODERN BOTANY

By PATRICK GEDDES, Professor of Botany, University College, Dundee. 12mo, Illustrated, $1.25 *net.*

Beginning with some of the strangest forms and processes of the vegetable world [Pitcher Plants], it exhibits these, not merely as a vegetable menagerie, but to give, as speedily and interestingly as may be:

(a) Some general comprehension of the processes and forms of vegetable life, and, from the very first,

(b) Some intelligent grasp of the experimental methods and reasoning employed in their investigation.

Other Insectiverous Plants, with their Movements and Nervous Action, are discussed. The Web of Life, Relations between Plants and Animals, Spring and its Studies, Geographical Distribution, Landscapes, Leaves, etc., form the subject of other chapters, and handled in a way to open the general subject of systematic botany most invitingly.

THE EARTH'S HISTORY

An Introduction to Modern Geology. By R. D. ROBERTS, M.A., Camb., D.Sc. Lond. With colored Maps and Illustrations. 12mo, $1.50 *net.*

A sketch of the methods and the results of geological inquiry to help those who wish to take up the study in its most interesting features. The purpose is to answer such questions as readily suggest themselves to the student, among which may be mentioned the following: What is the nature of the crust movements to which the land-areas and mountain ranges are due? What was the distribution of land and water that obtained in the area when each group of rocks was formed? What was the condition of its surface, and what the forms of life inhabiting it? What were the oceanic conditions; the depths in different parts; the forms of life inhabiting the water; and the nature and extent of the materials brought down by the rivers that poured into the seas from the land-areas of that period?